ACCA

Paper AFM

Advanced Financial Management

D1919401

Welcome to Emile Woolf's study text for *Advanced Financial Management (AFM)* which is:

- Written by tutors
- Comprehensive but concise
- In simple English
- Used around the world by Emile Woolf Colleges including China, Russia and the UK

EW
EMILE WOOLF INTERNATIONAL
Developing Trusted Professionals

Thirteenth edition published by
Emile Woolf International Limited
Bracknell Enterprise & Innovation Hub
Ocean House, 12th Floor, The Ring
Bracknell, Berkshire, RG12 1AX United Kingdom
Email: info@ewiglobal.com
www.emilewoolf.com

British Library Cataloguing in Publications Data
A catalogue record for this book is available from the British Library.

ISBN: 978-1-84843-959-7

Printed and bound in Great Britain

Acknowledgements
The syllabus and study guide are reproduced by kind permission of the Association of Chartered Certified Accountants.

C

Contents

S

Syllabus and study guide
September 2020 to June 2021

Aim

The aim of the syllabus is to apply relevant knowledge, skills and exercise professional judgement as expected of a senior financial executive or advisor, in taking or recommending decisions relating to the financial management of an organisation in private and public sectors.

Main capabilities

On successful completion of this paper, candidates should be able to:

A Explain and evaluate the role and responsibility of the senior financial executive or advisor in meeting conflicting needs of stakeholders and recognise the role of international financial institutions in the financial management of multinationals

B Evaluate potential investment decisions and assessing their financial and strategic consequences, both domestically and internationally

C Assess and plan acquisitions and mergers as an alternative growth strategy

D Evaluate and advise on alternative corporate re-organisation strategies

E Apply and evaluate alternative advanced treasury and risk management Techniques

Rationale

The aim of the syllabus is to apply relevant knowledge, skills and exercise professional judgement as expected of a senior financial executive or advisor, in taking or recommending decisions relating to the financial management of an organisation in private and public sectors.

This syllabus develops upon the core financial management knowledge and skills covered in the Financial Management syllabus and prepares candidates to advise management and/or clients on complex strategic financial management issues facing an organisation.

The syllabus starts by exploring the role and responsibility of a senior executive or advisor in meeting competing needs of stakeholders within the business environment of multinationals. The syllabus then re-examines investment and financing decisions, with the emphasis moving towards the strategic consequences of making such decisions in a domestic, as well as international, context. Candidates are then expected to develop further advisory skills in planning strategic acquisitions and mergers and corporate re-organisations.

The next part of the syllabus re-examines, in the broadest sense, the existence of risks in business and the sophisticated strategies which are employed in order to manage such risks. It builds on what candidates would have covered in the Financial Management syllabus.

Detailed syllabus

A Role of senior financial adviser in the multinational organisation

1. The role and responsibility of senior financial executive/advisor
2. Financial strategy formulation
3. Ethical and governance issues
4. Management of international trade and finance
5. Strategic business and financial planning for multinational organisations
6. Dividend policy in multinationals and transfer pricing

B Advanced investment appraisal

1. Discounted cash flow techniques
2. Application of option pricing theory in investment decisions
3. Impact of financing on investment decisions and adjusted present values
4. Valuation and the use of free cash flows
5. International investment and financing decisions

C Acquisitions and mergers

1. Acquisitions and mergers versus other growth strategies
2. Valuation for acquisitions and mergers
3. Regulatory framework and processes
4. Financing acquisitions and mergers

D Corporate reconstruction and re- organisation

1. Financial reconstruction
2. Business re-organisation

E Treasury and advanced risk management techniques

1. The role of the treasury function in multinationals
2. The use of financial derivatives to hedge against forex risk
3. The use of financial derivatives to hedge against interest rate risk

Approach to examining the syllabus

The Advanced Financial Management exam builds upon the skills and knowledge examined in the Financial Management exam. At this stage candidates will be expected to demonstrate an integrated knowledge of the subject and an ability to relate their technical understanding of the subject to issues of strategic importance to the organisation. The study guide specifies the wide range of contextual understanding that is required to achieve a satisfactory standard at this level.

Examination Structure

The syllabus is assessed by a three-hour 15 minutes examination.

Section A

Section A will always be a single 50 mark case study, which will contain four professional marks in which candidates are required produce a business document such as a report or a briefing paper for the board of directors.

Candidates should understand that they will be expected to undertake calculations, draw comparison against relevant information where appropriate, analyse the results and offer recommendations or conclusions as required.

Financial managers are required to look across a range of issues which affect an organisation and its finances, so candidates should expect to see the case study focus on a range of issues from at least two syllabus sections from A - E. These will vary depending on the business context of the case study.

Section B

Section B will consist of two compulsory 25 mark questions. All section B questions will be scenario based and contain a combination of calculation and narrative marks. There will not be any wholly narrative questions.

All topics and syllabus sections will be examinable in either section A or section B of the exam, but every exam will have question(s) which have a focus on syllabus sections B and E.

Total 100 marks

Study Guide

A ROLE OF THE SENIOR FINANCIAL ADVISER IN THE MULTINATIONAL ORGANISATION

1 The role and responsibility of senior financial executive/advisor

(a) Develop strategies for the achievement of the organisational goals in line with its agreed policy framework.

(b) Recommend strategies for the management of the financial resources of the organisation such that they are utilised in an efficient, effective and transparent way.

(c) Advise the board of directors or management of the organisation in setting the financial goals of the business and in its financial policy development with particular reference to:

- (i) Investment selection and capital resource allocation
- (ii) Minimising the cost of capital
- (iii) Distribution and retention policy
- (iv) Communicating financial policy and corporate goals to internal and external stakeholders
- (v) Financial planning and control
- (vi) The management of risk.

2 Financial strategy formulation

(a) Assess organisational performance using methods such as ratios and trends.

(b) Recommend the optimum capital mix and structure within a specified business context and capital asset structure.

(c) Recommend appropriate distribution and retention policy.

(d) Explain the theoretical and practical rationale for the management of risk.

(e) Assess the organisation's exposure to business and financial risk including operational, reputational, political, economic, regulatory and fiscal risk.

(f) Develop a framework for risk management, comparing and contrasting risk mitigation, hedging and diversification strategies.

(g) Establish capital investment monitoring and risk management systems.

(h) Advise on the impact of behavioural finance on financial strategies / securities prices and why they may not follow the conventional financial theories.

3 Ethical and governance issues

(a) Assess the ethical dimension within business issues and decisions and advise on best practice in the financial management of the organisation.

(b) Demonstrate an understanding of the interconnectedness of the ethics of good business practice between all of the functional areas of the organisation.

(c) Recommend, within specified problem domains, appropriate strategies for the resolution of stakeholder conflict and advise on alternative approaches that may be adopted.

(d) Recommend an ethical framework for the development of an organisation's financial policies and a system for the assessment of its ethical impact upon the financial management of the organisation.

(e) Explore the areas within the ethical framework of the organisation which may be undermined by agency effects and/or stakeholder conflicts and establish strategies for dealing with them.

(f) Establish an ethical financial policy for the financial management of the organisation which is grounded in good governance, the highest standards of probity and is fully aligned with the ethical principles of the Association.

(g) Assess the impact on sustainability and environmental issues arising from alternative organisational business and financial decisions.

(h) Assess and advise on the impact of investment and financing strategies and decisions on the organisation's stakeholders, from an integrated reporting and governance perspective.

4 Management of international trade and finance

(a) Advise on the theory and practice of free trade and the management of barriers to trade.

(b) Demonstrate an up to date understanding of the major trade agreements and common markets and, on the basis of contemporary circumstances, advise on their policies and strategic implications for a given business.

(c) Discuss how the actions of the World Trade Organisation, the International Monetary Fund, The World Bank and Central Banks can affect a multinational organisation.

(d) Discuss the role of international financial institutions within the context of a globalised economy, with particular attention to (the Fed, Bank of England, European Central Bank and the Bank of Japan).

(e) Discuss the role of the international financial markets with respect to the management of global debt, the financial development of the emerging economies and the maintenance of global financial stability.

(f) Discuss the significance to the organisation, of latest developments in the world financial markets such as the causes and impact of the recent financial crisis; growth and impact of dark pool trading systems; the removal of barriers to the free movement of capital; and the international regulations on money laundering.

(g) Demonstrate an awareness of new developments in the macroeconomic environment, assessing their impact upon the organisation, and advising on the appropriate response to those developments both internally and externally.

5 Strategic business and financial planning for multinationals

(a) Advise on the development of a financial planning framework for a multinational organisation taking into account:

- (i) Compliance with national regulatory requirements (for example the London Stock Exchange admission requirements)
- (ii) The mobility of capital across borders and national limitations on remittances and transfer pricing
- (iii) The pattern of economic and other risk exposures in the different national markets
- (iv) Agency issues in the central coordination of overseas operations and the balancing of local financial autonomy with effective central control.

6 Dividend policy in multinationals and transfer pricing

(a) Determine a corporation's dividend capacity and its policy given

- (i) The corporation's short- and long- term reinvestment strategy
- (ii) The impact of capital reconstruction programmes such as share repurchase agreements and new capital issues on free cash flow to equity.
- (iii) The availability and timing of central remittances
- (iv) The corporate tax regime within the host jurisdiction.

(b) Advise, in the context of a specified capital investment programme, on an organisation's current and projected dividend capacity.

(c) Develop organisational policy on the transfer pricing of goods and services across international borders and be able to determine the most appropriate transfer pricing strategy in a given situation reflecting local regulations and tax regimes.

B ADVANCED INVESTMENT APPRAISAL

1 Discounted cash flow techniques

(a) Evaluate the potential value added to an organisation arising from a specified capital investment project or portfolio using the net present value (NPV) model.

Project modelling should include explicit treatment and discussion of:

- (i) Inflation and specific price variation

- (ii) Taxation including tax allowable depreciation and tax exhaustion
- (iii) Single period and multi-period capital rationing. Multi-period capital rationing to include the formulation of programming methods and the interpretation of their output
- (iv) Probability analysis and sensitivity analysis when adjusting for risk and uncertainty in investment appraisal
- (v) Risk adjusted discount rates
- (vi) Project duration as a measure of risk.

(b) Outline the application of Monte Carlo simulation to investment appraisal. Candidates will not be expected to undertake simulations in an examination context but will be expected to demonstrate an understanding of:

- (i) The significance of the simulation output and the assessment of the likelihood of project success
- (ii) The measurement and interpretation of project value at risk.

(c) Establish the potential economic return (using internal rate of return (IRR) and modified internal rate of return) and advise on a project's return margin. Discuss the relative merits of NPV and IRR.

2 Application of option pricing theory in investment decisions

(a) Apply the Black-Scholes Option Pricing (BSOP) model to financial product valuation and to asset valuation:

- (i) Determine and discuss, using published data, the five principal drivers of option value (value of the underlying, exercise price, time to expiry, volatility and the risk-free rate)
- (ii) Discuss the underlying assumptions, structure, application and limitations of the BSOP model.

(b) Evaluate embedded real options within a project, classifying them into one of the real option archetypes.

(c) Assess, calculate and advise on the value of options to delay, expand, redeploy and withdraw using the BSOP model.

3 Impact of financing on investment decisions and adjusted present values

(a) Identify and assess the appropriateness of the range of sources of finance available to an organisation including equity, debt, hybrids, lease finance, venture capital, business angel finance, private equity, asset securitisation and sale, Islamic finance and initial coin offerings. Including assessment on the financial position, financial risk and the value of an organisation.

(b) Discuss the role of, and developments in, Islamic financing as a growing source of finance for organisations; explaining the rationale for its use, and identifying its benefits and deficiencies.

(c) Calculate the cost of capital of an organisation, including the cost of equity and cost of debt, based on the range of equity and debt sources of finance. Discuss the appropriateness of using the cost of capital to establish project and organisational value, and discuss its relationship to such value.

(d) Calculate and evaluate project specific cost of equity and cost of capital, including their impact on the overall cost of capital of an organisation. Demonstrate detailed knowledge of business and financial risk, the capital asset pricing model and the relationship between equity and asset betas.

(e) Assess an organisation's debt exposure to interest rate changes using the simple Macaulay duration and modified duration methods.

(f) Discuss the benefits and limitations of duration including the impact of convexity.

(g) Assess the organisation's exposure to credit risk, including:

- (i) Explain the role of, and the risk assessment models used by the principal rating agencies
- (ii) Estimate the likely credit spread over risk free
- (iii) Estimate the organisation's current cost of debt capital using the appropriate term structure of interest rates and the credit spread.

(h) Assess the impact of financing and capital structure upon the organisation with respect to:

- (i) Modigliani and Miller propositions, before and after tax
- (ii) Static trade-off theory
- (iii) Pecking order propositions
- (iv) Agency effects.

(i) Apply the adjusted present value technique to the appraisal of investment decisions that entail significant alterations in the financial structure of the organisation, including their fiscal and transactions cost implications.

(j) Assess the impact of a significant capital investment project upon the reported financial position and performance of the organisation taking into account alternative financing strategies.

4 Valuation and the use of free cash flows

(a) Apply asset based, income based and cash flow based models to value equity. Apply appropriate models, including term structure of interest rates, the yield curve and credit spreads, to value corporate debt.

(b) Forecast an organisation's free cash flow and its free cash flow to equity (pre and post capital reinvestment).

(c) Advise on the value of an organisation using its free cash flow and free cash flow to equity under alternative horizon and growth assumptions.

(d) Explain the use of the BSOP model to estimate the value of equity of an organisation and discuss the implications of the model for a change in the value of equity.

(e) Explain the role of BSOP model in the assessment of default risk, the value of debt and its potential recoverability.

5 International investment and financing decisions

(a) Assess the impact upon the value of a project of alternative exchange rate assumptions.

(b) Forecast project or organisation free cash flows in any specified currency and determine the project's net present value or organisation value under differing exchange rate, fiscal and transaction cost assumptions.

(c) Evaluate the significance of exchange controls for a given investment decision and strategies for dealing with restricted remittance.

(d) Assess the impact of a project upon an organisation's exposure to translation, transaction and economic risk.

(e) Assess and advise on the costs and benefits of alternative sources of finance available within the international equity and bond markets.

C ACQUISITIONS AND MERGERS

1 Acquisitions and mergers versus other growth strategies

(a) Discuss the arguments for and against the use of acquisitions and mergers as a method of corporate expansion.

(b) Evaluate the corporate and competitive nature of a given acquisition proposal.

(c) Advise upon the criteria for choosing an appropriate target for acquisition.

(d) Compare the various explanations for the high failure rate of acquisitions in enhancing shareholder value.

(e) Evaluate, from a given context, the potential for synergy separately classified as:

(i) Revenue synergy

(ii) Cost synergy

(iii) Financial synergy.

(f) Evaluate the use of the reverse takeover as a method of acquisition and as a way of obtaining a stock market listing:

2 Valuation for acquisitions and mergers

(a) Discuss the problem of overvaluation.

(b) Estimate the potential near-term and continuing growth levels of a corporation's earnings using both internal and external measures.

(c) Discuss, assess and advise on the value created from an acquisition or merger of both quoted and unquoted entities using models such as:

(i) 'Book value-plus' models

(ii) Market based models

(iii) Cash flow models, including free cash flows.

Taking into account the changes in the risk profile and risk exposure of the acquirer and the target entities

(d) Apply appropriate methods, such as: risk-adjusted cost of capital, adjusted net present values and changing price- earnings multipliers resulting from the acquisition or merger, to the valuation process where appropriate.

(e) Demonstrate an understanding of the procedure for valuing high growth start- ups.

3 Regulatory framework and processes

(a) Demonstrate an understanding of the principal factors influencing the development of the regulatory framework for mergers and acquisitions globally and, in particular, be able to compare and contrast the shareholder versus the stakeholder models of regulation.

(b) Identify the main regulatory issues which are likely to arise in the context of a given offer and

(i) assess whether the offer is likely to be in the shareholders' best interests

(ii) advise the directors of a target entity on the most appropriate defence if a specific offer is to be treated as hostile.

4 Financing acquisitions and mergers

(a) Compare the various sources of financing available for a proposed cash- based acquisition.

(b) Evaluate the advantages and disadvantages of a financial offer for a given acquisition proposal using pure or mixed mode financing and recommend the most appropriate offer to be made.

(c) Assess the impact of a given financial offer on the reported financial position and performance of the acquirer.

D CORPORATE RECONSTRUCTION AND RE-ORGANISATION

1 Financial reconstruction

(a) Assess an organisational situation and determine whether a financial reconstruction is an appropriate strategy for a given business situation.

(b) Assess the likely response of the capital market and/or individual suppliers of capital to any reconstruction scheme and the impact their response is likely to have upon the value of the organisation.

2 Business re-organisation

(a) Recommend, with reasons, strategies for unbundling parts of a quoted company.

(b) Evaluate the likely financial and other benefits of unbundling.

(c) Advise on the financial issues relating to a management buy-out and buy-in.

E TREASURY AND ADVANCED RISK MANAGEMENT TECHNIQUES

1 The role of the treasury function in multinationals

(a) Discuss the role of the treasury management function within:

- (i) The short term management of the organisation's financial resources
- (ii) The longer term maximisation of corporate value
- (iii) The management of risk exposure.

(b) Discuss the operations of the derivatives market, including:

- (i) The relative advantages and disadvantages of exchange traded versus OTC agreements
- (ii) Key features, such as standard contracts, tick sizes, margin requirements and margin trading
- (iii) The source of basis risk and how it can be minimised.
- (iv) Risks such as delta, gamma, vega, rho and theta, and how these can be managed.

2 The use of financial derivatives to hedge against forex risk

(a) Assess the impact on an organisation to exposure in translation, transaction and economic risks and how these can be managed.

(b) Evaluate, for a given hedging requirement, which of the following is the most appropriate strategy, given the nature of the underlying position and the risk exposure:

- (i) The use of the forward exchange market and the creation of a money market hedge
- (ii) Synthetic foreign exchange agreements (SAFEs)
- (iii) Exchange-traded currency futures contracts
- (iv) Currency swaps
- (v) FOREX swaps
- (vi) Currency options.

(c) Advise on the use of bilateral and multilateral netting and matching as tools for minimising FOREX transactions costs and the management of market barriers to the free movement of capital and other remittances.

3 The use of financial derivatives to hedge against interest rate risk

(a) Evaluate, for a given hedging requirement, which of the following is the most appropriate given the nature of the underlying position and the risk exposure:

(i) Forward Rate Agreements (FRAs)

(ii) Interest rate futures

(iii) Interest rate swaps

(iv) Interest rate options (including collars).

f

Formulae and tables

Formula Sheet

Modigliani and Miller Proposition 2 (with tax)

$$K_e = K_e^i + (1-T)(K_e^i - K_d)\frac{V_d}{V_e}$$

The Capital Asset Pricing Model

$$E(r_i) = R_f + \beta_i(E(r_m) - R_f)$$

The asset beta formula

$$\beta_a = \left[\frac{V_e}{(V_e + V_d(1-T))}\beta_e\right] + \left[\frac{V_d(1-T)}{(V_e + V_d(1-T))}\beta_d\right]$$

The Growth Model

$$P_o = \frac{D_o(1+g)}{(r_e - g)}$$

Gordon's growth approximation

$$g = br_e$$

The weighted average cost of capital

$$\text{WACC} = \left[\frac{V_e}{V_e + V_d}\right]K_e + \left[\frac{V_d}{V_e + V_d}\right]K_d(1-T)$$

The Fisher formula

$$(1+i)=(1+r)(1+h)$$

Purchasing power parity and interest rate parity

$$S_1 = S_o \times \frac{(1+h_c)}{(1+h_b)} \qquad f_o = S_o \times \frac{(1+i_c)}{(1+i_b)}$$

Modified internal rate of return

$$MIRR = \left[\frac{PV_R}{PV_I}\right]^{\frac{1}{n}}(1+r_e)-1$$

The Black Scholes Option Pricing Model

$$c = P_a N(d_1) - P_e N(d_2) e^{-rt}$$

Where:

$$d_1 = \frac{In(P_a / P_e) + (r + 0.5s^2)t}{s\sqrt{t}}$$

$$d_2 = d_1 - s\sqrt{t}$$

The Put Call Parity relationship

$$p = c - P_a + P_e e^{-rt}$$

Present value table

Present value of 1 i.e. $(1+r)^{-n}$

where r = discount rate

n = number of periods until payment

Periods	Discount rate (r)									
(n)	1%	2%	3%	4%	5%	6%	7%	8%	9%	10%	
1	0.990	0.980	0.971	0.962	0.952	0.943	0.935	0.926	0.917	0.909	1
2	0.980	0.961	0.943	0.925	0.907	0.890	0.873	0.857	0.842	0.826	2
3	0.971	0.942	0.915	0.889	0.864	0.840	0.816	0.794	0.772	0.751	3
4	0.961	0.924	0.888	0.855	0.823	0.792	0.763	0.735	0.708	0.683	4
5	0.951	0.906	0.863	0.822	0.784	0.747	0.713	0.681	0.650	0.621	5
6	0.942	0.888	0.837	0.790	0.746	0.705	0.666	0.630	0.596	0.564	6
7	0.933	0.871	0.813	0.760	0.711	0.665	0.623	0.583	0.547	0.513	7
8	0.923	0.853	0.789	0.731	0.677	0.627	0.582	0.540	0.502	0.467	8
9	0.914	0.837	0.766	0.703	0.645	0.592	0.544	0.500	0.460	0.424	9
10	0.905	0.820	0.744	0.676	0.614	0.558	0.508	0.463	0.422	0.386	10
11	0.896	0.804	0.722	0.650	0.585	0.527	0.475	0.429	0.388	0.350	11
12	0.887	0.788	0.701	0.625	0.557	0.497	0.444	0.397	0.356	0.319	12
13	0.879	0.773	0.681	0.601	0.530	0.469	0.415	0.368	0.326	0.290	13
14	0.870	0.758	0.661	0.577	0.505	0.442	0.388	0.340	0.299	0.263	14
15	0.861	0.743	0.642	0.555	0.481	0.417	0.362	0.315	0.275	0.239	15

(n)	11%	12%	13%	14%	15%	16%	17%	18%	19%	20%	
1	0.901	0.893	0.885	0.877	0.870	0.862	0.855	0.847	0.840	0.833	1
2	0.812	0.797	0.783	0.769	0.756	0.743	0.731	0.718	0.706	0.694	2
3	0.731	0.712	0.693	0.675	0.658	0.641	0.624	0.609	0.593	0.579	3
4	0.659	0.636	0.613	0.592	0.572	0.552	0.534	0.516	0.499	0.482	4
5	0.593	0.567	0.543	0.519	0.497	0.476	0.456	0.437	0.419	0.402	5
6	0.535	0.507	0.480	0.456	0.432	0.410	0.390	0.370	0.352	0.335	6
7	0.482	0.452	0.425	0.400	0.376	0.354	0.333	0.314	0.296	0.279	7
8	0.434	0.404	0.376	0.351	0.327	0.305	0.285	0.266	0.249	0.233	8
9	0.391	0.361	0.333	0.308	0.284	0.263	0.243	0.225	0.209	0.194	9
10	0.352	0.322	0.295	0.270	0.247	0.227	0.208	0.191	0.176	0.162	10
11	0.317	0.287	0.261	0.237	0.215	0.195	0.178	0.162	0.148	0.135	11
12	0.286	0.257	0.231	0.208	0.187	0.168	0.152	0.137	0.124	0.112	12
13	0.258	0.229	0.204	0.182	0.163	0.145	0.130	0.116	0.104	0.093	13
14	0.232	0.205	0.181	0.160	0.141	0.125	0.111	0.099	0.088	0.078	14
15	0.209	0.183	0.160	0.140	0.123	0.108	0.095	0.084	0.074	0.065	15

Annuity table

Present value of an annuity of 1 i.e. $\frac{1-(1+r)^{-n}}{r}$

where r = discount rate

n = number of periods

Periods (n)	Discount rate (r) 1%	2%	3%	4%	5%	6%	7%	8%	9%	10%	
1	0.990	0.980	0.971	0.962	0.952	0.943	0.935	0.926	0.917	0.909	1
2	1.970	1.942	1.913	1.886	1.859	1.833	1.808	1.783	1.759	1.736	2
3	2.941	2.884	20829	2.775	2.723	2.673	2.624	2.577	2.531	2.487	3
4	3.902	3.808	3.717	3.630	3.546	3.465	3.387	3.312	3.240	3.170	4
5	4.853	4.713	4.580	4.452	4.329	4.212	4.100	3.993	3.890	3.791	5
6	5.795	5.601	5.417	5.242	5.076	4.917	4.767	4.623	4.486	4.355	6
7	6.728	6.472	6.230	6.002	5.786	5.582	5.389	5.206	5.033	4.868	7
8	7.652	7.325	7.020	6.733	6.463	6.210	5.971	5.747	5.535	5.335	8
9	8.566	8.162	7.786	7.435	7.108	6.802	6.515	6.247	5.995	5.759	9
10	9.471	8.983	8.530	8.111	7.722	7.360	7.024	6.710	6.418	6.145	10
11	10.37	9.787	9.253	8.760	8.306	7.887	7.499	7.139	6.805	6.495	11
12	11.26	10.58	9.954	9.385	8.863	8.384	7.943	7.536	7.161	6.814	12
13	12.13	11.35	10.63	9.986	9.394	8.853	8.358	7.904	7.487	7.103	13
14	13.00	12.11	11.30	10.56	9.899	9.295	8.745	8.244	7.786	7.367	14
15	13.87	12.85	11.94	11.12	10.38	9.712	9.108	8.559	8.061	7.606	15

(n)	11%	12%	13%	14%	15%	16%	17%	18%	19%	20%	
1	0.901	0.893	0.885	0.877	0.870	0.862	0.855	0.847	0.840	0.833	1
2	1.713	1.690	1.668	1.647	1.626	1.605	1.585	1.566	1.547	1.528	2
3	2.444	2.402	2.361	2.322	2.283	2.246	2.210	2.174	2.140	2.106	3
4	3.102	3.037	2.974	2.914	2.855	2.798	2.743	2.690	2.639	2.589	4
5	3.696	3.605	3.517	3.433	3.352	3.274	3.199	3.127	3.058	2.991	5
6	4.231	4.111	3.998	3.889	3.784	3.685	3.589	3.498	3.410	3.326	6
7	4.712	4.564	4.423	4.288	4.160	4.039	3.922	3.812	3.706	3.605	7
8	5.146	4.968	4.799	4.639	4.487	4.344	4.207	4.078	3.954	3.837	8
9	5.537	5.328	5.132	4.946	4.772	4.607	4.451	4.303	4.163	4.031	9
10	5.889	5.650	5.426	5.216	5.019	4.833	4.659	4.494	4.339	4.192	10
11	6.207	5.938	5.687	5.453	5.234	5.029	4.836	4.656	4.486	4.327	11
12	6.492	6.194	5.918	5.660	5.421	5.197	4.988	4.793	4.611	4.439	12
13	6.750	6.424	6.122	5.842	5.583	5.342	5.118	4.910	4.715	4.533	13
14	6.982	6.628	6.302	6.002	5.724	5.468	5.229	5.008	4.802	4.611	14
15	7.191	6.811	6.462	6.142	5.847	5.575	5.324	5.092	4.876	4.675	15

Standard normal distribution table

	0.00	0.01	0.02	0.03	0.04	0.05	0.06	0.07	0.08	0.09
0.0	0.0000	0.0040	0.0080	0.0120	0.0160	0.0199	0.0239	0.0279	0.0319	0.0359
0.1	0.0398	0.0438	0.0478	0.0517	0.0557	0.0596	0.0636	0.0675	0.0714	0.0753
0.2	0.0793	0.0832	0.0871	0.0910	0.0948	0.0987	0.1026	0.1064	0.1103	0.1141
0.3	0.1179	0.1217	0.1255	0.1293	0.1331	0.1368	0.1406	0.1443	0.1480	0.1517
0.4	0·1554	0.1591	0.1628	0.1664	0.1700	0.1736	0.1772	0.1808	0.1844	0.1879
0.5	0.1915	0.1950	0.1985	0·2019	0·2054	0.2088	0.2123	0·2157	0·2190	0·2224
0.6	0.2257	0.2291	0.2324	0.2357	0.2389	0.2422	0.2454	0.2486	0.2517	0.2549
0.7	0.2580	0.2611	0.2642	0.2673	0.2703	0.2734	0.2764	0.2794	0.2823	0.2852
0.8	0.2881	0.2910	0.2939	0.2967	0.2995	0.3023	0.3051	0.3078	0.3106	0.3133
0.9	0.3159	0.3186	0.3212	0.3238	0.3264	0.3289	0.3315	0.3340	0.3365	0.3389
1.0	0.3413	0.3438	0.3461	0.3485	0.3508	0.3531	0.3554	0.3577	0.3599	0.3621
1.1	0.3643	0.3665	0.3686	0.3708	0.3729	0.3749	0.3770	0.3790	0.3810	0.3830
1.2	0.3849	0.3869	0.3888	0.3907	0.3925	0.3944	0.3962	0.3980	0.3997	0.4015
1.3	0.4032	0.4049	0.4066	0.4082	0.4099	0.4115	0.4131	0.4147	0.4162	0.4177
1.4	0.4192	0.4207	0.4222	0.4236	0.4251	0.4265	0.4279	0.4292	0.4306	0.4319
1.5	0.4332	0.4345	0.4357	0.4370	0.4382	0.4394	0.4406	0.4418	0.4429	0.4441
1.6	0.4452	0.4463	0.4474	0.4484	0.4495	0.4505	0.4515	0.4525	0.4535	0.4545
1.7	0.4554	0.4564	0.4573	0.4582	0.4591	0.4599	0.4608	0.4616	0.4625	0.4633
1.8	0.4641	0.4649	0.4656	0.4664	0.4671	0.4678	0.4686	0.4693	0.4699	0.4706
1.9	0.4713	0.4719	0.4726	0.4732	0.4738	0.4744	0.4750	0.4756	0.4761	0.4767
2.0	0.4772	0.4778	0.4783	0.4788	0.4793	0.4798	0.4803	0.4808	0.4812	0.4817
2.1	0.4821	0.4826	0.4830	0.4834	0.4838	0.4842	0.4846	0.4850	0.4854	0.4857
2.2	0.4861	0.4864	0.4868	0.4871	0.4875	0.4878	0.4881	0.4884	0.4887	0.4890
2.3	0.4893	0.4896	0.4898	0.4901	0.4904	0.4906	0.4909	0.4911	0.4913	0.4916
2.4	0.4918	0.4920	0.4922	0.4925	0.4927	0.4929	0.4931	0.4932	0.4934	0.4936
2.5	0.4938	0.4940	0.4941	0.4943	0.4945	0.4946	0.4948	0.4949	0.4951	0.4952
2.6	0.4953	0.4955	0.4956	0.4957	0.4959	0.4960	0.4961	0.4962	0.4963	0.4964
2.7	0.4965	0·4966	0.4967	0.4968	0.4969	0.4970	0.4971	0.4972	0.4973	0.4974
2.8	0.4974	0.4975	0.4976	0.4977	0.4977	0.4978	0.4979	0.4979	0.4980	0.4981
2.9	0.4981	0.4982	0.4982	0.4983	0.4984	0.4984	0.4985	0.4985	0.4986	0.4986
3.0	0.4987	0.4987	0.4987	0.4988	0.4988	0.4989	0.4989	0.4989	0.4990	0.4990

This table can be used to calculate $N(d_i)$, the cumulative normal distribution functions needed for the Black-Scholes model of option pricing. If $d_i > 0$, add 0·5 to the relevant number above. If $d_i < 0$, subtract the relevant number above from 0·5.

CHAPTER 1

The role and responsibilities of the senior financial executive

Contents

The role and responsibilities of the senior financial management executive

- The objectives of an organisation
- The primary corporate objective
- Policy frameworks
- Advising on financial goals and financial policy development

1 The role and responsibilities of the senior financial management executive

1.1 The objectives of an organisation

The role of the senior financial executive is to provide leadership and guidance on the financial aspects of the formulation and execution of an entity's strategy.

The identification of a primary objective is a starting point for the formulation of a strategy to achieve that objective.

- For companies, the main objective is usually stated as maximising the wealth of the company's owners, its equity shareholders
- For state-owned organisations, the main objective might be stated in terms of providing a certain standard of public service
- For a charity, the main objective might be to provide maximum aid or support for a particular group of people.

The process can be shown as follows:

Step 1:	Identify corporate objective (usually a financial objective)
Step 2:	Establish targets for the financial objective
Step 3:	Develop business strategies for achieving the financial objective/targets
Step 4:	Convert strategies into action plans
Step 5:	Monitor performance

Decision making criteria are strongly linked to the choice of objectives. Thus, if an objective is to maximise shareholder wealth, all decisions should be taken based on the impact that the decision would have on shareholder wealth.

When the main objective of an organisation is not a financial objective, there is always a financial constraint on its objective, such as providing the highest quality of public service with the available finance.

1.2 The primary corporate objective

The primary objective for companies is to maximise the wealth of its owners, the equity shareholders. It is worth exploring this statement in a little more depth.

Constraints on the primary objective

The above objective forms the basis of theoretical decision making in financial management. However, wealth maximisation is not an undertaking that takes place in a vacuum. Wealth must be maximised taking account of other constraints within which the entity must operate. These include:

- Legal constraints – there are many activities that are very profitable but which are also illegal. Wealth maximisation ignores such opportunities.
- Need to address the interests of other stakeholders. For example, to treat employees fairly and well, to treat customers and suppliers in a proper and ethical way, and to take into consideration the needs of society and the need to preserve the environment

Theoretical issue

Companies do not operate in a perfect world – they do not have perfect information. Therefore, a manager can never know if wealth is maximised or not in a given circumstance. Perhaps it would be better to talk of the objective as increasing shareholder wealth by as much as possible rather than maximising it.

Definitions and measurement

A company trying to maximise shareholder wealth must decide what the term means and how to measure it. Shareholder wealth is usually taken as being dividends plus the market value of the shares. Strategies are therefore desirable if they result in higher dividends, a higher share price or both.

This leads to practical problems:

- How does a company identify projects that will lead to higher share price and higher dividends?
- What time scale should be used?

Practical targets

The objective of maximising shareholder wealth is generally accepted as a sound basis for financial planning, but is not practical in terms of actually setting financial performance targets and measuring actual performance against the target. Other financial objectives might therefore be used instead, in the expectation that if these objectives are achieved, shareholder wealth will be increased by an optimal amount.

These include:

- maximising profits; and
- achieving growth in earnings per share.

These can be justified in terms of the pursuit of wealth maximisation as follows:

Stated objective	Link to wealth maximisation
To maximise profits	This would lead to the ability to pay out bigger dividends and to the ability to take advantage of favourable investment opportunities. This should lead to increased market value
To increase earnings per share year on year.	This would lead to a positive perception in the market place which in turn should lead to a higher demand for the shares thus increasing market value.

Other objectives

Companies might have other stated non-financial objectives but these can also be justified in terms of the pursuit of wealth maximisation.

Stated objective	Link to wealth maximisation
To pay staff competitive salaries	This should lead to happy and competent staff who will work hard for the company thus enabling it to achieve good performance. This should lead to increased market value
To invest in staff training	This should lead to staff with higher skills leading to improved performance. This should lead to increased market value
To invest in new product development	This would lead to bigger profits in the future (if successful). This should lead to increased market value
To take into account the needs of society and the need to preserve the environment	If the company was seen to do otherwise it would lead to bad publicity which would be reflected in the share price falling.

In summary

The objective of a company is to maximise the wealth of the equity shareholders. This is achieved by maximising the combined value of dividends and share price growth.

However, this is undertaken within the limits of having to satisfy the needs of other stakeholders.

1.3 Policy frameworks

The policy framework of a company will set out the corporate objectives and provide background information as to how they are to be achieved. This might include:

- project benchmarks (e.g. "investment projects must have a positive, NPV, a ROCE of 15% and a payback of 3 years");
- procedures that must be followed (e.g. all foreign currency transactions must be hedged);
- statements of environmental targets that must be met.

1.4 Advising on financial goals and financial policy development

A large part of the role of the senior financial manager is advisory, providing advice on financial strategy and policies.

A company must develop strategies in order to achieve its corporate objectives. To achieve an objective of maximising shareholder wealth, financial strategies should be formulated by the board of directors. Financial strategy is often (but not always) targeted towards achieving growth in annual earnings and achieving a return on investment in excess of the cost of the funds used to make the investment.

Financial managers provide advice concerned with three fundamental decisions supported by advice in other areas:

Three fundamental decisions

Decision	Questions to be answered	Chapter
Investment decisions	Which investments should be undertaken using the available capital resources? How can limited resources be used most effectively to achieve the corporate objectives?	Chapters 6 to 9 Capital rationing is covered in chapter 6
Financing decisions	How should finance be raised in order to minimise cost of capital (debt or equity)? What optimum finance structure will result in a minimised cost of capital?	Chapters 10 and 11
Dividend decisions	What should be the balance between the amount of profit distributed and that held back for reinvestment in the business? Whether alternatives to cash dividends might be used?	Chapter 21

Supporting decisions

Decision	Comment	Chapter
Financial planning and control	Target setting. Recommending internal controls Tax efficiency Setting transfer prices (Chapter 21)	Chapter 21
Risk management	What financial risks are faced by the business? How financial risks should be monitored, measured and addressed?	Chapters 2, 7 and 17 to 20
Communicating financial policy to internal and external stakeholders	Ensuring that the company meets its legal responsibilities (e.g. producing financial statements, meeting statutory filing deadlines etc.) Providing information as necessary to satisfy needs of stakeholder.	Chapter 3

Financial strategy formulation

- Assessment of corporate performance
- Optimum capital mix
- Distribution and retention policy
- Management of risk

2 Financial strategy formulation

Earlier it was noted that financial managers provide advice concerned with three fundamental decisions:

- **Investment decisions** – Which investments should be undertaken using capital resources
- **Financing decisions** – How finance should be raised in order to minimise cost of capital
- **Dividend decisions** – What the balance should be between the amount of profit distributed and that held back for reinvestment in the business.

Further responsibilities would include advice on the management of risk.

This section expands on some of these issues where others are covered in more detail in later chapters. Firstly though there is a brief reminder about performance measurement.

2.1 Assessment of corporate performance

An assessment of financial performance is important for two reasons:

- As a component of understanding strategic position
- To monitor progress of strategies that have been put into action

Financial ratios

Financial ratios are an important tool in measuring performance. The main financial ratios can be classified as:

- financial performance (return on capital, profitability and asset turnover)
- working capital ratios (average collection period; average inventory holding period etc)
- liquidity ratios (current ratio and quick ratio)
- debt ratios (gearing ratio (or debt to equity ratio) and interest cover ratio)
- investor ratios (earnings per share, price earnings ratio)

These have been covered elsewhere in your studies and will not be repeated here. If you need to revise these they are set out in detail in the F7 text book.

2.2 Optimum capital mix

Achieving the optimal capital mix for the company (mix of equity capital and debt capital) by minimising the company's weighted average cost of capital (WACC) will add to the value of the company and the wealth of the shareholders.

A financial manager must be able to calculate a cost of capital, and should advise management on what cost of capital should be used to evaluate particular capital expenditure projects. These aspects of the cost of capital are explained in later chapters.

A basic policy objective should be to minimise the company's cost of capital. This is because for a given annual return, the total value of a company is maximised when the weighted average cost of capital is minimised.

Example

The annual operational cash flows of Company YZ are $800,000 and are expected to remain $800,000 in perpetuity.

The total value of the company can be estimated by dividing the annual cash flows by the weighted average cost of capital.

- If the WACC is 10%, the total value of the company (equity and debt capital) is $8,000,000 ($800,000/0.10).
- If the WACC is 8%, the total value of the company (equity and debt capital) is $10,000,000 (800,000/0.08).
- If the WACC is 5%, the total value of the company (equity and debt capital) is $16,000,000 ($800,000/0.05).

When the total value of a company is maximised, the wealth of its shareholders is also maximised, in terms of dollars per share.

The WACC can be changed by altering the financial gearing of the company, and changing the relative amounts of debt capital.

The differing views on how WACC is affected by financial gearing are described in a later chapter on the cost of capital.

2.3 Distribution and retention policy

Companies retain earnings to reinvest in the business, and many companies rely extensively on retained profits as a source of new finance. There are several reasons why companies might prefer retained earnings to other sources of new capital:

- There are no issue costs with retained earnings, whereas there is a cost of issuing shares and some costs of arranging borrowing.
- No formalities are required to obtain the capital, and holding on to profits as retained earnings is very convenient.
- Shareholders usually expect some proportion of earnings to be retained in the business.

A company should apply a policy for dividend payments and profit retentions that achieves a suitable balance between the expectation of shareholders for annual dividend payments, and the need to retain some profits to reinvest in the business to achieve further growth in profits in the future. (Dividend policy is considered in more detail later in this chapter, and in detail in chapter 21).

Retentions and dividend growth: Gordon's growth model

Retained earnings should be invested for growth in future profits, earnings and dividends. The Gordon growth model will be dealt with in more detail in a later chapter. Briefly, however, the rate of annual growth in dividends can be expressed as:

$g = br$

where:

g is the annual rate of dividend growth
b is the proportion of earnings that is retained for reinvestment, and
r is the rate of return on investments by the company.

For example, if a company retains 40% of its earnings and the return on company capital investment is 8%, annual growth in earnings and dividends should be 3.2% (40% × 8%). If 60% of earnings are retained, only 40% of earnings are available for dividends, but the expected rate of annual earnings and dividend growth should be 4.8%.

Dividend policy

Stock market companies do not usually announce a dividend policy, and inform investors of the dividends they will expect to pay in future years. However, companies often adopt a consistent dividend policy, and investors might base their expectations of a company's future dividends on what the company has done in the past.

According to academic theory (for example, the theory put forward by Modigliani and Miller) the value of a company's shares does not depend on the dividend policy of the company. Shareholders ought to be indifferent about whether a company pays out its after-tax profits as dividends, or re-invests them. If a company does not pay out its profits to shareholders as dividends, it will reinvest the profits for growth in profits, so that future dividends will be larger and the share price will increase.

If a shareholder needs cash, he should not have to rely on dividend payments. He can borrow the money instead, or even sell the shares.

In practice, however, the dividend policy of a company can affect its share price and does matter to many shareholders.

- Some investors want cash returns from their investments, and expect companies in which they hold shares to pay dividends. On the other hand, some investors buy shares to invest in growth, and are not concerned in the short-term about receiving dividends. Investors can buy shares in companies that have a dividend policy consistent with their preferences. (For example, for many years Microsoft did not pay any dividends at all and reinvested all its profits to grow the business. Investors in Microsoft shares knew that they were investing in a high-growth stock, and dividend payments were not important to them).
- The tax position of investors might give them a preference for dividends or capital growth, when the tax rate on dividend payments is different from the tax rate on capital gains.
- Paying a dividend might send a signal from the company to the market. If the signal is that the board of directors are confident about the future of the company, this might give investors more confidence in the company and boost the share price.
- When a company reduces its dividend below the amount of dividends paid in previous years, this could be a signal that the company is in financial difficulty, and the share price is likely to fall.

Monitoring dividend policy

A company's dividend policy can be monitored with a few simple ratios.

- **Dividend per share as a percentage of earnings per share**. EPS is the maximum amount that a company could pay as dividends out of the year's profits. A low dividend/EPS ratio indicates high earnings retention. A high dividend/EPS ratio indicates low earnings retention – and this could restrict the ability of the company to finance investments in new capital projects for future growth.
- **Percentage growth or decline in annual dividends per share**.
- **Dividends as a proportion of free cash flow to equity**. Free cash flow can be defined in several ways, but for the purpose of analysing dividend policy, a useful measure of free cash flow to equity is after deduction of capital spending on investments in replacement non-current assets.

2.4 Management of risk

Financial managers are responsible for advising operational managers and the directors of a company about capital investment risk, and should establish a system for the management and monitoring of risk. Areas of responsibility include:

- establishing systems to monitor capital spending and for financial risk management; and
- developing a framework for financial risk management, with a variety of strategies for reducing and controlling risks, risk hedging and risk diversification

The treasury department should also be specifically responsible for monitoring and management of treasury risks, such as foreign currency risks and interest rate risks.

Framework for risk management

A risk management framework that is useful to remember is as follows. (It is based on the COSO risk management framework, developed some years ago by the Commission of Sponsoring Organisations in the US).

- There should be a well-established culture of risk management. Senior management should recognise the importance of risk and the need to balance the desire for high profits and returns with the need to avoid excessive risk exposures.
- There should be systems for identifying and measuring risks, and recognising which controls must be managed and controlled.
- Methods for managing risks should be applied to risks that are considered sufficiently serious, provided that the cost of controlling the risk does not exceed the potential benefit from reducing the risk of losses.
- The methods used to manage risks should be communicated to all managers concerned. Managers should be kept informed about risk as well as returns.
- There should be a regular monitoring of risk management systems, methods and measures, to ensure that they function effectively and achieve their intended purpose.

Risk assessment will be considered in later chapters, for example with respect to risk in capital investment projects. The risk in a proposed capital project should be assessed and the risk assessment should be included in the decision-making process leading to the decision of whether or not to undertake the investment.

After a capital investment has been undertaken, actual spending and actual returns should be monitored (in a 'post investment audit') to establish whether actual spending was kept within the planned limit and whether the expected returns were actually achieved.

Behavioural finance

- Definition and explanation of behavioural finance
- Concepts in behavioural finance

3 Behavioural finance

The efficient markets hypothesis and the methods of share valuation described earlier are based on an assumption that every investor is a 'rational economic man'. There is a logical and rational explanation for the valuation of financial assets, and these valuations should be their actual market value in an efficient market.

The assumption of rational behaviour and logical economic valuation has been challenged on the grounds that this is not what happens in the real world. Actual share prices and share price movements cannot be explained entirely or consistently by rational behaviour of investors.

It can be argued that other factors affect share prices and share price movements. In particular, market prices are affected by human psychology and the oddities of human behaviour.

For example, stock market 'bubbles' (often followed by a stock market 'crash') have shown beyond doubt that investors do not act in a rational way all the time, and behavioural factors are clearly important.

3.1 Definition and explanation of behavioural finance

Behavioural finance is closely linked to behavioural economics. It is the study of how psychology affects the behaviour of human investors (as distinct from computer investment models) and the effect that human behaviour has on financial markets and asset values.

Behavioural finance can explain both **why and how** markets might not be efficient (and why share prices might differ from what they perhaps ought logically to be). However, it cannot be used to predict share price movements.

Some definitions and explanations of behavioural finance are set out below.

- 'Behavioural finance is the study of the influence of psychology on the behaviour of financial practitioners and the subsequent effect on markets' (Sewell, 2005).
- 'Behavioural finance is the study of how psychology affects financial decision making and financial markets' (Shefrin, 2001).
- 'Behavioural economics combines the twin disciplines of psychology and economics to explain why and how people make seemingly irrational or illogical decisions when they spend, invest, save and borrow money' (Belsky and Gilovich, 1999).

- 'For most economists it is an article of faith that financial markets reach rational aggregate outcomes, despite the irrational behaviour of some participants, since sophisticated players stand ready to capitalise on mistakes of the naïve.... Yet financial markets have been subject to speculative fads, from Dutch tulip mania to junk bonds and to occasional dramatic losses in value such as occurred in October 1987, that are hard to interpret as rational.... Psychology can help to explain such aberrant macro phenomena' (Patel, Zeckhauser and Hendricks, 1991).

Supporters of the arguments of behavioural finance accept that many investors in the financial markets do act in a rational way, and seek to maximise returns. If investors identify shares or bonds in the market that are clearly over-valued or under-valued, they will sell or buy them until the market price changes to the point where the price anomaly no longer exists. This is called **arbitrage**. However it is argued that whereas some investors might make rational investment decisions, the actions of other investors can be more influential on market prices.

- Psychology can explain why many investors do not behave in a totally rational way.
- There are 'limits to arbitrage'. The actions of rational investors cannot offset the illogical effect on asset prices that are caused by less rational investors.

3.2 Concepts in behavioural finance

The recent origins of behavioural economics date back to the 1950s, but the origin of behavioural finance can probably be traced to an article by De Bondt and Thaler in 1985 'Does the Stock Market Over-react?' De Bondt and Thaler demonstrated that investors **over-react** systematically to unexpected and dramatic news.

There are many different behavioural or psychological concepts in behavioural finance. Some of these are explained below.

- **Loss aversion**. There is a noticeable lack of symmetry between decisions to buy and decisions to sell investment assets. Investors are often unwilling to sell shares when they would make a nominal loss on the sale. Loss aversion is also evident in the reluctance of house owners to reduce the selling price of their house, even in a period of weak demand from home buyers.
- **Under-reaction and over-reaction**. Share price movements are often characterised by under-reaction to new events or new information, followed by over-reaction.
- There is sometimes a '**herd instinct**' and investors simply do the same as other investors – and buy or sell shares – without considering the logic of what they are doing.
- **Status quo bias**. When there is uncertainty in the stock market about which shares should be 'winners' and which should be 'losers', there may be a bias towards the status quo, and share prices of both 'winners' and 'losers' might remain stable when they ought logically to move up or down.
- There is also evidence that people often prefer to **invest in what is familiar** to them, rather than using the rational principles of portfolio theory in their investment selection.

However, there are limitations to the value of behavioural finance.

- Behavioural finance can explain why investors might act irrationally and why share prices move higher or lower than should be expected on rational economic grounds. However, concepts of behavioural finance cannot be used to predict what share prices will be, or how they will move. It does not therefore provide a reliable basis for making investment decisions.
- It might also be argued that irrational behaviour affects share prices in the short term, but essentially investors are likely to act in a way they consider rational, in order to maximise their investment returns. In spite of the effects of psychology and irrational behaviour on share prices, the logical methods of share price valuation are probably the most reliable methods of valuation we can use.

CHAPTER

2

Theoretical and practical rationale for risk management

Contents

Risk and risk management

- Risk
- Nature and importance of business and financial risks
- Elements of a risk management system

1 Risk and risk management

1.1 Risk

Risk is usually associated with the possibility that things might go wrong, that events might turn out worse than expected or that something bad might happen.

However, risk has a broader meaning. Risk exists whenever a future outcome or future event cannot be predicted with certainty, and a range of different possible outcomes or events might occur.

Risks can be divided into two categories:

- pure risks; and
- speculative risks.

Pure risk (downside risk)

Pure risk, also called downside risk, is a risk where there is a possibility that an adverse event will occur. Events might turn out to be worse than expected, but they cannot be better than expected.

Pure risks are risks that can often be controlled either by means of internal controls or by insurance. These risks might be called **internal control risks** or **operational risks**.

Speculative risk (two-way risk)

Speculative risk, also called two-way risk, exists when the actual future event or outcome might be either better or worse than expected.

An investor in shares is exposed to a speculative risk, because the market price of the shares might go up or down. The investor will gain if prices go up and suffer a loss if prices go down.

Companies face two-way risk whenever they make business investment decisions. For example, a company might invest in the development of a new product, on the basis of sales and profit forecasts. Actual sales and profits might turn out to be higher or lower than forecast, and the investment might provide a high return, moderate return or low return (or even a loss).

Speculative risks cannot be avoided because risks must be taken in order to make profits. As a general rule, higher risks should be justified by the expectation of higher profits (although events might turn out worse than expected) and a company needs to decide what level of speculative risks are acceptable. Speculative risks are usually called **business risk**, and might also be called **strategic risk** or **enterprise risk**.

Business decisions taken by management could involve both business risk (strategic risk) and operational risk (downside risk).

It is easy to think of 'risk' as something undesirable, to be avoided. This attitude to risk focuses on downside risk. It is important to recognise that risk is unavoidable in business and that risks must be taken in order to make profits and a return on investment.

A key aspect of risk management is therefore managing the level of risk and:

- deciding which risks are acceptable and which are not: setting risk limits
- communicating the policy on risk, and
- monitoring risks, and taking appropriate measures to prevent the risks from becoming excessive.

1.2 Nature and importance of business and financial risks

The board of directors should consider business risk when it makes strategic decisions. It should choose strategies that are expected to be profitable, but that keeps the business risks to a level that it considers acceptable. Consequently, both risk and return should be assessed in strategic decision-making.

Business risks are strategic risks that threaten the health and survival of a business. They vary between companies and over time.

- The failure rate is greater for those businesses in cyclical industries like tourism.
- The failure rate among new start-up businesses is greater than that amongst more mature businesses.

Financial risk is a major cause of business risk. Cash flow and liquidity problems can be very damaging to the financial health of a business. Such problems can be caused by trading fluctuations but working capital management and financial structure also play a significant role.

Whilst debt finance might be preferable when interest rates are low or necessary when equity capital is unavailable it increases financial risk.

The major risks facing companies vary over time, and managers might have different opinions about which risks are more significant than others. Risks differ between companies in different industries or markets.

1.3 Elements of a risk management system

Risk management is the process of managing both downside risks and business risks. It can be defined as the culture, structures and processes that are focused on achieving possible opportunities yet at the same time control unwanted results.

This definition identifies the connection between risk and returns.

- The safest strategy is to take no risks at all. However, this is an unrealistic business strategy. All business activity involves some risk.

- Business decisions should be directed towards achieving the objectives of the company. The main objective is (usually) to increase value for shareholders over the long term.
- Strategies are devised for achieving this objective and performance targets are set. The strategies should be consistent with the amount of business risk that the company is willing to take, and the targets should be realistic for the chosen strategies.
- The strategies are implemented, and management should try to achieve the stated objectives and performance targets, but at the same time should manage the downside risks and try to limit the business risks.

Risk management is a corporate governance issue. The board of directors have a responsibility to safeguard the assets of the company and to protect the investment of the shareholders from loss of value. The board should therefore keep strategic risks within limits that shareholders would expect, and to avoid or control operational risks.

The elements of a risk management system:

- There should be a culture of risk awareness within the company. Managers and employees should understand the 'risk appetite' of the company, and that excessive risks are not justified in the search for higher profits.
- There should be a system and processes for identifying, assessing and measuring risks. When risks have been measured, they can be prioritised, and measures for controlling or containing the risk can be taken.
- There should be an efficient system of communicating information about risk and risk management to managers and the board of directors.
- Strategies and risks should be monitored, to ensure that strategic objectives are being achieved within acceptable levels of risk.

Process of risk management

- The need to categorise business/strategic risks
- Risk identification
- Assessing risks: impact and probability
- Different approaches to controlling risk
- Capital investment monitoring system (CIMS)

2 Process of risk management

Any process of risk management might contain the following components:

- Categorisation of risks
- Identification and assessment of risks
- Control measures

2.1 The need to categorise business/strategic risks

Categorisation is necessary to give some structure to the risk management process. The board of directors might use the same risk categories to provide their report on internal control and risk management, or to discuss risk in their annual business review (narrative report).

There are no standard risk classifications; the nature of business risks varies between different types of business. It is up to each business to identify and categorise the risks it faces as it sees fit.

Common broad categories of risk include:

- Operational risks
- Reputation risks
- Political risks
- Economic risks
- Regulatory risks
- Fiscal risks

Some of the above might be subdivided into more specific categories.

Operational risks

The risk of loss from a failure of internal business and control processes. Operational risks relate to things that could go wrong on a day-to-day basis. This category might include risks of:

- IT failure
- Production plant breakdown
- Fraud
- Supply chain problems

Reputation risks

Reputation risk is difficult to measure (quantify). It is the risk that a company's reputation with the general public (and customers), or the reputation of its product 'brand', will suffer damage. Damage to reputation can arise in many different ways: incidents that damage reputation are often reported by the media.

Companies that might suffer losses from damage to their reputation need to be vigilant and alert for any incident that could create adverse publicity. Public relations consultants might be used to assist with this task.

Political risks

This relates to the adverse effect that political decisions might have on company value. It can be used to describe impacts of change in policy both at home and in foreign countries in which an entity operates.

Political decisions can change the economic, regulatory and fiscal environments within which an organisation is operating.

Economic risks

This arises from changes in economic policies. For example, many western economies are reducing government spending in the current financial downturn. This has a direct impact on demand for companies that are suppliers to public sector bodies and an indirect impact for many others as there is less spending power in the economy.

Regulatory risks

This refers to risks arising from changes to the legal and regulatory environment within which a company operates.

Fiscal risk

This is the risk of changes in the tax system(s) faced by an organisation. It can be used to describe impacts of changes in policy both at home and in foreign countries in which an entity operates

Fiscal risk is unavoidable for companies that pay tax on their profits. However, the risk might sometimes be reduced for large companies. A large company can try to negotiate with the government of a country before deciding whether to invest in the country. They might argue that they will not invest unless the government gives an assurance of fiscal stability.

2.2 Risk identification

Risk identification is the initial stage in a system of risk management. A company needs to understand what risks it faces, both in its environment and markets (strategic risks) and internally (operational risks).

There are no standard rules about how risks should be identified.

- In a large company, it might be appropriate to identify risks at different levels in the organisation – on a group-wide basis, and for each business division and for each department or function.
- Management might be responsible for identifying strategic risks/business risks for the company, but the internal auditors or external auditors might be more efficient at identifying operational risks (and suggesting suitable internal controls to control the risks).

Risks identified by a company will vary in importance. Some risks might be unimportant, or easily controlled. Some risks will be very significant. Having identified risks, it is therefore necessary to assess the importance of each risk, in order to:

- rank the risks in order of significance (order of priority), and
- identify the risks that are the most significant, and
- identify the significant risks where control measures are urgently needed.

(Deciding on suitable control measures will depend on the significance of the risk, and the cost of taking control measures. Control measures are only justified if the cost of the control measures is less than the benefits obtained from reducing the risk).

2.3 Assessing risks: impact and probability

The assessment of risk is sometimes called '**risk profiling**' or '**risk mapping**'.

To assess each risk, it is necessary to consider the likelihood that losses will occur as a consequence of the risk, and the size or amount of the loss when this happens.

A simple approach to risk mapping involves taking each risk that has been identified and placing it on a map. The map is a 2×2 matrix, with:

- one side representing the **frequency** of adverse events or the **probability** that the risk will materialise and an adverse outcome will occur; and
- the other side representing the **impact (loss)** if an adverse event occurs or adverse circumstances arise.

The format of a simple risk map is shown below.

		Probability or frequency of the risk materialising	
		Low probability/ frequency	High probability/ Frequency
Impact/size of potential loss	High impact	**High impact** **Low probability** *Consider the need for control measures, such as insurance*	**High impact** **High probability** *Take immediate action to control the risk*
	Low impact	**Low impact** **Low probability** *Review periodically*	**Low impact** **High probability** *Consider the need for control action*

A risk map can help management to identify risks where immediate control measures are required, and where the need for control measures should be considered or reviewed periodically.

'High impact, low probability' risks might include the risks of damage to assets from fire or flooding, the risk of a terrorist attack or the risk of major legislation that will affect the company's business. Some of these risks, such as risks of fire, theft and criminal damage, can be insured. Insurance reduces the residual risk by the amount of the insurance cover obtained.

All key risks should be 'owned' by specific individual managers, who should be required to take the necessary control measures and report to their senior manager about what they have done.

Measuring risks

Whenever possible, risks should be measured. Measuring risk means quantifying the risk. When risks are quantified, the risk can be managed through setting targets for maximum risk tolerance and measuring actual performance against the target.

Risk measurements can be financial measurements (for example, a measurement of the expected loss) or non-financial (for example, a measurement of expected injuries to employees at work).

However, not all risks can be measured. Where risks are assessed in qualitative terms, risk management decisions become a matter of management judgement.

Prioritising risks

Within a system of risk management, companies need to establish a process for deciding which risks are tolerable and which might need more control measures to reduce the risk. (Sometimes, it might be decided that control measures are excessive, and that money can be saved by reducing the controls, without increasing risk above acceptable levels).

Deciding on priorities for risk management might be a matter of management judgement.

2.4 Different approaches to controlling risk

There are several different approaches to controlling risks. Risk management methods are much more sophisticated in some industries (and in some countries) than in others. For example, the financial services and banking industry has developed products (financial derivatives) that can be used to manage financial risks.

Approaches to the management of business risks that are described in this section are:

- risk transfer
- risk sharing
- hedging risks
- diversification of risks

Risk transfer

Risk transfer involves passing some or all of a risk on to someone else, so that the other person has the exposure to the risk.

A common example of risk transfer is insurance. By purchasing insurance, risks are transferred to the insurance company, which will pay for any losses covered by the insurance policy.

Using insurance to manage risk is appropriate for risks where the potential losses are high, but the probability of a loss occurring is fairly low.

Risk sharing

Risk sharing involves collaborating with another person and sharing the risks jointly.

Common methods of risk sharing in business are partnerships and joint ventures. In a joint venture, all the joint venture partners share in the investment, the management, the cost of the investment, the risks and the rewards.

Companies pursuing a strategy of developing their business in other countries might use joint ventures as a way of entering the market in a different country. For the 'global' company, the joint venture partner would be a local business whose management have knowledge of the local market. For a local business, a joint venture with a foreign company reduces the financial risk, and also improves the opportunities for expansion and growth.

Hedging risks

The term 'hedging' risks is used extensively in the financial markets, and hedging is commonly associated with the management of financial risks such as currency risk.

Hedging risk means creating a position (making a transaction) that offsets an exposure to another risk. For example, if a company has an exposure to currency risk, and will lose money if the US dollar falls in value against the euro, a hedge can be created whereby the company will make a profit if the US dollar falls in value against the euro. The loss on the original risk exposure will be offset by a gain on the hedge position.

Risks can be hedged with a variety of derivative instruments, such as futures, options and swaps.

Diversification

Risks can be reduced through diversification. Diversification is also called 'spreading risks'.

The purpose of diversification in business is to invest in a range of different business activities, and build up a portfolio of different business activities. Each individual business activity is risky, but some businesses might perform better than expected just as some might perform worse than expected. Taking the entire portfolio of different businesses, the good performers will offset the bad performers, and the portfolio as a whole might provide, on average, the expected returns.

2.5 Capital investment monitoring system (CIMS)

A capital investment monitoring system (CIMS) monitors how an investment project is progressing once it has been implemented.

Features of CIMS include the following

- A CIMS can be used to establish a plan and budget of how the project should proceed. The plan should include milestones for what needs to be achieved and by when and also consider possible risks (internal and external) that might affect the project.
- CIMS should set up contingency plans for dealing with the identified risks.
- CIMS monitors progress of the project by comparisons to the plan and budget.
- CIMS should identify the need for corrective action when needed.

Benefits of CIMS include the following:

- CIMS system should ensure, as far as possible, that the project meets what is expected of it in terms of revenues and expenses.
- CIMS helps ensure that the project is completed on time.
- CIMS is active in monitoring risk factors that might affect the project outcomes.
- CIMS encourages a proactive rather than reactive approach to the management of risk.
- CIMS is a communication and coordination device between managers charged with managing the project and the monitoring team.

Why manage risk? – Theory and practice

3 Why manage risk? – Theory and practice

This section is based on an article written by the examiner in Student Accountant (issue 19/2010).

The examiner pointed out that management of risk is a key area. He wrote that "it is vital that students are able to apply risk management techniques, such as using derivative instruments to hedge against risk, and offer advice and recommendations as required by the scenario in the question".

He went on to say "however, it is also equally important that students understand why corporations manage risk in theory and in practice, because risk management costs money but does it actually add more value to a corporation?"

3.1 Introduction

Business involves generating returns by undertaking risky projects. Important management decisions include:

- which projects to undertake;
- how they should be financed; and
- whether the volatility of its returns (its risk) should be managed.

Risk (volatility of returns) can be quantified through statistical measures such as probabilities, standard deviations and correlation coefficients.

Risk management involves decisions about changing the volatility of returns. Managing risk costs money. Therefore, risk should be managed if it results in increasing the value of a corporation. This could be either by increasing the future cash flows or by reducing investors' required rate of return (or both).

If markets were perfect the owners of large corporations would be well diversified. Such corporations would not increase value by diversifying company specific risk, as their equity holders have already achieved this level of risk diversification. In this situation it can be argued that risk management activity is at best neutral or at worst detrimental because costs would either equal or be more than the benefits accrued.

This argument would not apply to smaller companies whose owners might not be well diversified.

This implies that small companies might benefit from risk management but not large corporations. This is of course the opposite of what is found in practice with large corporations investing heavily in treasury management expertise.

This is because there are real world imperfections which result in outcomes which differ from those predicted by models based on assumptions based on market perfection. These imperfections include:

- managers might not act in the best interests of the shareholders
- The existence of other stakeholders whose requirements need to be met
- Corporations paying tax at different effective rates

Such factors mean that in reality there are opportunities to reduce volatility in cash flows at a cost which enhances corporate value.

3.2 Impact of reward structures for senior management

Managers might act in their own interests. A manager might be concerned that his salary and other benefits continue in the future. This might result in actions to reduce unsystematic risk. This would be of no benefit to the well diversified shareholder. In fact, it would use the company's resources unnecessarily thus reducing corporate value.

Reward structures including large equity stakes

Managers who hold concentrated equity stakes in a corporation face both systematic and unsystematic risk. Such managers may act in their own best interests rather than that of the other shareholders by trying to reduce unsystematic risk. This use of the corporation's resources to reduce unsystematic risk might reduce the corporation's value.

Why don't they diversify the risk of their concentrated equity investments themselves? They could sell equity in their own corporation and replace it by buying equity in other corporations. One possible explanation that has been suggested is that senior managers are reluctant to sell equity in their own company as this might be interpreted as a bad sign by the market.

Reward structures including equity options

Managers holding equity options (which will be converted into equity at a future date) are more inclined to undertake risky projects (and less inclined to manage risk). This is because they want to maximise future profits and the price of the equity in order to maximise the future share price.

Equity options have been criticised because they encourage managers to act in an overly risky manner.

3.3 Insolvency and financial distress

In situations of capital market perfection there would be no financial distress. In practice corporations do experience problems of financial distress and of insolvency (inability of meeting financial obligations as they fall due).

Financial distress is less severe than insolvency as the corporation can continue to operate but incurring greater costs as suppliers, for example, offer less favourable terms of trade due to concern that it may become insolvent in the future.

Thus even though the shareholders might be well diversified other stakeholders (suppliers and employees) are not. These are subject to the corporation's full risk, as opposed to only systematic risk, and therefore demand greater compensation for their participation.

Active risk management reduces the possibility of financial distress making it easier to contract with these other stakeholders and at a lower cost. The more volatile the cash flows of a corporation, the more likely the need to manage its risk in order to reduce the costs related to financial distress.

3.4 External funding and agency costs

Another consequence of financial distress is that it compromises a corporation's ability to raise finance and this in turn means that it might be unable to enter into favourable investment opportunities. This has been described as the "under investment" problem.

Lenders receive a fixed return on their investment with any additional benefit due to higher profits going to the shareholders.

Existence of possibility of financial distress

Suppose a corporation is considering two projects each requiring the same initial capital investment. Project A offers a return of 10% and project B offers a return of 15%. Project B is more risky than project A. The company can borrow at 6%.

The views of lenders and shareholders would differ on which project the company should undertake.

- The lender would prefer project A. Both projects would allow the lender to recover the required rate of return but project A has a lower risk. If the corporation undertook project B the lender would be subject to higher risk for no additional benefit.
- The shareholders would perhaps prefer project B as this would allow access to potentially higher returns

Lenders respond to this possibility by imposing higher borrowing costs and restrictive covenants. In other words, the existence of the possibility of financial distress means that a corporation faces higher agency costs.

Substantial financial distress

In circumstance of substantial financial distress this conflict becomes more extreme. A corporation may find it difficult to raise equity capital to finance new investment as profits earned would initially go to the debt holders and the equity holders will gain only residual profits. Shareholders would put pressure on management to reject good, low risk projects, which may have been acceptable to the lenders.

Lenders would be reluctant to lend to a severely distressed company in any case.

Financial distress may make the cost of external debt and equity funding so expensive that a corporation and its management may be forced to reject profitable projects.

This all means that risk management to reduce financial distress (by reducing cash flow volatility) may help management to achieve an optimal mix of debt and equity, and to undertake profitable projects.

3.5 Capital structure

Risk management reduces operating cash flow volatility. This would enable a corporation to borrow more and at a lower rate.

- A business with stable operating cash flows can borrow favourably as the lender perceives its investment to be safe.
- A business with volatile cash flows would find it more difficult and more expensive to borrow.

Since debt is cheaper to finance than equity because of lower required rates of return and the tax shield, taking on more debt should increase the value of the corporation.

Risk management can help a corporation obtain an optimal capital structure of debt and equity to maximise its value.

3.6 Information asymmetry

In practice the preferred source of funds is those that have been generated internally. Such funds are cheaper. It has been suggested that this is in part due to the fact that raising finance externally would involve parties who do not have the complete information about the corporation.

If risk management stabilises the cash flows that the corporation receives from year to year, then this would enable managers to plan when the necessary internal funds will become available for future investments with greater accuracy. They will then be able to align their investment policies with the availability of funding.

3.7 Taxation

A corporation might face progressive taxation rates where the tax rate increases with higher profits.

Risk management might reduce the tax burden of earnings volatility so that the corporation stays in the lower tax brackets.

CHAPTER 3

Ethical and governance issues

Contents

Conflicting stakeholder interests

- Stakeholders and their objectives
- Separation of ownership from control
- Agency theory
- Resolving stakeholder conflict

1 Conflicting stakeholder interests

1.1 Stakeholders and their objectives

The stakeholders in an entity are any individuals, groups of individuals or external organisations that have an interest (a 'stake') in what the entity does or is trying to achieve.

Some stakeholders have much more influence than others over the strategic decision-making of an entity, and the identity of the main stakeholders varies between different entities.

The stakeholders or stakeholder groups for a business entity usually include most of the following:

- the ordinary shareholders
- bondholders and other lenders
- the investment community
- suppliers, especially major suppliers
- customers
- the directors and other senior executive managers
- other managers and employees, or groups of employees
- the government (local or national government)
- local communities in which the entity operates
- the general public.

The expectations of stakeholders

Each stakeholder or stakeholder group has different expectations from a company. They expect to benefit from their association with the company, and the benefits they expect are different.

Stakeholder	Expectations
Shareholders	Share price growth Dividends Return on investment
Directors	Personal advancement – remuneration, status
Senior managers	Personal advancement – remuneration, status

Expectations of other stakeholder groups

Other stakeholder groups have different expectations from their company.

- Employees expect to receive fair pay for the work that they do. They will often want job security and possibly career progress. They might also expect good working conditions. The expectations of employees might be expressed by trade union representatives.
- Customers have expectations about the nature of the goods or services they receive from a company.
- Suppliers might expect to develop a good business relationship with the company and collaborate on achieving improvements in the value network.
- Communities might expect a company to provide employment and economic prosperity by investing in the local area
- The general public and government might expect a company to show concern for the environment and to reduce pollution and develop environment-friendly ways of operating.

1.2 Separation of ownership from control

Problems with agreeing the aims and objectives of a company and the resulting possible conflicts exist because of the separation of the ownership of a company from its control.

- Shareholders are the owners of the company.
- However, the company is a separate legal person, and decisions are made by the company in its own name, not in the name of the shareholders.
- The directors and senior managers of a company control the decisions that the company makes.

The legal rights of shareholders to make decisions for the company are very limited (by law, by stock market regulations and by the company's constitution) in all countries. The shareholders therefore rely on the directors and senior managers to govern the company in the interests of the shareholders and other stakeholders, and laws and codes of corporate governance are aimed at achieving this.

1.3 Agency theory

When directors and managers are appointed to run a company there is a separation of ownership from control and an agency-principal relationship is created. This agency relationship is a form of contract between a company's owners and its managers, where the owners (as principal) appoint an agent (the managers) to manage the company on their behalf. Within this arrangement, decision-making authority is delegated by the shareholders to the management.

Individuals are driven by self-interest so conflicts of self-interest may arise between shareholders and managers.

These agency problems create costs for the shareholders. The aim should be to minimise these costs, by improving the monitoring of management and/or providing management with incentives to bring their interests closer to those of the shareholders.

Possible conflicts of interest

Most shareholders want to increase their income and wealth over the long-term. The value of their shares depends on the long-term financial prospects for the company.

Managers might be concerned with meeting short term performance targets which might lead to them making decisions which are not in the long term interest of the company. The conflict is exacerbated when management remuneration is based on meeting such targets.

Agency conflicts are differences in the interests of owners and managers. Some of these conflicts that might have a direct impact on the financial management of a company are as follows:

- **Earnings retention**. The remuneration of directors and senior managers is often related to the size of the company (for example, annual sales). This gives managers an incentive to increase the size of the company, rather than to increase the returns to the company's shareholders. When this happens, companies might invest in capital investment projects where the expected return is quite small, or propose over-priced takeover bids for other companies.
- **Time horizon**. Shareholders are concerned about the long-term financial prospects of their company because the share price depends on expectations for the long-term future. In contrast, managers might only be interested in the short-term. This is partly because they might receive annual bonuses based on short-term performance, and partly because they might not expect to be with the company for more than a few years.
- **Risk minimisation**. Management might choose investments based on their impact on the total business risk of the company. However, this might not be in the best interests of well diversified shareholders who would only be concerned with the systematic risk of investments.
- **Risk minimisation**. Management might choose finance based on its impact on their perception of financial risk. Thus they might issue equity in preference to debt because they deem it to be safer. However, this might lead to a lost opportunity to reduce the cost of capital of the company as debt is cheaper than equity.

1.4 Resolving stakeholder conflict

Agency theory is based on the view that the system of corporate governance should be designed to minimise the agency problem, and reduce agency costs. For example, the management objectives could be aligned with shareholder objectives through the management remuneration system.

If the main financial management objective is the maximisation of shareholder wealth, management could be persuaded to pursue that objective by granting them share options. The grant of share options should motivate them to increase the market value of the shares as much as possible so as to maximise their wealth. Doing this would also increase the wealth of the shareholders.

In an ideal situation, the 'agency contract' between the owners and the managers of a company should ensure that the managers always act in the best interests of the owners. However, it is impossible to arrange the 'perfect contract', because decisions by the managers affect their own personal welfare as well as the interests of the owners.

Stakeholder theory

Agency theory makes the assumption that the main objective of a company should be to maximise the wealth of shareholders. Stakeholder theory is different. It is based on the view that the purpose of corporate governance should be to satisfy, as far as possible, the objectives of all key stakeholders – employees, investors, major creditors, customers, major suppliers, the government, local communities and the general public. A role of the company's directors is therefore to consider the interests of all the major stakeholders.

Managers should try to achieve a range of different objectives, not just the aim of maximising the value of the company for its shareholders. This is because different stakeholders each have their own (different) expectations from the company, which the company's management should attempt to satisfy. However, some stakeholders might be more important than others, so that management should give priority to their interests above the interests of other stakeholder groups.

Stakeholder theory also considers the role of companies in society, and the responsibility that they should have towards society as a whole. It might be argued that some companies are so large, and their influence on society is so strong, that they should be accountable to the public for what they do. The general public are taxpayers and as such they provide the economic and social infrastructure within which companies are allowed to operate. In return, companies should be expected to act as **corporate citizens** and act in ways that benefit society as a whole. This aspect of stakeholder theory is consistent with the arguments in favour of **corporate social responsibility**.

In the chapters that follow, the focus of attention will be largely on shareholder wealth maximisation, but it is always important to remember the potential significance of other stakeholder interests in a company, including the interest of the general public and the government.

Corporate governance

- Introduction to corporate governance
- Other aspects of the Combined Code

2 Corporate governance

2.1 Introduction to corporate governance

Corporate governance is the system by which companies are directed and controlled. (Cadbury Report).

Governance should not be confused with management.

- Management is concerned with running the business operations of a company.
- Governance is about giving a lead to the company and monitoring and controlling management decisions, so as to ensure that the company achieves its intended purpose and aims.

'If management is about running business, governance is about seeing that it is run properly': (Professor Bob Tricker, 1984).

Codes of governance

Codes of corporate governance, in different forms, have been developed in most countries where there is a stock exchange. The main reason for codes of good corporate governance is to help and protect investors.

- Investors need reliable information about companies, to decide whether to invest in shares or (if they already hold shares) whether to sell them. Financial reporting by companies and external auditing should therefore be reliable. Investors should also be given other information to help them make their investment decisions, such as information about future prospects of the company, internal control and risk management and directors' remuneration.
- Investors need to be protected against unethical or dishonest behaviour by company management. For example, there must be strict laws against insider dealing, to prevent managers from making personal profits at the expense of other investors.

Many investment institutions invest in the stock markets of many different countries. They can choose which markets to invest in, and can choose to avoid stock markets where they believe that governance practices are poor and investors are treated badly.

Countries have developed corporate governance codes and practices because they want to attract and keep investment capital, especially from global institutional investors. This is because investment capital helps the country's economy to develop and its companies to prosper. Pressure for better corporate governance has come mainly for two reasons:

- The collapse of major stock market companies in a major financial centre, where investors have lost substantial amounts of money and the cause of the collapse has been largely attributable to bad corporate governance.
- Pressure from institutional investors in countries with well-developed corporate governance codes or rules.

Ethics and company performance

Other reasons for encouraging the development of good corporate governance are that:

- Good corporate governance practices are an application of good business ethics.
- It might be argued that good corporate governance contributes to the efficiency and effectiveness of a company's leadership and management. If this view is correct, well-governed companies will be more successful in the long term than badly-governed companies. However, this has not yet been proved, one way or the other.

Corporate governance codes might be a voluntary code, or might be made a legal requirement.

In the UK, there is a mixture of voluntary code and legal requirements. For example, listed UK companies are required by the UK Listing Rules to comply with the Combined Code on Corporate Governance or explain their non-compliance in the annual report and accounts. In addition, quoted companies are required by UK law to disclose details of the remuneration of each individual director and to submit a directors' remuneration report to the shareholders for approval, at the annual general meeting of the company.

Measures recommended by the UK Combined Code for achieving good corporate governance relate to:

- the board of directors: the board's responsibilities and the composition of the board
- financial reporting and the independence of the external auditors
- directors' remuneration
- internal control and risk management
- communication between the company and its shareholders, and the rights and responsibilities of shareholders (particularly investment institutions such as pension funds and insurance companies).

The provisions of the UK Combined Code are described briefly below. These are a useful guideline to corporate governance issues generally, and how they might be dealt with in companies in any country.

2.2 Other aspects of the Combined Code

Directors' remuneration

The board should delegate to a remuneration committee (consisting of independent NEDs) responsibilities for:

- remuneration policy for executive directors, and
- negotiating the remuneration of individual executive directors.

In the UK, quoted companies are required by law to present a directors' remuneration report in the annual report and accounts and invite the shareholders to approve the report at the annual general meeting of the company.

Internal control and risk management

The board of directors must review the internal control system, and risk management system of the company, and satisfy themselves that suitable control systems are in place. The board should report to shareholders that they have done so.

The responsibility for carrying out an annual review of risk management and the internal control system may be delegated to the audit committee.

Communication with shareholders

The Combined Code requires the board of a company to promote good relations and good communications with their shareholders.

In addition, institutional investors have a responsibility for maintaining a dialogue with the company's board of directors.

A new legal requirement has been introduced throughout the European Union that listed companies should prepare an annual business review, setting out the operating and financial position of the company in easy-to-understand language.

Corporate governance and corporate social responsibility

In summary, the aims of good corporate governance should be to reduce the **conflicts of interest** between the board of directors and the shareholders.

The UK Combined Code does not include any provisions relating to Corporate Social Responsibility. However, some institutional investors seek to promote CSR in companies, and some institutions will not invest in companies that do not meet certain minimum CSR requirements.

Ethical issues in financial management

- Business ethics
- Corporate codes of ethics
- Contents of a corporate code of ethics

3 Ethical issues in financial management

3.1 Business ethics

In pursuing profits and shareholder wealth maximisation, companies should act ethically, and in giving advice financial managers should be conscious of any ethical issues that might be involved in the matter. Business ethics covers aspects of business behaviour such as:

- Honesty and integrity in business dealings with others: honesty is more than just remaining within the law!
- Concern for other stakeholders, such as employees, suppliers and customers.
- Respect for human rights: this might involve avoiding business dealings with unethical suppliers or suppliers who use child labour or slave labour.
- Concern for the environment: the need to reduce or avoid pollution and the need to develop a sustainable business.
- Recognition by large companies of the social responsibilities to the communities in which they exist and operate.

Some companies have expressed their concern for ethical conduct in a formal corporate code of ethics.

3.2 Corporate codes of ethics

A corporate code of ethics is a code of ethical behaviour, issued by the board of directors of a company. The decisions and actions of all employees in the company must be guided by the code. The effectiveness of a code of ethics depends on the leadership of the company – its directors and senior managers. These individuals must be seen to comply with the ethical code or other employees will see no purpose in complying with the code themselves.

It has been suggested that there are three reasons why companies might develop a code of ethics. These reasons are progressive, which means that companies might begin by having a code of ethics for the first reason, but then progress to the second and third reasons as they gain experience with implementing the code and appreciating its potential benefits.

- **Reason 1: Managing for compliance**. The company wants to ensure that all its employees comply with relevant laws and regulations, and conduct themselves in a way that the public expects. For example, companies providing a service to the general public need to ensure that their employees are polite and well-behaved in their dealings with customers.

- **Reason 2: Managing stakeholder relations**. A code of ethics can help to improve and develop the relations between the company and its shareholders, by improving the trust that shareholders have in the company. The code might therefore include the ethical stance of the company on disclosing information to shareholders and the investing public (openness and transparency) and on respecting the rights of shareholders.
- **Reason 3: Creating a value-based organisation**. A company might recognise the long-term benefits of creating an ethical culture, and encouraging employees to act and think in a way that is consistent with the values in its code of ethics. (It could be argued that an ethical company, like a well-governed company, is more likely to be successful in business in the long-term. However, there is no firm evidence to prove this point, and it is therefore a matter of opinion).

Note on global organisations.

Global companies might have difficulty in developing and implementing a code of ethics for the entire organisation world-wide, because of differences in ethical values in different cultures in different parts of the world. A criticism of codes of ethics of global companies is that they often focus on the company's relationships with stakeholders in their 'home country' and do not give enough thought to their operations in other countries.

3.3 Content of a corporate code of ethics

There is no standard format or content for a code of ethics, but a typical code contains:

- general statements about ethical conduct by employees
- specific reference to the company's dealings with each stakeholder group, such as employees, customers, shareholders and local communities.

A code of conduct should specify that **compliance with local laws** is essential. In addition, employees should **comply with the policies and procedures** of the company. There might be a statement that any employee who fails to comply with the company's code of conduct will face disciplinary action.

The code might also include an **overview of business conduct**, and the need to protect the company's reputation and 'good name'. It might also contain statements about the values of the company, such as:

- acting at all times with integrity
- protecting the environment
- the 'pursuit of excellence'
- respect for the individual.

A code of conduct might address its main concerns about its dealings with stakeholder groups and its ethical treatment of each group.

- **Employees**. A code of ethics might include statements about:
  - human rights, including the right of all employees to join legally-authorised organisations such as a trade union or political party
  - equal opportunities for all employees, regardless of gender, race, ethnic origin, religion, age, disability or sexual orientation
  - refusal to tolerate harassment of employees by colleagues or managers
  - concern for the health and safety of employees
  - respect for the privacy of confidential information about each employee
  - company policy on giving or receiving entertainment or bribes.
- **Customers**. A code of ethics might include statements about:
  - fair dealing with customers
  - product safety and/or product quality
  - the truthfulness of advertisements
  - respect for the privacy of confidential information about each customer.
- **Competitors**. A code of ethics might include statements about:
  - fair dealing with competitors
  - the use of techniques for obtaining information about competitors (industrial spying)
- **Shareholders**. A code of ethics might not include much about shareholders, because the relationship between a company and its shareholders might be contained in a code of corporate governance that the company follows. The key issue with shareholders is to maintain and develop trust and confidence, which might be achieved through disclosure of information (openness and transparency).

An exam question will focus more on a practical ethical situation or dilemma and ask you to comment on it rather than a theoretical discourse on ethics. Codes of ethics are not mentioned in the syllabus. However, establishing such a code could be a practical suggestion to deal with a problem in an exam scenario and the detail above provides a list of the kinds of situations that an exam question might raise.

Social and environmental footprints: environmental risk

- Environmental footprint (ecological footprint)
- Carbon neutrality
- Social footprint
- Sustainability and environmental risk
- Role of the environment agency

4 Social and environmental footprints: environmental risk

The purpose of economic activity is to create economic wealth. It is now recognised, much more than in the past, that economic activity also has an environmental impact and a social effect. An organisation is said to create an 'environmental footprint' and a 'social footprint' - a visible mark on the environment and on society. The social footprint may be either beneficial or damaging. The environmental footprint is almost inevitably damaging.

4.1 Environmental footprint (ecological footprint)

An environmental footprint, also called an ecological footprint, is a term that refers to the impact that an entity has on the environment, in terms of:

- the amount of raw materials that it uses to make its products or services, where the raw materials are subject to depletion (see note)
- non-renewable resources that it uses to make its products or services
- the quantity of wastes and emissions that it creates in the process.

Note: Raw materials subject to depletion are raw materials that can be renewed, but where the current total rate of consumption exceeds the current total rate of renewal. Fish stocks and hard wood timber are examples.

In the past, it was accepted that in order to grow, companies (and economic activity as a whole) had to increase its environmental footprint. With the recognition today that the world cannot go on increasing its environmental footprint, many leading companies are looking for ways to reduce the size of their own particular footprint and 'tread more softly'.

Reducing an environmental footprint involves the development and implementation of policies for:

- better (more efficient) resource management, and using different resources
- 'green' procurement policies
- waste minimisation and waste management (for example, policies on reducing pollution and recycling waste).

Countries that consume most environmental resources and create most environmental damage relative to other countries are those with the highest environmental footprint per head of the population.

4.2 Carbon neutrality

The effect on the environment of economic activities by individual companies may be measured in terms of emissions of carbon-based pollutants, such as the release of carbon dioxide into the atmosphere. (Carbon is only one of many different pollutants of air, water and land, but carbon dioxide emissions into the atmosphere have attracted extensive interest and concern).

Some environmentally-conscious companies already measure their impact on carbon pollution, and might have a stated environmental policy of being 'carbon neutral'.

Carbon neutrality exists when a company is able to counterbalance its use of carbon products, and particularly its carbon dioxide emissions, with activities that reduce the amount of carbon dioxide in the atmosphere such as growing trees or plants (which absorb carbon dioxide from the atmosphere). Some companies have also tried to reduce their impact on carbon dioxide pollution by switching to the use of fuel and energy that does not involve carbon consumption.

Example

The Du Pont Corporation is an example of a large environmentally-conscious company, which has stated as its mission the aim of seeking sustainable growth.

Du Pont listed some of the initiatives it has taken to create a sustainable business:

- Setting a target of zero waste generation and zero waste emissions
- Conserving energy and resources such as oil, coal, natural gas, water and minerals
- Recycling materials to reduce the need for disposals
- Reducing packaging waste
- Making, using, handling and transporting materials safely and in an environmentally-friendly way and in compliance with local regulations
- Managing land efficiently to increase habitats for wildlife
- Developing new products and processes that reduce the environmental risks.

4.3 Social footprint

A social footprint is the effect of economic activity on society and people. In general, economic activity is seen as providing benefits for society, although some companies are much more 'people-friendly' than others. Some companies, for example, use child labour and/or pay only subsistence-level wages to their workers.

Companies might seek to measure the contribution of their activities towards society in terms of:

- Total numbers employed or increase in the total number of employees
- The proportion of the total work force employed in different parts of the world
- The proportion of the total work force that is female or from different ethnic groups
- Health and safety at work (for example, numbers of employees injured each year per 1,000 of the work force).

Social ecologists argue that the environmental crisis has been caused by companies seeking growth, profits and economic self-interest. Nothing fundamental has changed. Companies are still trying to get bigger and more profitable, even though they use environmental ideology to express their plans and ambitions. They argue that the environmental crisis cannot be averted without a radical change in human society.

4.4 Sustainability and environmental risk

For companies there are two aspects to environmental risk:

- There is reputation risk for companies that are considered serious polluters of the environment and companies that are depleting the world's natural resources. Reputation risk is the risk that a company will acquire a bad reputation in the eyes of the general public customers, and so be at a competitive disadvantage to rival producers.
- There is also the risk that by continuing to use up natural resources and pollute the environment, companies might not have a business that can be sustained into the long-term future. Examples of concerns about sustainable business development have included the consumption of the world's fishing stocks by fishing fleets and the destruction of hardwood forests by forestry companies.

One way in which companies might recognise their responsibility towards the environment is to provide information about their environmental and social footprints.

Many companies now produce a voluntary social and environmental report each year (as a separate publication), or include comments on environmental issues in the chairman's statement or the chief executive officer's report in the published annual report and accounts. However, social and environmental reports often do not include quantified information, and reports often concentrate on the 'good' environmental measures taken by the company and ignore the 'bad' polluting and non-sustainable activities.

4.5 Role of the environment agency

The Environment Agency (EA) is a public body with responsibilities relating to the protection and enhancement of the environment in England. The Scottish Environment Protection Agency carries similar responsibilities in Scotland.

The Environment Agency's stated purpose is, "to protect or enhance the environment, taken as a whole" so as to promote "the objective of achieving sustainable development.

In particular it responsibilities covering:

- flood and coastal risk management;
- the regulation of discharges to air, water, and land through the issue of formal consents to discharge or permits;
- conservation and ecology specifically along rivers and in wetlands;
- the regulation of the release of air pollutants;
- the regulation of all waste management activities including the licensing of landfill sites and recycling facilities;
- the regulation of the movement of hazardous wastes and harmful chemicals;
- the quality of fresh water;
- the monitoring of discharges into rivers, lakes and the sea; and
- the management of the use and conservation of water.

Sustainability reporting and environmental audits

- Accounting and the economic model
- The need for objective environmental reporting
- Sustainability and sustainability reporting
- Triple bottom line reporting
- Integrated reporting
- Environmental audits

5 Sustainability reporting and environmental audits

5.1 Accounting and the economic model

The capitalist system creates incentives for maximising wealth, and it is based on the assumption that wealth can only be increased through continual economic growth. This is the 'economic model' of society. As a result, growth-seeking economic activities continue, in spite of growing concerns for the environment, and recognition that continual growth in its current form cannot be sustained.

Accounting has developed in support of the economic model. Financial reporting measures the consequences of a company's activities in terms of the use of the assets that it owns and the liabilities for which it has the direct responsibility for payment. Current accounting practice does not allow companies to report the consequences of their actions on external assets that it does not own, and the creation of liabilities for which it does not have to pay directly.

Investment decisions by large companies are made using accounting techniques such as discounted cash flow analysis, which focuses exclusively on economic consequences of investment, and does not measure or evaluate the environmental and social impact.

Financial reporting, management accounting and financial management have all therefore supported the economic model of business.

5.2 The need for objective environmental reporting

In the past, companies ignored their consumption of natural resources such as air and water because they assumed that supplies of these items were both limitless and free. This is no longer the case. It can now be argued that whereas companies are increasing economic wealth through growth and the search for profit maximisation, society may well be getting poorer because of the damage that economic activity is having on the environment and society.

As companies have become increasingly aware of environmental issues, and begin to accept that economic growth might not be sustainable, they have become more interested in measuring sustainability and environmental impact.

Traditional accounting methods do not provide for this type of measurement, and to the extent that companies (and society) want environmental and social impacts to be measured, traditional accounting is inadequate.

In order to help companies to set targets for achievement and assess their actual performance, there should be measurement. Environmental and social effects should be quantified, because managers find it easier to plan and control using numbers than using more general qualitative assessments.

Some accountancy bodies, including the ACCA, are contributing towards efforts to establish measurement and reporting systems for social and environmental issues, to complement traditional financial reporting.

Alternative measurement and reporting systems that recognise the need for economic activity to be **sustainable** have therefore been considered, although there is as yet no widely-accepted standard measurement and reporting system.

5.3 Sustainability and sustainability reporting

The concept of sustainability is that organisations and individuals should meet their own needs today without compromising the needs of future generations. It requires organisations and individuals to preserve the environment and better serve society at large.

More and more companies have are recognising the need to make their operations more sustainable. Over the past twenty years or so the number of organisations that have made sustainability a key strategic focus has increased significantly.

This increase is due to a number of factors, including:

- a broader understanding and acceptance of the links between economic activity and global sustainability issues;
- a recognition of the risk-management and economic benefits that organisations can gain from integrating sustainability into their strategies; and
- a growing demand from stakeholders, including investors, customers, employees and NGOs, for organisations to manage their operations in a more sustainable manner.

Also some governments and regulators have required companies to report on their environmental and social impacts.

Companies can enhance their value by developing an understanding about the connections between sustainability and business and communicating this to their stakeholders. This also allows companies to drive improvement and innovation.

Sustainability reporting

Organisations tend to communicate their sustainability activities through sustainability reports. Many companies worldwide (over 3,000) issue annual reports on sustainability and corporate responsibility. These companies represent all sectors and industries across the globe.

Sustainability reporting is largely voluntary although a few governments have introduced mandatory sustainability reporting. For example:

- French law requires the annual reports of companies to include information on their environmental and social performance.
- All state-owned companies in Sweden must present a sustainability report on a 'comply or explain' basis.

Furthermore some stock exchanges have sustainability reporting as a listing requirement. One such stock exchange is the Johannesburg Stock Exchange in South Africa, which has been a leading light in this area.

Greater transparency on sustainability and the consequent attention to sustainability issues is of benefit to both companies and their stakeholders.

Experience has shown that the process of sustainability reporting can add value in a number of ways, including:

- increased efficiency;
- higher levels of employee retention; and
- lower cost of capital.

A number of organisations have produced codes of practice and guidelines for companies to follow, but to date these are non-mandatory. This can lead to problems in comparability of the content of these reports, although having the information in the annual report is better than not disclosing at all.

5.4 Triple bottom line reporting

Sustainability reporting in the form of 'triple bottom line reports' have been developed as a method of presenting quantified and more objective information about the social and environmental effects of a company's activities.

The term 'triple bottom line' was 'invented' in 1994 by J Elkington. Its aim is to encourage companies to recognise social and environmental issues in their business models and reporting systems. This method of reporting is encouraged by the Global Reporting Initiative (GRI), an internationally-recognised body that promotes sustainability reporting.

The 'triple bottom line' gets its name because companies report their performance not simply in terms of profit: they provide key measurements for three aspects of performance:

- economic indicators
- environmental indicators, and
- social indicators.

Triple bottom line reporting is therefore providing a quantitative summary of a company's economic, environmental and social performance over the previous year. Economic indicators will include measurements relating to:

- sales revenue
- profits, earnings and earnings per share

- dividends per share
- global market share (as a percentage of the total market)
- in some industries, such as car production, units of sale worldwide.

Environmental indicators might include measurements relating to:

- reducing the 'intensity' of materials in products and services
- reducing energy intensity
- minimising the release of toxic materials/pollutants
- improving the ability to recycle material
- maximising the use of renewable resources
- extending the life of a product

Example

One major global company using triple bottom line reporting reported its environmental performance in terms of:

- global energy use, measured in thousands of GWh
- global carbon dioxide emissions, measured in metric tonnes
- production of non-recycled waste, measured in metric tonnes
- the number of manufacturing sites that had been awarded an ISO 14000 certificate (which is explained later).

The same company reported, as social indicators:

- its donations to communities and sponsorships, measured in US dollars
- diversity: the percentage of its employees who were female and the percentage who came from minority groups
- the number of discrimination charges brought against the company during the year
- employee satisfaction, based on a census of employee opinion
- the recordable injury rate per 1,000 employees.

Weaknesses in triple bottom line reporting

There are several weaknesses with triple bottom line reporting.

- There are no widely-established standards for triple bottom line reporting, and no standard methods for measuring social and environmental impacts. It is therefore difficult to compare the sustainability of one company with the sustainability of another. (The work of the Global Research Initiative or GRI is to standardise measurements for the triple bottom line. It has been publishing Sustainability Reporting Guidelines since 1999. These were updated and amended in 2002).
- If the social and environmental measures are not subject to independent audit, there might be doubts about the reliability of the data presented in a company's report.

5.5 Integrated reporting

There has been a growing acceptance that using traditional financial reporting as the sole measure of a company's performance and financial standing is a flawed approach. Financial reports are historical in nature, providing little information on the future potential of a company. Corporate sustainability reports help to fill this gap, but are not often linked to a company's strategy or financial performance, and provide insufficient information on value creation.

Businesses need a reporting environment that allows them to explain how their strategy drives performance and leads to the creation of value over time. This should make it easier to attract financial capital for investment. Integrated reporting is a new approach to reporting which, tries to do this.

The International Integrated Reporting Council define an integrated report as a concise communication about how an organisation's strategy, governance, performance and prospects, in the context of its external environment, lead to the creation of value in the short, medium and long term.

The Johannesburg Stock Exchange (JSE) has mandated integrated reporting through its listing requirements. This is the first national attempt to enforce integrated reporting across all listed companies.

International Integrated Reporting Council (IIRC)

The International Integrated Reporting Council (IIRC) is an influential global coalition of regulators, investors, companies, standard setters, the accounting profession and NGOs who share the view that communication about value creation should be the next step in the evolution of corporate reporting.

The International Integrated Reporting Council define an integrated report as a concise communication about how an organisation's strategy, governance, performance and prospects, in the context of its external environment, lead to the creation of value in the short, medium and long term.

The IIRC has developed and published The International <IR> Framework to provide a foundation for the development of integrated reports. Note that the symbol <IR> is used by the IIRC as a designation for integrated reports and reporting.

Content elements

An integrated report should answer the following questions

- What does the organisation do and what are the circumstances under which it operates?
- How does the organisation's governance structure support its ability to create value in the short, medium and long term?
- What is the organisation's business model?
- What are the specific risks and opportunities that affect the organisation's ability to create value over the short, medium and long term, and how is the organisation dealing with them?

- Where does the organisation want to go and how does it intend to get there?
- To what extent has the organisation achieved its strategic objective: for the period and what are its outcomes in terms of effects on the capitals?
- What challenges and uncertainties is the organisation likely to encounter in pursuing its strategy, and what are the potential implications for its business model and future performance?
- How does the organisation determine what matters to include in the integrated report and how are such matters quantified or evaluated?

5.6 Environmental audits

A social and environmental audit, or simply an environmental audit, can have several meanings.

- It can mean a formal audit of an environmental management system, to check that the system operates effectively.
- It could be an internal check of a particular aspect of the company's environment management system, such as its system for measuring the environmental costs of waste, or the methods used to measure the cost of site contamination at a particular manufacturing site. This audit might be carried out by members of the company's own internal audit team (who might be an environmental expert rather than an accountant).
- There may be a check on the company's compliance with environmental and social legislation and regulations.
- It could involve a verification of social and environmental information that will be included in a published report, such as an environmental performance report.
- Similarly it might be a check on the accuracy of figures supplied by the company to the government authorities responsible for environment regulation.
- It could also refer to the checks that the company's external auditors need to carry out on the company's financial statements, as far as they relate to environmental issues. For example, the introduction of new environmental laws might have an impact on the impairment of non-current assets, and a failure by the company to carry out environmental improvements required by law might create a requirement to make an accrual for remedial costs or a provision for the payment of a fine.

An international auditing practice statement has explained environmental audits as follows:
Environmental audits 'can be performed by external or internal experts…at the discretion of the company's management. In practice, persons from various disciplines can qualify to perform "environmental audits". Often the work is performed by a multi-disciplinary team. Normally "environmental audits" are performed at the request of management and are for internal use. They may address various subject matters, including site contamination, or compliance with environmental laws and regulations' (IAPS 1010).

How can environmental audits contribute to environmental accounting?

At the moment there is no legal requirement in any country for environmental audits. This type of audit is voluntary.

Similarly there is no legal requirement for environmental accounting, although professional accounting bodies such as the ACCA are encouraging more research by academics and practice by companies.

It seems quite possible, however, that environmental audits and environmental accounting will both become more common, as companies become increasingly aware of the problems of sustainability and sustainable growth, and include environmental objectives within their corporate strategy and investment decision-making.

The development of environmental accounting and environmental auditing will depend to a large extent on the development of environmental management systems, and how soon more companies establish environmental management systems. When environmental management systems are established:

- management needs reliable environmental information
- in general, managers prefer information in a quantified/measured form rather than in qualitative and descriptive terms
- as environmental management systems develop, with measurement systems for setting targets and monitoring performance, it seems likely that the need for audits of the information system will be necessary, to reassure management that the information systems are sound.

However, there still seems a long way to go before social and environmental reporting rivals financial reporting (economic reporting) as the main method of reporting by companies.

Carbon trading

- Origins of carbon trading
- Features of the EU Emissions Trading Scheme
- The significance of carbon trading for companies and financial management

6 Carbon trading

6.1 Origins of carbon trading

The Kyoto Protocol to cut greenhouse gas emissions was agreed by the governments of about 140 countries and came into force in 2005.

The implementation of the Kyoto agreement in the European Union has been in the form of the European Emissions Trading Directive, which sets out a framework for a European Emissions Trading Scheme (EU ETS). This is the first and largest greenhouse gas emissions trading scheme in the world.

The EU ETS is more commonly known as a carbon trading scheme, because the scheme applies only to emissions of carbon dioxide (CO_2) until 2007, although from 2008 it was extended to other greenhouse gases.

One of the most disappointing aspects concerning the Kyoto Protocol and measures to cut greenhouse gas emissions was the refusal of the United States to join the scheme. The US government began discussions on greenhouse gas emissions in 2007, but has so far still not taken any direct action. However, some individual states (e.g. California, the eighth largest economy in the world) and groups of states (e.g. nine north eastern and mid-Atlantic states) have since introduced their own schemes.

6.2 Features of the EU Emissions Trading Scheme

The scheme operates under a cap and trade principle. Under this principle, a maximum (cap) is set on the total amount of greenhouse gases that can be emitted by participating installations. Allowances for emissions (rights to pollute) are then auctioned off or allocated for free to the participating installations. These can be traded.

Installations must monitor and report their CO_2 emissions and hand sufficient allowances to the authorities to cover their emissions for a period. In practice some companies do not need all the allowances they have been given, and other companies need to make more emissions than they are allowed.

- Companies with surplus allowances or 'credits' can sell them in a carbon trading market, and companies needing more credits can buy them.
- The price for carbon credits depends on demand and supply.
- There are specialist carbon credit traders who act as intermediaries between buyers and sellers of credits.

There is another aspect to the carbon trading market. Companies that invest in projects that are environmentally friendly are given additional carbon credits by the government. The companies receiving these additional credits can sell them in the market.

Example

A company decides to build a wind farm. It receives carbon credits from the government because the technology to generate power from the wind has a zero carbon output.

This company does not need its carbon credits, because it does not produce any carbon dioxide emissions. The company can therefore sell its carbon credits to another company that does produce CO_2 emissions and needs to obtain more credits.

The company building the wind farm is able to use the money it receives from trading in carbon credits to help pay for the cost of its wind farm.

The scheme has been divided into a number of trading periods.

First trading period:

The first ETS trading period lasted three years, from January 2005 to December 2007.

In this phase carbon dioxide emissions in the EU countries were limited or 'capped' for companies in the power-generating and energy-intensive industrial sectors. Each country sets its own total emissions limit for these industries and the government then allocated 'free emissions allowances' or 'rights to pollute' to companies.

In the UK, the first phase of the ETS applied to about 1,500 sites.

Second trading period:

The second trading period ran from January 2008 until December 2012.

During this phase, every EU member state:

- Developed a national allocation plan (NAP) proposing caps on total emissions from relevant installations for approval by the European Commission.
- Distributed allowances:
  - Each cap was converted into allowances (known as EUAs where 1 EUA = 1 tonne of carbon dioxide).
  - The allowances were distributed to installations in the scheme according to the NAP
  - Up to 10% of the allowances could be auctioned instead of being given for free. These auctions were largest in the UK and in Germany.
- Operated the scheme. Installations had to monitor and report carbon emissions and surrender sufficient allowances to cover their emissions at the end of each year.

Third trading period:

The third trading period began in January 2013 and will span until December 2020.

It now applies to 31 countries (the 28 member states of the EU and Iceland, Norway and Lichtenstein). It covers 45% of all emissions and approximately 12,000 installations.

The proposed caps for 2020 represents a 21% reduction of greenhouse gases from 2005, when the EU ETS was first implemented

6.3 The significance of carbon trading for companies and financial management

Government actions to reduce greenhouse gases have an impact on companies affected by the regulations in their particular country. For many polluting companies, the consequences are higher costs. Higher costs take the form of both measures to reduce emissions and also the cost of buying carbon credits when permitted limits will otherwise be exceeded.

For companies that will receive carbon credits for environmentally-friendly investments, the system of carbon credits means that they can reduce their investment costs by selling the credits they are given.

Criticisms of carbon trading

Critics of carbon trading argue that the only way to reduce greenhouse gas emissions is through direct government action and regulation, and that the system of offsetting and trading carbon credits has no effect on the total amount of environmental pollution.

The scheme is also criticised on the grounds that some countries have been given fairly 'generous' limits for carbon dioxide emissions (notably China and India) and that in other countries the government has been too generous in awarding the free emissions allowances.

CHAPTER

4

Management of international trade and finance

Contents

Free trade and protectionism

- Free trade
- Protectionism
- Restrictions on movements of capital or currency
- World Trade Organisation (WTO)
- Trade agreements
- Common markets

1 Free trade and protectionism

1.1 Free trade

Free trade is where there are no restrictions on trade between countries. It is the conduct of international trade without protectionist measures. Free trade involves the absence of import tariffs (or the taxation of imported goods at the same rate as the tax on domestically-produced goods), and the absence of import quotas and government subsidies.

Arguments for free trade

The governments of many countries have accepted the principle that free trade will increase the total volume of international trade. Total output in the world economies will grow, there will be more employment. Economic growth creates additional wealth. Supporters of free trade argue that this additional wealth will benefit all the countries involved and will be shared between them.

1.2 Protectionism

Protectionism involves measures by a national government to protect its domestic Protectionist measures are used by governments to preserve jobs and businesses in their own country. Such measures exist, not only in developing and under-developed countries, but also in countries with advanced economies.

Protectionism takes several forms.

- Taxes on imports of particular types of goods. These are **import tariffs**, which are charged on goods entering the country.
- **Import quotas**. These are limits on the quantities of particular items that can be imported.
- **Import ban**. There might be a ban on the import of certain items.
- **Embargos** (temporary import bans)

- **Procedural regulations** that make it time-consuming and expensive to import goods (for example, documentation requirements, slow procedures by the customs authorities).
- Regulations relating to the required minimum standard of products, which imported goods may not meet. For example a country may impose regulations that require particular products (such as cars) to meet minimum environmental regulations.
- Regulations requiring a proportion of any new business to be owned by 'local' companies or individuals.
- Providing **government subsidies** to national companies. These enable them to compete unfairly against foreign companies. For example, the European Union is criticised in discussions on world trade for the large agricultural subsidies paid to its farmers.
- Legal restrictions on the purchase of domestic companies by foreign investors or foreign companies.
- Government action to weaken the domestic currency. This makes imports more expensive thus making it harder for foreign companies to sell goods in a country.

Regulations introduced in country (or jurisdiction) for reasons other than protectionism might be seen as protectionist by other countries. This is often the case where one country has lower standards in some areas than those applied in other countries.

- A jurisdiction might outlaw genetically modified ingredients in foodstuffs. This would be seen as a protectionist measure by a food manufacturer from a jurisdiction where GM ingredients were allowed.
- The existence of free universal healthcare in EU countries is a barrier to foreign private health companies setting up in the EU.
- Sale of cosmetics tested on animals is prohibited in the EU but animal testing is allowed in the US. Thus, US companies are unable to import animal tested products for sale in the EU.

The arguments for protectionism

Protectionism might be necessary to maintain social standards (see the references to GM food, free universal healthcare and animal testing above).

Whilst free trade might lead to growth in the world economy, but it might increase the wealth of some countries and reduce the wealth of others. For example, free trade might help the economies of the advanced industrialised nations to expand, but might prevent the economies of under-developed countries from growing. There is an argument that protectionist measures are necessary to give domestic industries in less developed countries an opportunity to develop, and to protect jobs in those industries.

There are also difficulties raised by the fact that protectionist measures exist and are used extensively by governments. Some countries refuse to abandon their measures for protection as long as another country still has different measures in place relating to different industries and products. For example, one country might refuse to remove tariffs on imports of agricultural produce when another country charges tariffs on imports of electronic goods.

There are also some difficulties relating to intellectual property, such as patents, trademarks and copyright. Although there are international agreements for the protection of intellectual property, not all countries have subscribed to them and intellectual property laws are not applied worldwide. This creates disputes between countries that have such laws and those that do not.

The World Trade Organisation seeks to achieve free trade internationally, but needs to win the agreement of all the countries affected. Progress towards the abolition of protectionism has therefore been and continues to be slow.

1.3 Restrictions on movements of capital or currency

Some developing countries seek to restrict the movement of capital or foreign currency out of the country, by imposing foreign exchange restrictions or restrictions on the movement of capital.

This can inhibit inward investment as companies investing in the country (by setting up a local subsidiary) are therefore unable to 'repatriate' the profits from their foreign investment, because:

- there is a ban on payments of dividends to foreign investors, so that companies cannot pay themselves dividends on the profits of their foreign subsidiary , or
- (more commonly) there is a withholding tax on the payment of dividends and interest to foreign investors, so that companies have to pay an additional tax if they want to repatriate profits of their foreign subsidiary.

1.4 World Trade Organisation (WTO)

The World Trade Organisation is an intergovernmental organisation established with the aim of regulating international trade.

Established in 1994 by signatories from 123 nations, it replaced the General Agreement on Trade and Tariffs (GATT).. GATT was a multilateral agreement regulating international trade set up in 1947. Membership of the WTO has grown to include most countries of the world. An amended version of the GATT remains as the WTO's umbrella treaty for trade in goods.

The WTO promotes the view that reducing barriers to world trade (protectionist measures) will promote economic growth and prosperity.

The aim of the WTO is to encourage countries to:

- adopt more free trade measures;
- remove protectionist barriers against imports of goods or services from other countries; and
- ban the practice of 'dumping' surplus goods at a low price on the markets of other countries. (Dumping can have a serious adverse effect on the domestic industry of the countries where the goods are 'dumped').

Member countries have met regularly over the years to try to agree packages of world-wide series of measures to enhance free trade and remove trade barriers. WTO negotiations occur in a series of cycles known as rounds.

- The Uruguay Round of discussions began in 1986 and agreement was eventually reached on measures, including the establishment of the WTO in 1994.
- The Doha round of talks started in 2001. So far, the talks have failed to make any significant progress.

It is generally accepted that there is still a long way to go in achieving the objective of free trade. Member countries meet regularly and try to come to agreements on trade. The WTO encourages direct discussions between particular countries or blocs of countries, such as the US and the European Union, and offers an arbitration service for the settlement of trade disputes.

Agreements contribute towards free trade and the removal of protectionist barriers, but they are not 'perfect' and many protectionist measures still exist. Some of these measures can lead to serious disputes between governments, which sometimes escalate. One country's government might demand the removal of protectionist measures against its exports by another country, and make threats of protectionist counter-measures in retaliation.

1.5 Trade agreements

A trade agreement is a treaty between countries covering a wide range of issues including taxation, tariffs and trade. They aim to reduce (or eliminate) tariffs, quotas and other trade restrictions on items traded between the signatories. The benefits and obligations of the trade agreements apply only to their signatories.

Common types of trade agreements include:

- Free trade agreements: These establish a free trade area (FTA) in which there is reduction or elimination of tariffs on substantially all trade. This allows for the free movement of goods. Some agreements also allow for the removal of restrictions on investment leading to the free movement of capital and services.
- Preferential trade agreements: These are a pact between countries to reduce tariffs for certain products. The tariffs are not necessarily eliminated, but are lower than those on trade with countries not party to the agreement.

Examples of trade agreements

- The North American Free Trade Agreement (NAFTA) is an agreement signed by Canada, Mexico, and the United States, creating a trilateral rules-based trade bloc in North America.
- The European Free Trade Association (EFTA) is an intergovernmental organisation set up for the promotion of free trade and economic integration to the benefit of its four member states (Iceland, Liechtenstein, Norway and Switzerland).

Trade agreements can involve different numbers of countries (jurisdictions).

- Bilateral trade agreement (BTA): A trade agreement between two sides (whether a country, trade bloc or an informal group of countries.

- Multilateral trade agreement: A trade agreement signed between more than two sides.
- Plurilateral trade agreement: A category of multilateral trade agreements. Multilateral implies a lot of countries where, plurilateral implies a more limited number.

Current negotiations

Trade pacts are frequently politically contentious since they may change economic customs and deepen interdependence with trade partners. Increasing efficiency through "free trade" is a common goal. For the most part, governments are supportive of further trade agreements whilst the populations they purport to represent can be very suspicious of them.

There are currently two major plurilateral trade agreements under discussion.

- Trans-Pacific Partnership (TPP) (covering 36% of world output). This a proposed deal between the USA and 11 other countries.
- Transatalantic Trade an Investment Partnership (TTIP) (covering 46% of world output). This is a proposed deal between the USA and the EU. Its main aim is to remove regulatory obstacles to trade. The detail of the negotiations is shrouded in secrecy but what information has been made available has resulted in strong resistance in Europe as it is believed that it will be to the detriment of citizens in many areas due to the acceptance of lower standards in many areas, for example, workers' rights, food quality and health care.

1.6 Common markets

Free trade and either a common currency or exchange rate stability create an environment in which international trade can grow.

Some countries have joined together to create common markets in which there is free trade between the member countries. The most notable example is probably the European Union with 28 member states. Many member states have gone as far as establishing a common currency. EU member states which have adopted the euro are collectively described as the Eurozone.

A free trade area like the European Union (EU) aims to remove barriers to trade and allow freedom of movement of production resources such as capital and labour. The EU also has an overarching common legal structure across all member countries and tries to limit any discriminatory practice against companies operating in these countries. Furthermore, the EU erects common external barriers to trade against countries which are not member states so that companies outside the EU may find it difficult to enter the EU markets due to these barriers.

The European Economic Area (EEA) is a single market that provides for the free movement of persons, goods, services and capital through three of the four member states of the European Free Trade Association (EFTA) (Iceland, Liechtenstein and Norway) and all the member states of the European Union (EU).

International financial institutions

- The World Bank
- The International Monetary Fund (IMF)
- Central banks
- The Federal Reserve (The Fed)
- Bank of England
- European Central Bank
- Bank of Japan

2 International financial institutions

2.1 The World Bank

The international capital and money markets are accessible for governments of many countries and large companies. However, they are not accessible to governments and companies in many developing countries or to governments of under-developed countries.

However, unless under-developed countries and developing countries can improve their infrastructure of transport and communication systems and standards of education, foreign companies might be reluctant to invest in new capital projects. Before companies invest large amounts of capital, governments therefore need to invest heavily in their economic infrastructure.

The difficulties of developing countries in gaining access to capital have been recognised, and a role of the World Bank is to provide loan finance to countries in need of capital. In practice, this means lending to developing countries, subject to certain conditions (such as the requirement for the borrowing country to maintain strict discipline over its economic policies).

The objective of the World Bank is to promote long-term economic development and reduce poverty, by providing technical and financial support to help countries reform particular sectors of their economy and implement specific projects such as building schools, providing water and electricity and protecting the environment.

Financial support provided to countries by the World Bank is generally long-term, and the World Bank obtains funding to provide this financial assistance:

- from contributions by governments of wealthy countries; and
- by issuing bonds in the international bond markets.

Even so, the funds provided by the World Bank are insufficient to meet the total needs of developing and under-developed countries.

The World Bank consists mainly of two institutions:

- the International Bank for Reconstruction and Development (IBRD)
- the International Development Association (IDA).

International Bank for Reconstruction and Development (IBRD)

The IBRD provides financial assistance to 'middle income' countries and creditworthy poorer countries. This financial assistance is in the form of loans to pay for projects that:

- will reduce poverty and promote sustainable economic growth, and
- private sector companies will not finance.

The IBRD obtains most of the finance for its loans from money raised through issues of bonds by the World Bank. The loans are repayable.

International Development Association (IDA)

The IDA provides assistance to poorer countries in the form of interest-free loans and grants (known as 'credits'). Interest-free loans are repayable over a period of about 35 – 40 years, often with a grace period of ten years during which no repayments at all are made. Grants and loans are provided for projects relating to health, education, infrastructure development and similar purposes.

Some examples of IDA projects in recent years are as follows:

- In Nicaragua, finance was provided to restore a section of the Pan American Highway, and other roads, after severe devastation by Hurricane Mitch.
- In Bangladesh the IDA has provided finance for the building of a number of secondary schools for girls.
- In Vietnam, finance was provided to improve electricity supply.

2.2 The International Monetary Fund (IMF)

The International Monetary Fund (IMF) was established in 1944 as an international organisation with member countries.

Finance for the IMF comes from quota subscriptions by member countries, which are denominated in Special Drawing Rights or SDRs. The maximum amount of temporary financing that a company can obtain from the IMF is related to the size of its quota subscriptions.

The role of the IMF is to oversee the global financial systems, in particular:

- to improve international monetary co-operation;
- to promote exchange rate stability;
- to help countries to achieve balance of payments and facilitate in the country's development through influencing the economic policies of the country in question foster economic growth; and
- provide temporary financial assistance to countries with balance of payments difficulties.

Temporary loans and austerity

The IMF can grant temporary loans, from member states' deposits, to countries facing severe financial and economic difficulties. These temporary loans are often offered with different levels of conditions or austerity measures. The IMF believes that in order to regain control of the balance of payments, the country should take action to reduce the level of demand for goods and services.

To achieve this, the IMF often requires countries to adopt strict austerity measures such as reducing public spending and increased taxation, as conditions of the loan. It believes these conditions will help control the inflationary pressures on the economy, and reduce the demand for goods and services. As a result, this will help the country to move away from a position of a trade deficit and achieve control of its balance of payments.

However, these deflationary pressures may cause standards of living to fall and unemployment to rise. The IMF regards these as short-term hardships necessary to help countries sort out their balance of payment difficulties and international debt problems.

The IMF has faced a number of criticisms for the conditions it has imposed, including the accusation that its policies impact more negatively on people with lower or mid-range incomes, hinder long-term development and growth, and possibly result in a continuous downward spiral of economic activity.

2.3 Central banks

A central bank is an institution that manages a state's currency, money supply, and interest rates. They also usually oversee the state's commercial banking system.

Examples include:

- the Federal Reserve of the United States;
- the Bank of England;
- the European Central Bank (ECB); and
- the bank of Japan; and

2.4 The Federal Reserve (The Fed)

The Federal Reserve (almost always referred to as "the Fed") is the central bank of the United States of America.

The Federal Reserve was founded by an act of congress in 1913. Its responsibilities have evolved since then to include the following:

- To serve as the central bank for the United States
- To maintain the stability of the financial system and contain systemic risk in financial markets
- To deal with crises in the banking system
- To supervise and regulate banking institutions
- To protect the credit rights of consumers
- To manage the nation's money supply through monetary policy.

- To act as a lender of last resort.
- To provide financial services to depository institutions, the U.S. government, and foreign official institutions, including playing a major role in operating the nation's payments system
- To strengthen U.S. standing in the world economy

Central bank

In its role as the central bank of the United States, the Fed serves provides banking services to US banks and other financial institutions and to the government.

As the government's bank, or fiscal agent, the Fed processes a variety of financial transactions involving trillions of dollars. The U.S. Treasury keeps an account with the Federal Reserve, into which are paid federal tax deposits. The account is used to make federal government payments.

The Federal Reserve is the lender of last resort in The USA. This means that it can provide credit to institutions unable to obtain credit elsewhere, the collapse of which might harm the US economy. Support is not automatic, for example in the 2008 banking crisis:

- the Fed authorised an $85 billion loan to prevent bankruptcy of international insurance giant American International Group (AIG); but
- it declined to support Lehman Brothers, a financial institution of long standing which was consequently forced to wind up.

Monetary policy

The term "monetary policy" refers to the actions undertaken by a central bank to influence the availability and cost of money and credit to help promote national economic goals. The Fed is able to influence the

The Fed is able to influence the federal funds rate. (This is the interbank lending rate – the rate that banks charge each other for loans). The following are the three main tools used to do this:

- Open market operations: purchase and sale of U.S. Treasury and federal agency securities;
- Discount rate: The interest rate charged to commercial banks and other financial institutions on loans from the Fed's regional lending facility (known as the discount window);
- Reserve requirements: The amount of funds that a bank must hold in reserve.

2.5 Bank of England

The Bank of England is the central bank of the United Kingdom.

It is an independent public organisation, wholly owned by the Treasury Solicitor on behalf of the government It has independence in setting monetary policy.

The Bank's most important role is maintaining price stability and supporting the economic policies of the UK Government, thus promoting economic growth. In particular it tries to ensure the following.

- Monetary stability by maintaining stable prices and market confidence. The Bank tries to meet government inflation targets by adjusting the base interest rate. This is set periodically by the Monetary Policy Committee.
- Financial stability by protecting against threats to the financial system. Threats are detected by the Bank's surveillance and market intelligence functions. The threats are then dealt with through financial and other operations, both at home and abroad.

The Bank also acts as the government's banker, and it maintains the government's Consolidated Fund account. It also manages the country's foreign exchange and gold reserves. The Bank also acts as the bankers' bank, especially in its capacity as a lender of last resort.

2.6 European Central Bank

The European Central Bank (ECB) is the central bank for the euro and administers monetary policy of the Eurozone. The Eurozone consists of 19 EU member states and is one of the largest currency areas in the world.

The primary objective of the ECB is to maintain price stability within the Eurozone. Its basic tasks are to define and implement the monetary policy for the Eurozone, to conduct foreign exchange operations, to take care of the foreign reserves of the European System of Central Banks and operation of the financial market infrastructure for settlement of securities in Europe.

The ECB has the exclusive right to authorise the issue of euro banknotes.

2.7 Bank of Japan

The Bank of Japan is the central bank of Japan. It decides and implements monetary policy with the aim of maintaining price stability.

Other roles and responsibilities include:

- Issuance and management of banknotes
- Providing settlement services and ensuring the stability of the financial system
- Treasury and government securities-related operations

International financial markets

- International lending
- International bond markets
- International money markets
- International equity
- Systemic risk in the global financial system

3 International financial markets

3.1 International lending

The capital markets, as well as many markets for goods and services, are international. Capital can be transferred freely between many countries, usually in one of the major international currencies (particularly the US dollar, euro and Japanese yen).

Large companies are able to obtain large syndicated bank loans in a major currency, from syndicates of international banks.

3.2 International bond markets

Companies can raise debt finance by issuing bonds. There are domestic bond markets in many countries, but these markets are often dominated by domestic government bonds. For example, in the UK the domestic bond markets are dominated by the market for UK government bonds (gilts). Some countries, notably the US, have large domestic bond markets for corporate bonds.

International companies are able to obtain bond finance by issuing bonds:

- in the international bond markets, or
- in a domestic bond market such as the US.

The international bond markets are still often called the **eurobond markets**.

The main features of the international bond markets are as follows:

- Governments, companies and other organisations are able to issue bonds in the market, with the advice and assistance of financial institutions in several countries.
- Bonds can be denominated in any major currency, but the most commonly-used currencies for the denomination of international bonds are US dollars and euros.
- The bonds are sold by banks in different countries to investment institutions in different countries.
- A second-hand market in the bonds is provided by some of the banks after the issue has been made.

How do companies raise capital in the international bond markets?

The ability of companies to raise debt capital by issuing bonds varies between countries as well as between different types of company.

- It is much easier to issue bonds in the domestic US bond market than in other countries. The UK, for example, has only a small sterling corporate bond market.
- When there is a large domestic bond market, it is easier for smaller companies to issue bonds, because investors in those markets are more willing to consider investing in smaller companies. In the European bond markets, in contrast, investors generally prefer to invest in bonds of large companies.
- It is possible for foreign companies to issue bonds in a domestic bond market. For example, foreign companies might be able to issue bonds in the US market. However, foreign issuers need to be aware of the regulations in the bond market, and they need to persuade investors in the market to buy their bonds. Investors might be reluctant to buy bonds of foreign companies that they do not recognise.

If you are asked in your examination about raising debt capital for a foreign investment, you should consider the possibility of using a foreign subsidiary to issue bonds in the country concerned. For example, it might be possible for a company wanting to invest in China to issue bonds in the Chinese bond market. Such a strategy might be possible, although this would depend on the size and nature of the domestic bond market concerned and the amount of debt finance that the company needs to obtain. You cannot be expected to know the current status of bond markets in every financial centre in the world, but you should be aware in general terms that a possibility of borrowing in other financial centres might exist.

(Bond issues are normally for large amounts of capital. Companies wanting smaller amounts of debt capital are much more likely to try to obtain a bank loan).

3.3 International money markets

The international money markets can be used to borrow short-term from banks in foreign currencies. For example, companies can borrow US dollars short-term (up to 12 months or possibly longer) in London. There are several major international money market centres around the world. The largest is London.

3.4 International equity

Investment institutions buy equity shares in countries throughout the world. Some countries have larger and more liquid stock markets than others. Investment institutions prefer to invest in stock markets that are properly regulated, and where the market is 'liquid'. (A liquid market for shares is a market in which shares can be readily bought or sold at a price that is a fair market price. The fair price is usually at or close to the most recent traded price for the shares).

However, although investment institutions might invest internationally, most stock exchanges are national. A company wishing to issue new shares (or to seek a flotation for its shares, when it is coming to the stock market for the first time) will issue them in a specific stock market, usually a domestic stock market in its own country.

There have been some movements towards the creation of international stock markets, but progress is slow. For example, the stock exchanges of Paris, Brussels and Amsterdam and also the London-based LIFFE futures exchange, are now combined within a single exchange organisation, Euronext.

3.5 Systemic risk in the global financial system

Systemic risk in the financial system refers to the risk that financial collapse in one part of the system, such as the financial collapse of a large international bank or a sharp fall in share prices in a major stock market, might have severe repercussions throughout the world's financial systems and lead to the collapse of other institutions and markets.

Systemic risk has grown as the global economy has developed, because financial institutions and markets are often very closely linked. International banks operate in many countries of the world, and banks in different countries make financial transactions with each other. Large investment institutions hold securities in many different countries, and might therefore be vulnerable to a major collapse in share prices in a foreign stock market.

The potential threat from systemic risk is recognised, and efforts have been made to reduce risks globally in financial systems. The regulation of financial markets is largely conducted at national level (or through EU Directives in the case of the European Union). In banking, the prudential regulation of international banks is based on rules developed by the Bank for International Settlements (BIS).

The financial crisis

- Roots of the crisis
- Securitisations
- Impact
- Government intervention

4 The financial crisis

4.1 Roots of the crisis

Since the 1990s until recent years there was a wave of aggressive selling of home loans (mortgages), often to individuals who had no realistic prospect of ever repaying their debt. These loans are known as "subprime mortgages". Lenders were prepared to do this because property prices had been rising steadily and provided good security for the loans in the event of default.

There are different views as to why lenders went into these markets:

- There is a view that many banks were forced to enter a high-risk section of the credit market which they would not have considered had they used normal commercial criteria. Successive US administrations have tried to improve the availability of credit for home loans across all levels of income, geographical locations, and social groups. Various government initiatives encouraged lenders to make loans available to individuals who would have previously been refused as a bad credit risk.
- Alternatively, there is a view that the market expansion allowed a valuable growth opportunity to the lenders. Which they were happy to exploit.

4.2 Securitisations

Banks hold many assets which give them access to future cash flows (e.g. mortgages, credit cards, loans etc.).

Banks often securitise such assets. This involves the transfer of the interest bearing assets to a 'special purpose vehicles' (SPVs). The SPV effectively purchases a bank's mortgage book for cash which is raised through the issue of bonds backed by the income stream flowing from the borrowers.

This results in the conversion of future cash receipts into cash today.

Securitisation through CDOs (Collateralised Debt Obligations)

Securitisation of sub-prime mortgages was affected through the issue of instruments known as 'collateralised debt obligations' or CDOs.

CDO securities are split into different risk classes, or tranches.

- Tranche 3: Known as the senior tranche this has the lowest risk and carries the lowest return.

- Tranche 2: This is known as the junior tranche (also mezzanine or intermediate tranche). It has higher risk than the senior tranche but also has higher coupon payments to compensate for the additional risk.
- Tranche 1: The most junior tranche is known as the "equity" tranche. This tranche carries the highest risk but also attracts the highest return. It is also described as subordinated debt.

The proportion of the principal of the underlying asset held in each tranche is known as the CDO structure.

- The percentage of value in the mortgage pool forming the equity and mezzanine tranches will be quite small if there is perceived to be little risk of default.
- There is a greater proportion of the principal in the equity and mezzanine tranches and a relatively smaller proportion in the senior tranche if the risk is high.

Cash flows are received from borrowers in the form of interest payments and loan repayments are paid to tranche 3 first until their obligation is fulfilled, then tranche 2 with the balance paid to the equity tranche.

Example

A bank has made a number of mortgage loans to customers with a current total value of $350 million.

The mortgages have an average term to maturity of ten years and deliver a net income of 7% per annum.

The bank will use 85% of the mortgage pool as collateral for a securitisation with the following structure:

Tranche	Percentage of collateralised debt (i.e. the 85% of 350m)	Return
Senior: AA rated	75%	6%
Junior: BB rated	15%	11%
Equity: Subordinated	10%	Balance

The estimated cash flows for this arrangement would be as follows:

	Value	Return(%)	Cash flow
Cash inflows	$m		$m
Inflows from mortgages	350	× 7%	24.5
Cash outflows			
To A-rated loan notes ($350m x 85% x 75%)	223.1	× 6%	13.4
To B-rated loan notes ($350m x 85% x 15%)	44.6	× 11%	4.9
			18.3
To subordinated tranche ($350m x 85% x 10%)	29.75		6.2

The return on the high-risk subordinated investment is $6.2m/$29.75m = 20.8%.

In simple terms, a CDO as a promise to pay cash flows to investors in a prescribed sequence, based on how much cash flow the CDO collects from the pool of bonds or other assets it owns. If cash collected by the CDO is insufficient to pay all of its investors, those in the lower layers (tranches) suffer losses first.

If the mortgages default then the equity tranche investors lose their principle first. When this is reduced to nothing the next level loses their investment and so on.

Sub-prime problem

When the sub-prime mortgages were issued, high employment and rising property prices led to the expectation that the vast majority of borrowers would repay their interest and their debt on the due date. In other words it was expected that all tranches would be safe from default.

In 2007, interest rates in the US were increased to slow down inflation. This made mortgage payments more expensive. Also, many homeowners had taken out mortgages with initially attractive lower rates for an introductory period. These lenders face the double problem of coming to the end of their introductory period and this facing higher payments at the same time as the higher payments themselves were increased. A further problem was that the level of unemployment increased.

The result was a rise in mortgage defaults particularly at the high risk (sub-prime) end of the market. Many institutional lenders who had invested in credit enhanced sub-prime mortgages lost billions of dollars. Banks had to write off large losses and this made them reluctant to make any further lending.

Under US Securities Exchange Commission rules, CDOs could only be traded between banks and other financial institutions. At the start of the credit crisis a trillion dollars of sub-prime debt was sitting on bank balance sheets in the form of what they believed to be very low risk securities.

The scale of the default led to erosion of the junior tranches but then also the more senior tranches. This had an adverse effect on the cash flow position of the banks that had invested in the CDOs.

In addition to this the CDOs had to be reflected at fair value in the financial statements of banks. The increase in default led the fair value to fall. Banks are very highly geared with typically less than 10% their asset value covered by equity. Falling asset values pushed certain banks towards negative equity.

Investors holding CDOs tried to sell their securities. It was difficult to find buyers and this pushed the price of the securities into freefall exacerbating the problem.

4.3 Impact

Banks that had stayed free of the problem began to suspect the credit worthiness of other banks and, as a result, became reluctant to lend on the inter bank market. This led to an increase in LIBOR threatening the liquidity of banking operations.

The result was that it became very difficult to raise funds and borrow money all around the world. The drying up of credit affected many firms who depended on being able to borrow in order to finance their operations. Furthermore, the drying up of lending led to a downturn in the construction industry as people who wanted to buy a house were unable to borrow the cash to do so. Factors such as these tilted economies into recession thus further exacerbating the risk of defaults.

The above factors led to a fall in house prices. Banks that had made loans secured on houses no longer had full security. This was another issue which made banks more reluctant to lend money.

The banking sector problems fed into the real economy. Banks tightened up their lending practices making credit harder to come by. As credit dried up and borrowing rates rose because of the scarcity of supply of willing lenders. Home buyers cannot raise mortgages and, as a result, property prices fall.

Recession in the real economy means that more people default on their home loans.

Consumer confidence begins to deteriorate and, as a result, previously strong economies began to slow down.

4.4 Government intervention

Governments had to intervene to prevent disaster.

United Kingdom

The government in the UK had to take several banks into public ownership. This was not necessarily due to direct sub-prime exposure. For example, Northern Rock operated under a business model that relied on the money markets for access to short term funding. The drying up of these markets led to the company experiencing severe short term liquidity problems.

USA

The Federal Reserve implemented a number of programs designed to support the liquidity of financial institutions and foster improved conditions in financial markets.

- The Fed (as lender of last resort) provided short-term liquidity to banks and other depository institutions and other financial institutions.
- The Fed approved bilateral currency swap agreements with several foreign central banks in order to assist them in their provision of dollar liquidity to banks in their jurisdictions.
- The Fed provided liquidity directly to borrowers and investors in key credit markets using various facilities.
- The Fed expanded its traditional tool of open market operations to support the functioning of credit markets, put downward pressure on longer-term interest rates, and improve broader financial conditions by purchasing longer-term securities for the Fed's portfolio. One such initiative involved spending $40 billion per month on mortgage-backed securities.

Ireland

The government had to step in and guarantee these loans in order to prevent the six main Irish banks from failing.

Problems for multinational companies

5 European debt crisis

5.1 Introduction

Countries with large balance of payment deficits and those in economic recession can use monetary policies to devalue their currency.

Devaluation of a country's currency is a step that can be taken to try to deal with various economic problems:

- Balance of payments deficit: Devaluing the currency discourages imports as they become more expensive and lowers the cost of exports for foreign customers thus increasing demand.
- Recession: Devaluing the currency lowers the cost of exports for foreign customers, thus increasing demand.

5.2 Development of the European debt crisis

Summary of causes

The causes of the debt crisis in Europe can be summarised as follows:

- countries being allowed to join the Eurozone without sufficient financial convergence and stability;
- the availability of borrowing to Eurozone members at rates not justified by the strength and structure of their economies;
- failure to keep national debt and budget deficits in agreed ranges;
- reduction in competitiveness;
- poor supervision in the financial sector leading to too much lending at rates which (with hindsight) could not be justified;
- the absence of an exit mechanism from the Eurozone.

Some of these causes are discussed in more detail below. Reference is often made to the problems of the Greek economy. These references are included for illustrative purposes and are in no way meant to be critical of Greece and its citizens in any way. We wish the country well as it tries to deal with its economic problems.

Introduction of the euro

The Maastricht Treaty led to the introduction of the euro in 1992 leading to countries of different economic strengths becoming members of the Eurozone.

Members of the Eurozone made undertakings to ensure that government debt would not exceed 60% of GDP and any budget deficit would not exceed 3% of GDP

The euro was established with no mechanism for a country to leave and bail outs of individual countries were not allowed for or expected.

It was believed that participation in a single currency would enhance trade. However, countries adopting the euro as their currency passed the responsibility for monetary policy to the ECB. This meant that any member state with economic problems is unable to use tools that were previously at their disposal.

The introduction of the euro lowered borrowing costs for those members of the Eurozone with weaker economies. It seems that markets assumed that the backing of all Eurozone members provided a guarantee that all Eurozone debt would be safe and had no risk of default.

- Some countries (e.g. Greece) used the available credit to consume more, build generous social systems and fund construction booms.
- Other countries (e.g. Ireland and Spain) used the borrowing to fuel a construction boom.
- In some countries the availability of borrowed cash fuelled wage increases without a corresponding increase in productivity leading to a fall in competitiveness. The strength of the Euro is too high for some Eurozone countries. However, it is difficult for these countries to improve their competitiveness without the option to devalue their currency.

Some countries failed to stay within the borrowing limits imposed by the Maastricht treaty. This resulted in some countries operating with very large amounts of debt in comparison to their GDPs. Amounts borrowed were often justified by the expectation that economic growth would enable countries to raise tax revenues to enable them to repay the loans.

Impact of the credit crunch

The financial crisis which started in 2007 caused problems with the liquidity of banks. In extreme cases some banks required government intervention to save them from collapse. The problems in the sector led to a reduction in lending and economic growth faltered. This in turn, pushed economies in some countries into recession.

The recession led to the collapse of property markets in many countries resulting in many bank loans secured against property, no longer being covered by that security. When customers with such loans defaulted the bank lost out, leading to further write offs and increased reluctance to lend.

During a recession, unemployment increases and commercial activity falls. These factors cause a downturn in tax revenues leading to governments needing to borrow more to fund their activities. However, this was at the same time as less money was available on the international markets.

It became increasingly apparent that some countries were suffering from lack of liquidity and some were even at risk of default.

- A lack of liquidity means that the country is unable to raise cash in the short term to fund its day to day needs.
- A risk of default means that a country is unable to service its debts.

Default by one country could lead to default of another (known as contagion).

As the crisis continued, international markets lost confidence in some countries leading to deteriorating credit ratings and increasing bond yields (borrowing rate) for these countries. The increase in bond yields meant that it became even more expensive for countries to borrow money at a time that they needed to increase the level of borrowing to deal with the fall in tax revenues due to the recession.

Countries in difficulty were unable to use monetary policy to try to deal with their problems. They might have benefited from a fall in the exchange rate but the exchange rate for the euro was maintained by the strength of other economies in the Eurozone.

For most countries with problems, the key issue is thought to be one of liquidity rather than insolvency. As long as these countries are provided with loans to keep them liquid when required, default can be avoided.

However, Greece is potentially insolvent and more drastic action is likely to be needed. Some Greek creditors have already had to agree to a significant write down of the value of their debt.

Commentary

The strength of the Euro is too high for some Eurozone countries. However, it is difficult for these countries to improve their competitiveness without the option to devalue their currency.

Countries in difficulties have been required to introduce austerity measures. These are likely to reduce economic activity leading to an increase in unemployment. They are also likely to lead to higher taxes. In this environment it will be hard to restart economic growth.

The interrelationship between the economies of European countries means that the impact of a reduction in demand in one or several countries will be felt by other countries in Europe (and elsewhere in the world). Therefore, there is a risk of a deflationary slump within Europe which would be made worse if there were significant defaults and consequent contagion.

5.3 Action taken by international financial institutions

EU institutions

EU institutions have taken actions which have prevented default to date. Emergency measures taken by the EU include:

- The **European Financial Stability Facility (EFSF)** was created to raise the funds to provide loans to countries in financial trouble, to buy sovereign debt and to recapitalise banks. The EFSF is jointly and severally guaranteed by the Eurozone countries.
- The **European Financial Stabilisation Mechanism (EFSM)** was set up to allow the European Commission to raise funds using the EU budget as collateral. The EFSM has made loans in conjunction with both the EFSF and the International Monetary Fund (IMF).
- **The European Stability Mechanisation (ESM)** is a permanent scheme which is superseded both the EFSF and EFSM. The role of the ESM is to provide guarantees thus limiting the risk of default by a country and reducing the chance of contagion.
- Increasing the minimum level of bank capitalisation to aid their stability and ability to deal with further default. This involves changing the ratios of assets to lending that banks must adhere to.

European Central Bank (ECB)

The ECB has acted with other leading central banks to try and ensure that both governments and major banks have sufficient liquidity. Actions include:

- the purchase of debt securities in the open market to provide liquidity to the government selling the securities;
- accepting Greek Government bonds as collateral for lending.

International Monetary Fund (IMF)

The IMF has made loans available in conjunction with the EU. The terms of the loans have required the recipient countries to adopt stringent fiscal austerity measures.

Countries aided

Eurozone states that have applied for and received rescue funds to repay their due debt or bailout their financial sector are Greece, Ireland, Portugal, Cyprus, and Spain.

5.4 Future of the Eurozone

Possibility 1: The Eurozone continues in its present form with its existing members. This will require the availability of funds to prevent default and might also result in closer fiscal union within the Eurozone. This will involve more stringent fiscal rules and greater penalties for countries not abiding by the rules. This is the most likely outcome.

Possibility 2: Greece is allowed to default and expelled from the Eurozone. Proponents of this course of action argue that the effects of a Greek default could be managed, helping to rebuild confidence in the Eurozone.

Possibility 3: Germany leaves the Eurozone and introduces its own or enters into a new currency union with other Northern European nations with more closely aligned economies. This is extremely unlikely.

Dark pool trading

- Dark pools
- Regulatory response

6 Dark pool trading

6.1 Dark pools

An offer to sell a large block of shares for sale on an open exchange is advertised to every participant. The offer itself could affect the price of the security and this could cause the trader to lose out.

The term "dark pool" refers to a place where trading shares exists but is not displayed for all to see. Dark pool trades are for large blocks of shares between anonymous parties. The trade is only announced once the trade is completed. It is estimated that over 20% of share trades in the USA and UK are in dark pools.

Dark pool trades are at a price which is not known to the exchange. This means that the price set by the exchange for trades in the same securities is undermined reducing the efficiency of those exchanges. This could in turn harm investors on these exchanges.

6.2 Regulatory response

In the USA the Securities and Exchange Commission (SEC) has proposed measures calling for fuller disclosure of dark pool trades and by dark pool participants.

The European Commission is engaged in research to examine how dark pool trades affect securities pricing.

Money laundering

- Introduction
- FATF: Financial Action Task Force against Money Laundering
- United Kingdom

7 Money laundering

7.1 Introduction

Money laundering is an international problem which is addressed on an international level by mutual co-operation between countries and international bodies.

Money laundering covers any activity by which the apparent source and ownership of money or property representing the proceeds of crime are changed, so that they appear to have been obtained legitimately.

The methods by which money may be laundered are varied and can range in sophistication from simple to complex.

Money laundering often occurs in three steps:

- cash is introduced into the financial system by some means ("placement"); then
- complex financial transactions camouflage the illegal source ("layering"); then
- wealth appears to have been generated from legal sources ("integration").

Money laundering takes several different forms although most methods can be categorized into one of a few types including:

- Structuring (smurfing): A method of placement by which cash is deposited with banks in smaller amounts in order to avoid suspicion.
- Bulk cash smuggling to jurisdictions with greater bank secrecy or less rigorous money laundering enforcement.
- Cash-intensive businesses that simply deposit both legitimate and criminally derived cash as legitimate earnings.
- Real estate may be purchased with illegal proceeds, and then sold. The proceeds from the sale appear to outsiders to be legitimate income

7.2 FATF: Financial Action Task Force against Money Laundering

Formed in 1989 by the G7 countries, the Financial Action Task Force on Money Laundering (FATF) is an intergovernmental body whose purpose is to develop and promote an international response to combat money laundering and combat the financing of terrorism.

FATF is a policy-making body, which brings together legal, financial and law enforcement experts to achieve national legislation and regulatory reforms.

FATF recommendations

Countries should criminalise money laundering on the basis of the United Nations Conventions

Countries should ensure that financial institution secrecy laws do not inhibit implementation of the FATF Recommendations.

Financial institutions should not keep anonymous accounts or accounts in obviously fictitious names.

Financial institutions should undertake customer due diligence measures, including identifying and verifying the identity of their customers, when:

- establishing business relations;
- carrying out occasional transactions above the applicable designated threshold or that are wire transfers;
- there is a suspicion of money laundering or terrorist financing; or
- the financial institution has doubts about the veracity or adequacy of previously obtained customer identification data.

Financial institutions should pay special attention to all complex, unusual large transactions, and all unusual patterns of transactions, which have no apparent economic or visible lawful purpose.

If a financial institution suspects or has reasonable grounds to suspect that funds are the proceeds of a criminal activity, or are related to terrorist financing, it should be required, directly by law or regulation, to report promptly its suspicions to the financial intelligence unit

Financial institutions should develop programmes against money laundering and terrorist financing. These programmes should include:

- The development of internal policies, procedures and controls, including appropriate compliance management arrangements, and adequate screening procedures to ensure high standards when hiring employees.
- An ongoing employee training programme.
- An audit function to test the system.

FATF assesses each member country against these recommendations in published reports. Countries seen as not being sufficiently compliant with such recommendations are subjected to financial sanctions.

7.3 United Kingdom

The Proceeds of Crime Act 2002 contains the primary UK anti-money laundering legislation. It requires businesses within the 'regulated sector' (banking, investment, money transmission, certain professions, etc.) to report to the authorities suspicions of money laundering by customers or others.

There is no obligation on banking institutions to routinely report monetary deposits or transfers above a specified value. Instead reports have to be made of all suspicious deposits or transfers, irrespective of their value.

Money laundering is widely defined in the UK to include any handling or involvement with the proceeds of any crime as well as activities which would fall within the traditional definition.

UK money laundering offences are not limited to the proceeds of serious crimes, nor are there any monetary limits, nor is there any necessity for there to be a money laundering design or purpose to an action for it to amount to a money laundering offence.

A money laundering offence under UK legislation need not involve money, since the money laundering legislation covers assets of any description. In consequence any person who commits an acquisitive crime (i.e. one from which he obtains some benefit in the form of money or an asset of any description) in the UK will inevitably also commit a money laundering offence under UK legislation.

This applies also to a person who, by criminal conduct, evades a liability (such as a taxation liability) - referred to by lawyers as "obtaining a pecuniary advantage" - as he is deemed thereby to obtain a sum of money equal in value to the liability evaded.

Solicitors, accountants, and insolvency practitioners who suspect that their clients (or others) have engaged in tax evasion or other criminal conduct from which a benefit has been obtained are required to report their suspicions to the authorities. It is an offence (tipping-off) if they also told the client what they had done.

Financial planning framework for multinational companies

- Operating internationally
- National regulatory requirements
- London Stock Exchange (LSE) listing rule
- Mobility of capital
- Risk exposures
- Agency issues

8 Financial planning framework for multinational companies

8.1 Operating internationally

Many industries operate in a global market. Global competition exists largely for products, but there is also global competition in many service industries, such as banking and financial services and telecommunications.

When an industry becomes global, there is usually a trend towards the creation of a number of large multinational companies or corporations (MNCs). Some large MNCs control very large amounts of resources, and have more economic power than many of the countries in which they invest.

Three fundamental decisions

Chapter 1 explained that financial managers provide advice concerned with three fundamental decisions supported by advice in other areas.

The financial planning framework of a multinational company has to address these decisions. However, operating internationally adds other dimensions and brings extra considerations to these decisions. These must be taken into account in the development of the financial planning framework.

Investment decisions (see chapters 6 to 9 and 12 to 14)

Issues addressed:

- Which investments should be undertaken using the available capital resources?
- How can limited resources be used most effectively to achieve the corporate objectives?

Additional considerations for MNCs:

The tax regime in the country under consideration (The factors that should be considered include the availability of incentives, tax on profits, tax allowable depreciation, tax on remittances and social security costs).

- Availability of other incentives for inward investment (e.g. government subsidies).
- Potential impact on exports.
- Level of education in the potential workforce.
- Infra-structure in the country.

- Access to markets in the region.
- Additional risks (see below).

Finance decisions (see chapters 10 and 11)

Issues addressed:

- How should finance be raised in order to minimise cost of capital (debt or equity)?
- What optimum finance structure will result?

Additional considerations for MNCs: Whether finance should be raised in the MNC's home markets, in the target countries markets or in some other market.

Dividend decisions (see chapter 21)

Issues addressed:

- What should be the balance between the amount of profit distributed and that held back for reinvestment in the business?
- Whether alternatives to cash dividends might be used?

Additional considerations for MNCs: Capital mobility (barriers to repatriating the return on investment and how to deal with these)

Risk management (see chapters 2, 7 and 17 to 20)

Issues addressed:

- What financial risks are faced by the business?
- How financial risks should be monitored, measured and addressed?

Additional considerations for MNCs:

- What are the additional financial risks faced by the business as a result of operating overseas? These would include foreign exchange risk which is covered in detail in chapters 17, 19 and 20).
- What other risks are faced by the business as a result of operating overseas?

8.2 National regulatory requirements

Multinational companies might be able to raise capital in different financial markets around the world, should they wish to do so. To be able to raise capital in any financial market, a company must meet the legal, regulatory and compliance requirements that apply in that particular market.

Legal requirements

There are certain legal requirements that must be met before a company can raise capital from investors on a stock market. In the UK for example, companies cannot raise capital from the general investing public unless they have the status of a public limited company.

Regulatory requirements

There are also regulatory requirements that have to be met. These include regulations relating to obtaining official permission to raise capital in the form of shares or bonds, and issuing a prospectus to potential investors. Having obtained approval from the regulatory authorities, the shares or bonds must be accepted for trading by a stock exchange.

Compliance requirements

Having issued shares or bonds, the company must then continue to comply with continuing obligations (rules) of the regulatory authorities and the stock market. These include rules relating to the regular provision of information about the company to the stock market (such as profit warnings and trading updates).

To meet the regulatory and compliance requirements for issuing shares or bonds on a stock market, a company might have to commit considerable time and money. The burden is greater for shares than for bonds. This is because bonds are often traded 'privately' between professional and institutional investors whereas shares are traded much more on public stock markets.

The process of raising capital by issuing shares in a stock market

Although the detailed rules vary between countries, the broad nature of the rules for issuing shares in a stock market are fairly similar in most countries with a large stock market. There is a two-stage process of acceptance before the shares can be issued.

- The company and its shares must be approved by a regulatory authority for the country's stock markets. In the UK, this involves getting the shares accepted on to an 'Official List' by the Listing Authority, which is a department of the financial markets regulator (the Financial Services Authority), or by a similar listing authority in any other EEA country of Europe. Obtaining a listing for the shares includes an approval process for a draft prospectus for the share issue. Companies whose shares have been accepted on to the Official List are called 'listed companies'. In the US, approval must be obtained from the US stock markets regulator, the Securities and Exchange Commission or SEC.
- The company must also apply to the country's stock exchange for the shares to be accepted for trading on the stock market operated by the exchange. In the UK, for example, companies apply to the London Stock Exchange for the new shares to be admitted to trading on the exchange. Similarly, in the US, a company might apply for its shares to be traded on the New York Stock Exchange or NASDAQ.

When the shares have been issued and are trading on the stock market, the company must comply with continuing regulations of both the financial markets regulator and the stock exchange. In the UK for example, listed companies must comply with the Listing Rules and the Disclosure and Transparency Rules of the financial markets regulator, and must also comply with the Admission and Disclosure Standards of the London Stock Exchange which require for example that securities must be eligible for electronic settlement.

Some multinational companies obtain listings for their shares in two or more countries. For example a company in Germany might obtain a listing in Germany and its shares might be traded on the German stock market. In addition, the company might obtain a listing for its shares in the USA or in the UK.

International companies might obtain a listing for their shares in a major international stock market such as London, in addition to their own country. In recent years, several major companies in countries such as Russia and Kazakhstan have sought a listing in the UK. The advantage of a London listing for these companies is that they gain access to global investment capital: it is much easier to raise capital by issuing shares in the UK than in countries with financial markets that are much less developed.

Raising capital by issuing bonds

In recent years, multinational companies have often preferred to raise capital by issuing bonds rather than shares. Debt capital has been much cheaper than equity, and institutional investors have been willing to invest in large quantities of bonds.

If a multinational company wants to raise capital in the international markets, it might prefer to consider the possibility of issuing bonds in a national bond market rather than consider the possibility of a share issue.

8.3 London Stock Exchange (LSE) listing rules

The syllabus makes specific reference to the London Stock Exchange listing rules as an example of national regulatory requirements that a multi-national company might have to comply with. These requirements are summarised below.

Public limited company

Only public limited companies (plcs) are allowed to issue shares to the public.

A private company must re-register as a public limited company (plc) before it can apply for a listing.

A plc must have an issued share capital of a least GBP50,000, of which at least one quarter must be paid up.

Track record

The company must have a track record of independent trading of at least three years.

Financial statements

The company must have published, audited accounts for the three years prior to the application for a listing (except in exceptional circumstances).

The accounts must not have a qualified audit report and comply in all material respects with acceptable accounting standards.

If the last published accounts were more than six months from the listing date, a set of interim accounts must be prepared.

Future

The directors must be satisfied and confirm in writing that the company has sufficient working capital for its needs and consequently will not become insolvent in the next 12 months.

The company must provide a general description of future plans and prospects

Controlling shareholder

A controlling shareholder is a person who owns 30% or more of the voting rights in the company.

A company must be able to demonstrate that all significant decisions are taken by directors independent of the controlling shareholder and there are arrangements in place to avoid detriment to other shareholders.

Transferability of securities

Listed shares must be freely transferable.

This means that a company may need to change its constitution to remove any restrictions on the transfer of shares.

Market value of securities to be listed

The minimum market value of shares to be listed is GBP700,000.

Public shareholders

A sufficient number of the shares must be in the hands of the public, to ensure that the secondary market for the shares is sufficiently liquid and the shares are marketable.

The minimum requirement is for 25% of the shares to be in public hands.

8.4 Mobility of capital

This refers to the ability to move funds across national boundaries.

- Perfect capital mobility means that there are no transaction costs or barriers in moving capital from one country to another.
- Capital immobility means it is difficult and expensive to move capital between countries.

Capital mobility is reduced by any regulations that increase the cost of moving capital from one country to another. Examples include the following:

- Tariffs or taxes on capital flows (e.g. tax on investment or on profits).
- Restrictions on capital flows. Some countries may impose restrictions on the amount of capital that can be taken into and out of a country.
- Foreign exchange controls. Some countries impose restrictions on the movement of foreign currency out of the country..

Impact of capital mobility

It is easier for a country to attract foreign direct investment into a country when capital is mobile. Restrictions discourage such investment as the investing company is unable to repatriate any profits it might make.

On the other hand, capital mobility could lead to a sudden outflow of capital under times of uncertainty. Large companies and wealthy individuals might transfer their wealth out of a country. This could cause a run on the banks, causing significant disruption to the economy with job losses and increased unemployment.

Location of other information

There is more information on exchange controls in paragraph 1.4 of chapter 13.

Information on managing barriers to remittance can be found at paragraph 3.4 of chapter 17.

8.5 Risk exposures

The main objective of a MNC is presumably to maximise the wealth of its shareholders. The main objective of many national governments is to provide for the well-being of their population. The objectives of MNCs and national governments therefore differ, particularly when the MNC is a 'foreign company' with its head office in another country.

National governments might expect MNCs to:

- invest in their country, and provide employment
- through investment, add to the economic wealth of the country and help to develop the country's economy
- pay taxes on their profits, that the government can spend on the well-being of its population.

MNCs might therefore be exposed to political and regulatory risks when they invest in another country, particularly when the local government and population suspect that the multinational is more concerned about the interests of its shareholders than in the welfare of the country.

Some MNCs are aware of their corporate social responsibility to the countries in which they invest, and are aware of the need to educate the local population, preserve the local environment and create a sustainable industry within that country. On the other hand, some MNCs might show little awareness of corporate social responsibility, and seek to avoid paying taxes if possible. As a consequence, in many countries, MNCs are treated with dislike and suspicion.

Investment decisions by multinationals might be affected by the perceived political and regulatory risks of investing in particular countries.

Political risk

Political risk is the risk for an international company that the government of a foreign country might take action that affects the operations or profitability of its investment in its country, or places restrictions on the ability of the foreign subsidiary to remit interest or dividends to the parent country.

Political action against an international company might include the nationalisation of some or all of the assets of its foreign subsidiary, punitive additional tax charges or exchange controls. The government might simply pursue economic policies and other policies that are 'unfriendly' to businesses and to foreign businesses in particular.

Potential risks include:

- the risk of confiscation of their assets by the government
- the risk of new regulations of the industry, such as regulations requiring minimum ownership in all businesses by 'nationals' of the country

- the risks of political unrest and violence.

Regulatory risk

Regulatory risk is the risk that a government might change regulations after a capital investment project has been implemented and that these regulations will affect the returns from a project.

For example, a government might introduce new environmental regulations which had not been budgeted for.

Most changes to law can be anticipated as they pass through a legislative procedure so a company should monitor proposed legal changes so that they are in a position to manage their impact.

Fiscal risk

Fiscal risk is the risk that after a capital investment project has been implemented, the government might increase the rate of tax payable on the profits or cash flows from the project. Higher tax payments could significantly affect the returns from a project.

Fiscal risk varies between countries. Some countries have a reputation for fiscal stability, so that any changes in tax are fairly insignificant. In other countries there is a much higher risk of tax changes. Obviously, companies considering an investment in a country, even their domestic country, should take fiscal risk into consideration when deciding whether or not to invest in a project.

Example

The oil and natural gas industry is an example of an industry where fiscal risk has had a significant impact on capital expenditure decisions.

Oil companies purchase concessions to explore for oil or gas, and extract any that they find. If they fail to find any oil or gas, they will lose their investment. However, they face a risk that if they are successful in finding and extracting oil, the government will decide to tax their profits. One way of doing this is to charge a windfall tax on the profits of firms in the industry that operate in the country. For example, the UK government introduced a windfall tax on the profits of companies in the North Sea oil business.

Reducing fiscal risk

Fiscal risk is unavoidable for companies that pay tax on their profits. However, the risk might sometimes be reduced for large companies. A large company can try to negotiate with the government of a country before deciding whether to invest in the country. They might argue that they will not invest unless the government gives an assurance of fiscal stability.

The risk of an unexpected additional tax (windfall tax) cannot be removed simply by a government's promise, because promises might be broken. Another approach that might be used by some companies is to offer to pay a royalty tax on their output. For example, an oil company might undertake to pay a royalty on every barrel of oil that it extracts under a concession agreement. If the company pays tax in this way, so that the royalty payments increase with the volume of business, the government might be less inclined to charge additional tax on what it sees as excessive profits.

8.6 Agency issues

Corporate governance issues were described in an earlier chapter. Corporate governance is a particular problem for MNCs. A part of the problem is that MNCs need to recognise the interests of local governments and populations as stakeholders in their foreign subsidiaries.

Another issue is the agency problem, and the requirement for management to act in the best interests of the company's shareholders. In large multinational companies, a considerable amount of authority is delegated to 'local' management in divisions and subsidiaries around the world. Delegation of authority is essential for the effective management of large global businesses.

On the other hand, when authority is delegated to local managers, head office management need to co-ordinate the worldwide activities of the MNC, and try to ensure that the strategic objectives of the MNC are met and the interests of its shareholders are satisfied.

The local management/central management relationship is an agency relationship with local management acting as agents for the principal (central management). This is true for any large company that delegates decision making to managers at another location. However, the difficulties that might arise can become exacerbated for investments overseas due to different cultural background.

Decisions by head office management might be resisted by local management in some countries, where head office managers might be trying to act in the interests of the shareholders, whereas local managers have more concern for their own position or for the interests of employees, customers and economic conditions in their own country.

Furthermore, the local management might believe that instruction received from central management is not in the best interests of the shareholders because central management do not understand the local situation. This too could lead to conflicts.

These issues can be reduced by management processes that allow for good two-way communication and set out guidelines specify authority for different classes of decisions.

CHAPTER

5

Dividend policy and transfer pricing in multinationals

Contents

Dividend policy

- The relationship between the dividend decision and the financing decision
- Shareholder preferences
- The nature of dividend policy
- Practical influences on the dividend decision
- Dividend capacity
- Alternatives to cash dividends

1 Dividend policy

1.1 The relationship between the dividend decision and the financing decision

Total earnings are retained or paid out in dividends. Retained earnings are the surplus profits available to the company for investment after dividend has been paid. Dividends reduce equity capital.

When a company wants to raise more capital for investment, it could do so by paying no dividend at all and retaining 100% of earnings. The only external capital it then needs to raise is the amount by which its capital requirements exceed its earnings.

In practice, however, not many companies would do this. Instead, they have a dividend policy that they make known to their shareholders and try to apply in practice (subject to profits being large enough). Even when they want to raise fresh capital, they will probably continue to pay dividends.

1.2 Shareholder preferences

Some shareholders prefer to receive dividends from their equity investments. Others are not concerned about dividends and would prefer the company to reinvest all its earnings in order to pursue growth strategies that will increase the market value of the shares. Many shareholders prefer a mixture of dividends and retaining some profits for share price growth. (For many years, for example, software giant Microsoft had a policy of retaining its earnings to invest in growth, with no dividend pay-outs.)

Shareholders will buy and hold shares of companies that pursue a dividend policy consistent with their preferences for dividends or share price growth, and companies might try to pursue a dividend policy consistent with the preferences of most of their shareholders

1.3 The nature of dividend policy

In practice dividend policy might be stated in terms of an intention of the board of directors to increase annual dividends in line with growth in earnings per share.

When dividends increase by the same proportionate amount as the rise in EPS, it is said to maintain a constant 'pay-out ratio'.

Shareholders can monitor the future profit expectations of the company to predict the amount of dividends they are likely to receive in the future.

There are several theories about dividend policy. These theories are intended to identify the optimal amount of dividends that a company should pay to the shareholders. Three of these theories are:

- the traditional view of dividend policy
- residual theory
- Modigliani and Miller's theory of the irrelevance of dividend policy.

Traditional view of dividend policy

The traditional view of dividend policy is that the amount of dividend payments should be at a level that enables the company to maximise the value of its shares. Retaining earnings adds to earnings growth in the future, and earnings growth will enable the company to increase dividends in the future.

For example, suppose that a company pays out 40% of its earnings in dividends and retains the remaining 60% of earnings which it can reinvest in the business to earn a return of 10% per year. For every $100 of earnings in the current year, it will pay dividends of $40 and by reinvesting $60 it will add to future annual earnings by 6% (= 60% × 10%) each year. Annual earnings next year will be $106.

Similarly if a company retains only 20% of its earnings which it can reinvest at 10%, for every $100 of earnings in the current year, it will pay dividends of $80 and by reinvesting $20 it will add to future annual earnings by 2% (= 20% × 10%) each year. Annual earnings next year will be $102.

There is a model for the valuation of shares based on expectations of future dividend growth, known as Gordon's growth model or the dividend growth model. This model is described in a later chapter on valuation.

According to traditional theory of dividend policy, the optimal dividend policy is the dividends and retentions policy that maximises the share price using the dividend growth model to obtain a share price valuation.

Residual theory of dividend policy

The residual theory of dividend policy is that the optimal amount of dividends should be decided as follows.

- If a company has capital investment opportunities that will have a positive NPV, it should invest in them because they will add to the value of the company and its shares.
- The capital to invest in these projects should be obtained internally (from earnings) if possible.

- The amount of dividends paid by a company should be the residual amount of earnings remaining after all these available capital projects have been funded by retained earnings.
- In this way, the company will maximise its total value and the market price of its shares.

A practical problem with residual theory is that annual dividends will fluctuate, depending on the availability of worthwhile capital projects. Shareholders will therefore be unable to predict what their dividends will be.

Modigliani and Miller's theory of the irrelevance of dividend policy

Modigliani and Miller (MM) developed a model that suggested that dividend policy is irrelevant, and the level of dividends paid out by a company does not matter. The total market value of a company will be the same regardless of whether the dividend payout ratio is 0%, 100% or any ratio in between.

MM argued that the value of a company's shares depends on the rate of return it can earn from its business. 'Earning power' matters, but dividends do not. They argued that if a company has opportunities for investing in capital projects with a positive NPV, they can either:

- use retained earnings to finance the investment, or
- pay out earnings and dividends and obtain the equity that it needs for capital investment from the stock market.

For example if a company has earnings of $100 million and investment opportunities costing $100 million that have a positive NPV, it does not matter whether it pays no dividend and invests all its earnings on the capital projects, or whether it pays dividends of $100 million and raises new equity capital of $100 million for the capital project investments.

If the company pays out dividends and raises new equity capital, the existing shares will fall in value by the amount of the dividend payments. However this loss of value will be replaced by the new equity raised in the market, so the total value of the company's equity will be unaffected.

- Loss in value of existing shares = Amount of dividends paid
- Total value of equity before the dividend payment and equity issue = Total value of equity after the dividend payment and equity issue

Whenever shareholders want cash, it does not matter whether they obtain it in the form of dividends or by selling their shares in the market.

The MM theory is based on simplifying assumptions (capital market perfection). They did not say that dividend policy was irrelevant. They said it would be irrelevant in the simplified world that they described.

Dividend policy does seem to affect market value in practice. There are several real world circumstances which prevent irrelevance in practice.

- The theory assumes that there are no costs involved in raising new equity capital, so that there is no cost difference between retaining earnings and raising new equity.

- Similarly, MM assumed that there are no costs involved in selling shares, so that shareholders should be indifferent between getting cash in the form of dividends or getting it by selling some shares.
- MM assumed that shareholders possess perfect information about the returns that will be obtained by companies from their new capital investments. Since future earnings can be predicted with confidence, MM argued that share prices would remain close to their real value. In practice, however, this is not the case. Shareholders cannot always assess the real value of their shares with confidence: this is one reason why many shareholders prefer high cash dividends instead of the prospect of bigger capital gains in the future.
- Some shareholders have a preference for high dividends, so dividend policy does matter. MM responded by arguing that companies often have a consistent dividend policy with a constant pay-out ratio. Shareholders will be attracted to holding shares in the companies whose dividend policy is consistent with their own dividend preference.

1.4 Practical influences on the dividend decision

There are several practical limitations and influences on the amount of dividends paid by companies.

Investment opportunities

The amount of earnings a company wishes to retain might be affected by the number of suitable investment opportunities available to the company. If there are few investment projects available which can generate sufficient return then surplus cash should be returned to shareholders. Companies might payout as dividends any surplus cash for which they have no long-term need

Legal constraints: There might be legal restrictions on the maximum dividend payments. Companies can only pay dividends out of accumulated net realised profits. There may also be restrictions imposed by loan agreements to protect lenders.

Liquidity: Retained profit is not the same as retained cash. A company might be highly profitable but still have low levels of surplus cash. The dividends paid must not threaten a company's liquidity and dividends might be limited by the availability of cash.

Dividends as a signal to investors and shareholder expectations

A dividend which differs from shareholders expectations about dividends might send signals to the market and affect share price.

- A higher than expected dividend may signal that the board of directors are confident about the future and may lead to an increase in share price
- A lower than expected dividend may signal that the company is in financial difficulties and lead to a fall in share price.

Investors usually expect a consistent dividend policy from year to year or steady dividend growth. This can lead to pay-out ratios fluctuating as companies seek to hold a steady dividend as earnings fluctuate.

A company might also use dividend policy to send signals to the stock market about its future prospects and intentions.

1.5 Dividend capacity

Dividend capacity is determined by the free cash flow available to equity investors after net reinvestment. This was covered in detail in chapter 12.

Reinvestment is that which is required to maintain the operating capacity of the business at the planned rate of growth specified by management as necessary to achieve the firm's strategic goals. Where new capital has been introduced this is deducted from the capital expenditure during the year to give the amount of investment financed from the free cash flow.

Dividend capacity can be represented as follows:

	$m
Revenue	X
Operating costs	(X)
Interest expense	(X)
Taxation	(X)
	X
Dividend income (from domestic and overseas subsidiaries)	X
Net investment in non-current assets	X/(X)
Net investment in working capital	X/(X)
Net debt issued (repaid)	X/(X)
Net share capital issued (repaid)	X/(X)
Dividend capacity	X

Several past exam questions have included a requirement to estimate dividend capacity resulting from a given scenario.

Example

X Plc's revenue for the year just ended was $60m. It is expected to grow by 25% next year.

X Plc has an operating margin of 20% of revenue.

X Plc will require the following capital investment in the coming year.

1. A 30% investment in additional non-current assets for every $1 increase in sales revenue.
2. $3·0 million additional investment in non-current assets for a new project.
3. A 10% investment in working capital for every $1 increase in sales revenue.

Overseas subsidiary

X Plc has a wholly owned overseas subsidiary called A Co.

A Co makes and sells a product with a variable cost of $25 per unit and a selling price of $40 per unit.

A Co's annual fixed costs are $1.0m.

A Co has budgeted to make 250,000 units next year.

A Co pays 60% of its post-tax profits to X Plc.

Other Information

1. X Plc's has long term debt of $40 million, on which it pays interest of 6% per year.
2. X Plc's profits are taxed at 25%.
3 A Co's profits are taxed at 20%.
3. X Plc does not pay tax on overseas dividends.

Required:

Calculate X Plc's dividend capacity for the coming year.

Answer

	$m
Revenue ($60m × 1.25)	75.00
Operating profit (20%)	15.00
Interest expense ($40m × 0.06)	(2.40)
Profit before tax	12.60
Taxation (25%)	(3.15)
	9.45
Dividend income (W)	1.32
Net investment in new project	(3.00)
Net investment in non-current assets (30% × ($75m – $60m))	(4.50)
Net investment in working capital (10% × ($75m – $60m))	(1.50)
Dividend capacity	1.77

Working: Dividend from A Co.

	$m
Revenue ($40 × 250,000 units)	10.00
Variable costs ($40 × 250,000 units)	(6.25)
Fixed costs	(1.00)
	2.75
Taxation (20%)	(0.55)
	2.20
Dividend (60%)	1.32

1.6 Alternatives to cash dividends

Scrip dividends

A company that wants to retain cash for reinvestment but does not want to reduce its dividends might offer its shareholders a scrip dividend. A scrip dividend is a dividend paid in the form of new shares. Instead of receiving cash, the shareholder receives new shares.

The rules of the stock exchange might require that when a company wants to make a scrip dividend, it must offer a cash dividend alternative, so that shareholders can choose between new shares and cash.

In practice, scrip dividend shave not proved popular and they are fairly uncommon.

Share repurchases

Share repurchases were mentioned in a previous section of this chapter. If a company has surplus cash and is over-capitalised, it might decide to repurchase some shares as an alternative to paying out the cash in the form of a higher dividend.

If a company chooses to pay a higher dividend, this might act as a signal to shareholders who then expect high dividends in future years too. If the cash is used for share repurchases instead of higher dividends, future dividend expectations will not be affected.

Transfer pricing

- Purpose of transfer pricing
- Corporate objectives and the relevance of tax and transfer pricing
- MNCs: transfer pricing and tax rules
- Multinationals and tax planning

2 Transfer pricing

2.1 Purpose of transfer pricing

When a company has a divisionalised structure, some of the divisions might supply goods or services to other divisions in the same company. Similarly, one subsidiary within a group may supply goods or services to another of the group's subsidiaries.

- One division sells the goods or services. This will be referred to as the 'selling division'.
- Another division buys the goods or services. This will be referred to as the 'buying division'.

For accounting purposes, these internal transfers of goods or services are given a value. Transfers could be recorded at cost. However, when the selling division is a profit centre or investment centre, it will expect to make some profit on the sale.

A transfer price is the price at which goods or services are sold by one division within an entity to another division in the same entity. Internal sales are referred to as transfers, so the internal selling and buying price is the transfer price.

The objectives of transfer pricing

A decision has to be made about what the transfer price should be.
For the purpose of performance measurement and performance evaluation in a divisionalised organisation, it is appropriate that:

- the selling division should earn some profit or return on sales to other divisions and
- the buying division should pay a fair price for the goods or services that it buys from other divisions.

Transfer prices are decided by management. The objectives of transfer pricing should be to:

- achieve goal congruence for the entity as a whole, and
- give autonomy (freedom to make decisions) to the managers of the profit centres or investment centres.

These two objectives are often in conflict with each other, and unless the transfer prices are set at a suitable level, it might be impossible to achieve both objectives.

The motivation of divisional managers

An assumption is that the managers of every profit centre will take decisions that maximise the profits of the division.

If every division maximises its profits, the profits of the entity as a whole will also be maximised.

However, a division might take action that maximises its own profit, but reduces the profits of another division. As a result, the profits of the entity as a whole might also be reduced.

Goal congruence

Every divisional manager should work towards the maximisation of the profits and returns of the entity as a whole. When every divisional manager has the same aim or goal, there is goal congruence.

- Transfer prices should therefore encourage divisional managers to take decisions that are in the best interests of the entity as a whole.
- Transfer prices should not encourage a divisional manager to take decisions that are against the interests of the entity as a whole and would reduce the profits of the entity.

Example

An entity has two divisions, Division K and Division L. Division K makes a product which it sells as a component to Division L. Division L uses this component to make an end product that it sells to external customers.

Division K as estimated that the variable cost to make the component is $5 per unit and with fixed costs of $7 per unit, the total cost per unit is $12. If Division K stopped making the component there would be no savings in fixed costs.

The manager of the division would like to make a profit from making and selling the component to Division L, and thinks that a transfer price of $14 would be reasonable. Similar components are sold in the market for about $15 per unit.

However, the manager of Division L has received an offer from an external supplier who, for a period of six months, would be prepared to sell the same component that is made by Division K at a special price of 11 per unit.

In this situation:

- The manager of Division L would be attracted by an offer of 11 per unit for buying the component, given a transfer price of $14 from Division K. Given free choice, Division L would accept the offer and buy the component externally.
- However this decision would reduce the profits of the company as a whole, because it costs just $5 per unit (the variable cost in Division K) to make the component internally. For each unit bought externally at $11 per unit, profit would therefore be reduced by $6.

In this situation, a transfer price of $14 per unit would not be 'ideal' and would encourage sub-optimal decision-making.

Divisional autonomy

Autonomy is freedom of action and freedom to make decisions. Divisional managers should be free to make their own decisions. Autonomy should improve motivation of divisional managers.

For example, when transfer prices have been decided, the managers of all divisions within the entity should be free to decide:

- whether to sell their output to other divisions (internal transfers) or whether to sell them to external customers, if an external market exists for the output
- whether to buy their goods from another division (internal transfers) or whether to buy them from external suppliers, if an external market exists.

Divisional managers should be allowed to make their own choices. They should not have to be told what to do by senior management at head office.

If there is a conflict between the objectives of goal congruence and divisional autonomy, goal congruence should have priority. If divisional managers cannot agree to do what is best for the entity as a whole, they should be instructed about what to do by senior management. However, this situation would be undesirable.

Ideally, transfer prices should be set so that divisional managers can agree on selling and buying between each other in a way that is in the best interests of all the divisions and the entity as a whole.

2.2 Corporate objectives and the relevance of tax and transfer pricing

The corporate objective of a multinational company, as for any other company, is linked to profitability and returns for shareholders. Multinational companies operate in different countries, and are therefore subject to differing tax regulations and systems. MNCs will try to improve earnings for shareholders by minimising their worldwide tax liabilities.

- Multinational companies will seek to invest in countries where the taxation system is more favourable. For example, companies might seek relief from taxation for making capital investments in a country, and will choose one country in preference to another on the basis of the tax advantages offered
- Some MNCs have been accused of using transfer pricing to minimise their tax liabilities. Transfer prices are used to charge for goods and services transferred between companies in the group. Transfer prices can be charged in such a way that:
  - transfers from a subsidiary in a high-tax country to a subsidiary in a low-tax country are fixed at high levels, and
  - low transfer prices are set for transfers from a low-tax to a high-tax country.

In this way, profits in the high-tax subsidiaries are reduced, and more profits are earned in the low-tax countries.

2.3 MNCs: transfer pricing and tax rules

Transfer prices are prices charged internally within a group, and have no effect on the total pre-tax profit of the group. Transfer prices are simply a way of sharing the profit between the two companies concerned.

Transfer prices between a company and a foreign subsidiary have implications for taxation, and the aim of a group of companies should be to minimise total tax payable on the group profits. Issues to consider are:

- the rate of taxation on profits in the two countries
- the existence of a double taxation agreement
- the existence of any withholding tax in the country of the foreign subsidiary
- tax rules on transfer pricing.

Tax rates

The rate of taxation on profits will vary between the two countries and two companies concerned. As a general principle, the aim of a group should be to set a transfer price that shares the profits in a way that reduces the profits of the company in the higher-tax country.

For example, suppose that a parent company in country A sells goods to its 100%-owned subsidiary in country B, and the rate of tax is 20% in country A and 30% in country B. The transfer price should be set as high as the tax rules permit, because this will increase profits of the parent company in lower-tax country A and reduce the profits of the subsidiary in higher-tax country B.

Double taxation agreement

There should usually be a double taxation agreement between the two countries. From the point of view of the parent company, this means that:

- If the rate of tax on profits is higher in the country of the foreign subsidiary than in the parent company's country, the subsidiary pays tax in its own country on its profits at the rate applicable in that country. No further tax is payable in the parent company's country on the profits of the foreign subsidiary.
- If the rate of tax on profits is lower in the country of the foreign subsidiary than in the parent company's country, the subsidiary pays tax in its own country on its profits at the rate applicable in that country. However, tax is also payable by the parent company in its own country. The tax payable is the difference between tax on profits at the rate in the parent company and the tax payable by the subsidiary in its own country.

Withholding tax

Withholding tax is additional tax that is 'withheld' when a company pays interest or dividends to a foreign investor. It affects international groups where foreign subsidiaries are located in a country where withholding tax is charged. Payments of interest or dividends by a subsidiary to the parent company will be subject to the withholding tax.

Tax rules on transfer prices

The tax rules in a country are likely to make it difficult for an international group to charge inter-company transfer prices that are significantly different from market prices (where these exist). This is because the tax authorities recognise that transfer prices might be set artificially so as to minimise the total tax burden for the group.

These various tax aspects of transfer pricing are illustrated by the following example.

Example

A UK company has recently acquired a foreign subsidiary in another country, Outland. A part of the operating arrangements of the new group is that the parent company will export a component to the subsidiary, and the subsidiary will use this component to make a product that it will sell in Outland. The management of the parent company have to decide what the transfer price for the component should be.

The following information is available:

UK (annual)		**Outland (annual)**	
Components transferred to Outland	100,000 units	Units of product sold	100,000 units
		Sales price per unit	$150
Variable cost per unit	£15	Local variable cost per unit	$40
Fixed costs	£900,000	Local fixed costs	$600,000
Tax rate	30%	Tax rate	25%

The exchange rate is £1 = $4.

Withholding tax of 10% is charged on all remittances of interest and dividends from Outland. The UK parent company intends to remit all available profits from Outland to the UK.

There is a double taxation agreement between the UK and Outland. Tax on income and distributions in one country may be credited against a tax liability on the same income in the other country.

Required

Calculate the group profits if the transfer price for the component is set at

(a) its market price, which is £26 per unit

(b) total UK cost per unit plus 25%.

Answer

Tax on profits in Outland will be 25%, but there will be an additional withholding tax of 10% since all available profits will be remitted to the UK. The total tax payable on income in Outland is therefore 35% which is higher than the rate of UK tax. This means that profits earned in Outland will not be taxed at all in the UK.

(a) **Transfer price = market price**

Parent company, UK	£	£
Component sales (£26 per unit)		2,600,000
Variable costs (£15 per unit)	1,500,000	
Fixed costs	900,000	
		2,400,000
Profit before tax		200,000
Tax at 30%		(60,000)
Profit after tax		140,000

The transfer price in Outland dollars is £26 × $4 = $104.

Subsidiary company, Outland	$	$	
Product sales ($150 per unit)		15,000,000	
Transfer costs ($104 per unit)	10,400,000		
Local variable costs ($40 per unit)	1,500,000		
Local fixed costs	600,000		
		12,500,000	
Profit before tax		2,500,000	
Tax at 25%		(625,000)	
Profit after tax		1,875,000	
Withholding tax at 10%		(187,500)	
Profit in the UK after tax		1,687,500	= £421,875

The total group profit will be £140,000 + £421,875= £561,875.

(b) **Transfer price = cost plus 25%**

Total UK costs are £2,400,000 or £24 per unit. Cost plus 25% = £30 per unit. The transfer price will therefore be £30, which is $120 per unit.

Parent company, UK	£
Component sales (£30 per unit)	3,000,000
Total costs (as above)	2,400,000
Profit before tax	600,000
Tax at 30%	(180,000)
Profit after tax	420,000

Subsidiary company, Outland	$	$	
Product sales ($150 per unit)		15,000,000	
Transfer costs ($120 per unit)	12,000,000		
Local variable costs ($40 per unit)	1,500,000		
Local fixed costs	600,000		
		14,100,000	
Profit before tax		900,000	
Tax at 25%		(225,000)	
Profit after tax		675,000	
Withholding tax at 10%		(67,500)	
Profit in the UK after tax		607,500	= £151,875

The total group profit will be £420,000 + £151,875 = £571,875.

The higher transfer price will provide a bigger after-tax profit for the group. However, the tax authorities in Outland might not agree to accept a transfer price of $20, because this is $4 per unit above the market price for the component.

2.4 Multinationals and tax planning

Multinationals are subject to tax on their profits in all the countries in which they operate. They are also subject to tax on their world-wide profits in their country of registration. As explained earlier, the tax burden is reduced by the existence of double taxation agreements between countries, and a multinational is able to set off tax paid in foreign countries against tax payable in the country of registration.

For example, a UK multinational may be liable to tax in Country X on the profits of a subsidiary in Country X. Suppose that the amount of this tax liability is the equivalent of £500,000. The UK parent company will also be liable to tax in the UK for the profits (or dividends) of the foreign subsidiary. If a double taxation agreement exists between the UK and Country X, the following tax positions might arise.

- If the UK tax liability for the foreign subsidiary is more than £500,000, tax payable in the UK will be reduced by the tax payable in Country X (£500,000).
- If the UK tax liability for the foreign subsidiary is less than £500,000, no tax is payable in the UK.

Tax planning to reduce a tax liability

A multinational may be able to reduce its world-wide tax liability through tax planning. One measure might be to establish a subsidiary company in a **tax haven**, and by channelling its profits and capital gains in other countries through the tax haven, its total tax liability might be reduced.

An example may help to illustrate this point.

Example

A UK multinational company has three wholly-owned foreign subsidiaries, in Country A, Country B and Country C. The profits of each subsidiary for the year are the equivalent of £100,000. The rate of corporate tax in the UK is 30%.

The tax rates in the other countries are set out below.

Country	Tax on profits	Withholding tax on dividends	% of after-tax profit remitted to the UK as dividends
Country A	20%	5%	90
Country B	25%	-	90
Country C	40%	10%	80

Double taxation agreements exist between the UK and each of the three countries.

Required

Calculate the world-wide tax liability of the UK multinational in each of the three following circumstances:

(a) The UK government charges companies tax on the dividends remitted from foreign subsidiaries. The amount of the dividend is grossed up at the local tax rate, before deduction of any withholding tax, and UK tax is calculated on this grossed-up dividend.

(b) The UK government charges multinationals tax on the gross income of their foreign subsidiaries. A tax credit is available for all corporate taxes paid in foreign countries, including withholding tax.

(c) The multinational sets up a subsidiary in a tax haven (Country D). All income from the foreign subsidiaries would be transferred to the UK via this tax haven company. The UK government would then treat all the foreign income as coming through a single source, the tax haven company in Country D.

Calculate the total tax payable on the foreign profits of the multinational if the tax rules are:

(i) the same as in (a)

(ii) the same as in (b).

Answer

(a)

		Country A		Country B		Country C
		£000		£000		£000
Taxable income		100.0		100.0		100.0
Local tax on profits	(20%)	20.0	(25%)	25.0	(40%)	40.0
		80.0		75.0		60.0
Dividend payment before withholding tax	(90%)	72.0	(90%)	67.5	(80%)	48.0
Withholding tax	(5%)	3.6			(10%)	4.8
Dividends to UK before deducting withholding tax		72.0		67.5		48.0
Gross up for local tax	(× 100/80)	90.0	(× 100/75)	90.0	(× 100/60)	80.0
UK tax liability at 30%		27.0		27.0		24.0
Foreign tax credit (see note below)	(20 + 3.6)	23.6		25.0		24.0
UK tax payable		3.4		2.0		0.0

Note: The foreign tax credit is the lower amount of tax payable in the foreign country and tax payable in the UK.

Summary	**£000**
Tax payable in other countries (20 + 25 + 40 + 3.6 + 4.8)	93.4
Tax payable in the UK (3.4 + 2.0)	5.4
Worldwide tax liability	98.8

(b)

		Country A		Country B		Country C
		£000		£000		£000
Taxable income		100.0		100.0		100.0
Local tax on profits	(20%)	20.0	(25%)	25.0	(40%)	40.0
		80.0		75.0		60.0
Dividend payment before withholding tax	(90%)	72.0	(90%)	67.5	(80%)	48.0
Withholding tax	(5%)	3.6			(10%)	4.8
Income for UK tax purposes		100.0		100.0		100.0
UK tax liability at 30%		30.0		30.0		30.0
Foreign tax credit (see note above)		23.6		25.0		30.0
UK tax payable		6.4		5.0		0.0

Summary	**£000**
Tax payable in other countries (20 + 25 + 40 + 3.6 + 4.8)	93.4
Tax payable in the UK (6.4 + 5.0)	11.4
Worldwide tax liability	104.8

Under these tax rules, more tax is payable in the UK than with the tax system in (a).

(c)

	Tax system in (a)	**Tax system in (b)**
	£000	£000
Tax payable in other countries	93.4	93.4
UK tax liability (90 + 90 + 80)	260.0	300.0
UK tax at 30%	78.0	90.0
Foreign tax credit	78.0	90.0
Tax payable in the UK	0.0	0.0

The worldwide tax payable is just £93,400 because no tax is now payable in the UK (because a tax credit of up to £93,400 would be available). Setting up the tax haven therefore reduces the word-wide tax burden for the multinational.

CHAPTER 6

Net present value

Contents

Discounted cash flow: net present value method

- Introduction
- Net present value (NPV) method of investment appraisal
- Assumptions about the timing of cash flows
- Changes in working capital and cash flows
- Calculating the NPV of a project
- Discount tables
- Annuities
- Present value of a perpetuity

1 Discounted cash flow: net present value method

1.1 Introduction

An important element of financial management is deciding how to invest funds in capital projects. The basic principle is that a company should not invest capital unless the expected return from the investment is expected to exceed the cost of the funds invested.

Proposed capital expenditure projects can be evaluated using discounted cash flow.

A crucial aspect of DCF is that capital expenditure is assessed by looking at the cash flows from the investment, not at accounting profits.

You should be familiar with the basic rules of DCF from your earlier studies. This chapter contains revision material for what you should already know. However, in your examination, you will be required to take DCF analysis to a more advanced stage. This chapter explains some advanced aspects of capital investment appraisal. Other aspects will be dealt with in later chapters.

1.2 Net present value (NPV) method of investment appraisal

With the NPV method of investment appraisal, all the future cash flows from an investment are converted into a present value, by discounting the cash flow at the investment cost of capital. This cost of capital is the return required from the investment.

The discount rate to apply to a cash flow at the end of year n is:
$1/(1 + r)^n$
where r is the cost of capital (so that 9% = 0.09, 12.5% = 0.125 and so on).

Cash flows at the beginning of the investment, in Year 0, are already stated at their present value. The present value of \$1 in Year 0 is \$1. (The discount factor for Year 0 is $1/(1 + r)^0$. This has a value of 1.000 for any and every value of r).

1.3 Assumptions about the timing of cash flows

The following assumptions are used in DCF about the timing of cash flows:

- The cash flows for each year (or time period) are assumed to occur at the end of the year (or time period). For example, if it is estimated that cash flows in Year 4 will be $100,000, it is assumed that the $100,000 is a cash inflow on the last day of Year 4.
- If a cash flow will occur early during a particular year, it is assumed that it will occur at the end of the previous year. Therefore a cash expenditure early in Year 1, for example, is assumed to occur at Year 0.

If greater accuracy is required for the timing of cash flows, each year can be divided into shorter time periods, such as three-month periods. The same assumptions about the timing of cash flows will apply, however, regardless of the length of these time periods.

1.4 Changes in working capital and cash flows

When there is an increase in working capital, cash inflows are lower than the accounting profit in the same period, by the amount of the increase.

Similarly, when there is a reduction in working capital, cash inflows are higher than accounting profits in the period, by the amount of the reduction.

This rule should be familiar to you from cash flow statements.

In DCF analysis, instead of adjusting the accounting profits in the years when working capital is increased or reduced, the increases or reductions in working capital are treated as separate cash flow items.

Example

A five-year project will require a working capital investment of $20,000 early in Year 1, and an additional working capital investment of $15,000 early in Year 2. The adjustments for working capital to the cash flows in each year of the project will be:

Year	$
0	(20,000)
1	(15,000)
5	35,000

There is a cash inflow at the end of the project because working capital is reduced to zero, and cash flows exceed accounting profits in that year by the amount of the working capital reduction.

1.5 Calculating the NPV of a project

The net present value (NPV) of a project is the net difference between the present value of all the costs incurred and the present value of all the cash flow benefits (savings or revenues).

- If the present value of benefits exceeds the present value of costs, the NPV is positive.
- If the present value of benefits is less than the present value of costs, the NPV is negative.
- The NPV is 0 when the PV of benefits and the PV of costs are equal.

The **decision rule** is that, ignoring other factors such as risk and uncertainty, and non-financial considerations, a project is worthwhile financially if the NPV is positive or zero. It is not worthwhile if the NPV is negative.

The **net present value** of an investment project is also **a measure of the value of the investment**. For example, if a company invests in a project that has a NPV of $2 million, the value of the company should increase by $2 million.

1.6 Discount tables

Discount tables will be provided in your examination. They take away the need to calculate the value of discount factors $\frac{1}{(1+r)^n}$. The discount factors in the tables are rounded to three decimal places.

The following example tests your basic understanding of the NPV method and the use of discount tables. It should also demonstrate that **when the cost of capital is lower, the NPV is higher**. (And when the cost of capital is higher, the NPV is lower).

Example

A company is considering an investment in equipment costing $70,000. Working capital of $5,000 will also be required early in Year 1. The equipment will have a resale value of $7,000 at the end of Year 5. The operating profits from the investment, in cash flows, will be:

Year	Cash flow
	$
1	25,000
2	20,000
3	30,000
4	20,000
5	3,000

Required

Using discount tables for the discount factors, calculate the NPV of the project if the cost of capital is:

(a) 12%, and

(b) 8%.

a

Answer

In this example, the investment in working capital is treated as a cash outflow of $5,000 in Year 0 (early in Year 1). When the working capital is recovered at the end of the project (at the end of Year 5, or early in Year 6), this is treated as a Year 5 cash inflow.

The resale value of the equipment is also a cash inflow at the end of Year 5.

The cash flows for each year are therefore calculated as follows:

Year	Equipment	Working capital	Cash profits	Annual cash flow
	$	$	$	$
0	(70,000)	(5,000)		(75,000)
1			25,000	25,000
2			20,000	20,000
3			30,000	30,000
4			20,000	20,000
5	7,000	5,000	3,000	15,000

These cash flows should be used to calculate the NPV at (a) 12% and (b) 8%.

Year	Cash flow	Cost of capital 12%		Cost of capital 8%	
		Discount factor	Present value	Discount factor	Present value
	$		$		$
0	(75,000)	1.000	(75,000)	1.000	(75,000)
1	25,000	0.893	22,325	0.926	23,150
2	20,000	0.797	15,940	0.857	17,140
3	30,000	0.712	21,360	0.794	23,820
4	20,000	0.636	12,720	0.735	14,700
5	15,000	0.567	8,505	0.681	10,215
			+5,850		+14,025

Conclusion

The NPV is **higher** when the cost of capital is lower.

1.7 Annuities

An annuity is a constant cash flow for a given number of time periods.

Examples of annuities are:

- $80,000 each year for years 1 – 7
- $50,000 each year for years 6 – 12
- $1,000 each month for months 1 – 36.

Annuity discount factors can be used in DCF investment analysis, mainly to make the calculations easier and quicker. Instead of discounting a constant annual cash flow each year by the discount factor for that year, and then adding up the present values of the annual cash flows, we can multiply the constant annual cash flow by an annuity factor.

The annuity factor is simply the sum of the discount factors for all the years in which the constant annual cash flow occurs.

Annuity discount tables

The cash flows of project might include an annuity. The discount factors for annuities ('annuity factors') are provided in discount tables at the beginning of this text, and in the examination.

An annuity factor for time periods 1 to n is the sum of the discount factors from time period 1 to time period n.

Example

You should refer to the annuity factor table at the beginning of this text to check the discount factors in the following examples.

- The annuity factor for years 1 – 2 at a cost of capital of 8% = 1.783. This is found from the annuity table, n = 2, discount factor 8%. This annuity factor is the sum of the discount factors at 8% for years 1, and 2 (0.926 + 0.857).
- The annuity factor for years 1 – 6 at a cost of capital of 10% = 4.355. This is found from the annuity table, n = 6, discount factor = 10%. This annuity factor is the sum of the discount factors at 10% for years 1, 2, 3, 4, 5 and 6 (0.909 + 0.826 + 0.751 + 0.683 + 0.621 + 0.564).
- The annuity factor for years 4 – 8 at a cost of capital of 12% is calculated from annuity tables as follows:

Annuity factor at 12%, Years 1 – 8	=	4.968
Annuity factor at 12%, Years 1 – 3	=	2.402
Annuity factor at 12%, Years 4 – 8	=	2.566

This is the sum of the discount factors at 12% for each of the years 4 to 8. (0.636 + 0.567 + 0.507 + 0.452 + 0.402 = 2.566.)

Formula for calculating an annuity factor

It is useful for the purpose of financial management to be aware of the formula for an annuity. This is shown at the top of the annuity table:

$$\text{Annuity factor} = \frac{1 - (1 + r)^{-n}}{r}$$

This formula can be re-arranged, as follows:

$$\text{Annuity factor} = \frac{1}{r}\left[1 - \frac{1}{(1+r)^n}\right]$$

For example, the annuity factor for years 1 – 6 at 10% is:

$$\frac{1}{0.10}\left[1 - \frac{1}{(1.10)^6}\right]$$

$$= \frac{0.4355}{0.10} = 4.355$$

A knowledge of this formula might be useful for calculating an annuity factor when the cost of capital is not a whole number; for example when the cost of capital is 8.5% or 11.25%.

Example

The expected cash flows for a project to purchase the patent rights to a product are as follows:

Year	Annual cash flow	Discount factor at 12%	Present value
	$		$
0	(100,000)		
1	10,000		
2	15,000		
3 – 15	20,000		
NPV			

If the cost of capital is 12%, the NPV of the project is calculated as follows:

Years	Annuity factor at 12%
1 – 15	6.811
1 – 2	1.690
3 – 15	5.121

Year	Annual cash flow	Discount factor at 12%	Present value
	$		$
0	(100,000)	1.000	(100,000)
1	10,000	0.893	8,930
2	15,000	0.797	11,955
3 – 15	20,000	5.121	102,420
NPV			+ 23,305

Annuity factors can be used to calculate a 'breakeven' or minimum annual cash flow for a project.

Example

A company is considering an investment of $70,000 in a project. The project life would be five years.

What must be the minimum annual cash returns from the project to earn a return of at least 9% per annum, if the returns are a constant amount each year?

Answer

Investment	$70,000
Annuity factor at 9%, years 1 – 5	3.890

The minimum annual cash flow must have a present value of $70,000. The PV of the returns for the five years is the annual return multiplied by the annuity factor.

Minimum annual return required = $70,000/3.890 = $17,995.

1.8 Present value of a perpetuity

A perpetuity is a constant annual cash flow 'for ever', or into the long-term future.

In investment appraisal, it might be assumed that there is an annual cash flow in perpetuity whenever a constant annual cash flow is expected **for a long time** into the future.

The **present value of a perpetuity is: C/r**

where:

- C is the constant annual cash flow in perpetuity
- r is the cost of capital: for example 0.08, 0.10 etcetera.

Example

(1) What is the present value of £2,000 in perpetuity, starting in Year 1, if the cost of capital is 8%?

(2) What is the present value of £5,000 in perpetuity, starting in Year 4, if the cost of capital is 11%?

Answer

(1) $\frac{£2,000}{0.08} = £25,000$

(2) Year 3 value of perpetuity	$\frac{£5,000}{0.11} = £45,456$
Year 3 discount factor at 11%	0.731
Year 0 (present value) of perpetuity	**£33,228**

Use of perpetuities in financial management

The PV of a perpetuity is used in the dividend valuation model for share valuations, when there are constant annual dividends. Share valuation methods are explained in a later chapter.

DCF and inflation

- Real cost of capital and money cost of capital
- The DCF rule on inflation

2 DCF and inflation

2.1 Real cost of capital and money cost of capital

Inflation will affect future cash flows. Future rates of inflation cannot be predicted with certainty, but can be estimated. It is therefore possible to estimate future cash flows to allow for expected inflation. If the future rate of inflation is expected to be i%:

Inflation-adjusted cash flow = [Cash flow at today's value $\times (1 + i)^n$]

where:

i = the annual rate of inflation, expressed as a proportion (4% = 0.04, and so on)
n = the number of years in the future that the cash flow will occur.

For example, if sales revenue at today's prices is expected to be $100,000 in four years' time, and the rate of sales price inflation is expected to be 3% each year, sales revenue in Year 4 at inflation-adjusted prices will be:
[$100,000 $\times (1.03)^4$] = $112,551.

There is a real cost of capital and a money cost of capital.

- The money cost of capital is the required return on investment, allowing for inflation
- The real cost of capital is the required rate of return at today's price levels.

There is a mathematical connection between the real cost of capital and the money cost of capital.

$(1 + r)(1 + i) = (1 + m)$

where:

r = real cost of capital
i = annual rate of inflation
m = money cost of capital

A cost of capital is normally calculated as and expressed as a money cost of capital. It is much less common to use a real cost of capital for DCF analysis.

Example: real cost and money cost of capital

The rate of inflation in the future is expected to be 5% each year. A business has a weighted average cost of capital of 11%. This is its money cost of capital.

The real cost of capital is calculated as follows:

$$(1+r)(1.05)=1.11$$

$$(1+r)=\frac{1.11}{1.05}$$

$$r=1.057-1=0.057 \text{or } 5.7\%$$

2.2 The DCF rule on inflation

When inflation is expected to have a significant effect on the future cash flows of a project, it should be included in the DCF analysis. There are two ways of dealing with expected inflation in DCF. Both methods are acceptable.

- **Method 1**. Estimate the cash flows of the project at today's prices, with no adjustment for inflation. Discount these cash flows at the real cost of capital.
- **Method 2**. Calculate the cash flows of the project to allow for inflation. Discount these inflation-adjusted cash flows at the money cost of capital.

Both methods give the same NPV. **You might be expected to use either method in your examination.**

Method 2 is usually the easiest in practice, especially when items of cost and revenue are expected to increase in price at different annual rates.

Example: real cost and money cost of capital

A company has a money cost of capital of 15.5%. The expected future rate of inflation is 10% each year. The real cost of capital is therefore 5%. (This is calculated as [(1.155/1.10) – 1]).

The company is considering an investment for which the expected future cash flows and NPV are as follows:

Year	Cash flows: today's prices
	$
0	(60,000)
1	18,000
2	35,000
3	20,000
4	10,000

What is the NPV of the project?

Answer

	Method 1 – Today's prices: Discount at the real cost of capital			Method 2 – Inflated prices: Discount at the money cost of capital		
Year	Cash flows: today's prices	Discount factor at 5%	PV	Cash flows: inflated prices	Discount factor at 15.5%	PV
	$		$	$		$
0	(60,000)	1.000	(60,000)	(60,000)	1.000	(60,000)
1	18,000	0.952	17,136	19,800	0.866	17,147
2	35,000	0.907	31,745	42,350	0.750	31,762
3	20,000	0.864	17,280	26,620	0.649	17,276
4	10,000	0.823	8,230	14,641	0.562	8,228
NPV			14,391			14,413

These numbers should be **exactly** the same. They differ slightly due to 'rounding errors' in the arithmetic.

Example: calculating an NPV with inflation in the cash flow

A business is planning an investment in new equipment that would have an expected useful life of three years. The cash flows from the project have been estimated as follows:

Year	0	1	2	3
	$	$	$	$
Equipment cost/residual value	(50,000)			20,000
Sales revenue		25,000	25,000	20,000
Running costs		(10,000)	(10,000)	(8,000)

The expected annual rates of inflation for the next three years are:

Equipment cost/residual value	5%
Sales revenue	4%
Running costs	7%

In addition, the project will require a working capital investment of $10,000 immediately, with an increase to $11,000 at the end of Year 1 and a further increase to $12,000 at the end of Year 2. This estimate allows for inflation. The weighted average cost of capital, which is the money cost of capital, is 10%.

Required

Calculate the NPV of the project and recommend whether the project should be undertaken.

Answer

Since different rates of inflation apply to different items of cash flow, the NPV should be calculated by discounting inflation-adjusted cash flows at the money cost of capital.

Workings

Equipment residual value = 20,000 × $(1.05)^3$ = 23,153

Sales, Year 1 = 25,000 × (1.04) = 26,000
Sales, Year 2 = 25,000 × $(1.04)^2$ = 27,040
Sales, Year 3 = 20,000 × $(1.04)^3$ = 22,497

Running costs, Year 1 = 10,000 × (1.07) = 10,700
Running costs, Year 2 = 10,000 × $(1.07)^2$ = 11,449
Running costs, Year 3 = 8,000 × $(1.07)^3$ = 9,800.

These cash flows should be discounted at the money cost of capital, which is 10%.

Year	**0**	**1**	**2**	**3**	**NPV**
	$	$	$	$	$
Equipment	(60,000)			23,153	
Working capital	(10,000)	(1,000)	(1,000)	12,000	
Sales revenue		26,000	27,040	22,497	
Running costs		(10,700)	(11,449)	(9,800)	
Net cash flow	(70,000)	14,300	14,591	47,850	
Discount factor at 10%	1.000	0.909	0.826	0.751	
Present value	(70,000)	12,999	12,052	35,935	**(9,014)**

Conclusion

The project has a negative NPV. The decision should therefore be: Do not invest.

DCF and taxation

- Taxation cash flows in investment appraisal
- Interest costs and taxation
- Timing of tax cash flows
- Tax-allowable depreciation (capital allowances)
- Tax exhaustion

3 DCF and taxation

3.1 Taxation cash flows in investment appraisal

In capital investment appraisal, cash flows arise due to the effects of taxation.

- When an investment by a company results in higher profits, there will be higher taxation. For example, if taxation on profits is 25% and a company earns $10,000 each year from an investment, the annual pre-tax cash inflow is $10,000, but there is a tax payment of $2,500 each year.
- Similarly, if an investment results in lower profits, tax is reduced. For example, if an investment causes higher spending of $5,000 each year and the tax on profits is 30%, there will be a cash outflow of $5,000 but a cash benefit from a reduction in tax payments of $1,500.

Tax cash flows should be included in DCF analysis.

3.2 Interest costs and taxation

Interest costs are allowable for tax purposes. However, interest cash flows are not included in DCF analysis, because the interest cost is in the cost of capital (discount rate). In DCF analysis, an **after-tax cost of capital** is used to calculate present values. An after-tax cost of capital is a discount rate that allows for the benefit of the tax relief on interest payments.

3.3 Timing of tax cash flows

The payment of tax on extra profits or the savings in tax due to lower profits could occur either:

- in the same year as the profits or losses to which they relate, or
- one year later ('one year in arrears').

Either of these assumptions could be correct. An examination question should specify which assumption you should use.

e

Example

The after-tax cost of capital is 8%. A project costing $60,000 will be expected to earn cash profits of $40,000 in year 1 and $50,000 in year 2. Taxation at 30% occurs one year in arrears of the profits or losses to which they relate. There will be no tax relief on the initial investment of $60,000.

Required
Calculate the NPV of the project.

a

Answer

Year	Investment	Pre-tax cash profit	Tax at 30%	Net cash flow	Discount factor at 8%	PV
0	(60,000)			(60,000)	1.000	(60,000)
1		40,000		40,000	0.926	37,040
2		50,000	(12,000)	38,000	0.857	32,566
3			(15,000)	(15,000)	0.794	(11,910)
					NPV	(2,304)

3.4 Tax-allowable depreciation (capital allowances)

When a business buys a non-current asset, depreciation is charged in the financial accounts. However, depreciation in the financial accounts is not an allowable expense for tax purposes.

Instead, the tax rules provide for 'tax-allowable depreciation' or capital allowances, according to rules determined by the government.

Tax-allowable depreciation affects the cash flows from an investment, and the tax effects must be included in the project cash flows.

There are two ways of allowing depreciation for tax purposes.

- straight line method
- reducing balance method.

Straight-line method

With the **straight-line method**, the amount allowed for tax purposes is a constant amount each year. The tax-allowable depreciation is calculated as:

$$= \frac{\text{(The cost of the asset minus any expected residual value)}}{\text{Expected years of life}}.$$

Example

An asset costs $80,000 and has an expected economic life of four years with no residual value.

If depreciation is allowed for tax purposes over four years using the straight-line method, the allowable depreciation would be $20,000 each year.

If the rate of tax on profits is 25%, the annual reduction in tax from the capital allowance is $20,000 × 25% = $5,000 for four years.

These cash flows should be treated as cash inflows for the project.

The reducing balance method

With the reducing balance method, the tax allowable depreciation is a constant percentage each year of the written down value (WDV) of the asset as at the beginning of the year. The WDV of the asset is its cost less all accumulated capital allowances to date.

The reducing balance method is much more likely to feature in an examination question on DCF than the straight-line method.

Example

A company purchases an asset costing $80,000. Tax-allowable depreciation is 25% on a reducing balance basis. Tax on profits is payable at the rate of 30%. Tax is payable/saved one year in arrears.

It should be assumed that the first claim for tax-allowable depreciation is made against the profits of the company for Year 1.

Required

(a) Calculate the tax-allowable depreciation (capital allowances) that would be claimed against profits of Year 0 to Year 4, the tax saving, and the year of the cash flow benefit from the tax saving.

(b) Calculate the effect on tax if the asset is sold in Year 5 for $24,000.

Answer

(a) The capital allowances for Years 1 – 4, and their effect on cash flows, are calculated as follows:

Year		WDV at start of year	Tax allowable depreciation (25%)	Tax saved (30%)	Year of cash flow benefit
		$	$	$	
1		80,000	20,000	6,000	2
2	(80,000 – 20,000)	60,000	15,000	4,500	3
3	(60,000 – 15,000)	45,000	11,250	3,375	4
4	(45,000 – 11,250)	33,750	8,438	2,531	5
5	(33,750 – 8,438)	25,312			

(b) If the asset is sold in Year 5, it is assumed for DCF purposes that a balancing charge or a balancing allowance will arise.

- There is no annual capital allowance in the year of disposal.
- If the asset is sold for more than its WDV at the beginning of the year of disposal, a **balancing charge** will arise. This increases taxable profits, and so increases the amount of tax payable (in the following year, since it is assumed that tax payments occur one year in arrears of profits).
- If the asset is sold for less than its WDV at the beginning of the year of disposal, a **balancing allowance** will arise. This reduces taxable profits, and so reduces the amount of tax payable (in the following year).

In this example:

	$
Sale value in Year 5	24,000
WDV at the start of the year	25,312
Balancing allowance	1,312

Since there is a balancing allowance of $1,312 for Year 5, there will be a tax saving of $1,312 × 30% = $394 in Year 6, one year in arrears. The effect of capital allowances on the cash flows of the project is therefore as follows:

Year		WDV at start of year	Capital allowance (25%)	Tax saved (30%) = cash flow benefit	Year of cash flow benefit
		$	$	$	
1		80,000	20,000	6,000	2
2		60,000	15,000	4,500	3
3		45,000	11,250	3,375	4
4		33,750	8,438	2,531	5
5		25,312			
5	Disposal value	(24,000)			
5	Balancing allowance	1,312		394	6

The disposal value of the asset in Year 5, $24,000, is also a cash flow of the project.

e

Example

A company is considering an investment in a non-current asset (fixed asset) costing £80,000. The project would generate the following cash profits:

Year	£
1	30,000
2	40,000
3	20,000
4	10,000

The asset is eligible for capital allowances each year at 25%, by the reducing balance method. It is expected to have a residual value of £40,000 at the end of year 4. The after-tax cost of capital is 9%. The rate of tax on profits is 30%. Taxation cash flows occur one year in arrears.

The first annual capital allowance can be claimed against the company's profits for Year 1.

Required

Calculate the NPV of the project.

a

Answer

The balancing charge or balancing allowance?

The previous example shows that if the first annual capital allowance is claimed against Year 1 profits, the WDV of the asset at the beginning of year 4 (the year of disposal) will be £33,750. The disposal value of the asset at the end of year 4 is £40,000. This means that there is a balancing charge in Year 4, because the disposal value is higher than the WDV.

Balancing charge = £40,000 - £33,750 = £6,250.

There will be extra tax payable in Year 5 for the balancing charge. Extra tax payment = £6,250 × 30% = **£1,875**.

(If the residual value had been lower than £33,750, there would have been a balancing allowance and a saving in tax the following year).

Project cash flows and NPV

Year	Investment	Cash profits	Tax on profits at 30%	Tax-allowable dep'n – tax saved/ (extra tax)	Net cash flow	Disc factor at 9%	PV
	£	£	£	£	£		£
0	(80,000)				(80,000)	1.000	(80,000)
1		30,000			30,000	0.917	27,510
2		40,000	(15,000)	6,000	31,000	0.842	26,102
3		20,000	(12,000)	4,500	12,500	0.772	9,650
4	40,000	10,000	(6,000)	3,375	47,375	0.708	33,542
5			(3,000)	(1,875)	(4,875)	0.650	(3,169)
						NPV	**+ 13,635**

3.5 Tax exhaustion

It is normally assumed in DCF analysis that when capital allowances are available, the company has sufficient taxable profits against which the capital allowances can be set. This means that the tax benefit from the capital allowances can be claimed as soon as possible.

A different situation would apply if a company does not have sufficient taxable profits, for example if it has accumulated losses. In this situation, the company might be unable to claim the capital allowances until sufficient taxable profits existed.

If tax allowances are not claimed as soon as possible, the cash flow benefit from the tax savings will be deferred, and this will affect the cash flows and the NPV of the proposed investment project.

Capital rationing

- The nature of capital rationing
- Single period capital rationing
- Multi-period capital rationing and the simplex method
- The simplex method and your examination

4 Capital rationing

4.1 The nature of capital rationing

Capital investment decisions might be affected by capital rationing. Capital rationing occurs when there is not enough capital available to invest in every project with a positive NPV that the company would like to undertake. Since capital is in short supply, a decision has to be made about which projects to invest in with the capital that is available.

A distinction is sometimes made between 'hard' and 'soft' capital rationing.

- Hard capital rationing occurs when there is a real shortage of capital for investment. For example, a company might be unable to raise new capital in the capital markets or borrow large amounts from a bank. Its capital for investment might therefore be limited to the amount of capital it adds to the business each year as cash flows from retained profits.
- Soft capital rationing occurs when there is sufficient capital to invest in every project, but management has taken a policy decision that spending on capital investment should be limited to a budgeted maximum amount. The policy decision therefore sets a limit on the amount of capital available.

Several methods have been devised for indicating which projects should be selected for investment when there is capital rationing. These methods are based on the following assumptions:

- The choice of projects or investments should have the objective of maximising total NPV.
- The projects that are available for investment are comparable in terms of risk.

The method used to identify which projects to select depends on how many years of capital rationing there will be. Capital rationing might be for one year only (single period capital rationing) or might be for several years, and the investment projects will require some additional investment in each of the years when there will be capital rationing (multi-period capital rationing).

4.2 Single period capital rationing

When there is capital rationing in one year only (usually Year 0), the selection of projects for investment is normally straightforward. The method used depends on which of two assumptions should be used:

- Alternative assumption 1: The projects available for selection are indivisible. The choice is between investing in 100% of a project or not investing in the project at all.
- Alternative assumption 2: The projects available for investment are divisible, although there is a maximum amount that can be invested in any project. This second assumption might seem unusual, although it is likely to feature in an examination question on capital rationing.

When alternative 1 is the assumption, the combination of projects should be selected:

- for which there is sufficient capital and
- which will maximise the total NPV.

When alternative 2 is the assumption, the combination of projects should be selected:

- which uses all the capital available for investment, and
- maximises the NPV per $1 invested in the year of capital rationing.

Example

A company has $20 million to invest in Year 0. There are four projects available for investment, all similar in terms of risk. The amount of investment required and the NPV of each project are as follows:

Project	Capital required in Year 0	Capital required in Year 1	NPV
	$m	$m	$m
A	8	0	+ 3.0
B	5	1	+ 2.0
C	6	0	+ 2.5
D	10	2	+ 4.2

Required

(a) Which projects should be selected if they are not divisible?

(b) Which projects should be selected if they are divisible?

Answer

(a) **Projects are not divisible**

If the projects are not divisible, the first step is to identify the combinations of projects that may be selected with the capital available in Year 0. The total

NPV for each combination should be calculated and the combination with the highest total NPV should be selected.

Combination of projects	Total capital required in Year 0		Total NPV
	$m		$m
A + B + C	19	(3 + 2 + 2.5)	+ 7.5
A + D	18	(3 + 4.2)	+ 7.2
B + D	15	(2 + 4.2)	+ 6.2
C + D	16	(2.5 + 4.2)	+ 6.7

Here, the combinations are easy to identify, and total NPV will be maximised by investing in projects A, B and C.

(b) **Projects are divisible**

If the projects are divisible and there is a maximum investment in each project, the aim should be to maximise the NPV per $1 invested in Year 0 (the year of capital rationing: Year 1 is ignored because there is no capital rationing in Year 1).

Project	NPV	Capital required in Year 0	NPV per $1 invested in Year 0	Priority for investment
	$m	$m	$m	
A	3.0	8	0.375	4th
B	2.0	5	0.400	3rd
C	2.5	6	0.417	2nd
D	4.2	10	0.420	1st

The choice of investments should be as follows:

Project	Priority	Capital required in Year 0	NPV per $1 invested in Year 0	Total NPV
		$m	$m	$m
D	1st	10	0.420	4.2
C	2nd	6	0.417	2.5
		16		
B (balance)	3rd	4	0.400	1.6
		20		8.3

Total NPV is maximised by spending the $20 million in Year 0 by investing in 100% of Projects D and C, and investing the remaining $4 million in 80% of Project B. The total NPV will be (in $ million) 4.2 + 2.5 + (80% × 2) = $8.3 million.

The total NPV should always be higher when projects are divisible than when they are not divisible.

4.3 Multi-period capital rationing and the simplex method

When there is capital rationing in more than one year, and some or all of the projects require additional finance in each year where there will be capital rationing, a different method is needed to identify the combination of projects that will maximise total NPV, **where the projects are divisible**.

The mathematical technique used to identify the NPV-maximising combination of projects is called **linear programming**, and the technique of linear programming you are most likely to encounter is the **simplex method**.

For your examination, you are not required to solve a linear programming problem. However, you should understand how to formulate a linear programming problem, and how the simplex method works.

The method will be explained using a simple example. (The example is simple because there is capital rationing in two years only, and there are only three projects. The same technique can be applied to problems when there is capital rationing in more than two years, and when there are many different divisible projects available for selection).

Example

A company has $9 million to invest in Year 0 and $6 million to invest in Year 1. There are three projects available for investment, all similar in terms of risk. The amount of investment required and the NPV of each project are as follows:

Project	Capital required in Year 0	Capital required in Year 1	NPV
	$m	$m	$m
X	6	3	+ 4.0
Y	2	1	+ 2.0
Z	5	2	+ 2.0

Required
Which projects should be selected if they are all divisible?

Answer

There is capital rationing in both Year 0 and Year 1 because in each year the capital available for investment is less than the total needed to invest in all three projects.

Formulating the linear programming problem

A linear programming problem is stated as an objective function that is subject to certain constraints or limitations. The objective function is to maximise or minimise something. With capital rationing, the objective function should be to maximise the total NPV, and the objective function can be stated as follows:

Objective function:
Maximise 4x + 2y + 2z

where x, y and z are the proportion of Projects X, Y and Z respectively chosen for investment.

There are five constraints on investment. These are the amounts of capital available in Year 0 and Year 1, and the fact that it is impossible to invest in more than 100% of a project.

The **five constraints** can be stated as follows:

Year 0 capital	$6x + 2y + 5z$	$\leq$	10.2
Year 1 capital	$3x + y + 2z$	$\leq$	6.0
Maximum investment in X	x	$\leq$	1.0
Maximum investment in Y	y	$\leq$	1.0
Maximum investment in Z	z	$\leq$	1.0

(Note: The symbol $\leq$ means 'is less than or equal to'.)

There are also non-negativity constraints, which mean that the value of x, y and z cannot be a negative amount.

If there is a more complex problem, with capital rationing in more years, there will be a constraint for each year in which the capital rationing will occur.

Formulating and interpreting the initial simplex tableau

The simplex method can be used to find the optimal solution to the linear programming problem. The method is to test feasible solutions to the linear programming, one feasible solution at a time, until the optimal solution is found that maximises (or minimises) the value of the objective function.

Each feasible solution is tested in a table or 'tableau'. A tableau should have:

- one column for each variable in the problem, one column for each constraint, and a total column
- one row for each variable in the solution and a row for the objective function. There will always be exactly as many variables in the solution as there are constraints in the linear programming problem. In our example, this is 5.

In addition, we need to introduce some new variables into the problem. There should be one variable for each constraint.

- Let Y_0 = the number of unused capital in Year 0
- Let Y_1 = the number of unused capital in Year 1.
- Let U_x = the proportion of Project X not invested in.
- Let U_y = the proportion of Project Y not invested in.
- Let U_z = the proportion of Project Z not invested in.

The initial tableau for this problem is constructed as follows:

Variable in the solution	x	y	z	Y_0	Y_1	U_x	U_y	U_z	Total (million)
Y_0	6	2	5	1	0	0	0	0	9
Y_1	3	1	2	0	1	0	0	0	6
U_x	1	0	0	0	0	1	0	0	1
U_y	0	1	0	0	0	0	1	0	1
U_z	0	0	1	0	0	0	0	1	1
Objective function	- 4	- 2	- 2	0	0	0	0	0	0

Notice that the figures in each row of the x, y and z columns are taken directly from the linear programme, and the objective function on the bottom row shows the NPV of each project with a minus sign.

The initial tableau tests the feasible solution that there is 9 million of unused capital in Year 0 and 6 million of unused capital in Year 1. The proportion of each project not invested in is 1.0 (100%) Y_0, Y_1, U_x, U_y and U_z are therefore the five variables in this feasible solution, and the values of x, y and z are 0. The total NPV (bottom row, total column) is $0 million.

Testing other feasible solutions

This is clearly not the optimal solution, and the simplex method now produces another feasible solution where the value of the objective function is higher. The second tableau might be as follows:

Variable in the solution	x	y	z	Y_0	Y_1	U_x	U_y	U_z	Total (million)
Y_0	0	2	5	1	0	- 6	0	0	3.0
Y_1	0	1	2	0	1	- 3	0	0	3.0
Project X (x)	1	0	0	0	0	1	0	0	1.0
U_y	0	1	0	0	0	0	1	0	1.0
U_z	0	0	1	0	0	0	0	1	1.0
Objective function	0	- 2	- 2	0	0	4.0	0	0	4.0

This tableau has introduced x into the solution in place of U_x.

In this solution, there will be an investment in 100% of project X (since x = 1.0 in the tableau). This will leave unused capital of $3.0 million in Year 0 and $3.0 million in Year 2. The total NPV will be $4 million.

This is not the optimal solution, because there are still some minus signs in the objective function row, and for every unit of y or z that is introduced into the solution, the total NPV can be increased by $2 million.

The final solution and its interpretation: dual prices or shadow prices

Variable in the solution	x	y	z	Y_0	Y_1	U_x	U_y	U_z	Total (million)
Project Z (z)	0	2	5	1	0	- 6	0	0	0.2
Y_1	0	1	2	0	1	- 3	0	0	1.6
Project X (x)	1	0	0	0	0	1	0	0	1.0
Project Y (y)	0	1	0	0	0	0	1	0	1.0
U_z	0	0	1	0	0	0	0	1	0.8
Objective function	0	0	0	0.6	0	1.6	0.8	0	6.4

The final tableau is shown here, with the solution that maximises total NPV. The problem in this example is fairly simple, so the solution is quite straightforward.

To maximise total NPV, the company should invest in 100% of Project X, 100% of Project Y and 20% of Project Z (since x = 1.0, y = 1.0 and z = 0.2). This will leave unused capital of $1.6 million in Year 1 (since Y_1 = 1.6). The proportion of Project Z not invested in is 0.8.

Total NPV will be $6.4 million.

The solution also shows the dual prices or shadow prices of the variables that are not in the solution. These are Y_0, U_x and U_y.

- All the available capital in Year 0 is used up by the solution. The dual price indicates that if $1 of extra capital could be made available in Year 0, the total NPV could be increased by $0.6.
- The maximum investment is made in project X, so U_x = 0 in the final solution. The dual price for U_x indicates that if the maximum investment in project X could exceed 100%, the total NPV could be increased by $1.6 million for every additional project X that is available.
- The maximum investment is made in project Y, so U_y = 0 in the final solution. The dual price for U_y indicates that if the maximum investment in project Y could exceed 100%, the total NPV could be increased by $0.8 million for every additional project Y that is available.

Dual prices for projects are not particularly significant. However, **the dual price or shadow price for capital is significant**. It shows by how much total NPV could be increased if more capital could be made available in that year (given no change in any other constraint in the problem).

For example, this solution indicates that if the available capital in Year 0 could be increased by, say, $1 million, from $9 million to $10 million, there would be a different optimal solution and the total NPV for this solution would be higher by $600,000 ($1 million × 0.6).

4.4 The simplex method and your examination

The study guide for the examination syllabus indicates that you need to know about 'multi-period capital rationing to include the formulation of programming methods and the interpretation of their output'. This indicates that some knowledge is required for the examination of linear programming and the use of the simplex method for solving capital rationing problems.

You should therefore try to familiarise yourself with the nature of a simplex tableau, and what the solution tells you (including the meaning of dual prices or shadow prices).

CHAPTER 7

DCF and risk

Contents

Risk and uncertainty in capital investment appraisal

1 Risk and uncertainty in capital investment appraisal

1.1 The problem of risk and uncertainty

Investment projects are long-term projects, often with a time scale of many years. When the cash flows for an investment project are estimated, the estimates might be incorrect.

Estimates of cash flows might be wrong for two main reasons:

- risk in the investment, and
- uncertainty about the future.

Risk

Risk exists when the actual outcome from a project could be any of several different possibilities, and it is not possible in advance to predict which of the possible outcomes will actually occur.

The simplest example of risk is rolling a dice. When a dice is rolled, the result will be 1, 2, 3, 4, 5 or 6. These six possible outcomes are known in advance, but it is not possible in advance to know which of these possibilities will be the actual outcome.

With risk assessment, it is often possible to estimate the probabilities of different outcomes. For example, we can predict that the result of rolling a dice will be 1, 2, 3, 4, 5 or 6, each with a probability of 1/6.

Risk can often be measured and evaluated mathematically.

Uncertainty

Uncertainty exists when there is insufficient information to be sure about what will happen, or what the probability of different possible outcomes might be. For example, a business might predict that sales in three years' time will be £500,000, but this might be largely guesswork, and based on best-available assumptions about sales demand and sales prices.

Uncertainty occurs due to a lack of sufficient information about what is likely to happen.

It is possible to assess the uncertainty in a project, but with less mathematical precision than for the assessment of risk.

Management should try to evaluate the risk and uncertainty, and take it into account, when making their investment decisions. In other words, investment decisions should consider the risk and uncertainty in investment projects, as well as the expected returns and NPV.

1.2 Methods of assessing risk and uncertainty

There are several methods of analysing and assessing risk and uncertainty. Some of these are fairly simple and straightforward. Others are more complex. The available methods include:

- calculating the expected value of the NPV;
- sensitivity analysis;
- using risk adjusted discount rates;
- simulation modelling;
- calculating a project value at risk (VaR).

1.3 Expected value of the NPV

An expected value is a weighted average value, calculated using estimated probabilities of different possible outcomes. To calculate an expected value, the probability of each possible outcome is estimated, and the mean (average) outcome is calculated.

Expected value (EV) = Σpx

where:

p represents the probability of each outcome and

x represents the value of each particular outcome.

When expected values are used to assess the risk in capital investment appraisal, x would be the NPV for each possible outcome, and the EV would be the expected value of the project net present value (the EV of the NPV).

The basic decision rule is that an investment project should be undertaken if the expected value of its NPV is positive.

However, a project with a positive EV of NPV might not be undertaken if the risk involved seems too great in relation to the amount of the return expected.

e

Example

A company is considering an investment in a project. The project would be a five-year project, and would cost £200,000. The actual returns from the investment are subject to uncertainty, but the following estimates have been prepared for the different possible outcomes:

Probability	NPV
	£
0.10	(8,000)
0.30	4,000
0.40	12,000
0.20	20,000

The EV of the NPV is calculated as follows:

Probability p	NPV x	EV px
	£	£
0.10	(8,000)	(800)
0.30	4,000	1,200
0.40	12,000	4,800
0.20	20,000	4,000
EV of NPV		9,200

The EV of the NPV is positive, + £9,200. The decision would therefore be to undertake the investment, provided that the risk does not seem too great. In this example, there is a 10% probability that the NPV will be negative, – £8,000. Management might therefore consider whether they consider the investment worth undertaking, in view of this risk.

Expected value of cash flows for specific items

An alternative approach to using EVs is to use estimates of probabilities for individual items of cash flow, such as EVs for annual sales revenue from a project and EVs for the expected annual running costs.

Example

A company is considering an investment in a project where the prospects for winning market share have been estimated as follows:

Market share		Probability
High	40%	0.10
Medium	25%	0.50
Low	10%	0.40

The total value of market sales is expected to be $1,000,000 in Year 1, rising to $6 million in Year 5.

For the purpose of DCF analysis, we could calculate the EV of sales revenue in each year and use this EV as the cash flow for sales revenue.

EV of market share = (0.10 × 40%) + (0.50 × 25%) + (0.40 × 10%) = 20.5%.

Estimates of sales revenue for the DCF analysis would therefore be $205,000 in Year 1 (20.5% of $1 million) rising to $1,230,000 in Year 5.

Disadvantages of using expected values

The advantage of using expected values of the NPV is that it provides a weighted average value that allows for all the different possible outcomes.

The disadvantages of using expected values of the NPV are as follows:

- The estimates of probabilities might be subjective, and based on judgement and guesswork.
- The EV of the NPV is not a value for any of the actual possible outcomes. In other words, the EV will not happen.
- An EV is much more reliable for estimating the average outcome from events that will happen repeatedly, many times over. A weighted average is not nearly as suitable for estimating the expected outcome for a once-only investment project.
- Most important of all, an EV does not provide any analysis of the risk or uncertainty. When capital investment projects are evaluated, and a decision is made whether or not to undertake the investment, there should be a thorough analysis of the risk as well as the expected returns.

1.4 Sensitivity analysis

Sensitivity analysis is a useful but simple technique for analysing risk and uncertainty in an investment, when it is recognised that estimates of cash flows could be inaccurate, or that events might occur that will make the estimates wrong.

Sensitivity analysis can be used:

- To calculate the effect on the NPV of a given percentage reduction in benefits or a given percentage increase in costs. For example, what would the NPV of the project be if sales volumes were 10% below estimate, or if annual running costs were 5% higher than estimate?
- To calculate the percentage amount by which benefits must fall below estimate or costs rise above estimate before the project NPV becomes negative. For example, by how much would sales volumes need to fall below the expected volumes, before the project NPV became negative?
- To assess the effect of an unexpected event occurring in the future that would make the cash flow estimates for the project wrong.
- To assess the effect of a delay so that the expected cash inflows from the project occur later than planned.

Example

A company is considering the following project:

Year	Equipment	Income	Running costs	Net cash flow	DCF factor at 10%	PV
	£	£	£	£		£
0	(8,000)				1.000	(8,000)
1		6,000	3,500	2,500	0.909	2,273
2		8,000	4,500	3,500	0.826	2,891
3		10,000	5,500	4,500	0.751	3,379
4		4,000	2,500	1,500	0.683	1,025
NPV						+ 1,568

Required

Estimate the sensitivity of the project to:

- income being lower than estimate, and
- running costs being higher than estimate.

a

Answer

We can calculate the PV of the equipment cost, the income and the running costs separately, as follows:

Year	Equipment PV	Income PV	Running costs PV	NPV
	£	£	£	£
0	(8,000)			
1		5,454	(3,181)	
2		6,608	(3,717)	
3		7,510	(4,131)	
4		2,732	(1,707)	
PV	(8,000)	22,304	(12,736)	+ 1,568

The sensitivity of the project to errors in the estimates can now be assessed as follows:

- Income. The project would cease to have a positive NPV if income is below the estimate by more than: $\frac{1,568}{22,304}$ = 0.070 or 7.0%.
- Running costs. The project would cease to have a positive NPV if running costs are above the estimate by more than: $\frac{1,568}{12,736}$ = 0.123 or 12.3%.

An assessment of risk and uncertainty could then be made on the basis of the likelihood that income will fall below estimate or running costs will increase above the estimate by more than these amounts.

1.5 Risk modelling

The risk in an investment can be assessed by constructing a 'model' for the investment, and then considering possible variations in the possible outcomes.

For capital investment appraisal, a risk model might be constructed using a spreadsheet.

Having constructed the model, the risk in the investment can be assessed by testing different scenarios, such as delays in achieving the benefits from an investment, and combinations of variations in costs and benefits.

Risk modelling can be used to consider any aspect of risk. One aspect of risk that can be particularly significant for investment decisions by companies in certain industries is fiscal risk.

Risk adjusted discount rates

- Introduction
- Certainty equivalents
- Risk adjusted discount rates

2 Risk adjusted discount rates

2.1 Introduction

The calculation of NPV involves modelling the project cash flows and then discounting them. It is possible to take account of the riskiness of the project cash flows in this process. Two approaches are possible;

- Cash flows can be restated to the risk free equivalent (certainty equivalents) and discounted at the risk free cost of capital; or
- The cash flows as modelled can be discounted at the risk adjusted discount rate.

2.2 Certainty equivalents

A certainty equivalent is the risk free equivalent of a risky cash flow. This is difficult to understand at first and is best illustrated by way of example.

Example

Suppose Mr A was offered a chance to win $1,000,000 on the flip of a coin. Under the offer Mr A would receive $1,000,000 if the coin landed on heads but zero if it landed on tails.

Mr A owns an asset (being the opportunity to win $1,000,000) and this asset has an expected value of $500,000. However, Mr A is not being offered any course of action that would result in this amount as he would either receive $1,000,000 or nothing.

Now suppose that Mr B offered to buy the asset off him for $100. It is likely that Mr A would reject this as a certain amount of $100 is not much compensation for a 50% chance of receiving a million.

However, if Mr B kept increasing the offer there would be a point where Mr A would be indifferent between the certainty of the sum offered and a 50% chance of receiving a million. That point is the certainty equivalent.

For example suppose that Mr B's increased his offer by increments until Mr A accepted an offer of $310,000 for his right.

The $310,000 is the certainty equivalent of the risky asset.

2.3 Risk adjusted discount rates

The discount rate should always reflect the risk of the underlying cash flows being discounted. (This is the case under the certainty equivalent approach where the risk free equivalent cash flows are discounted at the risk free rate).

The WACC of a company is the rate of return required by its owners to compensate them for tying up their capital in that company. The owners decide on the level of return they require for investing in a company by comparing the risk of the company to the risk of alternative investment opportunities. Therefore, in a very real sense, the WACC of a company reflects the risk of that company's assets and returns. The WACC of a company reflects the risk of that company.

It is only appropriate for a company to use its WACC as a discount rate if the risk of the project is the same as the overall risk of the company. If this is not the case an alternative rate should be used to reflect the risk of the project.

Discount rates are increased to reflect future cash inflows of higher risk. The use of a higher discount rate results in a lower NPV. This is as would be expected.

Suppose a business expected two receipts of $10,000 in one year's time but one of these was more risky than the other. In that case the riskier asset would be worth less. A higher discount rate would achieve this.

Source of risk adjusted discount rates

In practice the treasury department of a multinational might provide a list of rates to be used to appraise projects of different types. For example they might specify 10% for asset replacement decisions but 12% for expansion decisions which by their nature are more risky. Such rates should be derived from a CAPM based approach but this is not always the case.

The CAPM was explained in an earlier chapter. It is a technique which provides the required rate of return for an appropriate level of risk (measured as β) by adding a risk premium to the risk free rate.

A later chapter explains how the β of a project might be derived from that of a proxy company in order to use the CAPM approach (see the sections 4 and 5 of chapter 11).

Certainty equivalents or risk adjusted discount rates

The certainty equivalent approach keeps the risk and time value separate, whereas the risk adjusted discount rate approach deal with both in a single measure. On these grounds the certainty equivalent approach sounds to be superior but it is the risk adjusted discount rate approach that is used more in practice. This is due to the difficulty in estimating certainty equivalent cash flows.

Theoretically, both approaches should give the same answer.

Example

An asset is expected to give rise to one of the following cash inflows in a years' time.

Cash inflow	Likelihood of cash flow	Expected value
$100	25%	$25
$150	50%	$75
$200	25%	$50
		$150

The expected value of the inflow in 1 years' time is $150. However there is a possibility that the cash flow will not be $150 but $100 or $200.

The company is risk averse and would accept an amount of $140 in 1 year's time in return for the asset. This is the certainty equivalent of the expected value of $150.

The risk free rate is 10%.

The present value of the certainty equivalent is: $140 \times \frac{1}{1.10} = 127.27$

The present value of the expected value should be the same and this implies a risk adjusted discount rate of 17.9% (this was calculated as a balancing figure in the following expression).

The present value of the expected value is: $150 \times \frac{1}{1.179} = 127.27$

Risk adjusted discount rates for negative cash flows

Discount rates are **increased** to reflect future cash **inflows** of higher risk. The use of a higher discount rate results in a lower PV.

Discount rates are **decreased** to reflect future cash **outflows** of higher risk. The use of a lower discount rate results in a higher PV. This is as would be expected.

Suppose a business faced two payments of $10,000 in one year's time but one of these was more risky than the other. In that case the riskier liability would be more expensive. A third party would demand a greater sum to take the risky liability than it would to take the less risky. A lower discount rate would achieve this.

Example

A provision is expected to give rise to one of the following cash outflows in a years' time.

Cash outflow	Likelihood of cash outflow	Expected value
$100	25%	$25
$150	50%	$75
$200	25%	$50
		$150

The expected value of the outflow in 1 years' time is $150. However there is a possibility that the cash flow will not be $150 but $100 or $200.

The company is risk averse and would pay a third party $160 to settle the liability in 1 year's time. This is the certainty equivalent of the expected value of $150.

The risk free rate is 10%.

The present value of the certainty equivalent is: $160 \times \frac{1}{1.10} = 145.45$

The present value of the expected value should be the same and this implies a risk adjusted discount rate of 3.1% (this was calculated as a balancing figure in the following expression).

The present value of the expected value is: $150 \times \frac{1}{1.031} = 145.45$

In the above example the risk adjusted discount rate is less than the risk free rate of return. This means that the β value of these flows is negative. It is very difficult to try to understand negative β of cash inflows but here we are talking about cash outflows.

- The securities market line is upward sloping (+ve β) for assets implying that there will be a higher return for accepting higher risk investments.
- The securities market line is downward sloping (-ve β) for liabilities implying that there will be a higher cost for accepting higher risk liabilities.

Monte Carlo simulation

- The nature of Monte Carlo simulation
- Monte Carlo simulation and capital investment appraisal
- The significance of the results from a Monte Carlo simulation
- Project volatility

3 Monte Carlo simulation

3.1 The nature of Monte Carlo simulation

Monte Carlo simulation is a method of measuring an expected outcome by means of generating multiple trials or iterations, in order to determine the expected value of the outcome and also to measure the variability or risk.

This method of determining the EV of an outcome gets its name from the large number of random outcomes that are used to obtain the measurement, which can be compared with the random outcomes that would be expected on the gambling tables of a casino in Monte Carlo.

Monte Carlo simulation depends on the fact that by taking the outcomes of a large number of individual random events (iterations), an accurate measurement of the expected value and probability distribution of the outcome will be obtained.

There are various software packages that can be used for Monte Carlo simulation. Simulation models can be constructed, for example, in a spreadsheet.

3.2 Monte Carlo simulation and capital investment appraisal

There are many different cash flows in a project whose value might be uncertain, but which can be estimated as a probability distribution. A Monte Carlo simulation model can be created, and the model can be used to calculate the NPV of the project for many iterations, in order to obtain an expected value of the project NPV and a standard deviation of the expected NPV.

Example

Suppose that you want to use a Monte Carlo simulation model to estimate the NPV of a proposed capital investment project, where there is some uncertainty about the units of sale each year and the variable cost per unit sold.

Probability distributions might be prepared for each of these unknown variables, and random numbers allocated to each possible value, as follows:

Units per year	Probability	Random numbers	Variable cost	Probability	Random numbers
5,000	0.15	00 – 14	$5.00	0.25	00 – 24
6,000	0.20	15 – 34	$5.50	0.60	25 – 84
7,000	0.30	35 – 64	$6.00	0.15	85 – 99
8,000	0.25	65 – 89			
9,000	0.10	90 – 99			

With a more complex model, a large number of different variables could be given various possible values, with associated probabilities and random number allocations.

The model is then used to produce a large number of possible outcomes and NPVs for the project. For each possible outcome, random values are given to each of the uncertain variables by generating random numbers and deciding the value in accordance with the random number generated.

Alternatively, a model might be constructed based on the assumption that sales units might be anywhere in the range 5,000 to 9,000 each year and the variable cost per unit might be anywhere between $5.00 and $6.00. Random numbers can be generated for both units of sale and variable cost per unit, in many iterations, using the same method as described above for the project total costs.

For your examination, you are not required to construct a Monte Carlo simulation model for capital investment appraisal and risk analysis, but you are expected to know how a simulation model would be constructed, and to interpret the output obtained from using the model.

3.3 The significance of the results from a Monte Carlo simulation

The output from a Monte Carlo simulation is the results from a large number of iterations. These results are used to calculate an expected value (average value) for the item that is being measured, and a standard deviation.

The standard deviation provides a measure of risk. A large standard deviation relative to the average or expected value indicates high risk. The actual result could be significantly higher or lower than the expected value. A small standard deviation relative to the size of the EV indicates lower risk and a greater probability that the actual result will be close to the expected value.

Risk analysis using the standard deviation

A significant feature of Monte Carlo simulation is that the range of outputs from the many iterations usually follow a normal distribution (provided that the number of iterations is large enough). If it can be assumed that there is a normal distribution of possible results around the expected value, normal distribution analysis can be used to assess probabilities of what the actual outcome might be.

In the previous example of the project activity costs, if the outputs from the iterations follow a normal distribution, the EV of total cost and the standard deviation can be used to assess:

- the probability that the total project cost will not exceed a particular amount, say \$95,000
- what the maximum total cost of the project should be, at the 95% or 99% level of probability.

Note
If you are not familiar with normal distribution and the analysis of risk with normal distribution, you should read the final section of this chapter. This provides a **short beginner's guide to normal distribution analysis**.

How accurate is the estimate of the expected value?

It is also possible to estimate the accuracy of the estimate of the EV of a project NPV using Monte Carlo simulation. The accuracy of the estimated EV can be measured statistically as a total error, as follows:

$$\text{Error} = (3 \times \sigma) / \sqrt{N}$$

where
σ = the standard deviation of the expected value of the NPV, obtained from the simulation model
N = the number of iterations used.

For example, if the EV of the NPV is + \$500,000, the standard deviation of the EV of the NPV is \$10,000 and 400 iterations of the simulation model were made to produce these results, the total error in the estimate of the EV of the NPV would be:

$$\text{Error} = (3 \times 10{,}000) / \sqrt{400} = \$1{,}500.$$

For a larger value of N (the larger the number of iterations), the error is smaller. Not surprisingly, this indicates that greater accuracy is obtained from simulation by doing a larger number of iterations of the model.

3.4 Project volatility

You might come across the term 'project volatility'. Volatility in this context refers to the possibility that a project's NPV might be much higher or lower than the expected value of the NPV. (In the financial markets, volatility refers to the extent to which share prices, interest rates or exchange rates might fluctuate up and down).

High volatility indicates much greater variability and so much greater risk.

In financial management, volatility is measured statistically, usually as a standard deviation. The volatility of a capital investment project can be measured as either:

- the standard deviation of the expected NPV of the project, or
- the standard deviation of the PV of the annual net cash flows from the project.

If you are given the volatility of a project in an examination question, check carefully to see whether volatility is defined. If it is not specifically defined in the question, you should assume that it is the standard deviation of the expected NPV of the project.

Example

Monte Carlo simulation has been used to calculate the expected value of the NPV of a proposed capital investment project and the volatility of the project.

The EV of the NPV is + $106,000 and the project volatility, measured as the standard deviation, is $80,000.

This indicates that the EV of the NPV is greater than $0 ('break-even') by a Z score of:

106,000/80,000 = 1.325 standard deviations.

Normal distribution tables show that the probability of a value greater than 1.325 standard deviations below the mean of a normal distribution is 0.5000 – 0.4079 = 0.0921 – about 9.2%.

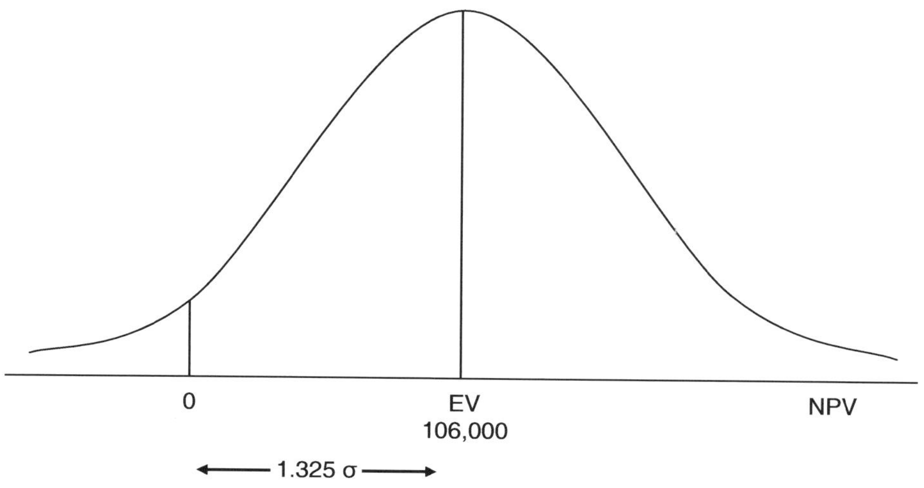

Normal distribution tables can also be used to calculate the following probabilities:

- At the 95% confidence level, the NPV will not be lower than 1.645 standard deviations below the mean or EV.

  $N(0.95)\sigma = 1.645 \times \$80,000 = \$131,600$.

  At the 95% confidence level, the NPV will not be worse than $106,000 - $131,600 = - $25,600.

- At the 99% confidence level, the NPV will not be lower than 2.327 standard deviations below the mean or EV.

  $N(0.99)\sigma = 2.327 \times \$80,000 = \$186,160$.

  At the 99% confidence level, the NPV will not be worse than $106,000 - $186,160 = - $80,160.

Project value at risk

- Annual volatility of a project
- The meaning of value at risk and project value at risk
- Calculating project value at risk

4 Project value at risk

4.1 Annual volatility of a project

Volatility can be measured over differing periods of time. In the previous example of project volatility, the volatility was measured over the entire life of the project.

Volatility can also be measured over shorter time periods, such as annual volatility. In capital investment appraisal, annual volatility is the standard deviation of the PV of annual cash flows from the project.

For any item with a variable value, for which volatility is measured, the statistical volatility increases with the length of the time period over which it is measured. The relationship is as follows:

$$\sigma_L = \sigma_S \times \sqrt{T}$$

where

σ_L is the volatility (standard deviation) over the longer time period
σ_S is the volatility (standard deviation) over the shorter time period
T is the number of short time periods that make up the long time period.

Example

Expected annual cash flows are $100,000 and the volatility of annual cash flows is $15,000. Cash flows in any one year are independent of what the cash flows were in the previous years.

Over a five year period, expected cash flows are $500,000 and the five-year volatility of cash flows is:
$\$15,000 \times \sqrt{5} = \$33,541$.

4.2 The meaning of value at risk and project value at risk

The concept of Value at Risk (VaR) has been developed in the financial services industry, mainly by banks. In banking, Value at Risk can be measured for items such as the risk of losses from credit risk (bad debts) and the risk of losses from a fall in the market value of investments.

For a given period of time, such as one day, one week, one month, three months or one year, and at a given confidence level, Value at Risk can be stated as a single figure. For example, a bank might use its VaR computer model to calculate that on any one day at the 95% confidence level, the Value at Risk is $10 million. This means that at the 95% level of confidence, the maximum loss the bank will suffer on any one day is $10 million.

The concept of VaR can be extended to capital investment appraisal, although at the moment it is not widely used in practice.

A project value at risk is the maximum amount, at a given confidence level, by which the actual NPV from a project will be worse than the expected value of the NPV. It can therefore be used to assess the risk in a capital investment project, which should help management to decide whether or not to invest in the project, taking into consideration the risk as well as the expected return (expected NPV).

4.3 Calculating project value at risk

Project value at risk can be calculated in either of two ways:

- using the standard deviation of the project NPV: this was illustrated by the example in the previous section of this chapter
- using the annual volatility of the PV of cash flows.

Example

A simulation model has been used to calculate the expected value of the NPV of a project. This is $282,000. The project has an expected life of ten years, and the volatility of the PV of the annual cash flows is $30,000.

Normal distribution tables can also be used to calculate the following probabilities:

- At the 95% confidence level, the project value at risk is:

  N(0.95) 30,000 $\sqrt{10}$ = 1.645 × $94,868 = $156,058.

  At the 95% confidence level, the NPV will not be worse than $282,000 – $156,058 = $125,942.

- At the 99% confidence level, the project value at risk:

  N(0.99) 30,000 $\sqrt{10}$ = 2.327 × $94,868 = $220,758.

  At the 99% confidence level, the NPV will not be worse than $282,000 - $220,758 = $61,242.

This suggests a low level of risk with this capital investment project, because the NPV is expected to be positive even at the 99% confidence level for project value at risk.

Beginner's guide to normal distribution tables

- The features of a normal distribution
- A standard normal distribution table
- Using a standard normal distribution table
- Normal distribution tables and confidence levels
- Applications of normal distribution tables in financial management

5 Beginner's guide to normal distribution tables

When a measurement is taken of a population or a sample of items, we can calculate an average value for the population or sample.

For example, a business can calculate its average daily sales from a sample of daily sales figures. The actual sales on any day will usually be above or below the average, so there is a range of daily sales figures that the average sales figure represents. Actual daily sales are therefore 'distributed' around the average or mean value. So daily sales might average $2,400, but actual daily sales might be anywhere in a range of, say, $1,200 to $3,700.

It has been found from experience that the distribution of actual values around the average is often very close to a normal distribution. A normal distribution is a distribution that can be defined mathematically, and whose properties are measurable. If a population of items has a distribution that is similar to a normal distribution, the distribution can be analysed statistically using normal distribution tables.

5.1 The features of a normal distribution

A normal distribution is a symmetrical distribution of values around an average ('mean'). The distribution of values below the average is mirrored exactly by the distribution of values above the average.

This symmetrical distribution can be drawn as a bell-shaped curve as follows:

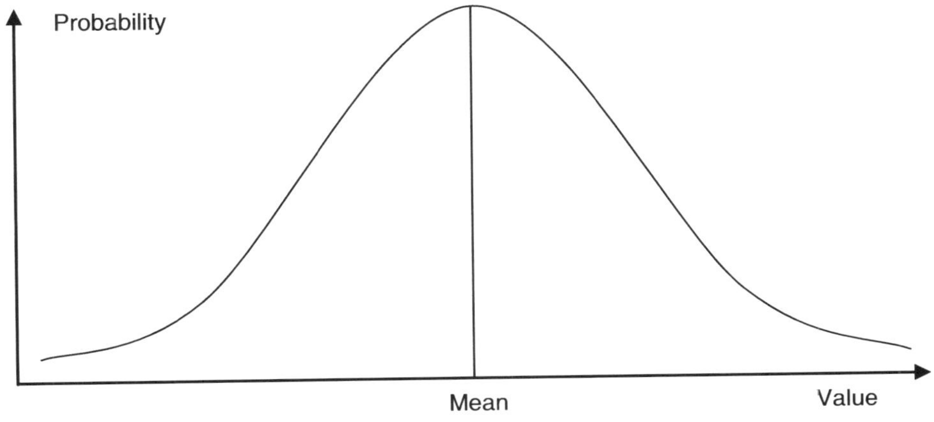

This is a graph where the y axis represents probability and the x axis represents the value of the item being measured (such as daily sales). The total area under the curve represents 100% of total values.

A normal distribution therefore shows that the most likely actual value is the mean value, but the actual value can be above or below the mean. Values close to the mean are more probable (more likely to happen) than values a long way above or below the mean.

Because of the mathematical properties of a normal distribution, it is possible to measure the probability of a value being:

- above a specified amount
- below a specified amount, or
- within a specified range of values.

A key statistical feature of a normal distribution is that the probability of a value being more or less than a specified amount can be measured in terms of standard deviations above or below the average/mean.

- The normal distribution is symmetrical. Because the distribution is symmetrical, there is a 50% probability that a value will be higher than the average ('above the mean' and a 50% probability that a value will be less than the average ('below the mean').
- Because of the mathematical properties of the normal distribution, it is also possible to predict the probability that a value will be within a given number of standard deviations above or below the mean. For example:
  - there is a probability of 34.13% that a value will be within a range of one standard deviation below the mean and the mean
  - there is a probability of 34.13% that a value will be within a range of the mean and one standard deviation above the mean
  - there is therefore a probability of 68.26% (2 × 34.13%) that a value will be in a range of one standard deviation below the mean to one standard deviation above the mean.
- For similar reasons we can predict that there is a probability of 15.87% (50% - 34.13%) that a value will be more than one standard deviation below the mean and there is also a probability of 15.87% that a value will be more than one standard deviation above the mean.

These probabilities can be obtained from normal distribution tables. A normal distribution table is provided in the formula sheet in your examination.

5.2 A standard normal distribution table

A standard normal distribution table is shown in the introductory pages to this text, in the pages for the formulae and tables.

The table represents the probabilities in one half of a normal distribution. Since the normal distribution is symmetrical, the table represents either the half of the distribution below the mean or the half that is above the mean.

- The rows and columns represent the number of standard deviations above or below the mean.
- The figures in the table are the probabilities that a value will be within that number of standard deviations of the mean.

For example:

- The value for 1 standard deviation is in the row 1.0 and the column 0.00. The value here is 0.3413. This shows that in a normal distribution, there is a probability of 0.3413 or 34.13% of a value between the mean and 1 standard deviation below the mean. There is a similar probability of 0.3413 or 34.13% of a value between the mean and 1 standard deviation above the mean.
- The value for 1.25 standard deviations is in the row 1.2 and the column 0.05. The value in the table is 0.3944. This shows that in a normal distribution, there is a probability of 0.3944 or 39.44% of a value between the mean and 1 standard deviation below the mean. There is a similar probability of 0.3944 or 39.44% of a value between the mean and 1 standard deviation above the mean. This also means that the probability that a value will be somewhere between 1.25 standard deviations below the mean and 1.25 standard deviations above the mean is 78.88%.

5.3 Using a standard normal distribution table

For any value whose variability can be approximated by a normal distribution, normal distribution tables can be used for probability analysis and so for risk analysis. The following examples show how this can be done:

Example

A simulation model has been used to calculate the expected value of the NPV of a project. This is + $31,950. The standard deviation of the project is $18,000.

The variability in the NPV approximates to a normal distribution. (This is usual for the output results from a simulation model).

(a) What is the probability that the NPV will be greater than $0?
(b) What is the probability that the NPV will be greater than $40,000?

Answer

(a) An NPV of $0 is below the mean value of $31,950, by $31,950. We need to convert this into a number of standard deviations, or 'Z score'.

Z = 31,950/18,000 = 1.775 standard deviations.

The probability that the NPV will be between the mean (the EV of the NPV) and a value that is 1.775 standard deviations below the mean is between 0.4616 (1.77 standard deviations) and 0.4625 (1.78 standard deviations). Since 1.775 is exactly half-way between 1.77 and 1.78, we can estimate by interpolation that the probability for 1.775 standard deviations is 0.46205 (0.4616 + (0.4625 – 0.4616) × 50%).

This can be rounded to 0.4620.

The probability that the NPV will be between the mean (the EV of the NPV) and a value that is 1.775 standard deviations below the mean is therefore 0.4620. The probability that the NPV will be above the mean (the EV of the NPV) is 0.5000 (50%). The probability that the NPV will be higher than $0 is therefore 0.9620 or 96.20%.

	Probability
NPV between $0 and the EV(mean)	0.4620
Above the mean	0.5000
Above $0	0.9620

(b) An NPV of $40,000 is $8,050 above the mean value of $31,950.

The Z score is 8,050/18,000 = 0.447.

The probability that the NPV will be between the mean value (EV) and 0.447 standard deviations above the mean is somewhere between 0.1700 (0.44 standard deviations) and 0.1736 (0.45 standard deviations). We can estimate by interpolation that the probability for 0.447 standard deviations is 0.1726 (0.1700 + (0.1736 – 0.1700) × 70%).

The probability that the NPV will be more than 0.447 standard deviations above the mean is therefore 0.5000 – 0.1726 = 0.3274 or 32.74%.

5.4 Normal distribution tables and confidence levels

A normal distribution table can also be used to establish confidence levels. In risk analysis, it is usual to assess risk at the 95% confidence level or the 99% confidence level.

- A 95% confidence level means that there is a 95% probability.
- A 99% confidence level means that there is a 99% probability.

Confidence levels for values within a range

We can use normal distribution tables to calculate, at a given confidence level, that the value of an item will be within a specified range of values above and below the mean.

For example, suppose that a simulation model produces results showing that the EV of the NPV for a project is $125,000 and the standard deviation (project volatility) is

$40,000. We can predict at the 95% confidence level that the NPV of the project will be within a specified range around the EV.

To establish a 95% confidence level for the range around the NPV, we need to identify the range of values below the mean that represent 47.5% of total probabilities and the range of values above the mean that represent 47.5% of total probabilities (since 2 × 47.5% = 95%).

We therefore need to identify the number of standard deviations from the mean that cover 47.5% of all probabilities. From the normal distribution table, we can identify that this is 1.96 standard deviations.

At a 95% confidence level, we can therefore predict that the NPV will be somewhere in the range between 1.96 standard deviations below the mean and 1.96 standard deviations above the mean.

Similarly, at a 99% confidence level, we can predict that the NPV will be somewhere in the range between 2.575 standard deviations below the mean and 2.575 standard deviations above the mean. (This is because there is a probability of 0.4950 that the value will be 2.575 standard deviations below the mean and a probability of 0.4950 that the value will be 2.575 standard deviations above the mean.)

Example

A simulation model has been used to calculate the expected value of the NPV of a project. This is + $150,000. The standard deviation of the project is $55,000.

The variability in the NPV approximates to a normal distribution. (This is usual for the output results from a simulation model).

At the 95% confidence level, we can predict that the NPV of the project will be in the range of 1.96 standard deviations above and below the mean. 1.96 × $55,000 = $107,800. At the 95% confidence level, we can therefore predict that the NPV will be somewhere in the range $42,800 to $257,800.

At the 99% confidence level, we can predict that the NPV of the project will be in the range of 2.57 standard deviations above and below the mean. 2.57 × $55,000 = $141,350. At the 99% confidence level, we can therefore predict that the NPV will be somewhere in the range + $8,650 to $291,350.

Confidence levels for values above or below a specified amount

Confidence levels can also be established to identify the probability that the actual value will be above or below a specified amount. For example, we can establish at the 95% or 99% level of confidence that a value will be more than $X or less than $X (or not more than $X or not less than $X).

With this type of calculation we are looking at only one side of the normal distribution table (and carrying out a 'one-tailed test'). This differs from confidence levels for a range above and below the mean, where we are looking at both sides of the normal distribution, above and below the mean.

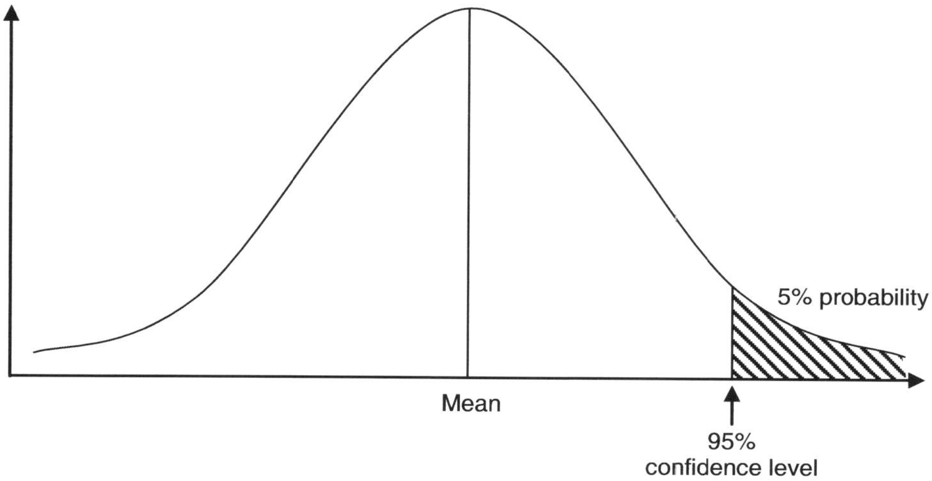

The diagram shows that if we want to establish a 95% confidence level for a value that is above the mean, we need to calculate the number of standard deviations above the mean for which there is a 45% probability. There is a 50% probability that the value will be less than the mean, so taken together we have a 95% probability level.

From the normal distribution table, we can find that 0.4500 of probabilities are within 1.645 standard deviations of the mean, on one side of the normal distribution table.

At the 95% level of confidence we can therefore state that the value will be less than an amount equal to 1.645 standard deviations below the mean. We can also state that at the 95% confidence level, the value will not exceed an amount that is more than 1.645 standard deviations above the mean.

Example

A simulation model has been used to calculate the expected value of the NPV of a project. This is + $70,000. The standard deviation of the project is $28,000.

The variability in the NPV approximates to a normal distribution.

At the 95% confidence level, we can therefore predict that the NPV will be not less than $46,060 (1.645 × $28,000) below the EV of $70,000. This means that at the 95% confidence level the NPV will be not less than $23,940.
To establish the 99% confidence level, we can establish that 0.4900 of probabilities are between the men and about 2.33 standard deviations of the mean. At the 99% confidence level, we can therefore predict that the NPV will be not less than $65,240 (2.33 × $28,000) below the EV of $70,000. This means that at the 99% confidence level the NPV will be not less than + $4,760.

5.5 Applications of normal distribution tables in financial management

Normal distributions are found in many 'populations' and can be used for detailed statistical analysis of risk. For your examination, the most likely use of normal distribution tables will be for:

- analysing the output from a Monte Carlo simulation model for the purpose of assessing project risk, or
- the valuation of financial options, which is explained in another chapter.

CHAPTER

8

Internal rate of return and modified internal rate of return

Contents

internal rate of return (IRR)

- The investment decision rule with IRR
- Calculating a project IRR
- NPV, IRR and financial management

1 Internal rate of return (IRR)

The internal rate of return (IRR) of a project is the discounted rate of return on the investment.

- It is the average annual investment return from the project.
- Discounted at a cost of capital equal to the IRR, the NPV of the project cash flows must come to 0.

1.1 The investment decision rule with IRR

An organisation might establish the minimum rate of return that it wants to earn on an investment. If other factors such as non-financial considerations and risk and uncertainty are ignored, the investment decision using IRR should be based on the following rule:

- If a project IRR is equal to or higher than the minimum acceptable rate of return, it should be undertaken.
- It the IRR is lower than the minimum required return, it should be rejected.

Since NPV and IRR are both methods of DCF analysis, the same investment decision should normally be reached using either method.

1.2 Calculating a project IRR

The IRR of an investment can be calculated by inputting the project cash flows into a financial calculator. An **approximate IRR** can be calculated using interpolation.

Calculating IRR by interpolation

To calculate the approximate IRR by interpolation, you must have the NPV for the project at two different discount rates (cost of capital). Ideally, one NPV should be positive and the other NPV should be negative.

If the NPV at A% is positive, + \$P, and if the NPV at a higher cost of capital B% is negative, - \$N, then:

$$\text{IRR} = \text{A\%} + \left[\frac{\text{P}}{\text{P}+\text{N}} \times (\text{B}-\text{A})\%\right]$$

Ignore the minus sign for the negative NPV. For example, if P = + 75 and N = - 30, then P + N = 105.

The interpolation method is only approximate and is not exact. This is because it assumes that the IRR decreases at a constant rate between the two NPVs.

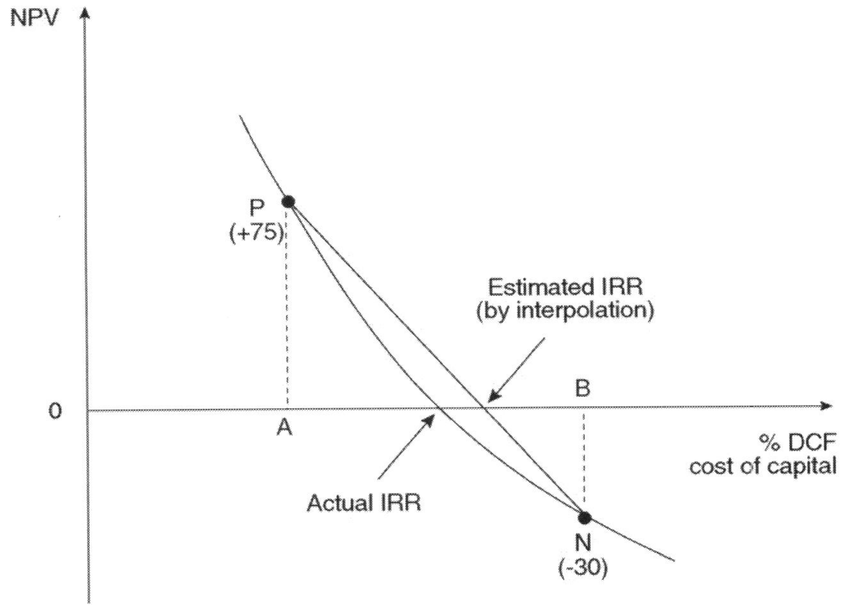

For a 'typical' project, the IRR estimated by the interpolation method is slightly higher than the actual IRR. The interpolation method gives a more accurate estimate of the IRR when:

- both NPVs in the calculation are close to 0, and
- the NPV at A% is positive and the NPV at B% is negative.

Example

A business requires a minimum expected rate of return of 12% on its investments. A proposed capital investment has the following expected cash flows:

Year	$
0	(80,000)
1	20,000
2	36,000
3	30,000
4	17,000

Required

Calculate the NPV at a cost of capital of 10% and a cost of capital of 15%. Use these NPV figures to estimate the IRR.

Answer

Year	Cash flow	Discount factor at 10%	Present value at 10%	Discount factor at 15%	Present value at 15%
0	(80,000)	1.000	(80,000)	1.000	(80,000)
1	20,000	0.909	18,180	0.870	17,400
2	36,000	0.826	29,736	0.756	27,216
3	30,000	0.751	22,530	0.658	19,740
4	17,000	0.683	11,611	0.572	9,724
NPV			+ 2,057		(5,920)

The IRR is above 10% but below 15%.

Using the interpolation method:

The NPV is + 2,057 at 10%.

The NPV is – 5,920 at 15%.

The NPV falls by 7,977 (2,057 + 5,920) between 10% and 15%.

The estimated IRR is:

$$\text{IRR} = 10\% + \left[\frac{2{,}057}{(2{,}057 + 5{,}920)} \times (15 - 10)\%\right]$$

= 10% + 1.3%

= 11.3%

Recommendation

The project is expected to earn a DCF return below the target rate of 12%, and on financial grounds it is not a worthwhile investment.

1.3 NPV, IRR and financial management

In strategic financial management, the NPV method of investment appraisal is more important than the IRR method. This is because the value of an investment or a financial instrument is the present value of the expected future cash flows that it will produce, discounted at a suitable cost of capital.

The expected NPV of a new investment by a company could possibly be taken as an estimate of the change that should result in the total value of the company, if the investment is undertaken, provided that investors are aware of the project and its expected NPV.

However, although the NPV method is used much more often, the IRR method might sometimes be used for project appraisal.

Relative merits of NPV and IRR

2 Relative merits of NPV and IRR

2.1 Advantages of DCF techniques

NPV and IRR have several advantages in common.

- Both techniques are based on cash flows rather than accounting profits which are easier to manipulate and more difficult to interpret.
- Both techniques take account of time value. This is a very important variable that is not considered by less sophisticated techniques like return on capital employed.
- Both techniques take account of all cash flows modelled and not just those in a payback period.

2.2 Advantages and disadvantages of the NPV method

Advantages of the NPV method (compared to the IRR method)

NPV provides a single absolute value which indicates the amount by which the project should add to the value of the company.

The NPV decision rule is consistent with the objective of maximisation of shareholders' wealth.

Disadvantages of the NPV method (compared to the IRR method)

The following are often stated as the main **disadvantages** of the NPV method (compared to the IRR method).

The time value of money and present value are concepts that are not easily understood by those without a financial education. (**Commentary:** This might be true but decision makers tend to be intelligent and educated people. If they do not understand something, they can have it explained to them).

There might be some uncertainty about what the appropriate cost of capital or discount rate should be for applying to any project. The NPV approach would give a perfect answer in a perfect world but companies do not operate with perfect information so this undermines the usefulness of NPV. (**Commentary:** This is true to a point. No company knows its cost of capital with certainty but they may be able to make a reasonable estimate of it so that it allows for NPV appraisal. It could be further argued that the approach would give an efficient answer in an efficient world. Companies operate in efficient markets and can strive to enhance the efficiency of their decisions by spending time and effort to obtain good quality information).

2.3 Advantages and disadvantages of the IRR method

Advantages of the IRR method (compared to the NPV method)

The main **advantage** of the IRR method of investment appraisal (compared to the NPV method) is often given as it is easier to understand an investment return as a percentage return on investment than as a money value NPV.

Commentary: People are used to receiving information based on percentages and so would be more comfortable with the notion of IRR but this does not mean that they would understand it. The supposed simplicity of IRR is an illusion. The percentage return is an average which takes account of time value. Without a certain level of financial education it is difficult to fully appreciate what the percentage answer actually means. Also remember that the decision makers are not the average man on the street. They are clever, educated people so would understand NPV or be in a position to do so.

Another advantage of the IRR method is that it does not require an estimate of the cost of capital.

Commentary: It is true that it is not necessary to know the cost of capital to calculate the IRR. However, once calculated it must be compared to something and this is usually the cost of capital. Therefore, the cost of capital may not be necessary in the calculation of the IRR but is important in its use.

Disadvantages of the IRR method (compared to the NPV method)

One **disadvantage** of the IRR method compared to NPV is that it is a relative measure, not an absolute measure. The technique cannot choose between a 10% IRR based on an initial investment of $10,000 or a 10% IRR based on an initial investment of $10,000,000 or would choose a project with an IRR of 11% on an initial investment of $10,000 instead of a 10% IRR based on an initial investment of $10,000,000.

Commentary: This is a weakness of the technique but techniques do not make decisions – people do. A decision-maker should be able to understand the difference between the above projects even if the technique does not provide that information.

The following disadvantages of IRR compared to NPV are more fundamental.

Mutually exclusive projects

For accept/reject decisions on individual projects, the IRR method will give the same decision as the NPV method. However, if making a choice between two mutually exclusive projects IRR might give a decision that is in conflict with NPV.

Consider the following graphs which illustrate NPV profiles at different costs of capital for two projects.

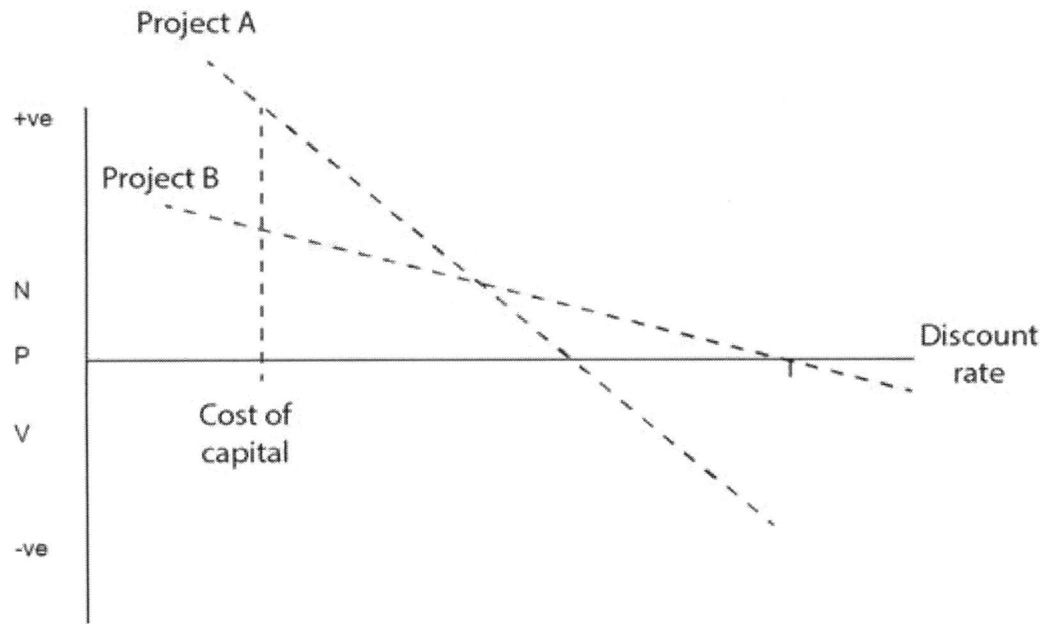

Project A has the higher NPV at the company's cost of capital but project B has the higher IRR.

Resolving the conflict is easy – use NPV! This can be justified on the basis that NPV has a more realistic reinvestment assumption than IRR. The concept of the reinvestment assumption refers to the discount rate used to re-express cash flows in different time terms. The NPV approach "time shifts" values using the cost of capital, whereas the IRR method "time shifts" values using the IRR. It is argued that using the cost of capital is more realistic as this is the cost faced by the company at the date of the appraisal.

Multiple IRRs

Another disadvantage of the IRR method is that a project might have two or more different IRRs, when some annual cash flows during the life of the project are negative. How should the different IRRs be interpreted?

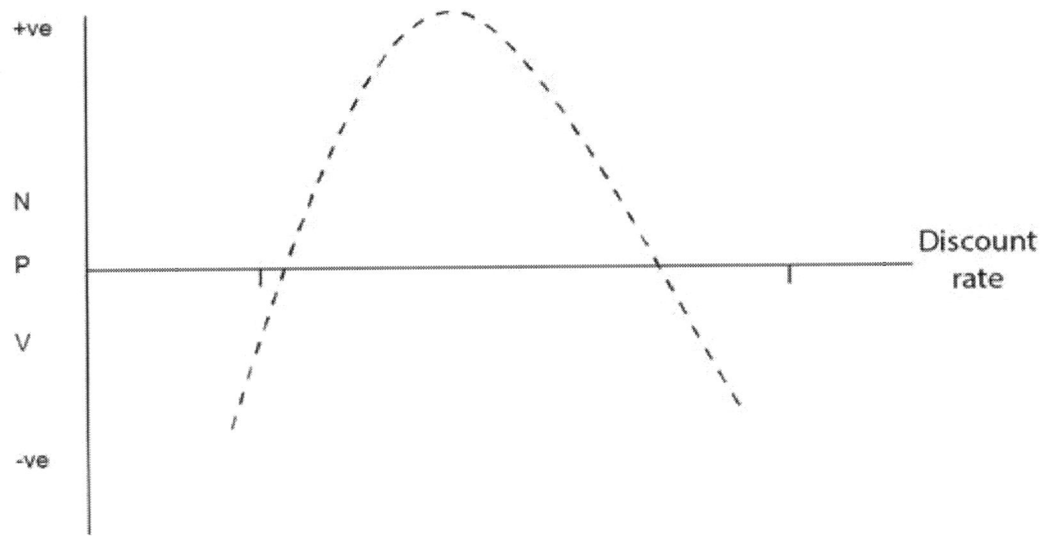

Modified internal rate of return (MIRR)

- Modified internal rate of return (MIRR)
- Calculating MIRR

3 Modified rate of return (MIRR)

3.1 Modified internal rate of return (MIRR)

A criticism of the IRR method is that in calculating the IRR, an assumption is that all cash flows earned by the project can be reinvested to earn a return equal to the IRR.

For example, suppose that a project has an NPV of + $300,000 when discounted at the cost of capital of 8%, and the IRR of the project is 14%. In calculating the IRR, an assumption would be that all cash flows from the project will be reinvested as soon as they are received to earn a return of 14% - even though the company's cost of capital is only 8%.

Modified internal rate of return is a calculation of the return from a project, as a percentage yield, where it is assumed that cash flows earned from a project will be reinvested to earn a return equal to the company's cost of capital. So in the previous example of the project with an NPV of $300,000 at a cost of capital of 8%, MIRR would be calculated using the assumption that project cash flows are reinvested when they are received to earn a return of 8% per year.

Using MIRR for project appraisal

It might be argued that if a company wishes to use the discounted return on investment as a method of capital investment appraisal, it should use MIRR rather than IRR, because MIRR is more realistic because it is based on the cost of capital as the reinvestment rate.

3.2 Calculating MIRR

The MIRR of a project is calculated as follows:

- Step 1. Take the negative net cash flows in the early years of the project, and discount these to a present value. The total PV of these cash flows is the PV of the investment phase of the project. If the only year of negative cash flow is Year 0, the PV of the investment phase is the cash flow in Year 0. However, if there are negative cash flows in Year 1, or Year 1 and 2, discount these to a present value and add them to the Year 0 cash outflow.
- Step 2. Take the cash flows from the year that the project cash flows start to turn positive and compound these to an end-of-project terminal value, assuming that cash flows are reinvested at the cost of capital. For example, if cash flows are positive from Year 1 of a five-year project:

- compound the cash flow in Year 1 to end-of-year 5 value using the cost of capital as the compound rate
- compound the cash flow in Year 2 to end-of-year 5 value using the cost of capital as the compound rate
- compound the cash flow in Year 3 to end-of-year 5 value using the cost of capital as the compound rate
- compound the cash flow in Year 4 to end-of-year 5 value using the cost of capital as the compound rate
- add the compounded values for each year to the cash flow at the end of Year 5.

The total of the compounded values is the total value of returns during the 'recovery' phase of the project, expressed as an end-of-project value.

- Step 3. The MIRR is then calculated as follows:

$$\text{MIRR} = n\sqrt{\frac{A}{B}} - 1$$

where

n = the project life in years

A = the end-of-year investment returns during the recovery phase of the project (as calculated in Step 2)

B = the present value of the capital investment in the investment phase (as calculated in Phase 1).

Study the following example carefully:

Example

A business requires a minimum expected rate of return of 8% on its investments. A proposed capital investment has the following expected cash flows and NPV.

Year	Cash flow	Discount factor at 8%	Present value
	$		$
0	(60,000)	1.000	(60,000)
1	(20,000)	0.926	(18,520)
2	30,000	0.857	25,710
3	50,000	0.794	39,700
4	40,000	0.735	29,400
5	(10,000)	0.681	(6,810)
NPV			+ 9,480

The IRR of the project is about 11.5% (workings not shown).

The modified internal rate of return (MIRR) is calculated as follows:

Step 1. The PV of investment in the investment phase

Year	Cash flow	Discount factor at 8%	Present value
	$		$
0	(60,000)	1.000	(60,000)
1	(20,000)	0.926	(18,520)
			(78,520)

Step 2. Reinvest cash flows in the recovery phase at the cost of capital, 8%

Year	Cash flow	Compound at 8% to end of Year 5	Present value
	$		$
2	30,000	$\times (1.08)^3$	37,791
3	50,000	$\times (1.08)^2$	58,320
4	40,000	$\times (1.08)^1$	43,200
5	(10,000)		(10,000)
Total			129,311

Step 3. Calculate MIRR using the formula

$$\text{MIRR} = \sqrt[5]{\frac{129{,}311}{78{,}520}} - 1$$

MIRR = 0.1049 or 10.49%, say 10.5%.

The IRR is 11.5%, but the MIRR is lower because it assumes a lower reinvestment rate of cash inflows.

CHAPTER

9

Option pricing theory and investment decisions

Contents

Features of options

- Definition of an option
- Financial options, commodity options and real options
- Call options and put options
- Expiry date: American, European and Bermudan options
- OTC and exchange-traded options

1 Features of options

1.1 Definition of an option

An option is something that gives its holder the right, but not the obligation, to take a particular course of action at some time in the future. Typically, an option gives its holder the right, but not the obligation, either to buy or to sell a quantity of a particular item on or before a specified date in the future, at a price that is fixed in the contract.

1.2 Financial options, commodity options and real options

There are different types of option.

- A **financial option** is a contract that gives its holder the right, but not the obligation, either to buy or to sell a quantity of a financial item on or before a specified date in the future, at a price that is fixed in the contract. There are financial options in currencies, interest rates, share prices and stock index values. For example, an option in shares of company Z might give its holder the right to sell 1,000 shares in company Z on 31st March at a price of $10 per share.
- With a **commodity option**, the option holder has the right to buy or sell a quantity of a specified commodity, such as a quantity of wheat, or a quantity of a metal such as gold or copper.

Real options are somewhat different. Real options relate to the choices facing a company when it is considering whether to invest in a new capital project. The company has the following **choices (which are not obligations)**:

- **to make a further investment** or additional investment if the project is a success
- **to abandon the investment** after it has been started, if it now appears that it will not be successful
- **to wait before investing**, instead of investing immediately.

These types of option are called real options, which will be described in more detail later.

1.3 Call options and put options

Financial options are either call options or put options.

- A **call option** gives its holder the right to **purchase** the underlying item in the option agreement.
- A **put option** gives its holder the right to **sell** the underlying item in the option agreement.

For example, a call option on 1,000 shares in company Z gives its holder the right to buy 1,000 shares in company Z at the price agreed in the option contract, and a put option on 1,000 shares in company Z would give its holder the right to sell 1,000 shares in company Z at the agreed price.

1.4 Expiry date: American, European and Bermudan options

An option agreement has an expiry date, after which the option lapses and the agreement comes to an end.

- An American-style option can be exercised by its holder at any time on or before the expiry date.
- A European-style option can be exercised only at the expiry date for the option and not before.
- A Bermudan option can be exercised on a restricted series of dates.

The terms do not refer to the countries where these types of option are available. All three types of option agreement are made throughout the world.

For example, if a company holds an American-style call option to buy US$500,000 in exchange for euros at a rate of 1.2000 (US$/€1) with an expiry date of 20 September, the company can exercise its right to buy the $500,000 at the agreed rate at any time up to and including 20th September. However, if the option is not exercised by that date, it will lapse (cease to exist).

1.5 OTC and exchange-traded options

Some financial options are arranged directly between buyer and seller. Directly-negotiated options are called over-the-counter options or OTC options. Examples of OTC options include borrowers' and lenders' interest rate options, caps, floors and collars. Currency options might also be arranged in OTC agreements.

Some options are traded on an exchange. Traded share options and some currency options are exchange-traded. In addition, there are options on futures contracts, and all options on futures are traded on the futures exchange where the underlying futures are traded.

Buying and selling (writing) options

- Exercise price or strike price
- Rights and obligations of buyer and seller
- Option premium = option price
- Options: a zero-sum game
- Exercising options

2 Buying and selling (writing) options

2.1 Exercise price or strike price

The exercise price for an option is the price at which the holder can:

- buy the underlying item, in the case of a call option, or
- sell the underlying item, in the case of a put option.

With OTC options, the exercise price is agreed between the option buyer and the option seller. With exchange-traded options, options are available for buying or selling at a limited range of fixed strike prices, and buyers and sellers agree on the price at which they will make a transaction in the options at one of these prices.

For example, the following table shows exercise prices that might be available on the CME exchange for US dollar/euro currency options on a day in August, and the prices of the most recent transactions in those options.

	CALLS			PUTS		
Expiry:	**Sep**	**Dec**	**Mar**	**Sep**	**Dec**	**Mar**
Strike price:						
12200	0.34	2.03	3.22	1.62	3.15	3.91
12300	0.18	1.62	2.81	2.16	3.53	4.49
12400	0.09	1.33	2.44	3.06	4.20	5.12
12500	0.04	1.18	2.11	3.66	4.90	-

Notes

(a) A strike price of 12200 indicates an exchange rate of €1 = $1.2200.

(b) At this date, currency options were being traded at just four strike prices, for expiry dates in September, December and March.

2.2 Rights and obligations of buyer and seller

Options are bought and sold. The seller of an OTC option is often called the **option writer**. Selling an OTC option is often called 'writing an option'. For exchange-traded options, it is more usual to refer to 'sellers' of options, who have a short position in the options.

- The option buyer or option holder has the right to exercise the option but is not obliged or contractually required to do so.

- On the other hand, the seller or writer of the option is contractually obliged to sell or buy the underlying item if the option is exercised by its holder.

2.3 Option premium = option price

Options are bought and sold at a price, which is called the option premium. This is paid by the buyer of the option to the option seller/writer when the option agreement is made. The option writer therefore receives the premium no matter whether the option is subsequently exercised or not.

The table of currency options above shows current prices for US dollar/euro traded currency options. For example, September call options at a strike price of $1.22 in $/€ were being traded at a price of 0.34. In this particular example, this premium price is stated in US cents per euro. Each traded option on the CME exchange is for 125,000 euros in exchange for US dollars, and the cost of one September call option was therefore $425 (125,000 × $0.0034).

Similarly, the premium for a December put option at a strike price of $1.25 was $6,125 (125,000 × $0.0490).

2.4 Options: a zero-sum game

Options can be described as a zero-sum game between the option buyer and the option seller. Any gain for the buyer is matched by an equal loss for the seller. Similarly, any gain for the seller is matched by an equal loss for the buyer. The combined sum of their profits and losses is always zero.

Example

A company buys a European-style call option on 1,000,000 euros at a strike price of 1.2500 (US$/€1). The option premium is 2.4 US cents per euro, therefore the cost of the option is $24,000.

What would be the net gain or loss for the option buyer and the option writer if the exchange rate at expiry is:

(a) $1.2350 = €1,

(b) $1.2670 = €1, and

(c) $1.2930 = €1.

Answer

(a) The option will not be exercised, because it is cheaper to buy the 1 million euros at the spot market price of $1.2350. The option will lapse.

(b) The option will be exercised, because it is cheaper to buy euros at the strike price of $1.2500 than the spot rate of $1.2670.

(c) The option will be exercised because it is cheaper to buy euros at the strike price of $1.2500 than the spot rate of $1.2930.

Option buyer	(a) spot price 1.2350	(b) spot price 1.2670	(c) spot price 1.2930
		$	$
Spot price	Not	1.2670	1.2930
Exercise price	exercised	1.2500	1.2500
Gain from exercising option (per €1)		0.0170	0.0430
	$	$	$
Total gain on option (€1,000,000)	0	17,000	43,000
Cost of option	(24,000)	(24,000)	(24,000)
(Loss)/gain to the buyer	(24,000)	(7,000)	19,000

The **option writer** would make a gain of $24,000 if the spot rate at expiry is $1.2350, a net gain of $7,000 if the spot rate is 1.2670 and a net loss if the spot rate is 1.2930.

2.5 Exercising options

Terminology

Options are in-the-money, at-the-money or out-of-the-money.

- An option is **in-the-money** when its exercise price (strike price) is more favourable to the option holder than the current market price of the underlying item.
- An option is **at-the-money** when its exercise price (strike price) is exactly equal to the current market price of the underlying item.
- An option is **out-of-the-money** when its exercise price (strike price) is less favourable to the option holder than the current market price of the underlying item.

An option will only be exercised if it is in-the-money.

When an option is exercised, the value of the option is the difference between the exercise price and the current market price of the underlying item.

Exercising call options

A call option will only be exercised if the market price of the underlying item is higher than the exercise price for the option. For example, a European call option on 1,000 shares in company Z with a strike price of $10 per share will only be exercised if the market price of the share is above $10 at expiry.

Exercising put options

Similarly, a put option will only be exercised if the market price of the underlying item is lower than the exercise price for the option. For example, a European put option on 2,000 shares in company XY with a strike price of $8 per share will only be exercised if the market price of the share is below $8 at expiry.

Factors influencing option values

- Option premium and option value
- Intrinsic value and time value
- The main factors affecting time value
- The five factors affecting option prices

3 Factors influencing option values

3.1 Option premium and option value

The option premium is the price paid by an option buyer to the option seller for an option. The premium represents the value of the option at the time it is written.

Between the time the option is written and the option's expiry date, the value of the option will change. The value will go up or down, according to changes in the likelihood that the option will be exercised, and if it is exercised, what the size of the gain for the option holder is likely to be.

Every option that has not yet expired therefore has some value, unless it is deeply out-of-the-money.

- The value of an option can be calculated by the option writer when the option is written, and this value is the premium charged for the option to the option buyer.
- After the option has been written but before its expiry, options can be re-valued to a current value. This revaluation process is now required by international accounting standard IAS 39, for financial reporting for financial instruments.

You need to be able to use the **Black-Scholes option pricing model** to calculate the value of a European-style call option. This model is explained later.

3.2 Intrinsic value and time value

The value of an option can be analysed into an intrinsic value and a time value.

Intrinsic value + Time value = Total value of the option

- Only in-the-money options have intrinsic value. **Intrinsic value** is the difference between the strike price for the option and the market price of the underlying item. If an option is at-the-money or out-of-the-money, its intrinsic value is 0.
- **Time value** is the value placed on the option that relates to the probability that the option will become in-the-money before expiry, or will become even more in-the-money before expiry, and if so by how much it is likely to be in-the-money at expiry.

3.3 The main factors affecting time value

Several factors influence the time value of an option:

- **The length of time remaining to expiry**. If there are two identical options with the same strike price but different times to expiry, the option with the longer time to expiry is more valuable. This is because there is more time for the option to become in-the-money, or to become even more deeply in-the-money in the period remaining to expiry.
- **The size of the difference between the strike price for the option and the current market price of the underlying item.** An option that is at-the-money will be worth more than a similar option that is out-of-the-money. This is because in the time remaining to expiry, an at-the-money option is more likely than an out-of-the-money option to become in-the-money. For the same reason, an option that is slightly out-of-the-money is worth more than an option that is deeply out-of-the-money.
- **The volatility in the market price of the underlying item**. An option is more valuable when there is higher volatility in the price of the underlying item. This is because when volatility is greater, the probability is greater that the market price will move up or down by a large amount in the remaining time to expiry of the option.
- **The risk-free rate of interest**. Another factor in the calculation of an option price is the risk-free rate of interest. This is included in the Black-Scholes option pricing model.

Example

Compare the following two call options on shares:

	Option on shares of Company X	**Option on shares of Company Y**
Exercise price	850	750
Current market value of shares	825	500
Time remaining to expiry	1 year	3 months
Volatility of share price (annual)	35%	10%

The value of the options on shares of Company X will be worth much more than the options on shares of Company Y, even though both options are currently out-of-the-money.

- The strike price on the Company X options is only 25 higher than the current market value, and the annual volatility is quite high relative to the current market price. There is also one year to the expiry date, during which time the price of the shares might rise.
- The strike price on the Company Y options is much higher than the current market price, indicating that the options are deeply out-of-the-money. The share price volatility is much lower than for Company X and there are only three months to expiry of the options. It is difficult to imagine that these options will be in the money by the expiry date, and the options are probably worthless.

3.4 The five factors affecting option prices

There are five factors that affect options prices:

- The time remaining to expiry of the option
- The current price of the underlying item (such as the current market price of the share)
- The strike price or exercise price for the option
- The volatility in the market price of the underlying item
- The risk-free interest rate.

These five factors are all elements in the Black-Scholes option pricing model.

Information about the market value of traded options in company shares are published regularly in the financial press. The published prices indicate the significance for the option price of the current market price of the underlying, the exercise price and the time to expiry

Example

Traded options in shares of publishing company Pearson Group were being traded at the following prices during early June, when the actual share price on the London Stock Exchange was 866 pence. Premium prices are shown in pence per share.

	CALLS			PUTS		
Expiry:	**Jun**	**Sep**	**Dec**	**Jun**	**Sep**	**Dec**
Strike price:						
860	17.5	34.0	44.5	10.0	22.0	29.5
880	8.0	23.5	33.5	21.0	32.0	39.0

Notes

(a) The premium varies with the difference between the strike price and the current market price for the shares. Call options with a higher strike price have a lower value. Put options with a higher exercise price have a higher value.

(b) Premiums vary with time to expiry. For each exercise price, the premium for both call options and put options is higher for a later expiry date.

The Black-Scholes option pricing model

- The model formulae
- Underlying assumptions
- Notes on the model
- Using the Black-Scholes model

4 The Black-Scholes option pricing model

The Black-Scholes option pricing model is used to derive the price of a European-style call option. This model, or variants of it, is used by banks to calculate the premium for an over-the-counter (OTC) option. The model is quite complex if you are not familiar with mathematics, but you might be required to calculate an option value with the model in your examination.

4.1 The model formulae

Formulae for the Black-Scholes model are given in the formula sheet in the examination. There are three formulae.

$c = P_a N(d_1) - P_e N(d_2) e^{-rt}$

where

$$d_1 = \frac{\ln(P_a / P_e) + (r + 0.5s^2)t}{s\sqrt{t}}$$

$d_2 = d_1 - s\sqrt{t}$

c = Price of the call option (call option value)

P_a = the price of the underlying item, such as the current share price (stock option) or current exchange rate (currency option)

$N(d)$ = a normal distribution probability density function – the probability that the value is less than d standard deviations above the mean

P_e = the exercise price or strike rate for the option

e = the constant e. You will need a calculator that calculates values to the power of e

r = the risk-free interest rate (as an annual rate: for example, 5% = 0.05)

t = time to expiry of the option, in years. For example, if the option has three months to expiry, t = 0.25

s = standard deviation of the value/returns of the underlying item. This should be the annual volatility, for consistency with the values of r and t

4.2 Underlying assumptions

The model rests on a series of assumptions:

- Capital market perfection
- The underlying asset is tradable. This means that it is assumed that there is a market for the asset.
- The return on the underlying asset is follows a lognormal distribution. (A lognormal distribution is a continuous probability distribution of a random variable whose logarithm is normally distributed).
- Risk free rate is constant and determinable
- Volatility is constant and determinable

The above assumptions can each be mentioned as limitations of the model as they may not hold in practice. Note in particular that determining some of the model inputs might be quite difficult. For example it is tricky to determine volatility of a new asset as there is no history from which to derive the volatility.

4.3 Notes on the model

If you are not familiar with mathematics, the following notes might be useful.

- To calculate the price of a European-style call option, it is necessary to calculate values for d_1 and d_2. To calculate d_2, it is necessary to know the value of d_1. The starting point is therefore to calculate the value of d_1.
- The first item in the formula for the value of d_1 is $\ln(P_a / P_e)$. The letters 'ln' mean 'natural logarithm of'. Natural logarithms are logarithms to the base of the constant e. You need a calculator that can work out natural logarithms, and you need to make sure that you can use the natural logarithm function on the calculator.

(Note: a natural logarithm is a number expressed as a value to the power of e. The constant 'e' has a value of 2.71828. This means, for example, that the natural logarithm of 4 is 1.3863 because 4 is equal to 2.71828 to the power of 1.3863).

The standard deviation is a measurement of volatility of the price of the underlying item. In the case of a stock option, it is the standard deviation of the annual returns from the share. An annual standard deviation of 15%, for example, would be 0.15 in the formula. Remember that the standard deviation is the square root of the variance. If an examination gives you the variance of the returns, remember to take the square root to obtain the standard deviation.

Having calculated values for d_1 and d_2, the final step is to calculate the option price. To do this, you need to establish values for $N(d_1)$ and $N(d_2)$. These are values obtained from normal distribution tables. These statistical distribution tables are provided in the examination, as a standard normal distribution table. These tables also explain how the tables should be used to find the values for $N(d_1)$ and $N(d_2)$.

The rules are as follows:

- Having established a value for d_1 (or d_2), find the corresponding value in the normal distribution tables. For example, if $d_1 = 1.75$, look for the value in the row 1.7 and the column 0.05 - this value is 0.4599.
- If the value of d_1 is positive, add 0.5 to the value you have obtained from the table. Similarly, if the value of d_2 is positive, add 0.5 to the value you have obtained from the table.
- If the value of d_1 is negative, subtract the value you have obtained from the table from 0.5. Similarly, if the value of d_2 is negative, subtract the value you have obtained from the table from 0.5.

This gives you the value for $N(d_1)$ (or $N(d_2)$).

The **call option price** is calculated as:

- the value of P_a multiplied by the value for $N(d_1)$
- minus the value of P_a multiplied by the value for $N(d_2)$ and multiplied by the value of e^{-rt}.

The value of e^{-rt} is the inverse of the constant e to the power of rt. In other words, e^{-rt} is $1/e^{rt}$. Use your calculator to calculate the value of e^{rt}, then calculate the inverse of your answer.
It is not immediately obvious but this a discount factor. The normal discount factor to calculate a present value say at 5% for 5 years would be $1/(1.05)^5$. However this assumes that the amount being discounted arises at a single point in time at the end of five years. The Black Scholes Model assumes that values change on a continuous basis (rather than suddenly arrive as is normally assumed in DCF). In this case the discount factor must be constructed on a continuous basis. In other words an equivalent period rate must be calculated for an infinite number of tiny time periods. This all sounds quite tricky but it is quite easy to do by using e^{-rt}. In truth, you do not really need to think about this as it is a component of the formulae provided in the exam.

4.4 Using the Black-Scholes model

The formulae might seem very complex. The following example shows how they should be applied:

Example

The current share price of BS Company is $17.

What should be the price of a European-style call option on the company's shares at an exercise price of $16.50, if the expiry date is in six months, the standard deviation of annual returns on the share is 12% and the risk-free rate of return is 7% per year?

a

Answer

Step 1. List the variables

P_a = 17
P_e = 16.5
r = 7% (= 0.07)
t = six months to expiry, t = 0.50.
s = 0.12

Step 2. Calculate d_1

$$d_1 = \frac{\ln(^{Pa}/_{Pe}) + (r + 0.5s^2)t}{s\sqrt{t}}$$

$$d_1 = \frac{\ln(^{17.00}/_{16.50}) + [0.07 + (0.5 \times 0.12^2)]\ 0.5}{0.12\sqrt{0.5}}$$

$$d_1 = \frac{\ln(1.0303) + [0.07 + 0.0072]\ 0.5}{0.08485}$$

$$d_1 = \frac{0.02985 + 0.0386}{0.08485}$$

$$\mathbf{d_1} = \frac{0.06845}{0.08485} = \mathbf{0.8067\ (say\ 0.81)}$$

Step 2. Calculate d_2

$d_2 = d_1 - s\sqrt{t}$

$d_2 = 0.8067 - 0.12\ \sqrt{0.5}$

$d_2 = 0.8067 - 0.08485$

d_2 = 0.7219 (say 0.72)

Step 3. Obtain values for $N(d_1)$ and $N(d_2)$

$N(d_1)$.

When $d_1 = 0.81$ the corresponding value in the normal distribution table is 0.2910.

The value of d_1 is positive, so add 0.50.

$N(d_1) = 0.2910 + 0.50 = 0.7910$.

$N(d_2)$.

When $d_2 = 0.72$, the corresponding value in the normal distribution table is 0.2642.

The value of d_2 is positive, so add 0.50.

$N(d_2) = 0.2642 + 0.50 = 0.7642$.

Step 4. Calculate the option price (for a call option)

$c = P_a N(d_1) - P_e N(d_2) e^{-rt}$

Tip – calculate the value of e^{-rt} first

$rt = (0.07)(0.5) = 0.035.$

$e^{-0.035} = 1/e^{0.035}$

$e^{0.035} = 1.0356$

Therefore $1/e^{0.035} = 0.9656.$

$$\text{Option price} = P_s N(d_1) - P_e N(d_2) e^{-rt}$$
$$= 17(0.7910) - 16.50\ (0.7642)\ (0.9656)$$
$$= 13.45 - 12.18 = \mathbf{1.27}$$

Example

In this similar example, the values of d_1 and d_2 are negative.

The current share price of CB Company is 400. What should be the price of a European-style call option on the company's shares at an exercise price of 440, if the expiry date is in six months, the standard deviation of annual returns on the share is 30% and the risk-free rate of return is 6% per year?

Answer

Step 1. List the variables

P_a	=	400
P_e	=	440
r	=	6% (= 0.06)
t	=	six months to expiry, t = 0.50.
s	=	0.30

Step 2. Calculate d_1

$$d_1 = \frac{\ln(400/440) + [0.06 + (0.5 \times 0.30^2)]\ 0.5}{0.30\sqrt{0.5}}$$

ln (400/440) = ln 0.9091. Using a calculator, the natural logarithm of 0.95238 can be obtained. This is – 0.0953.

$$d_1 = \frac{-0.0953 + 0.0525}{0.30\sqrt{0.5}} = -0.0428/0.2121 = \mathbf{-\ 0.202}$$

Step 3. Calculate d_2

$$d_2 = d_1 - s\sqrt{t} = -0.202 - (0.30)\sqrt{0.5} = \mathbf{-\ 0.414}$$

Step 4. Obtain values for $N(d_1)$ and $N(d_2)$

$N(d_1)$.

When d_1 = – 0.202, the corresponding value in the normal distribution table is about 0.0801.

The value of d_1 is negative, so subtract 0.0801 from 0.50.

$N(d_1) = 0.5000 - 0.0801 = 0.4199$

$N(d_2)$.

When d_2 = – 0.414, the corresponding value in the normal distribution table is about 0.1613.

The value of d_2 is negative, so subtract 0.1613 from 0.50.

$N(d_2) = 0.5000 - 0.1613 = 0.3387$.

Step 4. Calculate the option price (for a call option)

The value of rt is (0.06)(0.5) = 0.030.
$e^{0.03} = 1.03045$.
Therefore $e^{-0.03} = 1/1.03045 = 0.9704$.

Option price = $P_s N(d_1) - P_e N(d_2) e^{-rt}$

= 400(0.4199) – 440 (0.3387) (0.9704)

= 167.96 – 144.62

= 23.34

Value of a put option: put-call parity

- Value of a put option: put-call parity pricing model
- Value of a put option: alternative put-call parity pricing model

5 Value of a put option: put-call parity

5.1 Value of a put option: put-call parity pricing model

The Black-Scholes model calculates the value of a European-style call option. It can also be used to calculate the value of a European-style put option with the same expiry date and exercise price, using the put-call parity pricing model:

Value of put	+	Current market price of underlying item	=	Value of call	+	Present value of the exercise price.

This can be rearranged to:

Value of put	=	Value of call	+	Present value of the exercise price.	–	Current market price of underlying item

Remember that the present value of the exercise price is measured using continuous discounting. The discount rate to find the present value of the exercise price is found using e^{-rt}.

Example

Shares in BS Company have a current market value of $17.

The value of a call option with an exercise price of $16.50 and an expiry date in six months is $1.27.

The risk-free rate of return is 7% per year.

The present value of the exercise price is:

$\$16.50 \times e^{-(0.07 \times 0.5)} = \$16.50 \times 0.9656 = \$15.93$.

Applying the put-call parity pricing model:

Value of put = $1.27 + $15.93 – $17

Value of put = $0.20.

5.2 Value of a put option: alternative put-call parity pricing model

An alternative formula for the put-call parity is given in the formula sheet in the examination. Allowing for rounding differences, it gives the same valuation for a put option as the formula described above.

The alternative formula is:

$p = c - P_a + P_e e^{-rt}$

where
p = the price of a put option
c = the price of a call option with the same exercise price and expiry date
P_a is the current market price of the underlying item
P_e is the exercise price of the option
r = the risk free rate of interest
t = the time to expiry in years

Example

Shares in BS Company have a current market value of $17.

The value of a call option with a strike price of $16.50 and an expiry date in six months is $1.27.

The risk-free rate of return is 7% per year, and the option has six months to expiry, so rt = (0.07)(0.5) = 0.035. The value of $e^{0.035}$ is 1.03562 so $e^{-0.035}$ is 0.9656.

$p = c - P_a + P_e e^{-rt}$

$p = 1.27 - 17 + (16.5)(0.9656)$

$p = 0.22.$

This differs from the valuation above using the alternative formula by 0.01, due to mathematical rounding differences.

Real options

- Definition of a real option
- Real options theory
- Real options: the theoretical framework
- Different types of real option
- The valuation of real options

6 Real options

6.1 Definition of a real option

Options are normally associated with financial market derivative instruments and share options of companies. A different type of option is a real option, sometimes called an 'embedded real option'.

A real option is an alternative or choice that exists with an investment project or investment opportunity. They are real choices that management will be able to make at some stage during the life of the project. For example, if a company undertakes a particular project, there might be a real option (a choice, and not an obligation) to take one or more of the following courses of action at some stage during the project's life:

- Make a further incremental investment, and increase the total amount invested in the project.
- Abandon the project early because it is losing money.
- Defer the investment in the project, instead of having to invest immediately.

For example, a mining company might be negotiating a ten-year lease on a mine, and it might want to include a 'break clause' (an option) in the lease contract that will enable it to cancel the lease after five years. The option to cancel the lease and abandon the investment would be a real option. The company would have to consider how much it would be prepared to pay for the break clause to be included in the terms of the lease.

They are called 'real' options because they are generally associated with choices in relation to 'real' tangible assets.

Real options provide flexibility by giving choice – the flexibility for example to avoid losses and to take opportunities that unexpectedly emerge.

6.2 Real options theory

Real options theory can be used for investment appraisal, as an alternative to simple net present value analysis.

- Like NPV analysis, investment appraisal with real options analysis calculates a present value for a project by discounting future cash flows.
- Unlike NPV analysis, a real options approach also puts a financial value to the real options that are embedded in the investment opportunity, and which have some value. The value of the real options is taken into consideration in deciding whether to invest, or which of two or more alternative projects to invest in.

There are two aspects to real options theory:

- providing a theoretical framework for the valuation of real options in investment appraisal
- developing methods of measuring the value of real options for the purpose of investment appraisal.

6.3 Real options: the theoretical framework

When a company decides to invest in a capital project, it faces the risk that actual results will be different from what was expected when the investment decision was made. The risk in a project comes from a combination of:

- the uncertainty about the future, and the different situations that might arise, and
- the means that management have at their disposal to deal with any of these situations if they arise.

There are many different sources of uncertainty in a project. They include the risks from:

- changes in the condition of the overall economy
- technological change
- a change in regulations
- unforeseen actions by a competitor.

Any of these events or changes in situation could affect the value of the investment.

Management deals with uncertainty in two stages.

- **Stage 1**. At the **project selection stage**. When the investment decision is made, management considers the different possible outcomes and assesses the risk in the project. Different investment options are considered, and management decides to invest in the projects that appear to offer the best prospects for a good return.
- **Stage 2. Project management**. After the decision has been made to invest in a project, the project is managed. Management takes action to reduce the risks and uncertainty in the project, and seeks to enhance the positive effects of unexpected events.

Using the NPV method of project selection, the financial analysis focuses entirely on the project selection stage. All the different possible outcomes for the project are considered, and these are aggregated into a single expected value of future cash flows. The NPV analysis does not consider all the future decisions that might be made during the project management stage that will be contingent or dependent on how the project develops.

Example

A simple example is a management decision about whether to invest in Project A or Project B, which are mutually exclusive projects. Both projects would last for ten years. Estimated cash flows have been prepared and evaluated for each project and Project A has a higher NPV.

However, with Project B there would be an opportunity to withdraw from the project after five years if the returns are poor and the project is value-destroying. This option does not exist with Project A.

Simple NPV analysis would not consider the real option with Project B to withdraw after five years, and Project A would be selected. With a real options analysis, the comparison between Project A and Project B would put a value on the real option with Project B, and take this option into consideration when making the choice between the two projects.

Real options: analysing project management risk and flexibility

The NPV approach to project appraisal helps management with the project selection process but is not concerned with active risk management. In making choices between alternative projects for investment, it does not allow for the different amounts of flexibility (real options) that each project provides. For example, one project involving the use of more expensive but more flexible technology might have a lower NPV than an alternative investment involving the use of cheaper but more rigid technology. The flexible use of the more expensive technology provides a real option with value, but with simple NPV analysis this factor would be ignored.

An approach to project appraisal using real options considers all the different possibilities that might arise during the project management stage of a capital investment project. Instead of starting with an 'aggregate' or 'expected value' scenario of what might happen in the future, real options analysis starts by trying to identify all the future events or developments that might occur that would affect the project's value. The differing 'volatilities' of alternative investments are critical, and some projects will involve more uncertainty than others.

Once the risk profile of each investment alternative has been understood, the next step in the analysis is to identify the major project management decisions that could be made (the real options available with each investment alternative). Real options provide flexibility for project management, and these real options should be evaluated and taken into consideration (both at the project selection stage and during project management).

6.4 Different types of real option

There are different types of real option. The examination syllabus refers to real options to 'delay, expand, re-deploy and withdraw'. A more detailed analysis of the types of real option is set out below.

Invest/grow options	Scale up	Make sequential, incremental investments as the markets grow. This type of real option includes start-up options.
	Switch up	A speedy commitment to a first-generation of a technology might give a company an advantage if the opportunity eventually occurs to switch to a next-generation of the technology. This might be called a 'market power option'.
	Scope up	Real option that provides an opportunity to increase the scope or range of activities. For example, investing in one industry might give a company the opportunity to invest in another industry at the same time and at a low cost.
Defer/delay/learn options	Sundry start	Option to delay an investment until new information is available or new skills are acquired. A deferral option.
Divest/withdraw/ reduce options	Scale down	Option to reduce the size of a project part-way through its life, or to disinvest entirely and withdraw from the investment. This option might be used if new information changes the expected payback from the project.
	Switch down	Where the company has invested in flexible assets, there might be an option to switch to a more cost-effective use of the assets
	Scope down	There might be an option for a company to reduce the scope of its operations at a low cost if it is discovered that there is no potential for further business development.

6.5 The valuation of real options

To estimate the value of a project using a real options approach, it is necessary to identify when and under what conditions each real option would be exercised, and a value has to be calculated for each option. For each real option that is identified for a particular project, the following data should be obtained:

- When the option will be available during the project life, and for how long.
- How the option might have a positive effect on the value of the project, and what that effect might be.
- What additional investment would be needed to exercise the option.
- Whether any additional investment is needed now to make the option available in the future.
- Whether the exercise of the option will then make other follow-up options available at a later time.

Each investment project should be assessed both for their NPV and the value of the future opportunities they might provide during the project management stage, such as the opportunity to expand in the same or related markets, or the flexibility to change the level or scale of operations, or for the ease of halting further expenditure or withdrawing entirely from an investment at a low cost.

Real options analysis puts a financial value to flexibility in the management of projects, and the value of real options is therefore higher when the project risk and uncertainty is high.

However, the real options approach has an important weakness. A considerable amount of academic research has been carried out into the valuation of real options, but a simple and satisfactory approach to valuation has not yet been established. Some academics believe that real options can be valued using a model based on the Black-Scholes option pricing model.

Some companies have also used a real options approach to project evaluation, particularly where real options can have a significant impact on capital investment project selection – for example in the pharmaceuticals industry and other industries where expenditure on research and development is high, and also in mining (where mining leases might include important real options for the mining company).

Example

X Plc is considering a major investment to build and operate social housing in the capital city of Ruritania.

The project would require an initial investment of \$300m. The project would result in positive cash inflows with a present value of \$310m giving an NPV of \$10m.

In order to encourage investment of this type the Ruritanian government have agreed that X Plc can sell the project back to the government without recourse for \$200m after 4 years.

The risk free rate is estimated to be 5% in the foreseeable future. A cash flow simulation of similar investments has shown a standard deviation of 30%

Calculate the value of the abandonment option and hence the total NPV of the project. (Note that this is a put option).

a

Answer

Step 1. List the variables

P_a = \$310m (this is the value of the underlying asset at the start of the project)
P_e = \$200m
r = 5% (= 0.05)
t = 4 years to expiry (t = 4)
s = 0.30

Step 2. Calculate d_1

$$d_1 = \frac{\ln(P_a/P_e) + (r + 0.5s^2)t}{s\sqrt{t}}$$

$$d_1 = \frac{\ln(310/200) + [0.05 + (0.5 \times 0.30^2)]\,4}{0.3\sqrt{4}}$$

$$d_1 = \frac{\ln(1.55) + [0.05 + 0.045]\,4}{0.6}$$

$$d_1 = \frac{0.4383 + 0.38}{0.6}$$

$$\mathbf{d_1} = \frac{0.8183}{0.6} = \mathbf{1.368\ (say\ 1.37)}$$

Step 2. Calculate d_2

$d_2 = d_1 - s\sqrt{t}$

$d_2 = 1.368 - 0.3\sqrt{4}$

$d_2 = 1.368 - 0.6$

d_2 = 0.7638 (say 0.76)

Step 3. Obtain values for $N(d_1)$ and $N(d_2)$

$N(d_1)$.

When $d_1 = 1.37$ the corresponding value in the normal distribution table is 0.4147.

The value of d_1 is positive, so add 0.50.

$N(d_1) = 0.4147 + 0.50 = 0.9147$.

$N(d_2)$.

When $d_2 = 0.76$, the corresponding value in the normal distribution table is 0.2764.

The value of d_2 is positive, so add 0.50.

$N(d_2) = 0.2764 + 0.50 = 0.7764$.

Step 4. Calculate the option price (for a call option)

$c = P_a\, N(d_1) - P_e\, N(d_2)\, e^{-rt}$

Tip – calculate the value of e^{-rt} first

$rt = (0.05)(4) = 0.2.$

$e^{-0.2} = 1/e^{0.2}$

$e^{0.2} = 1.2214$

Therefore $1/e^{0.035} = 0.8187$

Option price = $P_s N(d_1) - P_e N(d_2) e^{-rt}$

= 310(0.9147) – 200 (0.7764) (0.8187)

= 283.56 – 127.12 = **156.44**

Step 5. Calculate the option price (for a put option)

$p = c - P_a + P_e\, e^{-rt}$

p = 156.44 – 310 + 200 (0.8187)

p = 10.18

Conclusion

The value of the option to abandon the project is $10.18m. This gives an overall project value of $10m + $10.18 = $21.18m

Example

X Plc is considering a major investment to build and operate social housing in the capital city of Ruritania.

The project would require an initial investment of $300m. The project would result in positive cash inflows with a present value of $310m giving an NPV of $10m.

Currently there is a major offshore oil and gas exploration project in Ruritania. If X Plc were to accept the project under consideration they would be well placed to secure a further government construction project if and when oil and gas production commences.

Initial investment in the future project would be $400 in 4 years' time. The present value of cash inflows from the project are estimated at $240m but there is a great deal of uncertainty associated with this. An analyst has estimated volatility on the cash inflows could be as high as 30%. Risk free rate is 5%

Calculate the value of the follow on opportunity. (Note that this is a call option).

Answer

Step 1. List the variables

P_a = \$240m (this is the value of the underlying asset at the start of the project)
P_e = \$400m
r = 5% = 0.05)
t = 4 years to expiry, t = 4.
s = 0.30

Step 2. Calculate d_1

$$d_1 = \frac{\ln(P_a / P_e) + (r + 0.5s^2)t}{s\sqrt{t}}$$

$$d_1 = \frac{\ln(240/400) + [0.05 + (0.5 \times 0.30^2)]\,4}{0.3\sqrt{4}}$$

$$d_1 = \frac{\ln(0.6) + [0.05 + 0.045]\,4}{0.6}$$

$$d_1 = \frac{-0.5108 + 0.38}{0.6}$$

$$\mathbf{d_1} = \frac{-0.1308}{0.6} = \mathbf{-0.218\ (say\ -\ 0.22)}$$

Step 2. Calculate d_2

$d_2 = d_1 - s\sqrt{t}$

$d_2 = 0.218 - 0.3\sqrt{4}$

$d_2 = 0.218 - 0.6$

d_2 = − 0.818 (say 0.82)

Step 3. Obtain values for $N(d_1)$ and $N(d_2)$

$N(d_1)$.

When $d_1 = -0.22$ the corresponding value in the normal distribution table is 0.0871.

The value of d_1 is negative, so subtract 0.0871 from 0.5

$N(d_1) = 0.5 - 0.0871 = 0.4129$.

$N(d_2)$.

When $d_2 = -.82$, the corresponding value in the normal distribution table is 0.2939.

The value of d_1 is negative, so subtract 0.2939 from 0.5

$N(d_2) = 0.5 - 0.2939 = 0.2061$

Step 4. Calculate the option price (for a call option)

$c = P_a\, N(d_1) - P_e\, N(d_2)\, e^{-rt}$

Tip – calculate the value of e^{-rt} first

$rt = (0.05)(4) = 0.2.$

$e^{-0.2} = 1/e^{0.2}$

$e^{0.2} = 1.2214$

Therefore $1/e^{0.035} = 0.8187$

Option price = $P_s N(d_1) - P_e N(d_2) e^{-rt}$

$= 240(0.4129) - 400\ (0.2061)\ (0.8187)$

$= 99.1 - 67.5 =$ **31.6**

Conclusion

The value of the option to enter a further project is \$31.6m. This gives an overall project value of \$10m + \$31.6 = \$41.6m

CHAPTER 10

Sources and costs of finance

Contents

Sources of finance

- Equity
- Debt
- Hybrids
- Leases
- Venture capital
- Business angels
- Private equity
- Asset securitisation and sale
- Initial coin offering (ICO)

1 Sources of finance

An important aspect of financial management is the choice of methods of financing for a company's assets. Companies use a variety of sources of finance and the aim should be to achieve an efficient capital structure that provides:

- a suitable balance between short-term and long-term funding
- adequate working capital
- a suitable balance between equity and debt capital in the long-term capital structure.

Factors that must be considered include:

- Amount needed
- Cost
- Duration
- Flexibility
- Repayment
- Impact on financial statements

1.1 Equity

Features

Finance raised through sale of shares to existing or new investors (existing investors often have a right to invest first – pre-emption rights).

Providers of equity are the ultimate owner(s) of the company.

Issue costs can be high.

Cost of equity is higher than other forms of finance.

New issues to new investors will dilute control of existing owners.

When appropriate

Used to provide long-term finance. May be used in preference to debt finance if company is already highly geared.

Private companies may not be allowed to offer shares for sale to the public at large (e.g. in the UK).

Methods of issuing new shares for cash

There are three main methods of issuing new shares for cash:

- Issuing new shares for purchase by the general investing public: this is called a **public offer**.

A public offer might be used to bring the shares of a company to the stock market for the first time (described as an **initial public offering (IPO)** or a 'stock market flotation'.

- Issuing new shares to a relatively small number of selected investors: this is called a **placing**
- Issuing new shares to existing shareholders in a **rights issue.**

1.2 Debt

Can be short-term or long-term.

Short-term debt includes:

- bank overdrafts
- bank loans

Bank overdrafts – Features

Flexible with regard to amount and available immediately within pre-arranged limits.

Interest and fees are tax deductible.

Interest is only paid when the account is overdrawn.

Penalties for breaching overdraft limits can be severe.

Overdrafts are repayable on demand.

When appropriate

Used to finance day-to-day operations.

An important component of working capital management policies

Bank loans – Features

Available for specified periods and must be repaid according to a pre-agreed schedule. This means that the company knows where it stands in terms of needing to meet cash payments.

Interest and fees are tax deductible.

Once the loan is taken interest is paid for the duration of the loan.

A loan might be repayable if loan covenants are breached but failing that the cash is available for the term of the loan.

Can be taken out in a foreign currency as a hedge of a foreign investment.

A company can offer security in order to secure a loan.

When appropriate

Short-term loans are suitable for funding smaller investments.

Long-term loans are suitable for funding major investments.

1.3 Hybrids

Features

A hybrid is a financial instrument that combines features of equity and debt, for example convertible debt.

Interest is paid at an agreed rate for a specified period. At the end of the period the holder can choose to be repaid in cash or to change the debt into equity shares. Whether or not conversion occurs depends on the share price at the conversion date.

The issuing company will need to raise cash in order to pay back the amount if conversion is not chosen.

Lower interest rates than straightforward (vanilla) debt as the lender is, in effect, lending money and buying a call option on the company's shares.

Interest and fees are tax deductible.

When appropriate

For long-term investments. Useful if the share price is low at the time of issue thus making equity issue too dilutive.

1.4 Leases

Features

Two types:

- operating leases – off-balance sheet
- finance leases – on-balance sheet

Legal ownership of the asset remains with the lessor.

Lessee has the right of use of the asset in return for a series of rental payments.

Tax deductibility of rental payments depends on the tax regime but typically they are tax deductible in one way or another.

Finance leases are capitalised and affect key ratios (ROCE, gearing)

When appropriate?

Operating leases

- For the acquisition of smaller assets but also for very expensive assets.
- Common in the airline industry

Finance leases – Can be used for very big assets (e.g. oil field servicing vessels)

1.5 Venture capital

Features

The term 'venture capital' is normally used to mean capital provided to a private company by specialist investment institutions, sometimes with support from banks in the form of loans.

The company must demonstrate to the venture capitalist organisation that it has a clear strategy and a convincing business plan.

A venture capital organisation will only invest if there is a clear 'exit route' (e.g. a listing on an exchange).

Investment is typically for 3-7 years.

When appropriate?

An important source of finance for management buy-outs.

Can provide finance to take young private companies to the next level.

May provide cash for start-ups but this is less likely.

1.6 Business angels

Features

Business angels are wealthy individuals who invest directly in small businesses, usually by purchasing new equity shares but do not get involved in the management of the company.

Business angels are not that common.

There is too little business angel finance available to meet the potential demand for equity capital from small companies.

When appropriate?

A way for small companies to raise equity finance.

1.7 Private equity

Features

Private equity is equity in operating companies that are not publicly traded on a stock exchange.

Private equity as a source of finance includes venture capital and private equity funds.

A private equity fund looks to take a reasonably large stake in mature businesses.

In a typical leveraged buyout transaction, the private equity firm buys majority control of an existing or mature firm and tries to enhance value by eliminating inefficiencies or driving growth.

Their view is to realise the investment possibly by breaking the business into smaller parts.

When appropriate?

If used as a source of funding a private equity fund will take a large stake (30% is typical) and appoint directors.

It is a method for a private company to raise equity finance where it is not allowed to do so from the market.

1.8 Asset securitisation and sale

Features

Securitisation is the process of conversion of existing assets or future cash flows into marketable securities.

Typically the following occur simultaneously:

- Company A sets up Company B (described as a special purpose vehicle or SPV) and transfers an asset to it (or rights to future cash flows).
- Company B issues securities to investors for cash. These investors are then entitled to the benefits that will accrue from the asset.
- The cash raised by Company B is then paid to Company A.

In substance this is like Company A raising cash and using the asset as security. Accounting rules might require Company A to consolidate Company B even though it might have no ownership interest in it.

Conversion of existing assets into marketable securities is known as asset-backed securitisation and the conversion of future cash flows into marketable securities is known as future-flows securitisation.

Used extensively in the financial services industry.

When appropriate?

Allows the conversion of assets which are not marketable into marketable ones.

Securitisation allows the company to borrow at rates that are commensurate with the rating of the asset. A company with a credit rating of BB might hold an asset rated at AA. If it securitises the asset it gains access to AA borrowing rates.

1.9 Initial coin offering (ICO)

Features

Similar in some respects to an IPO.

An IPO allows a company that was previously private or unquoted to gain wider access to equity finance by offering shares for sale to the wider public.

- The company making the IPO issues a prospectus detailing (amongst other things) the reason that extra capital is being raised.
- Investors buy shares in the hope of increasing their wealth through increase in share value and/or dividends in the future.

An ICO involves the sale of a new cryptocurrency coin "minted" for the purpose, to investors who pay using established cryptocurrency (e.g. bitcoin or etherium) or in some cases fiat (traditional) currency.

- The company making the ICO will issues a prospectus detailing (amongst other things) the reason that extra capital is being raised.
- Investors buy the new cryptocurrency coins (tokens) in the hope of increasing their wealth through increase in coin value.

There are important differences between ICOs and IPOs:

- ICOs are decentralised, with no single authority governing them.
- ICOs are largely unregulated, meaning that there is no regulatory oversight by government organisations.

A fundamental issue with ICOs is most of them raise money in order to provide finance for a project to be undertaken in the future. This makes the investment extremely speculative and risky. In addition, the lack of oversight and regulation can allow opportunities to scammers and fraudster.

ICOs can be risky and investors need to take care to reduce exposure to scams and fraudulent activity.

When appropriate?

ICOs are mainly used to fund new digital projects including cloud-based projects, new cryptocurrency projects, apps or other digital services.

They can also be used to fund start-ups of digital enterprises.

Sources of finance

- Introduction
- Types of sukuk
- Growth in Islamic finance

2 Islamic finance

2.1 Introduction

Note that the Islamic Finance Resource is an excellent website full of useful information and examples. It is recommended that you visit the site (http://ifresource.com)

Islamic finance rests on the application of Shariah. Sharia law is derived from the Quran (believed to be Allah's divine revelation to the prophet Muhammed) and the teachings of Muhammed.

Muslims believe that Sharia law shows the path to be followed as ordained by Allah. It covers all aspects of life and Muslims believe that following this path will lead to physical and spiritual wellbeing.

The main principles of Islamic finance are that:

- Wealth must be generated from legitimate trade and asset-based investment (the use of money for the purposes of making money is expressly forbidden).
- Investment should have a social and an ethical benefit to wider society beyond pure return.
- Risk should be shared.
- Charging and receiving interest (riba) is prohibited. This contradicts the principle that risk must be shared and is also contrary to the ideas of partnership and justice.

The following Islamic financial instruments provide Shariah-compliant finance. Often the cash flows from these techniques might be the same as they would have been under standard western practice. However, the key difference is that the rate of return is based on the asset transaction and not based on interest on money loaned.

Murabaha

In traditional western finance a customer would borrow money from a bank in order to finance activity, say the purchase of an asset. However, under Sharia the bank cannot charge interest.

Murabaha is a form of trade credit for asset acquisition that avoids the payment of interest. The bank buys the asset and then sells it on to the customer on a deferred basis at a price that includes an agreed mark-up for profit. Payment can be made by instalments but the mark-up is fixed in advance and cannot be increased, even if there is a delay in payment.

Ijara

A form of lease finance agreement where a bank buys an asset for a customer and then leases it to the customer over a specific period at agreed rentals which allows the bank to recover the capital cost of the asset and a profit margin.

Mudaraba

The bank provides capital and the customer provides expertise to invest in a project. Profits generated are distributed according to a predetermined ratio but cannot be guaranteed. The bank does not participate in the management of the business. This is like the bank providing equity finance.

The project might make a loss. In this case the bank loses out. The customer cannot be made to compensate the bank for this loss as that would be contrary to the mutual sharing of risk.

Musharaka

This is a joint venture or investment partnership between two parties who both provide capital towards the financing of new or established projects. Both parties share the profits on a pre-agreed ratio, allowing managerial skills to be remunerated, with losses being shared on the basis of equity participation.

Salam

Salam is a contract in which advance payment is made for goods to be delivered at a future date for a price paid in full at the time of contract.

A Salam contract must specify the quantity and quality of the commodity intended to be purchased and the exact date and place of delivery.

Sukuk

This is debt finance but Islamic bonds cannot bear interest. Sukuk holders must have an ownership interest in the assets which are being financed. The sukuk holders' return for providing finance is a share of the income generated by the assets. Modern sukuk share many features with western securitisations.

There are many different types of sukuk including:

- Ijara sukuk (sukuk al-ijara)
- Mudaraba sukuk (sukuk al-mudaraba)
- Murabaha sukuk (sukuk al-murabaha)
- Musharaka sukuk (sukuk al-musharaka)

2.2 Types of sukuk

Sukuk are shariah compliant "bonds". Typically sukuk are certificates that represent ownership of an asset or its usufruct. (Usufruct refers to all of the benefits that the ownership of an asset would convey).

This section explains types of sukuk arrangements in more detail. There are different ways in which each type of sukuk might be structured. The detail of a structure might vary from those in the following explanations.

Sukuk al-ijarah

This is a sale and leaseback transaction.

Suppose Business A wishes to raise finance.

A sponsor (say Business A's bank) would set up a special purpose vehicle (SPV) with the purpose of buying an asset off Business A (which would be later leased back to it) at a pre-agreed price.

The SPV would issue ownership certificates (sukuk) to investors for cash. The amount raised would be the amount needed to buy the asset off Business A.

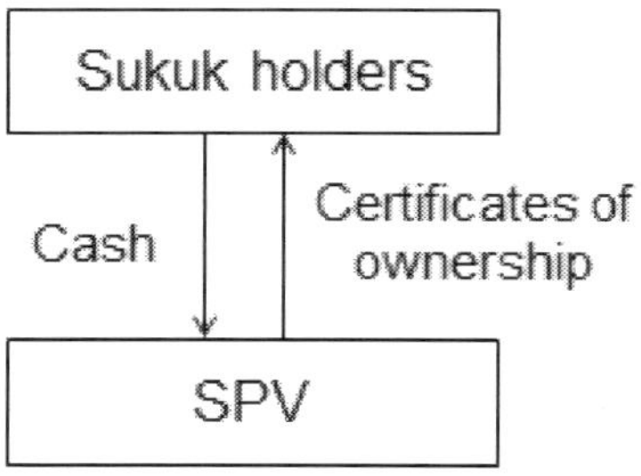

The SPV would buy the asset off Business A. The SPV would own the asset and in turn be owned by the sukuk holders.

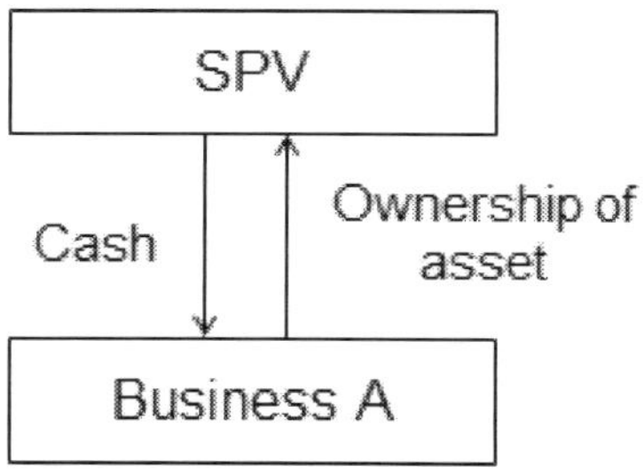

Business A would lease the asset back from the SPV for a series of pre-agreed rentals. The cash thus collected by the SPV would be paid as distributions to the sukuk holders.

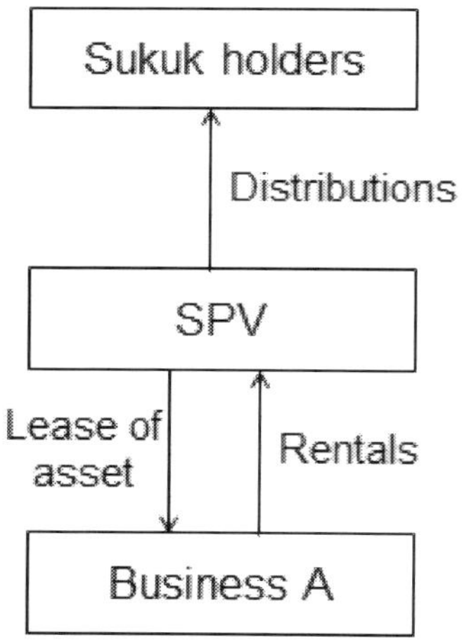

Note that Business A would be described as being the "obligator" in this transaction.

Mudaraba sukuk (sukuk al-mudaraba)

Business B wishes to raise finance for a major, new, construction project. The approach is to set up an SPV which would own the project and engage Business B to run it.

A sponsor (say Business B's bank) would set up a special purpose vehicle (SPV) with the purpose of investing in the project.

The SPV would issue ownership certificates (sukuk) to investors for cash. The amount raised would be the amount needed to finance the project.

Business B is contracted to run the project and would be entitled to a fee/share of profit.

On completion of the project the SPV transfers ownership of the asset to the customer.

The fees received from the customer are used to pay Business B's fee and to provide distributions to the sukuk holders.

Murabaha sukuk (sukuk al-murabaha)

Business C wishes to raise finance to buy a large amount of iron ore.

A sponsor (say Business C's bank) would set up a special purpose vehicle (SPV) with the purpose of buying the ore.

The SPV would issue ownership certificates (sukuk) to investors for cash. The amount raised would be the amount needed to buy the ore.

The SPV buys the ore.

The SPV then sells the ore to Business C at a profit. Business C pays for the ore according to a pre-agreed schedule of payments and these are passed on to the sukuk holders.

Musharaka sukuk (sukuk al-musharaka)

Business D wishes to raise finance for a major, new, construction project. The approach is to set up an SPV which would enter into a joint venture with Business D. Business D would provide the expertise needed to run the project and the sukuk holders (through) the JV would provide the finance.

The sukuk holders participate in the management of the joint venture.

The profits and losses of the JV are shared between Business D and the sukuk holders.

2.3 Growth in Islamic finance

The global Islamic economy, which includes the Islamic finance industry, is estimated to have a total value of $8 trillion. The industry represents less than 2% of banking assets worldwide but this comprises an estimated $1.6 trillion in global assets.

The Islamic finance market has grown by more than 10%-15% annually, from 2000-2012. Sharia-compliant assets rose by more than 160% between 2009 and 2011. Islamic finance investments are now worth $1.6 trillion and are forecast to increase to $2.5 trillion by 2015.

Reasons for the growth

There is a large and expanding international Muslim population who increasingly use Sharia compliant products.

There has been an increase in oil wealth among many Muslim nations.

The global crisis and liquidity squeeze has led to strong growth in Islamic finance. Many non-Muslim investors are viewing Islamic finance products as an ethical and, safer alternative to conventional banking products. (Perhaps they are viewed as safer because they have been subject a review which is based on ethics and fairness rather than commercial return alone).

For example, sukuk give the holder a stake in the underlying asset rather than a share of debt. A conventional bond holder receives interest on a loan but the sukuk holder receives a share of profit derived from the operation of the business, rather than on interest (which is strictly forbidden under Sharia law).

Weighted average cost of capital (WACC)

- Cost of equity, cost of debt and the weighted average cost of capital (WACC)
- WACC and capital investment appraisal
- Comparing the cost of equity and the cost of debt

3 Weighted average cost of capital (WACC)

3.1 Cost of equity, cost of debt and the weighted average cost of capital (WACC)

The **cost of capital for investors** is the return that investors require from their investment. Companies must be able to make a sufficient return from their own capital investments to pay the returns required by their shareholders and holders of debt capital. The cost of capital for investors therefore establishes a cost of capital for companies.

- For each company there is a cost of equity. This is the return required by its shareholders, in the form of dividends or share price growth
- There is a cost for each item of debt finance. This is the yield required by the lender or bond investor
- When there are preference shares, there is also a cost of preference share capital, which is the dividend yield required by the shareholders.

The **cost of capital for a company** is the return that it must make on its investments so that it can afford to pay its investors the returns that they require.

The cost of capital for investors and the cost of capital for companies should theoretically be the same. However, they are different because of the differing tax positions of investors and companies.

- The cost of capital for investors is measured as a pre-tax cost of capital. This is a return ignoring taxation.
- The cost of capital for companies recognises that interest costs are an allowable expense for tax purposes, and the cost of debt capital to a company should allow for the tax relief that companies receive on interest payments, reducing their tax payments. The cost of debt capital for companies is measured as an after-tax cost.

The **weighted average cost of capital** is the average cost of all the sources of capital that a company uses. This average is weighted, to allow for the relative proportions of the different types of capital in the company's capital structure.

Example: pre-tax and after-tax cost of debt

A company has a bank loan of $100,000 on which it pays interest at 8%. The rate of tax on company profits is 25%.

Gross interest on the loan each year is $8,000 and the pre-tax cost of the debt is 8%. This means that the company needs to make a profit of $8,000 each year before tax and interest in order to cover the interest cost of the debt. Tax relief on the interest is $2,000, which means that the tax charge for the company is reduced by $2,000 each year. The company therefore needs to make a profit after tax of $6,000 to cover the cost of the debt interest, and the after-tax cost of the debt is just 6%. The $6,000 after tax profit plus the reduction in the tax charge of $2,000 together provide the return of $8,000 that is needed to cover the cost of the debt interest.

The after tax cost of debt is simply:

- the pre-tax cost of debt
- multiplied by a factor (1 – t) where t is the rate of tax on profits.

3.2 WACC and capital investment appraisal

One approach to the evaluation of capital investments by companies is that all their investment projects should be expected to provide a return equal to or in excess of the WACC. If all their investment projects earn a return in excess of the WACC, the company will earn sufficient returns overall to meet the cost of its capital and provide its investors with the returns they require.

This principle is often applied in practice. The general rule is that when capital investment projects are evaluated using the NPV method, the cost of capital to be used is the WACC. This is on the assumption that the capital project **will not alter the risk profile of the company's investments** and the risk with the new project is similar to the risks with the rest of the company's business operations.

The principle is often applied when the financing for a new capital investment **changes the company's WACC**. On the assumption that the capital project will not alter the risk profile of the company's investments, the NPV of the new project should be calculated using the new WACC that will exist after the project has been undertaken and financed.

An alternative approach to the evaluation of capital investment projects, which does not use these assumptions, is the adjusted present value method or APV method. (This is explained in another chapter).

3.3 Comparing the cost of equity and the cost of debt

For investors and for companies, the cost of their equity is always higher than the cost of their debt capital. This is because equity investment in a company is always more risky than investment in the debt capital of the same company.

In addition, from a company's perspective, the cost of debt is also reduced by the tax relief on interest payments. This makes debt finance even lower than the cost of equity.

The effect of more debt capital, and higher financial gearing, on the WACC is considered in more detail later.

Cost of equity

- Methods of calculating the cost of equity
- Cost of equity: the dividend valuation model method
- Cost of equity: the dividend growth model method
- Gordon's growth approximation
- Cost of equity: CAPM method

4 Cost of equity

4.1 Methods of calculating the cost of equity

There are several methods for estimating the cost of equity in a company. These are the dividend valuation model method, the dividend growth model method and the CAPM method. The three methods are described briefly in this section, though you might be familiar with them already.

4.2 Cost of equity: the dividend valuation model method

The dividend valuation model says that the market value of a share is the present value of the future cash flows (dividends) expected by the shareholders discounted at the shareholders' required rate of return. If it is assumed that future annual dividends are expected to remain constant into the foreseeable future the market value is given by:

$$MV = \frac{d}{K_E}$$

This can be rearranged to give the following expression for the cost of equity:

$$K_E = \frac{d}{MV}$$

where:

K_E is the cost of equity (the shareholders' required rate of return)

d = the expected future annual dividend

MV is the share price ex-dividend. The ex-dividend share price is a price that excludes any dividend that has been declared and is payable in the near future.

Example

A company's shares are currently valued at $11.70 and the company is expected to pay an annual dividend of $1.40 per share for the foreseeable future. The cost of equity in the company can therefore be estimated as:

(1.40/11.70) = 0.1197 or 11.97%, say 12%.

4.3 Cost of equity: the dividend growth model method

If it is assumed that the annual dividend will grow at a constant percentage rate into the foreseeable future, the market value can be calculated as follows:

$$MV = \frac{d(1+g)}{K_E - g}$$

This can be rearranged to give the following expression for the cost of equity:

$$K_E = \frac{d(1+g)}{MV} + g$$

where:

K_E is the cost of equity
d = the annual dividend for the year that has just ended
g is the annual growth rate in dividends, expressed as a proportion (8% = 0.08, etc.)
MV is the share price ex-dividend
d (1 + g) is therefore the expected dividend next year.

Example

A company's share price is $11.70. The company has just paid an annual dividend of $1.40 per share, and the dividend is expected to grow by 3% into the foreseeable future.

The cost of equity in the company can be estimated as follows:

$$K_E = \frac{1.40\,(1.03)}{11.70} + 0.03$$

= 0.153 = 15.3%.

4.4 Gordon's growth approximation

A problem with the dividend growth model as a method of calculating the cost of equity is that estimates of future dividend growth might be unreliable.

Gordon's growth approximation is a method of estimating what the future rate of growth might be. It is based on the assumption that a company pays dividends out of profits (earnings). Growth in future profits, and so future growth in dividends is achieved by reinvesting some of the current profits. The reinvested profits earn additional earnings which can then be used to pay higher dividends.

The same principle might be applied to reinvestment of free cash flows rather than reinvestment of profits. However, the concept is the same: dividend growth is achieved by reinvesting some of the returns that could otherwise be paid as current year dividends.

Gordon's growth approximation is an estimate of future dividend growth, expressed by the formula:

$g = br_e$

where
g = the annual rate of dividend growth
b = the proportion of earnings (or free cash flow) reinvested for growth, and
r_e = the rate of return on those reinvested earnings (a rate of return on equity since the reinvested earnings represent equity profits).

Example

A company reported profits after interest and tax of $6 million and paid dividends of $4 million. This ratio of dividend payments to earnings is fairly typical of the company's dividend policy. The company's cost of equity is 12%.

The proportion of profits reinvested for growth is 0.33 (2/6).
An estimate of the future growth rate in annual dividends, using Gordon's growth approximation, is:
$0.33 \times 0.12 = 0.04$ or 4.0%.

Example

Gordon's growth approximation can also be applied to free cash flows, as the following example shows:

A company has a cost of equity of 10%. The company's cash flows for the financial year just ended are as follows:

	$ million
Net cash inflow from operating activities	84
Interest payments less interest receipts	(17)
Taxation paid	(23)
	44
Capital expenditure	(21)
Financing cash flows: repayment of debt	(16)
Increase in cash for the year	7

Free cash flow to equity will be defined as the net cash inflow from operating activities less net interest payments and less payments of tax, but before reinvestment. Here, the free cash flow to equity (FCFE) is $44 million.

The rate of reinvestment is assumed to be the total amount of capital expenditure in the year (net of disposal proceeds), which is $31 million.

We can estimate the rate of reinvestment of cash flows that could otherwise be paid as dividends as: 21/44 = 0.4773.

An estimate of the future growth rate in annual dividends, using Gordon's growth approximation, is:
$0.4773 \times 0.10 = 0.04773$, say 4.8%.

Because the estimate is only an approximation, this growth estimate might be rounded to 5% per year.

4.5 Cost of equity: CAPM method

Another approach to calculating the cost of equity in a company is to use the CAPM and the equity beta for the company's shares.

$K_E = R_{RF} + \beta\ (R_M - R_{RF})$

where
K_E = the cost of equity in the company
R_{RF} = the risk-free rate of return
R_M =the return on the market portfolio of securities that are not risk-free
β = the beta factor for the company's equity.

The CAPM method of estimating the cost of equity is an alternative to a dividend-based estimate using the dividend growth model. The two methods will normally produce differing estimates.

Example

A company's shares have a current market value of $13.00. The most recent annual dividend has just been paid. This was $2.00 per share.

Required

Calculate the cost of equity in this company in each of the following circumstances:

(a) The annual dividend is expected to remain $2.00 into the foreseeable future.

(b) The annual dividend is expected to grow by 2% each year into the foreseeable future

(c) The CAPM is used, the equity beta is 1.20, the risk-free cost of capital is 5% and the expected market return is 9%.

Answer

(a) Cost of equity $= \frac{2.00}{25.00} = 0.08$ or 8.0%.

(b) Cost of equity $= \frac{2.00\ (1.02)}{25.00} + 0.02 = 0.1016$ or 10.16%.

(c) Cost of equity = 5% + 1.20 (9 – 5)% = 9.8%.

Cost of debt capital

- Cost of variable rate debt (floating rate debt)
- Cost of irredeemable fixed rate debt (perpetual bonds)
- Cost of redeemable fixed rate debt (redeemable fixed rate bonds)

5 Cost of debt capital

Each item of debt finance for a company has a different cost. This is because debt capital has differing risk, according to whether the debt is secured, whether it is senior or subordinated debt, and the amount of time remaining to maturity.

5.1 Cost of variable rate debt (floating rate debt)

The **pre-tax cost of variable rate debt** (also called floating rate debt), such as the cost of a bank loan, is the current interest rate payable on the debt.

The **after-tax cost of variable rate debt** is the pre-tax cost multiplied by a factor (1 – t), where t is the rate of tax on company profits.

For example, suppose that a company is currently paying interest at 7.5% on its bank loan of $10 million, and the rate of tax on company profits is 30%. The pre-tax cost of the debt is 7.5% and the after-tax cost is 7.5 (1 – 0.30) = 5.25%.

For the purpose of calculating a weighted average cost of capital, the cost of the debt should be its after-tax cost of 5.25% and its market value (for the purpose of weighting the cost of capital) would be $10 million, which is the amount of the loan.

5.2 Cost of irredeemable fixed rate debt (perpetual bonds)

The cost of irredeemable fixed rate bonds, which might be described as perpetual bonds, is calculated as follows:

Pre-tax cost

$$K_D = \frac{i}{MV}$$

Post-tax cost

$$K_D = \frac{i(1-t)}{MV}$$

where:

K_D is the cost of the debt capital
i is the annual interest payable on each $100 (nominal value) of the bonds.
t is the rate of tax on company profits.
MV is the market value of $100 nominal value of bonds, excluding any interest currently payable.

For example, suppose that the coupon rate of interest on some irredeemable bonds is 6% and the market value of the bonds is 103.60. The tax rate is 25%.

(a) The pre-tax cost of the debt is 6/103.60 = 0.058 or 5.8%.

(b) The after-tax cost of the bonds is 6 (1 – 0.25)/103.60 = 0.043 or 4.3%.

5.3 Cost of redeemable fixed rate debt (redeemable fixed rate bonds)

The cost of redeemable bonds is their redemption yield. This is calculated as the rate of return that equates the present value of the future cash flows payable on the bond (to maturity) with the current market value of the bond. In other words, it is the IRR of the cash flows on the bond to maturity, assuming that the current market price is a cash outflow.

A problem arises with calculating the pre-tax and the after-tax cost of redeemable bonds, because the redemption of the principal at maturity is not an allowable expense for tax purposes. The post-tax cost of redeemable debt could therefore be calculated in either of two ways. Each gives a different cost of capital:

- **Method 1**. Calculate the pre-tax cost of debt (the IRR of the cash flows ignoring debt) and then apply the factor (1 – t) to reach the post-tax cost of debt.
- **Method 2**. Calculate the post-tax cost of debt as the IRR of the future cash flows, allowing for tax relief on the interest payments and the absence of tax relief on the principal repayment.

If in doubt, use Method 2. However, Method 1 might be more appropriate if it is assumed that the company will replace the redeemable debt at maturity with a new issue of similar debt capital. So either Method 1 or Method 2 might be valid. Read the requirements of the question carefully, to see whether you are given any instructions about which method to use.

Example

The current market value of a company's 7% loan stock is 96.25. Annual interest has just been paid. The bonds will be redeemed at par after four years. The rate of taxation on company profits is 30%.

Required
Calculate the after-tax cost of the bonds for the company.

a

Answer

(a) Method 1

Year	Cash flow		Try 8%		Try 10%	
			Discount factor	PV	Discount factor	PV
0	Market value	(96.25)	1.000	(96.25)	1.000	(96.25)
1	Interest	7.00	0.926	6.48	0.909	6.36
2	Interest	7.00	0.857	6.00	0.826	5.78
3	Interest	7.00	0.794	5.56	0.751	5.26
4	Interest	7.00	0.735	5.15	0.683	4.78
4	Redemption	100.00	0.735	73.50	0.683	68.30
	NPV			+ 0.44		(5.77)

Using interpolation, the before-tax cost of the debt is:

$$8\% + \frac{0.44}{(0.44 + 5.77)} \times (10 - 8)\% = 8.14\%$$

The after-tax cost of the debt is therefore estimated as 8.14% × (100 – 30) = 5.698% or 5.70%.

(**Note: deciding which cost of capital to try first**. If you don't know which cost of capital to try first, calculate the average annual net cash flow as a percentage of the current market value. Here the total annual net cash inflows = 7 + 7 + 7 + 107 – 96.25 = 31.75 which averages 7.9375 each year. As a percentage of the market value 96.25, this is 8.2%. So try 8% first).

(b) Method 2

It is assumed here that tax savings on interest payments occur in the same year as the interest payments.

Year	Cash flow		Try 6%		Try 5%	
			Discount factor	PV	Discount factor	PV
0	Market value	(96.25)	1.000	(96.25)	1.000	(96.25)
1	Interest less tax	4.90	0.943	4.62	0.952	4.66
2	Interest less tax	4.90	0.890	4.36	0.907	4.44
3	Interest less tax	4.90	0.840	4.12	0.864	4.23
4	Interest less tax	4.90	0.792	3.88	0.823	4.03
4	Redemption	100.00	0.792	79.20	0.823	82.30
	NPV			(0.07)		+ 3.41

Using interpolation, the after-tax cost of the debt is:

$$5\% + \frac{3.41}{(3.41 + 0.07)} \times (6 - 5)\% = 5.98\%, \text{ say } 6.0\%.$$

If in doubt, use Method 2.

Calculating the WACC

- Method of calculating the WACC
- WACC and market value

6 Calculating the WACC

6.1 Method of calculating the WACC

The WACC is a weighted average of the (after-tax) cost of all the sources of capital for the company. It is calculated as follows:

Source of finance	Market value	×	Cost	Market value × Cost
			r	MV × r
Equity	MV_E	×	K_E	$MV_E \times K_E$
Preference shares	MV	×	K_P	$MV_P \times K_P$
Debt	MV_D	×	K_D	$MV_D \times K_D$
Total	ΣMV			$\Sigma MV \times r$
WACC =	$\frac{\Sigma MV \times r}{\Sigma MV}$			

The WACC for a company is found using the method shown above. K_D is the after-tax cost of debt capital. If there is more than one source of debt, each with a different cost, you can either:

- have a separate line in the table for each item of debt, or
- calculate a weighted average cost of all debt capital first (after-tax), then have just one line in the table with the total market value of all debt capital and the weighted average after-tax cost of the debt.

Example

A company has 8 million shares each with a value of $7.90, whose cost is 8.4%. It has 6% bonds with a market value of $50 million and an after-tax cost of 3.6%. It has a bank loan of $10 million whose after-tax cost is 4.1%. It also has 2 million 8% preference shares of $1 whose market price is $1.33 per share and whose cost is 6%. Calculate the WACC.

Answer

Source of finance	Market value	Cost	Market value × Cost
	$ million	r %	MV × r
Equity	63.20	8.4	530.88
Preference shares	2.66	6.0	15.96
Bonds	50.00	3.6	180.00
Bank loan	10.00	4.1	41.00
	125.86		767.84

$$\text{WACC} = \frac{767.84}{125.86} = 6.10\%$$

Example

You should be prepared in your examination to calculate the cost of equity in a company, given the WACC, the cost of debt and the market value of equity and debt. Here is an example.

A company has a weighted average cost of capital of 8.2%. It has 100 million shares currently valued at $6 each, and it has a bank loan of $200 million on which the rate of interest is 6.5%. The rate of taxation is 30%.

Required

Calculate the current cost of equity in the company.

Answer

The cost of equity can be calculated as the solution to a mathematical problem.

Let the cost of equity be r.

The after-tax cost of debt is 6.5% × (1 – 0.30) = 4.55%.

The WACC , which is 8.2%, is calculated as follows:

Source of finance	Market value	Cost	Market value × Cost
	$ million	%	MV × r
Equity	600.0	r	600r
Debt	200.0	4.55	910.0
	800.0		600r + 910

$$\text{WACC} = 8.2\% = \frac{600r + 910}{800}\%$$

8.2 (800) = 600r + 910

600r = 5,650

r = 9.417%

The cost of equity is 9.417%, say 9.4%.

6.2 WACC and market value

For a company with constant annual 'cash profits', there is an important connection between WACC and market value. (Note: 'Cash profits' are cash flows generated from operations, before deducting interest costs.)

If we assume that annual cash profits are a constant amount in perpetuity, the total value of a company, equity plus debt capital, is calculated as follows:

$$\text{Total market value of the company} = \frac{\text{Annual cash profits}}{\text{WACC}}$$

From this formula, the following conclusions can be made:

- The lower the WACC, the higher the total value of the company will be (equity + debt capital), for any given amount of annual profits.
- Similarly, the higher the WACC, the lower the total value of the company.

For example, if annual cash profits are $12 million, the total market value of the company would be:

- $100 million if the WACC is 12% ($12 million/0.12)
- $120 million if the WACC is 10% ($12 million/0.10)
- $200 million if the WACC is 6% ($12 million/0.06).

The **aim should therefore be to achieve a level of financial gearing that minimises the WACC**, in order to maximise the value of the company.

Important questions in financial management are:

- How does the WACC change with changes in gearing?
- For each company, is there an 'ideal' level of gearing that minimises the WACC?

Duration

- The concept of duration
- McCauley's duration
- Modified duration
- Characteristics of duration
- Use of duration
- Limitations of duration
- Capital investment projects and duration

7 Duration

7.1 The concept of duration

Duration can be defined as the time to recover one half of the project value. It measures the average time it takes for a bond to pay its interest and principal. It measures the redemption period of a bond.

The concept of duration is widely used by analysts in the bond markets. It is a measure of how long an investor in bonds must wait before his investment in the bond is recovered.

Duration of bonds

For example, suppose that there are two bonds X and Y, each with a maturity of four years. The returns for the investor on the bonds will be as follows:

	Year	Year	Year	Year	Total return
	$	$	$	$	$
Bond X	10	10	10	110	140
Bond Y	20	20	20	120	180

For the investor, investing in a bond would be a four-year capital investment. This is the lifespan of the bond.

An investor might be interested in how long it will take to recover the investment. This can be calculated as the average time that this will take. Average time can be calculated as the weighted average number of years that this will take.

To calculate a weighted average period for obtaining the investment returns, the cash flows in each year should be given a weighting. For an investment with n years, the weighting for Year 1 should be 1, for Year 2 it should be 2 and for year 3 it should be 3, and so on. The weighting for the cash flow in Year n is n.

With four-year bonds, the weighting for the return in Year 1 is therefore 1, and so on.

Year	Bond X Return (R)	Bond X Weighting (W)	Bond X R × W	Bond Y Return (R)	Bond Y Weighting (W)	Bond Y R × W
1	10	1	10	20	1	20
2	10	2	20	20	2	40
3	10	3	30	20	3	60
4	110	4	440	120	4	480
	140		500	180		600

The non-discounted average time to recover the investment is:

- For Bond X, 500/140 = 3.57 years
- For bond Y, 600/180 = 3.33 years.

7.2 Macauley's duration

The average times calculated above are similar to the calculation of a non-discounted payback period. The calculation fails to recognise the time value of money by discounting the returns in each year before weighting them.

Macaulay's duration, provides a value for duration after using the present value of the returns in each year.

Macaulay's duration is the weighted average term to maturity of the cash flows from a bond. The weight of each cash flow is determined by dividing the present value of the cash flow by the price, and is a measure of bond price volatility with respect to interest rates.

In the previous example of the two bonds, suppose that the gross redemption yield (cost of debt) on each bond is 10%.

The value for Macaulay's duration of each bond is calculated as follows:

Bond X

Year	Return (R)	Discount factor at 10%	PV of return	Weighting (W)	PV × W
1	10	0.909	9.09	1	9.09
2	10	0.826	8.26	2	16.52
3	10	0.751	7.51	3	22.53
4	110	0.683	75.13	4	300.52
Market value of Bond X			99.99		
					348.66

Duration of Bond X = 348.66/99.99 = 3.49 years.

Bond Y

Year	Return (R)	Discount factor at 10%	PV of return	Weighting (W)	PV × W
1	20	0.909	18.18	1	18.18
2	20	0.826	16.52	2	33.04
3	20	0.751	15.02	3	45.06
4	120	0.683	81.96	4	327.84
Market value of Bond Y			131.68		
					424.12

Duration of Bond Y = 424.12/131.68 = 3.22 years.

7.3 Modified duration

Modified duration measures the sensitivity of bond price to changes in interest rates.

Modified duration is calculated as:

$$\text{Modified duration} = \frac{\text{Macauley's duration}}{1 + r}$$

Where r = gross redemption yield of the bond

Using the information from the example above:

	Bond X	Bond Y
Macauley's duration	3.49	3.22
÷ 1 + r	1.1	1.1
Modified duration	3.17	2.93

The modified duration is a measure of the sensitivity of the price of a bond to a change in interest rates.

The size of the modified duration determines how much the value of a bond or loan will change when there is a change in interest rates. The value of 3·17 above means that the value of Bond X will change by 3·17 times the change in interest rates multiplied by the original value of the bond or loan.

A higher modified duration means that the fluctuations in the value of a bond or loan will be greater. Thus, the price of Bond X is more sensitive to interest rate changes than the price of Bond Y.

Predicting change in value

The change in price of a bond brought about by a change in interest rates can be estimated using the following formula.

$$\text{Change in price} = \Delta P = -D \times \Delta i \times P$$

Where:

ΔP = change in price of the bond

D = modified duration of the bond (this is used as a negative in the formula to reflect the inverse relationship between interest rates and bond price).

P = original price of the bond

Δi = change in interest rates

Returning to the above examples:

	Bond X	Bond Y
Macauley's duration	3.49	3.22
Price	99.99	131.68

The change in price of each bond caused by a 0.5% change in interest rates is estimated as follows:

Change in price of Bond X = –3.17 × 0.005 × 99.99 = $1.58

Change in price of Bond Y = –2.93 × 0.005 × 131.68 = $1.93

Note that the change in Bond X is proportionately larger than the change in Band Y

7.4 Characteristics of duration

The following statements are true for both Macauley's duration and the modified duration.

- Bonds with longer terms have longer durations. This of course is obvious.
- The duration of a bond is an indication of the price sensitivity of the bond to a change in market yields on bonds. When there is a rise in interest rate, the fall in price of a bond (as a percentage) is greater for bonds with a higher/longer duration. The actual amount by which bonds will change in price following a change in market interest rates can also be calculated using $\Delta P = -D \times \Delta i \times P$ as shown above.
- **Bonds with lower yields have longer durations.** This can be demonstrated by looking at the impact on Bond X if interest rates were 5% instead of 10%

Bond X

Year	**Return (R)**	**Discount factor at 5%**	**PV of return**	**Weighting (W)**	**PV × W**
1	10	0.952	9.52	1	9.52
2	10	0.907	9.07	2	18.14
3	10	0.864	8.64	3	25.92
4	110	0.823	90.50	4	361.99
Market value of Bond X			117.73		
					415.57

Duration of Bond X (at interest rate of 5%) = 348.66/99.99 = 3.49 years.

Duration of Bond X (at interest rate of 10%) = 415.57/117.73 = 3.3.52ears.

- **Bonds with lower coupons have longer durations.** If two bonds have the same redemption date, the bond with the higher coupon will have a shorter duration. This means that in effect, investment is returned sooner. This is because a higher coupon bond results in the investor receiving income sooner than if he held a lower coupon bond of the same redemption date. This is demonstrated by the example above where Bond X paying lower interest has a higher duration than Bond Y.

Other features

Macauley's duration of a zero coupon bond is the same as the term of the bond.

Bond Z

Year	Return (R)	Discount factor at 5%	PV of return	Weighting (W)	PV × W
4	146.41	0.683	100.00	4	400.00

Therefore, the duration of Bond Z = 400/100 = 4 years.

Macauley's duration falls over the life of a bond. The decrease in duration is less than the decrease in the lifespan.

For example, assume Bond X has only 3 years to redemption.

Bond X

Year	Return (R)	Discount factor at 10%	PV of return	Weighting (W)	PV × W
1	10	0.909	9.09	1	9.09
2	10	0.826	8.26	2	16.53
3	110	0.751	82.63	3	247.93
Market value of Bond X			99.99		
					273.55

Therefore, the duration of Bond X = 273.55/99.99 = 2.74 years.

	Lifespan	Macauley's duration
Macauley's duration	4	3.49
Price	3	2.74
Change	1	0.75

7.5 Use of duration

Duration allows bonds with different coupon rates and maturities to be compared directly. Investors in bonds can therefore manage the risk in their bond portfolio by selecting bonds with a suitable duration.

Duration can be used to estimate price change in response to changes in interest rates.

7.6 Limitations of duration

Duration assumes that the relationship between the change in interest rates and the corresponding change in the value of a bond is linear. The actual relationship between interest rates and bond price is represented by a curve which is convex to the origin.

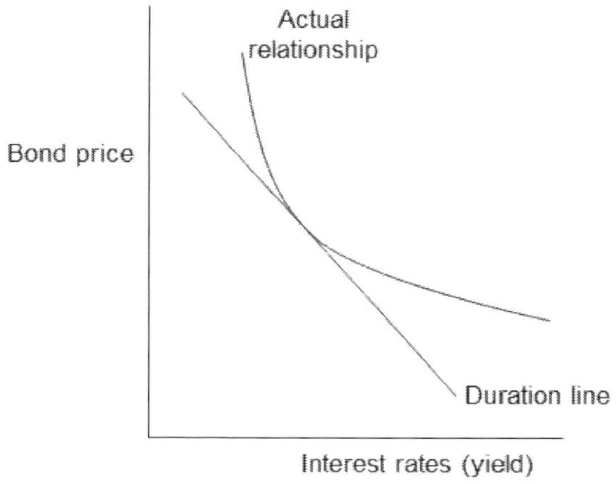

Therefore, duration only provides a reasonable estimation of the change in the value of a bond or loan due to small changes in interest rates. Duration understates price movement in response to larger changes.

This can be demonstrated using information for Bond X found above.

	Bond X
Market value at interest rates of 10%	99.99
Market value predicted using duration	
Predicted change	
$-D \times \Delta i \times P = -3.17 \times -0.05 \times 99.99 =$	15.85
Predicted market value	115.84
Market value at interest rates of 5%	117.73

Another limitation is that duration is further distorted by changes in shape of the yield curve. Changes in interest rates caused by a change in the shape of the yield curve result in duration being a less accurate indicator of the price change.

7.7 Capital investment projects and duration

Duration can be calculated for a capital investment project in exactly the same way as for a bond. It is a measure of the average time to obtain the returns from the investment. Another way of saying this is that the duration of a project is the time required to cover one half of the value of the investment returns.

Duration can be used in capital investment appraisal to assess the payback on a project. Unlike payback and discounted payback, however, it takes into consideration the total expected returns from the entire project (at their discounted value), not just the returns up to the payback time.

- If the duration of a project is short relative to the life of the project – for example, if the duration is less than half the expected total life of the project – this means that most of the returns from the project will be recovered in the early years.
- If the duration of a project is a large proportion of the total life of the project – for example if the duration is 75% or more of the total life of the project – this means that most of the returns from the project will be recovered in the later years.

It could therefore be argued that duration is the best available method of assessing the time for an investment to provide its return on the capital invested.

Example

The cash flows and present values of a project are as follows:

Year	Annual cash flow	Discount factor at 10%	PV of cash flow
	$		$
0	(200,000)	1.000	(200,000)
1	(40,000)	0.909	(36,360)
2	30,000	0.826	24,780
3	120,000	0.751	90,120
4	150,000	0.683	102,450
5	100,000	0.621	62,100
6	50,000	0.564	28,200
NPV			+ 71,290

To calculate duration for a project, the negative cash flows at the beginning of the project are ignored. Duration is calculated using cash flows from the year that the cash flows start to turn positive.

However, if there are negative cash flows in any year after the cash flows turn positive, such as in the final year of the project, these negative cash flows are included in the calculation of duration (as negative values).

In this example, the cash flows start to turn positive from Year 2, so duration is calculated using the present values of the cash flows from Year 2 to Year 6. The Year 2 cash flow is given a weighting of 2, the Year 3 cash flow a weighting of 3, and so on.

Duration is therefore calculated as follows:

Year	Annual cash flow	Discount factor at 10%	PV of cash flow	Weighting	PV × Weighting
	$		$		
2	30,000	0.826	24,780	2	49,560
3	120,000	0.751	90,120	3	270,360
4	150,000	0.683	102,450	4	409,800
5	100,000	0.621	62,100	5	310,500
6	50,000	0.564	28,200	6	169,200
			307,650		1,209,420

The duration of the project is 1,209,420/307,650 = 3.93 years.

Yield curves

- Background
- Shape of the yield curve (term structure of interest rates)
- Bond valuation using the yield curve
- Estimating the yield curve

8 Yield curves

Each item of debt finance for a company has a different cost. This is because debt capital has differing risk, according to whether the debt is secured, whether it is senior or subordinated debt, and the amount of time remaining to maturity.

Furthermore, the cost of debt differs for different periods of borrowing. This is because lenders might require compensation for the risk of having their cash tied up for longer and/or there might be an expectation of future changes in interest rates. The relationship between length of borrowing and interest rates is described by the yield curve. This session looks at the derivation and use of yield curves.

8.1 Background

An earlier section covered the relationship that exists between the market value of a bond, the cash flows that must be paid to service that bond and the cost of debt inherent in that bond.

The market value of a bond is the present value of the future cash flows that must be paid to service the debt, discounted at the lender's required rate of return (pre-tax cost of debt).

The lender's required rate of return (the pre-tax cost of debt) is the IRR of the cash flows (pre-tax) that must be paid to service the debt.

Example

A company has issued a bond that will be redeemed in 4 years. The bond has a nominal interest rate of 6%.

The required rate of return on the bond is 6%.

Required

Calculate what the market value of the bond would be if the required rate of return was 5% or 6% or 7%.

a

Answer

Year		Cash flow	Discount factor (5%)	PV (5%)	Discount factor (6%)	PV (6%)	Discount factor (7%)	PV (7%)
1	Interest	6	0.952	5.71	0.943	5.66	0.935	5.61
2	Interest	6	0.907	5.44	0.890	5.34	0.873	5.24
3	Interest	6	0.864	5.18	0.840	5.04	0.816	4.90
4	Interest + redemption	106	0.823	87.21	0.792	83.96	0.763	80.87
	Market value			103.54		100.00		96.62

Note that there is an inverse relationship between the lender's required rate of return and the market value. The cash flows do not change. The investor can increase his rate of return by offering less for the bond. If the investor offers more the rate of return falls. In 2011 UK Government debt was showing the lowest yields for many years. This was good news for the government! It meant that their debt was in demand by investors so it pushed up the amount that they were willing to pay for a given bond. This in turn meant that the UK government was able to borrow at a low rate.

It follows from the above example, that if the cash flows were given as above together with a market value of $103.54, the required rate of return could have been calculated as the IRR of these amounts, i.e. 5%. This would then be the pre-tax cost of debt.

Similarly, a market value of $100 would give a cost of debt of 6% and a market value of $96.62 would give a cost of debt of 7%.

The IRRs calculated in this way can be described in a number of ways including:

- lenders' required rate of return;
- cost of debt (pre-tax);
- gross redemption yield;
- yield to maturity.

The implied yield for a market value of $103.54 is 5%. This implies that an investor in the bond discounts each of the future cash flows at 5% in order to arrive at the market value of the bond.

This is a simplification. The 5% is an average required rate of return over the life of the bond. In fact, an investor might require a higher rate of return for the year 2 cash flows than for the year 1 cash flows and a higher rate of return for the year 3 cash flows than for the year 4 cash flows and so on. In other words, cash flows with different maturities are looked on differently by investors.

A plot of required rates of return (yields) against maturity is called a yield curve.

The normal expectation is that the yield curve will slope upwards (as described above) though this is not always the case.

8.2 Shape of the yield curve (term structure of interest rates)

The cost of fixed-rate debt is commonly referred to as the 'interest yield'. The interest yield on debt capital varies with the remaining term to maturity of the debt.

- As a general rule, the interest yield on debt increases with the remaining term to maturity. For example, it should normally be expected that the interest yield on a fixed-rate bond with one year to maturity/redemption will be lower than the yield on a similar bond with ten years remaining to redemption. Interest rates are normally higher for longer maturities to compensate the lender for tying up his funds for a longer time.
- When interest rates are expected to fall in the future, interest yields might vary inversely with the remaining time to maturity. For example, the yield on a one-year bond might be lower than the yield on a ten-year bond when rates are expected to fall in the next few months.
- When interest rates are expected to rise in the future, the opposite might happen, and yields on longer-dated bonds might be much higher than on shorter-dated bonds.

Interest yields on similar debt instruments can be plotted on a graph, with the x-axis representing the remaining term to maturity, and the y-axis showing the interest yield. This type of graph, showing the 'term structure of interest rates', is called a yield curve.

- As indicated above, a normal yield curve slopes upwards, because interest yields are normally higher for longer-dated debt instruments.
- However, on occasions, the yield curve might slope downwards, when it is said to be 'negative' or 'inverse'.
- Sometimes it might slope upwards, but with an unusually steep slope (steeply positive yield curve).

Normal (positive) yield curve

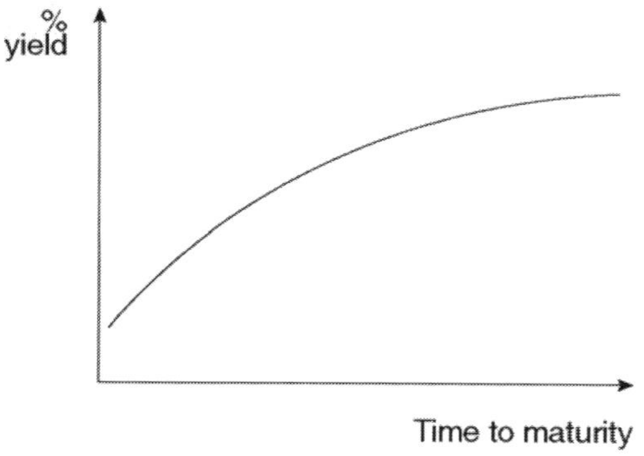

Inverse (negative) yield curve

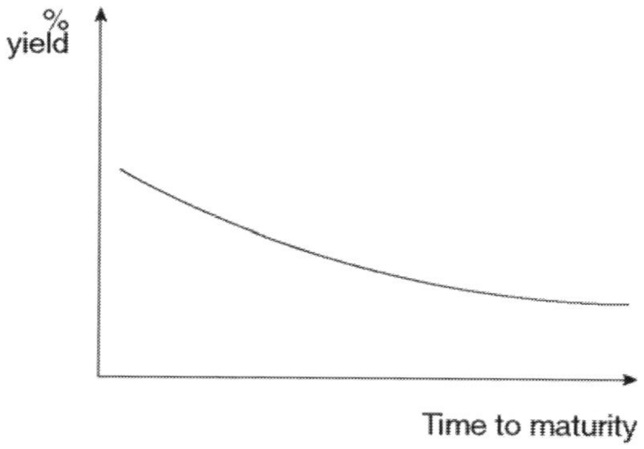

When the yield curve is inverse, this is usually an indication that the markets expect short-term interest rates to fall at some time in the future.

When the yield curve has a steep upward slope, this indicates that the markets expect short-term interest rates to rise at some time in the future.

Yield curves are widely used in the financial services industry. Two points that should be noted about a yield curve are that:

- Yields are **gross yields**, ignoring taxation (pre-tax yields).
- A yield curve is constructed for **'risk-free' debt securities**, such as government bonds. A yield curve therefore shows 'risk-free yields'.

As the name implies, risk-free debt is debt where the investor has no credit risk whatsoever, because it is certain that the borrower will repay the debt at maturity. Debt securities issued by governments with AAA credit ratings (see later) in their domestic currency by the government should be risk-free.

8.3 Bond valuation using the yield curve

Annual spot (valid on the day they are published) yield curves are published in the financial press.

The cost of new debt can be estimated by reference to a yield curve.

Example

A company wants to issue a bond that is redeemable at par in four years and pays interest at 6% of nominal value.

The annual spot yield curve for a bond of this class of risk is as follows:

Maturity	Yield
One year	3.0%
Two years	3.5%
Three years	4.2%
Four years	5.0%

Required

Calculate the price that the bond could be sold for (this is the amount that the company could raise) and then use this to calculate the gross redemption yield (yield to maturity, cost of debt).

Answer

An investor will receive a stream of cash flows from this bond and will discount each of those to decide how much he is willing to pay for them.

The first year flow will be discounted at 3.0%, the second year flow at 3.5% and so on. (Note that the two year rate of 3.5% does not mean that this is the rate in the second year. It means that this is the average annual rate for a flow in 2 years' time).

Year		Cash flow	Discount factor	PV (4%)
1	Interest	6	$1/1.03 = 0.971$	5.83
2	Interest	6	$1/1.035^2 = 0.934$	5.60
3	Interest	6	$1/042^3 = 0.884$	5.30
4	Interest + redemption	106	$1/1.05^4 = 0.823$	87.21
	Market value			103.94

The company would need to issue a $100 nominal value bond for $103.94.

The cost of debt (gross redemption yield) of the bond can be calculated in the usual way by calculating the IRR of the flows that the company faces.

Year	Cash flow		Try 4%		Try 6%	
			Discount factor	PV	Discount factor	PV
0	Market value	(103.94)	1.000	(103.94)	1.000	(103.94)
1	Interest	6.00	0.962	5.77	0.943	5.66
2	Interest	6.00	0.925	5.55	0.890	5.34
3	Interest	6.00	0.889	5.33	0.840	5.04
4	Interest + redemption	106.00	0.855	90.61	0.792	83.96
	NPV			+ 3.32		(3.94)

Using interpolation, the before-tax cost of the debt is:

$$4\% + \frac{3.32}{(3.32 + 3.94)} \times (6 - 4)\% = 4.91\%$$

The cost of the debt is therefore estimated as 4.91%. This is the average cost that the entity is paying for this debt.

8.4 Estimating the yield curve

A yield curve was provided in the previous section. The next issue to consider is how these are constructed.

This session looks at a technique called "bootstrapping". There are other methods but the examiner has indicated they are beyond the scope of the P4 syllabus.

Example

There are three bonds in issue for a given risk class.

All three bonds pay interest annually in arrears and are to be redeemed for par at maturity.

Relevant information about the three bonds is as follows:

Bond	Maturity	Coupon rate	Market value
A	1 year	6.0%	102
B	2 years	5.0%	101
C	3 years	4.0%	97

Required

Construct the yield curve that is implied by this data.

a

Answer

Step 1 – Calculate the rate for one year maturity

Work out the rate of return for bond A.

The investor will pay $102 for a cash flow in one year of $106.

This gives an IRR of (106/102) -1 = 0.0392 or 3.92%

Step 2 – Calculate the rate for two year maturity

The market value bond B is made up of the present value of the year one cash flow discounted at 3.92% (from step 1) and the present value of the two year cash flow discounted at an unknown rate.

This can be modelled as follows:

t		Cash flow	Discount factor	PV (4%)	
1	Interest	5	1/1.0392	4.81	
2	Interest + redemption	105	$1/(1+r)^2$	96.19	(Balancing figure)
	Market value (given)			101.00	

Therefore:

$$105 \times 1/(1+r)^2 = 96.19$$

Rearranging:

$$105/96.19 = (1 + r)^2$$

$$r = \sqrt{105/96.19} - 1 = 0.0448 \text{ or } 4.48\%$$

Step 3 – Calculate the rate for three year maturity

The market value of the three year bond is made up of the present value of the year one cash flow discounted at 3.92% (from step 1), the present value of the two year cash flow discounted at 4.48% (from step 2) and the present value of the three year cash flow discounted at an unknown rate.

This can be modelled as follows:

t		Cash flow	Discount factor	PV (4%)	
1	Interest	4	1/1.0392	3.85	
2	Interest	4	$1/1.0448^2$	3.66	
3	Interest + redemption	104	$1/(1+r)^3$	89.49	(Balancing figure)
	Market value (given)			97.00	

Therefore:

$$104 \times 1/(1+r)^3 = 89.49$$

Rearranging:

$$104/89.49 = (1 + r)^3$$

$$r = \sqrt[3]{104/89.49} - 1 = 0.051 \text{ or } 5.1\%$$

Step 4 – Summarise in a table

Maturity	Yield
1 year	3.92%
2 year	4.48%
3 year	5.1%

Credit risk

9 Credit risk

9.1 Introduction

The cost of a company's debt is the rate of return that lenders require for lending to that company. In other words, the interest yield on corporate debt is higher than the yield on risk-free debt with the same maturity.

The higher yield is to compensate investors in corporate bonds for the fact that the debt is not risk-free. The company might default.

Example

The interest rate on a sterling bond of ABC Company with two-years to maturity will be higher than the interest yield on a two-year UK government bond.

The amount that a lender requires is made up of:

Risk free rate (for debt of that maturity) + credit risk premium

Credit risk (default risk) is the risk that a party to whom cash is loaned will not be able to service the debt. A lender demands an extra rate of return to compensate for this extra risk.

The credit risk premium is called a 'spread'. The spread is the difference between the cost of debt under consideration and the risk-free rate of return. (Note that the credit spread can be estimated by comparing the cost of debt for a given bond to the risk free rate of the same maturity).

Example

A company wishes to issue a 5 year bond.

The risk-free return on five-year government bonds is 5.4%.

The spread for the company's five-year bonds is 80 basis points

Therefore the yield on the company bonds is: = 5.40% + 0.80% = 6.20%.

(**Note**: 1 basis point = 0.01% and 100 basis points = 1%, so 80 bp = 0.80%).

The size of spreads

The size of the spread allows for the additional risk in the debt that is not risk-free. The spread is therefore higher for debt that has a higher risk for investors or lenders.

9.2 Credit ratings

Many large companies are given a credit rating by a credit rating agency, such as Moody's, Standard & Poor's and Fitch. (Strictly, the company's debt is given a credit rating, but it is common to speak of companies having a credit rating rather than the debt having a credit rating.)

- The top credit rating is a 'triple-A' credit rating.
- Spreads are lowest for the top credit ratings, and higher for lower credit ratings.

Each credit rating agency uses its own credit rating system. The most well-known are the rating systems of Standard & Poor's and Moody's. Their ratings for bonds are set out in the table below.

	Standard & Poor's	Moody's
Investment grade		
Prime	AAA	Aaa
High grade:	AA+	Aa1
	AA	Aa2
	AA–	Aa3
Upper medium grade	A+	A1
	A–	A2
	AA	A3
Lower medium grade	BBB+	Baa1
	BBB	Baa2
	BBB–	Baa3
Sub-investment grade ('junk')		
Speculative	BB+	Ba1
	BB	Ba2
	BB–	Ba3
Highly speculative	B+	B1
	B	B2
	B–	B3
Substantial risks	CCC+	Caa1
Extremely speculative	CCC	Caa2
	CCC–	Caa3
In default/low prospect of recovery	CC	Ca
	C	
	D	D

Sub-investment grade debt, also called 'junk bonds', is a speculative investment for the lender or bondholder, and yields required by investors are normally much higher than on investment grade debt.

What drives credit ratings?

The rating agencies each employ their own risk models. These models assign a score in respect of variables which the agency has chosen as being vital indicators of credit risk. These are then multiplied by constants used to reflect the relative importance of each variable and the amounts totalled to give a credit score. This score is then expressed as a credit rating.

Key variables might include:

- firm size;
- financial gearing;
- the risk characteristics of the industry;
- the risk characteristics of the country;
- standing of the company compared to others in the same industry and country;
- perceived strength of management;
- asset backing of the company;
- cash generating ability.

9.3 Cost of debt from term structure and credit spreads

Example

Yield spreads on US bonds for companies in the construction industry are as follows:

Spreads:			**Years to maturity**			
Rating	**1**	**2**	**3**	**5**	**7**	**10**
AAA/ Aaa	2	4	10	15	20	25
AA+/Aa1	6	10	16	24	30	38
AA/Aa2	9	15	24	34	44	55
AA-/Aa3	15	24	30	40	**52**	64
A+/A1	24	35	45	60	75	88
A/A2	32	45	58	78	95	112
A-/A3	45	60	75	100	120	142

Example

A US company wishes to issue a 7 year bond.

The credit rating for the bonds is expected to be AA–

The yield curve shows the risk-free rate on US government bonds ('Treasuries') to be 6.6%

The yield on the company's bonds will be 6.6% + 0.52% = 7.12%.

9.4 Expected loss

The degree of credit risk reflects the expected loss from a loan. The expected loss is a function of the loss given default (LGD) and the probability of default (p(d)). This is a simple expected value calculation.

The loss given default is the amount that could be lost if a lender defaults. It is not necessarily the amount of the loan as the lender might hold some form of collateral or the borrower may be able to pay a percentage of the amount owed.

Example

A bank has loaned $10,000,000 to X Inc.

The bank holds collateral worth $8,000,000.

The probability of default is estimated at 2%.

The expected loss is = LGD × p(d) = (10,000,000 – $8,000,000) × 2% = $40,000.

The loss given default might be presented as a percentage. The same information might be presented as a recovery rate (100% – LGD%).

Example

A bank has loaned $10,000,000 to X Inc. The expected recovery is 80% due to collateral held.

The probability of default is estimated at 2%.

The expected loss is = LGD × p(d) = (10,000,000 – (80% of $10,000,000) × 2% = $40,000.

CHAPTER 11

Financing of projects

Contents

Choosing the method of financing an investment

- Theories about selecting the financing method for an investment
- Static trade-off theory
- Pecking order theory
- Market timing theory
- Agency effects on capital structure

1 Choosing the method of financing an investment

1.1 Theories about selecting the financing method for an investment

Capital investments have to be financed, and management must choose which method of financing they will use. There are different theories about how the method of financing is decided. These include:

- static trade-off theory
- pecking order theory
- market timing theory.

There is also a view that the choice of financing method is affected by agency costs.

These differing theories are considered in this section.

1.2 Static trade-off theory

Static trade-off theory argues that for each company there is an optimal capital structure, with an optimal level of gearing.

There is a trade-off between the benefits of taking on more debt and the costs of higher indebtedness.

- The benefits of taking on debt (rather than equity) are mainly in the tax relief that is obtained on debt interest. Modigliani and Miller have argued that although the cost of equity rises as gearing increases, the tax relief on debt means that the company's weighted average cost of capital falls as gearing rises. It is therefore beneficial to take in more debt and increase gearing up to the point where the marginal costs of extra debt start to exceed the marginal benefits of extra debt.
- The marginal costs of extra debt are related to the greater risks from 'financial distress.' If lenders perceive that a company with high levels of debt could be in financial distress (and in danger of failing to make payments of interest and repayments of loan capital on schedule), it becomes much more difficult to raise extra debt finance. The cost of debt might therefore increase substantially to compensate a lender for the high credit risk.

The optimal gearing level for a company is reached at a point where:

- the marginal benefits of taking on additional debt capital
- equals the marginal costs of taking on the extra debt.

The optimal gearing level varies between companies, depending on their profitability. A very profitable company can take on higher gearing because the marginal costs of financial distress will not become significant until the gearing level is very high.

For a company with low profitability, the situation is different. These companies provide low returns to their shareholders, and increasing the gearing level by borrowing more would increase the risks of bankruptcy and the cost of borrowing. Companies with low profits will therefore try to avoid additional borrowing, and they will also be reluctant to incur the costs of making new equity issues. To finance an investment, they will therefore rely on retained profits. They might even decide against investing in a capital project with a positive NPV unless they can finance it with funds from retained profits.

Static trade-off theory summarised

Static trade-off theory therefore states that:

- Companies have an optimal level of gearing.
- In choosing the method of financing for a new investment, they will try to maintain or achieve the optimal gearing level.
- The optimal gearing level is higher for companies with high profits than companies with low profits.
- This means that there is a **positive** correlation between profitability and gearing level.

1.3 Pecking order theory

Pecking order theory takes a different view of gearing and methods of financing new investments. It was put forward by Myers in 1984 as a challenge to static trade-off theory.

This theory states that companies show preferences for the source of finance that they use. There is an order of preference or 'pecking order'.

- 1st. The source of finance that is preferred most is **retained earnings**.
- 2nd. **Debt capital** is the source of finance second in the order of preference.
- 3rd. **New equity capital** (an issue of new shares) is the least preferred source of finance for investment.

This means that if a company has an opportunity to invest in a capital project with a positive NPV, it will prefer to fund the project from retained profits. If it is unable to do this, it will look for debt capital to finance the investment. Only if retained profits and debt capital are unavailable (because cash flows are weak and profitability is low) will the company consider a new issue of shares.

Companies are likely to choose a long-term dividend policy that will allow them to finance future investments largely through retained earnings.

The reasons for the pecking order of preferences for sources of finance can be explained by practical considerations.

- Using retained earnings is convenient. If a company wants to finance a new investment with equity, it is much simpler and cheaper to use retained earnings than to arrange a new share issue. Retained earnings are also much more convenient than new borrowing.
- If a company cannot finance an investment with retained earnings, it will prefer new borrowing to a new issue of shares because borrowing is cheaper. It is cheaper to arrange a loan than to issue new shares. The cost of debt is also less because of the tax relief on interest payments.

Pecking order theory states that the gearing of a company is the result of a series of financing decisions based on these preferences for sources of finance. An optimal level of gearing does not exist, and companies do not try to achieve an optimal gearing level.

Pecking order theory summarised

Pecking order theory therefore states that:

- Companies do not have an optimal level of gearing.
- In choosing the method of financing for a new investment, they have an order of preference: retained earnings followed by new debt capital followed by an issue of new shares.
- Companies with high profits can rely on retained profits as a source of finance more than companies with low profits.
- This means that there is a **negative** correlation between profitability and gearing level.

1.4 Market timing theory

Market timing theory states that the choice of financing method for companies can be driven by opportunities in the capital markets. These opportunities occur because of 'asymmetries of information'. These occur when the managers of a company have more information and better information about the company than shareholders and other investors.

Management should know when the future prospects for the company are better than investors are expecting, and when the prospects for the future are worse than investors are expecting. Company management might therefore recognise occasions when the company's shares are currently under-valued or over-valued.

- Companies will therefore wish to make a new issue of shares when they consider the share price to be over-valued.
- They will consider share repurchases when they consider the share price to be under-valued.

Taking advantage of opportunities in the market to issue new shares or buy back existing shares affects the gearing level. A company therefore does not have a target optimal gearing level. Its financing decisions are determined more by market opportunity and market timing.

1.5 Agency effects on capital structure

Agency theory can be used to explain the capital structure of a company and its choices of financing for new investment. Agency theory, which was developed by Jensen and Meckling (1976), states that the governance of a company is based on conflicts of interest between the company's owners (shareholders), its managers and major providers of debt finance.

Each of these groups has different interests and objectives.

- The **shareholders** want to increase their income and wealth. Their interest is with the returns that the company will provide in the form of dividends, and also in the value of their shares. The value of their shares depends on the long-term financial prospects for the company. Shareholders are therefore concerned about dividends, but they are even more concerned about long-term profitability and financial prospects, because these affect the value of their shares.
- The **directors and managers** are employed to run the company on behalf of the shareholders. However, if the managers do not own shares in the company, they have no direct interest in future returns for shareholders, or in the value of the shares. Unless they own shares, or unless their remuneration is linked to profits or share values, their main interests are likely to be the size of their remuneration package, and other benefits from their job and position such as their status as company managers.
- The **major providers of debt** have an interest in sound financial management by the company's managers, so that the company will be able to pay its debts in full and on time. Major lenders will often be concerned that a company will borrow more because the cost of borrowing is fairly low, and invest the money in high-risk ventures.

These conflicts of interest can have implications for capital gearing and preferences for financing method.

- Shareholders might prefer debt finance as a new source of funding. When managers own shares in the company, a new issue of shares might dilute their interest in the company's equity, and other shareholders should want to prevent this from happening. Borrowing to finance growth rather than relying on equity also reduces the amount of free cash for managers to spend on personal interests and benefits.
- Providers of debt capital might be worried by the fact that debt capital gives shareholders an incentive to invest in high-risk projects. They might therefore oppose new borrowing by a company when they think that this will put their interest (the security of their investment and returns) at risk.

Jensen and Meckling argued that the 'optimal' capital structure for a company is obtained by trading off not just the marginal benefits and marginal costs of extra debt (as suggested by static trade-off theory) but also by trading off the 'agency costs' of additional debt and the 'agency costs' of additional equity.

Cost of capital and gearing

- The traditional view of gearing and WACC
- The Modigliani-Miller propositions: ignoring corporate taxation
- The Modigliani-Miller view: allowing for corporate taxation

2 Cost of capital and gearing

For a given level of annual cash profits before interest and tax, the value of a company (equity + debt) is maximised at the level of gearing where WACC is lowest. This should also be the level of gearing that optimises the wealth of equity shareholders.

The question is therefore:
How does a change in gearing affect the WACC, and is there a level of gearing where the WACC is minimised?

The most important analysis of gearing and the cost of capital, for the purpose of your examination, is the analysis provided by Modigliani and Miller that allows for tax relief on debt interest.

However, the traditional view of WACC and gearing, and Modigliani and Miller's propositions ignoring tax relief on debt are also described briefly.

2.1 The traditional view of gearing and WACC

The traditional view of gearing is that there is an optimum level of gearing for a company. This is the level of gearing at which the WACC is minimised.

- As gearing increases, the cost of equity rises. However, as gearing increases, there is a greater proportion of debt capital in the capital structure, and the cost of debt is cheaper than the cost of equity. Up to a certain level of gearing, the effect of having more debt capital has a bigger effect on the WACC than the rising cost of equity, so that the WACC falls as gearing increases.
- However, when gearing rises still further, the increase in the cost of equity has a greater effect than the larger proportion of cheap debt capital, and the WACC starts to rise.

The traditional view of gearing is therefore that an optimum level of gearing exists, where WACC is minimised and the value of the company is maximised.

Traditional view of gearing and the WACC

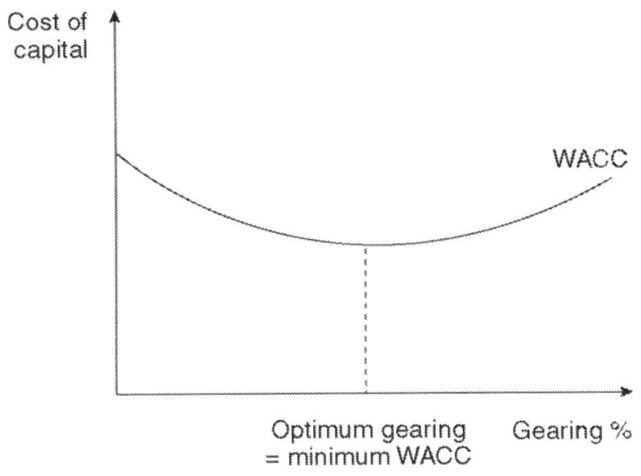

2.2 The Modigliani-Miller propositions: ignoring corporate taxation

The traditional view of gearing and WACC was challenged by Modigliani and Miller in the 1950s. Initially, their arguments were based on the assumption that corporate taxation, and the tax relief on interest, could be ignored.

You do not need to know Modigliani and Miller's arguments, only the conclusions they reached. They argued that if corporate taxation is ignored, an increase in gearing will have the following effect:

- As the level of gearing increases, there is a greater proportion of cheaper debt capital in the capital structure of the firm.
- However, the cost of equity rises as gearing increases.
- As gearing increases, the net effect of the greater proportion of cheaper debt and the higher cost of equity is that the WACC remains unchanged.
- **The WACC is the same at all levels of financial gearing**.
- The total value of the company is therefore the same at all levels of financial gearing

Modigliani and Miller therefore reached the conclusion that the level of gearing is irrelevant for the value of a company. There is no optimum level of gearing that a company should be trying to achieve.

Modigliani-Miller view of gearing and the WACC: no taxation

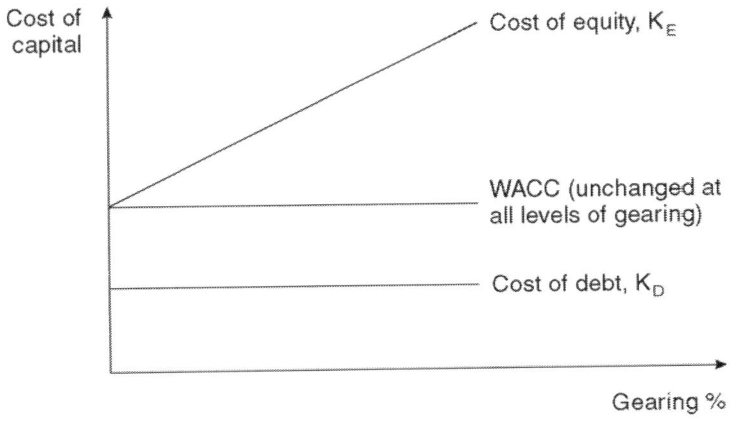

Modigliani and Miller's propositions: ignoring taxation

Modigliani and Miller's arguments, ignoring taxation, can be summarised as two propositions.

- **Proposition 1**. The WACC is constant at all levels of gearing. For companies with identical annual profits and identical business risk characteristics, their total market value (equity plus debt) will be the same regardless of differences in gearing between the companies.
- **Proposition 2**. The cost of equity rises as the gearing increases. The cost of equity will rise to a level such that, given no change in the cost of debt, the WACC remains unchanged.

Modigliani-Miller formulae: ignoring taxation

There are three formulae for the Modigliani and Miller theory, ignoring corporate taxation. These are shown below. The letter 'U' refers to an ungeared company (all-equity company) and the letter 'G' refers to a geared company.

(1) **WACC**

The WACC in a geared company and the WACC in an identical but ungeared (all-equity) company are the same:

$WACC_G = WACC_U$

This formula expresses a part of proposition 1.

(2) **Total value of the company (equity plus debt capital)**

The total value of an ungeared company is equal to the total value of an identical geared company (combined value of equity + debt capital):

$V_G = V_U$

This formula expresses another part of proposition 1.

(3) **Cost of equity**

The cost of equity in a geared company is higher than the cost of equity in an ungeared company, by an amount equal to:

- the difference between the cost of equity in the ungeared company and the cost of debt ($K_{EU} - K_D$)
- multiplied by the ratio of the market value of debt to the market value of equity in the geared company (D/E).

$$K_{EG} = K_{EU} + \frac{D}{E}(K_{EU} - K_D)$$

This formula expresses proposition 2.

Example

An all-equity company has a market value of $150 million and a cost of equity of 10%. It borrows $50 million of debt finance, costing 6%, and uses this to buy back and cancel $50 million of equity. Tax relief on debt interest is ignored.

Required

According to Modigliani and Miller, if taxation is ignored, what would be the effect of the higher gearing on (a) the WACC (b) the total market value of the company and (c) the cost of equity in the company?

Answer

According to Modigliani and Miller:

(a) **WACC**. The WACC in the company is unchanged, at 10%.

(b) **Total value**. The total market value of the company with gearing is identical to the market value of the company when it was all equity, at $150 million. This now consists of $50 million in debt and $100 million equity ($150 million – $50 million of debt)

(c) **Cost of equity**. The cost of equity in the geared company is

$$10\% + \left[\frac{50}{100} \times (10 - 6)\right]\% = 12.0\%$$

Example

A company has $500 million of equity capital and $100 million of debt capital, all at current market value. The cost of equity is 14% and the cost of the debt capital is 8%.

The company is planning to raise $100 million by issuing new shares. It will use the money to redeem all the debt capital.

Required

According to Modigliani and Miller, if the company issues new equity and redeems all its debt capital, what will be the cost of equity of the company after the debt has been redeemed? Assume that there is no corporate taxation.

Answer

In the previous example, the Modigliani-Miller formulae were used to calculate a cost of equity in a geared company, given the cost of equity in the company when it is ungeared (all-equity). This example works the other way, from the cost of equity in a geared company to a cost of equity in an ungeared company. The same formulae can be used.

Using the known values for the geared company, we can calculate the cost of equity in the ungeared company after the debt has been redeemed.

$K_{EG} = K_{EU} + D/E\ [K_{EU} - K_D]$

$14.0 = K_{EU} + 100/500\ [K_{EU} - 8.0]$

$1.2\ K_{EU} = 14.0 + 1.6$

$\mathbf{K_{EU} = 13.0\%}$ (15.6/1.2).

2.3 The Modigliani-Miller view: allowing for corporate taxation

Modigliani and Miller revised their arguments to allow for the fact that there is tax relief on interest. You do not need to know the arguments they used to reach their conclusions, but you must know what their conclusions were. You should also know and be able to apply the formulae described below.

(The formula for the cost of equity is given in the formula sheet in your examination, so you do not need to learn it.)

Modigliani and Miller argued that allowing for corporate taxation and tax relief on interest, an increase in gearing will have the following effect:

- As the level of gearing increases, there is a greater proportion of cheaper debt capital in the capital structure of the firm. However, the cost of equity rises as gearing increases.
- As gearing increases, the net effect of the greater proportion of cheaper debt and the higher cost of equity is that the WACC becomes lower. Increases in gearing result in a reduction in the WACC.
- The WACC is therefore at its lowest at the highest practicable level of gearing. (There are practical limitations on gearing that stop it from reaching very high levels. For example, lenders will not provide more debt capital except at a much higher cost, due to the high credit risk).
- The total value of the company is therefore higher for a geared company than for an identical all-equity company. The value of a company will rise, for a given level of annual cash profits before interest, as its gearing increases.

Modigliani and Miller therefore reached the conclusion that because of tax relief on interest, there is an optimum level of gearing that a company should be trying to achieve. A company should be trying to make its gearing as high as possible, to the maximum practicable level, in order to maximise its value.

Modigliani-Miller view of gearing and the WACC: with taxation

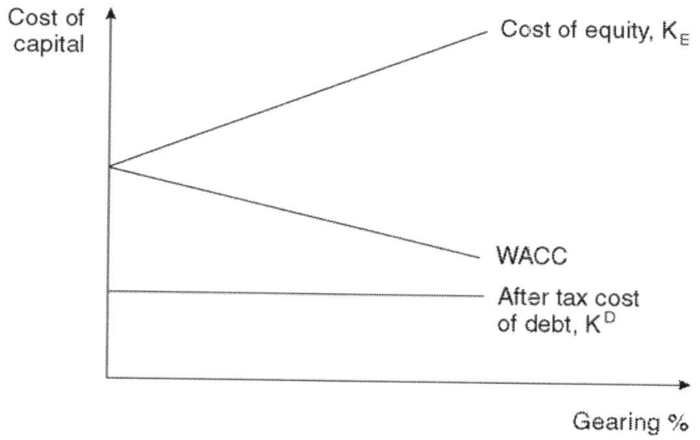

Modigliani and Miller's propositions: allowing for taxation

Modigliani and Miller's arguments, allowing taxation, can be summarised as two propositions.

- **Proposition 1**. The WACC falls continually as the level of gearing increases. In theory, the lowest cost of capital is where gearing is 100% and the company is financed entirely by debt. (Modigliani and Miller recognised, however, that 'financial distress' factors have an effect at high levels of gearing, increasing the cost of debt and the WACC.) For companies with identical annual profits and identical business risk characteristics, their total market value (equity plus debt) will be higher for a company with higher gearing.
- **Proposition 2**. The cost of equity rises as the gearing increases. There is a positive correlation between the cost of equity and gearing (as measured by the debt/equity ratio).

Modigliani-Miller formulae: allowing for taxation

There are three formulae for the Modigliani and Miller theory, allowing for corporate taxation. These are shown below. The letter 'U' refers to an ungeared company (all-equity company) and the letter 'G' refers to a geared company.

(1) **WACC**

The WACC in a geared company is lower than the WACC in an all-equity company, by a factor of $1-\frac{Dt}{(D+E)}$.

$$WACC_G = WACC_U\left[1-\frac{Dt}{(D+E)}\right]$$

This formula expresses a part of proposition 1.

(2) **Value of a company**

The total value of a geared company (equity + debt) is equal to the total value of an identical ungeared company plus the value of the 'tax shield'. This is the market value of the debt in the geared company multiplied by the rate of taxation (Dt).

$$V_G = V_U + Dt$$

where:

V_G = value of geared company

V_U = value of an identical but ungeared (all-equity) company

D = market value of the debt in the geared company

t = the rate of taxation on company profits.

This formula expresses another part of proposition 1.

(3) **Cost of equity**

The cost of equity in a geared company is higher than the cost of equity in an ungeared company, by a factor equal to:

- the difference between the cost of equity in the ungeared company and the cost of debt, $(K_{EU} - K_D)$
- multiplied by the ratio $(1-t)\times\frac{D}{E}$.

$$K_{EG} = K_{EU} + (1-t)(K_{EU} - K_D)\frac{D}{E}$$

This formula expresses proposition 2. It is given to you in your examination, in a formula sheet. Although you do not need to learn the formula, you should become familiar with it, and know how to use it.

Example

An all-equity company has a market value of $60 million and a cost of equity of 8%. It borrows $20 million of debt finance, costing 5%, and uses this to buy back and cancel $20 million of equity. The rate of taxation on company profits is 25%.

According to Modigliani and Miller:

(a) **Market value**

The market value of the company after the increase in its gearing will be:

$$V_G = V_U + Dt$$

V_G = $60 million + ($20 million × 0.25) = $75 million.

The market value of the debt capital is $20 million; therefore the market value of the equity in the geared company is $55 million ($75 million – $20 million).

(b) **WACC of the geared company**

The WACC of the company after the increase in its gearing is calculated as follows:

$$WACC_G = WACC_U\left[1 - \frac{Dt}{(D+E)}\right]$$

$$WACC_G = 8\%\left[1 - \frac{(\$20\text{ million} \times 25\%)}{(\$65\text{ million})}\right] = 8\%\,(0.9231) = 7.38\%$$

(c) **Cost of equity in the geared company**

$$K_{EG} = K_{EU} + (1-t)(K_{EU} - K_D)\frac{D}{E}$$

K_{EG} = 8% + [(1 – 0.25) (8 – 5) 20/45] = 8% + 1% = 9%

Check: the WACC can now be calculated as follows:

Source of finance	Market value	Cost	Market value x Cost
	$ million	r	MV x r
Equity	45.00	9.00	405
Debt (after-tax cost)	20.00	3.75	75
	65.00		480

$$WACC = \frac{480}{65.00} = 7.38\%$$

Change in gearing, the WACC and capital investment appraisal

- Modigliani and Miller with taxation: from one level of gearing to another
- The method
- Relevance for capital investment appraisal

3 Change in gearing, the WACC and capital investment appraisal

3.1 Modigliani and Miller with taxation: from one level of gearing to another

When a company is considering a major new capital investment project (where the business risk is similar to the risk with the company's other business operations), the method of financing the investment might alter the company's gearing. For example, if a project is financed entirely by new debt capital, its gearing level will increase.

- A change in gearing will alter the cost of equity (Modigliani and Miller proposition 2).
- There might be a change in the cost of debt, where the gearing level rises to such a high level that 'financial distress' concerns make debt capital more expensive. However, at lower levels of gearing it is assumed that the cost of debt is unaffected by changes in the gearing level.
- There will be a reduction in the WACC (Modigliani and Miller proposition 1).

If the project is evaluated using the WACC to estimate the NPV, the new WACC should be used for the NPV evaluation.

This means that when a new capital project will result in a change in gearing, it is necessary to calculate a new WACC before going on to the NPV calculations.

The Modigliani and Miller formulae can be used to do this. The explanation that follows concentrates on the formula for the cost of equity, because this is the formula that you will be given in the examination.

3.2 The method

The approach should be as follows:

- **Step 1**. Start with the company at its original level of gearing. You should be given the value of the company (the value of its equity and the value of its debt capital) and the cost of its equity and debt capital.
- **Step 2**. Use these values to calculate the value of a comparable ungeared company, and the cost of equity in the ungeared company. Use the Modigliani and Miller formulae to do this.
- You now have the cost of equity in a comparable ungeared company.

- **Step 3**. Use these values for the ungeared company to work out values for the company at its new level of gearing: total value, value of equity, WACC and cost of equity.

Example

A company has a total current value of $100 million, consisting of $80 million equity and $20 million of debt capital. The cost of equity is 10% and the pre-tax cost of the debt capital is 6%. The rate of tax on company profits is 25%.

The company proposes to borrow an additional $20 million of debt capital, and use the money to buy back and cancel $20 million of its equity.

Required

According to Modigliani and Miller, what will be the following values for the company at its new level of gearing?

(a) Its total value, divided into a value for the equity and a value for the debt capital

(b) Its WACC

(c) The cost of its equity capital.

This is a long example, but you should work through the solution carefully.

Answer

(a) **Total value of the company**

(i) Step 1: Value of a similar all-equity company.

We have the current value of the geared company, which is $100 million, consisting of $80 million equity and $20 million debt capital. We can calculate the cost of a similar company that is all-equity financed.

$V_G = V_U + Dt$

100 million = V_U + (20 million × 0.25)

V_U = 95 million.

(ii) Step 2: Value of the company at the new level of gearing.

The company will be replacing $20 million of equity with $20 million of debt capital, so in the new gearing structure, debt capital increases.

The market value of the debt will be $20 million + $20 million = $40 million.

We can calculate the total cost of the company at its new gearing level, using the same MM formula.

$V_G = V_U + Dt$

V_G = 95 million + (40 million × 0.25)

= 105 million.

The total value of the company at the new gearing level will be $105 million. Of this, $40 million will be debt capital; therefore the value of the remaining equity will be $65 million.

(b) **WACC**

(i) Step 1: WACC of a similar all-equity company.

The WACC of the company at its current level of gearing is calculated as follows:

Source of finance	Market value	Cost	Market value x Cost
	$ million	r	MV x r
Equity	80.00	0.10	8.00
Debt (after-tax cost)	20.00	0.045	0.90
	100.00		8.90

WACC = 8.9/100 = 0.089 or 8.9%.

We can use the MM formula for WACC to calculate what the WACC would be in a similar ungeared company.

The WACC of a similar ungeared company is:

$$0.089 = WACC_U \times \left[1 - \frac{20 \times 0.25}{(20 + 80)}\right]$$

$0.089 = 0.95\ WACC_U$

$WACC_U = 0.09368$

(ii) Step 2: WACC of the company at the new level of gearing.

Having established the WACC in an all-equity company, we can now use the same formula to calculate the WACC in the company at its new level of gearing, with $40 million debt and $65 million of equity.

(The value of equity and debt capital at the new level of gearing were calculated in (a)).

$$WACC_G = 0.09368 \times \left[1 - \frac{40 \times 0.25}{(40 + 65)}\right]$$

$WACC_G = 0.09368 \times 0.90476$

$WACC_G = 0.085 = 8.5\%$.

(c) **Cost of equity**

(i) Step 1: Cost of equity of a similar all-equity company.

A similar approach is taken for calculating the cost of equity. We start by calculating the cost of equity in a similar all-equity company, using the MM formula for Proposition 2. We know the value of K_{EG} and we need to calculate a value for K_{EU}.

In the original geared company, the value of equity is \$80 million and the value of debt capital is \$20 million.

The cost of equity in a similar all-equity company is calculated as follows:

$$K_{EG} = K_{EU} + (1-t)(K_{EU} - K_D)\frac{D}{E}$$

$10 = K_{EU} + [(1 - 0.25)\ (K_{EU} - 6)\ 20/80]$

$10 = K_{EU} + 0.1875\ K_{EU} - 1.125$

$1.1875\ K_{EU} = 11.125$

$K_{EU} = 9.3684.$

(ii) Step 2: Cost of equity of the company at the new level of gearing.

Having calculated the cost of equity in a similar all-equity company, we can now calculate the cost of equity in the company at its new level of gearing. Debt capital is \$40 million and equity is \$65 million.

(The value of equity and debt capital at the new level of gearing were calculated in (a).)

$$K_{EG} = K_{EU} + (1-t)(K_{EU} - K_D)\frac{D}{E}$$

$K_{EG} = 9.3684 + (1 - 0.25)\ (9.3684 - 6)\ 40/65$

$K_{EG} = 9.3684 + 1.5546 = 10.923$, say 10.9%.

3.3 Relevance for capital investment appraisal

The Modigliani and Miler formulae can be used to re-calculate the cost of equity and the WACC in a company where the level of gearing changes, provided there is no change in the overall business risk and the company is therefore similar in all respects except for its gearing.

When a company plans a new capital investment that will alter its gearing, without affecting its business risk profile, the MM formulae can be used to calculate the cost of equity and WACC at the new level of gearing. The new WACC can then be used as the discount rate for calculating the NPV of the proposed project.

If you are given an examination question of this type in your examination, you might prefer to use the formula for Proposition 2 (cost of equity) because this is given to you in the formula sheet in the examination, and you do not need to learn it.

Study the following example carefully.

Example

A US company has a current total market value of $12 billion, consisting of $10 billion of equity and $2 billion of debt capital. The debt capital will mature in four years' time. The current weighted average cost of capital is 6.5%.

The company is considering a new investment costing $3 billion, which it would finance entirely by $3 billion of new ten-year bonds.

The yield curve for US government bonds (Treasuries) shows that the risk-free cost of four-year debt is 4% and the risk-free cost of ten-year debt is 4.25%. The credit rating on the company's current debt capital is AA, but if the new bond issue takes place there is a 75% probability that all the company's debt will be re-rated to AA- and a 25% probability that all the company's debt will be re-rated to A+. (This applies to both the existing debt and the new bonds.)

The spreads for yields on corporate bonds above the US Treasuries yield curve are as follows:

Credit rating	**Spreads (basis points)**	
	4-year bonds	**10-year bonds**
AA	30	50
AA -	40	60
A +	45	70

The rate of taxation on company profits is 30%

Required
Calculate the weighted average cost of capital in the company if the project goes ahead and is financed entirely by ten-year bonds. Assume that there will be no change in the company's business risk.

Answer

Total value of the company

In the previous example, it was possible to re-calculate the total value of the company using the Modigliani and Miller formula $V_G = V_U + Dt$.

In this example, this is not possible, because the company is raising additional debt capital. The MM formula applies only when the size of the company is unchanged, and equity replaces debt or debt replaces equity. The formula cannot be used when additional debt capital is raised.

An assumption will therefore be made (even though it is unsatisfactory) that when the company obtains its additional debt capital of $3 billion, the value of the equity will be unchanged at $10 billion.

Preliminary workings

We need to calculate the current cost of equity in the company, in order to use the MM formula for Proposition 2. We know the current WACC which is 6.5%. We also know that the current credit rating for the four-year debt capital is AA, which means that the pre-tax cost of debt is the risk-free yield of 4.00% plus a spread of 30 basis points. The pre-tax cost of debt is therefore 4.30% and the after-tax cost of debt is 4.30% (1 – 0.30) = 3.01%.

We now have enough data to calculate the **current cost of equity**.

The WACC, which is 6.5%, is calculated as follows:

Source of finance	**Market value**	**Cost**	**Market value × Cost**
	$ billion	%	MV × r
Equity	10.0	r	10r
Debt	2.0	3.01	6.02
	12.0		10r + 6.02

$$\text{WACC} = 6.5\% = \frac{10r + 6.02}{12}\%$$

6.5 (12) = 10r + 6.02
10r = 71.98
r = 7.198%

The current cost of equity is 7.198%.

We also need to calculate the **cost of debt in the company after the new bond issue**.

	If AA -		**If A +**	
	4 year	**10 year**	**4 year**	**10 year**
Risk-free	4.00	4.25	4.00	4.25
Spread	0.40	0.60	0.45	0.70
Pre-tax cost	4.40	4.85	4.45	4.95

We can calculate a weighted average pre-tax cost of the debt capital, as follows:

	Market value	**AA -**		**A +**	
	$bn	**Cost**	**Cost × MV**	**Cost**	**Cost × MV**
4 year	2	4.40	8.80	4.45	8.90
10 year	3	4.85	14.55	4.95	14.85
	5		23.35		23.75

Weighted average before-tax cost of debt if credit rating is AA - = 23.35/5 = 4.67%.
Weighted average before-tax cost of debt if credit rating is A + = 23.75/5 = 4.75%.

Expected weighted average before tax cost of debt = (0.75 × 4.67) + (0.25 × 4.75)% = 4.69%.

Expected weighted average after-tax cost of debt = 4.69% (1 – 0.30) = 3.283%.

Calculate the cost of equity in the company after the new bond issue

Step 1. Calculate the cost of equity in an ungeared company at the current level of gearing. We know that the current cost of equity at the current level of gearing is 7.198%.

$$K_{EG} = K_{EU} + (1-t)(K_{EU} - K_D)\frac{D}{E}$$

$7.198 = K_{EU} + [(1 - 0.30)\ (K_{EU} - 4.30)\ 2/10]$

$7.198 = K_{EU} + 0.14\ K_{EU} - 0.602$
$1.14\ K_{EU} = 7.8$
$K_{EU} = 6.842.$

Step 2. Calculate the cost of equity in the company at the new level of gearing, making the assumption about market value discussed above, but **assuming no change in the cost of debt**. (Changing the cost of debt in this calculation would produce an incorrect valuation for the cost of equity.)

$$K_{EG} = K_{EU} + (1-t)(K_{EU} - K_D)\frac{D}{E}$$

$K_{EG} = 6.842 + 0.890$

$K_{EG} = 7.732.$

Calculate the WACC at the new level of gearing

We can now calculate the WACC after the bond issue.

Source of finance	**Market value**	**Cost**	**Market value × Cost**
	$ billion	%	MV × r
Equity	10.0	7.732	77.320
Debt (weighted average)	5.0	3.283	16.415
	15.0		93.735

WACC = 93.735/15 = 6.249, say 6.25%.

A discount rate of 6.25% should be used to calculate the NPV of the proposed new capital investment.

Asset beta

- Changes in gearing, the cost of equity and equity beta factors
- Definition of asset beta
- The asset beta formula
- Using the asset beta formula
- The asset beta formula: changing from one level of gearing to another
- Calculating a project beta factor
- Estimating an equity beta factor for a private company

4 Asset beta

4.1 Changes in gearing, the cost of equity and equity beta factors

Modigliani and Miller's theories are used to demonstrate that as the level of gearing in a company increases, assuming no change in business risk, the cost of equity also increases. This also means that as gearing increases, the beta factor of the company's equity must also increase, since there is no change in the risk-free rate of return or the returns on the market portfolio.

Companies that are otherwise identical except for their level of gearing will therefore have different costs of equity and different equity beta factors.

Similarly, if a company changes its gearing level without changing its business risk profile, there will be a change in its cost of equity and equity beta factor.

4.2 Definition of asset beta

An asset beta is the beta factor that would be applied to a company's assets if financing risk is removed from the calculation. It is therefore a beta factor that applies to entire companies or individual projects. It provides a measure of the underlying business risk faced by the entire firm regardless of its financing structure.

An asset beta is sometimes called unlevered beta or ungeared beta, and could be described as the beta of equity in a company that is totally equity-financed.

4.3 The asset beta formula

Modigliani and Miller argued that there is a difference between the beta factor in an ungeared (all equity) company and the beta factor in a similar geared company. The beta factor in a totally ungeared company (the ungeared beta) is the asset beta for the firm.

The formula, adjusted for taxation, is:

$$\beta_A = \beta_{EG} \times \frac{E}{E + D(1-t)} + \beta_D \times \frac{D(1-t)}{E + D(1-t)}$$

where

β_A = the asset beta or ungeared beta

β_{EG} = the beta of the equity in a geared company

β_D = the beta of the debt capital in the geared company

E = the market value of the equity in the geared company

D = the market value of the debt capital in the geared company

t = the rate of taxation on profits (the rate of tax relief on interest payments on debt capital).

This formula is included in the formula sheet for your examination. You do not need to learn it, but you must be able to apply it.

For the purpose of examination questions, it is often assumed that debt capital in a company is risk-free. This is a simplifying assumption which makes the calculations much easier!

If it is assumed that debt is risk-free, the asset beta formula simplifies to:

$$\beta_A = \beta_{EG} \times \frac{E}{E + D(1-t)}$$

Modigliani and Miller therefore argued that the beta factor in an all-equity company is lower than the beta factor in an identical but geared company, by a factor of $\frac{E}{[E+D(1-t)]}$

Example

A company is all-equity financed, and its equity beta factor is 1.05. Its total market value is $240 million. This includes debt capital with a market value of $80 million.

It is assumed that the debt capital is risk-free. The rate of tax is 30%.

Required

Calculate the asset beta for the company.

Answer

Using the asset beta formula and assuming a risk-free cost of debt.
(meaning that $\beta_D = 0$):

$$\beta_A = 1.05 \times \frac{160}{160 + 80(1 - 0.30)}$$

$\beta_A = 1.05 \times 0.74074 = 0.778$

4.4 Using the asset beta formula

The asset beta formula might be used in the following circumstances:

- when a company uses the CAPM to estimate a cost of equity and WACC, in a situation where a capital expenditure project will change the gearing of the company
- to estimate the beta factor for a capital investment project (a project beta), where the gearing will be different from the company's current capital structure
- in order to estimate a cost of equity in a private company by comparing it with a similar public company.

4.5 The asset beta formula: changing from one level of gearing to another

A company might be planning a capital investment that will alter its level of gearing. In these cases, to work out the equity beta factor and cost of equity at the new level of gearing, it is necessary to calculate the asset beta first (the beta for a similar ungeared company).

To calculate a cost of equity using the CAPM, where the level of gearing changes, we can calculate the asset beta and then convert this asset beta to an equity beta on the basis of the new expected level of gearing.

The approach should be as follows:

- Start with the company at its original level of gearing. You should be given the value of the company (the value of its equity and the value of its debt capital) and the cost of its equity and debt capital, and the equity beta factor.
- You may assume, unless instructed otherwise, that the debt capital in the company is risk-free, and the simplified version of the asset beta formula can be used.
- Having calculated the asset beta, you can calculate a new equity beta for the company at its new level of gearing, using the same formula.

Example

A company has a total current value of $80 million, consisting of $60 million equity and $20 million of debt capital. The cost of equity is 12% and the pre-tax cost of the debt capital is 7%. The rate of tax on company profits is 30%. The equity beta factor is 0.925. The debt capital is risk-free. The return on the market portfolio is 13.67%.

Required
What will be the equity beta factor and the cost of equity in the company, if the company issues new equity to raise $10 million and uses this money to repay $10 million of debt?

a

Answer

The equity beta of the company at its current level of gearing is 0.925.

The asset beta of the company (the equity beta of a similar ungeared company) will be:

$$\beta_A = \beta_{EG} \times \frac{E}{E + D(1 - t)}$$

$\beta_A = 0.925 \times 60/[60 + 20\ (1 - 0.30)]$
$\beta_A = 0.925 \times 60/74$
$\beta_A = 0.75$

We can calculate the total value of the company if it is ungeared, using the data for the company at its current gearing level.

Total value of an all-equity company:

$V_G = V_U + Dt$
\$80 million = V_U + (\$20 million × 0.30)
V_U = \$74 million.

At the new level of gearing, the market value of the debt capital will be \$10 million (\$20 million minus \$10 million redeemed). We can calculate the total value of the company at the new gearing level, using the value of the company if it is ungeared.

$V_G = V_U + Dt$
V_G = \$74 million + (\$10 million × 0.30)
V_G = \$77 million.

Of this total value, \$10 million is debt capital; therefore the value of the equity is \$67 million.

We now have the information to calculate a beta factor for the equity at the new level of gearing. The asset beta was calculated earlier, and is 0.75.

$$\beta_A = \beta_{EG} \times \frac{E}{E + D(1 - t)}$$

$$0.75 = \beta_{EG} \times \frac{67}{67 + 10\,(1 - 0.30)}$$

$0.9054\ \beta_{EG} = 0.75$

$\beta_{EU} = 0.828$, say 0.83.

Using the CAPM, we can calculate the cost of equity at the new gearing level as:

7% + 0.83 (13.67 – 7.0)
= 12.5361, say 12.5%.

4.6 Calculating a project beta factor

The CAPM can be applied to capital expenditure appraisal. The cost of capital for a project can be determined according to the risk of the project. If the beta factor for a project can be determined, the CAPM can then be used to decide what the cost of capital for the project should be, allowing for its beta and systematic risk.

In addition, adjustments can be made for differences in gearing.

Example

An all-equity company operates in an industry where its beta factor is 0.90. It is considering whether to invest in a completely different industry. In this other industry, the average debt/equity ratio is 40% and the average beta factor is 1.25. The risk-free rate of return is 4% and the average market return is 7%. If the company does invest in this other industry, it will remain all-equity financed. The rate of taxation is 30%. Assume that debt is risk-free.

Required
What cost of capital should be used to evaluate the proposed investment?

Answer

The appropriate discount rate should be one that applies to the industry in which the investment will be made. We know that the geared beta in this industry is 1.25, with a debt: equity ratio of 0.40. We can calculate the asset beta (ungeared equity beta) for the industry as:

$$\beta_A = 1.25 \times \frac{60}{[60 + 40(1 - 0.30)]} = 1.25 \times \frac{60}{88} = 0.85$$

Since the company will be all-equity financed, the cost of equity to apply to the project is therefore:
4% + 0.85 (7 – 4)% = 6.55%.
Note: If the company has proposed to finance the project with some debt, the asset beta could be used to calculate a new geared beta for the appropriate level of gearing, and a new cost of equity and new WACC could be calculated.

4.7 Estimating an equity beta factor for a private company

The asset beta formula can also be used to estimate the equity beta for a private company (and its cost of equity) where the private company is comparable in size, business mix and business risk to a public company whose shares are traded on a stock market.

Data for the public company can be used to estimate an asset beta, and the asset beta can then be applied to the private company to obtain an equity beta for the private company.

Since there is no market data for the private company, an assumption has to be made that accounting book b=values in the balance sheet are a reasonable approximation to market values, and the calculations use book values for equity and debt rather than market values.

Example

An investor is interested in acquiring Greenco, which is a private company with net assets of $240 million and debt capital of $160 million in its balance sheet.

Greenco can be compared to a public company Redco, which operates in the same industry and has a similar business mix and business risk. The following information is available about Redco:

Market value of equity	$450 million
Equity beta	1.60
Debt capital	Risk-free (debt capital beta = 0)
Price to book value of equity	1.50 times
Gearing (total debt to equity value)	1.25

The rate of tax on profits is 30%. The risk-free rate of interest is 5% and the equity risk premium is 3%.

Required
Use this information to estimate a cost of equity in Greenco.

Answer

Greenco is a private company and estimating a cost of equity has to be based on a comparison with the similar public company, Redco.
The asset beta formula uses market values for debt and equity. Although we have these market values for Redco, we do not have them for Greenco. An assumption should therefore be that book values are a reasonable approximation for market values, and book values will be used in the calculations.

It is also assumed that debt in Greenco is risk-free.

Taking data about Redco and book values rather than market values, we can estimate an asset beta for Redco and then assume that the same asset beta applies to Greenco.

Market value of Redco equity = $450 million
Price to book value of equity = 1.5
Book value of equity = $450 million/1.5 = $300 million

Debt: equity ratio = 1.25 times
Book value of debt = $300 million × 1.25 = $450 million

$$\beta_A = 1.60 \times \frac{300}{300 + 450(1 - 0.30)}$$

$\beta_A = 1.60 \times 0.4878 = 0.78$

This asset beta can be used to estimate an equity beta for Greenco:

$$0.78 = \beta_{EG} \times \frac{240}{240 + 160\,(1 - 0.30)}$$

$0.6818\ \beta_{EG} = 0.78$
$\beta_{EG} = 1.14$

The CAPM can now be used to estimate a cost of equity in Greenco:

$K_E = 5\% + 1.14\ (3\%)$
$K_E = 8.42\%$

Weaknesses with this method

Using the asset beta formula to estimate a cost of equity in a private company, using data from a comparable public company, has some weaknesses and limitations.

- It is assumed that book values are a reasonable approximation for market values, but this assumption is questionable.
- It is assumed that the business risk faced by both companies is the same, which might not be true.
- It is assumed that the cost of debt and equity in the private company is not affected by factors such as greater default risk, its private company status, and its smaller size. This assumption is also questionable.

Adjusted present value method (APV method) of project appraisal

- Introduction to the APV method
- The decision rule for the APV method
- Base case NPV
- PV of other costs
- Present value of the tax shield (PV of the tax relief on interest costs)
- Summary of the APV method
- Reasons for using the APV method
- Comparison of NPV and APV methods

5 Adjusted present value method (APV method) of project appraisal

5.1 Introduction to the APV method

The most common method for a company to evaluate a proposed capital expenditure project is the discount the expected future cash flows of the project at the WACC. Where appropriate, the cost of equity and WACC may be adjusted to allow for the different systematic risk characteristics of the project.

An alternative approach to capital investment appraisal is the adjusted present value (APV) method.

The APV method may be used when a business entity is considering an investment in a project that will have **different business risks** and **different financial risks** from its current operations. For example, a business entity might wish to evaluate an investment in a different industry or a different market, and raise new capital to finance the investment.

The APV method is an alternative to calculating a new cost of equity and a new WACC, for example using the Modigliani-Miller formulae or the asset beta formula.

5.2 The decision rule for the APV method

A project is financially viable and should be undertaken if its adjusted present value (APV) is positive. The APV of a project contains three elements, and is calculated as follows:

Base case NPV	X
minus: PV of other costs	(X)
plus: PV of tax relief on interest	X
Adjusted present value (APV)	X

To calculate the NPV of a project, we must therefore calculate three amounts: the base case NPV, the PV of other costs and the PV of tax relief on interest.

5.3 Base case NPV

The approach with the APV method is to calculate an NPV ignoring entirely the way in which the project will be financed. The cost of capital should therefore be calculated using an asset beta that is typical for the industry or type of business in which the investment will be made. Having estimated an appropriate asset beta, a cost of equity (cost of equity in an ungeared company) can be calculated using the CAPM, and this is the discount rate.

The base case NPV is therefore calculated assuming the project is financed entirely by equity, so that the method of financing is ignored.

It is therefore necessary to calculate the cost of equity in an all-equity company in the same industry or the market in which the capital investment will be made. To do this:

- convert a geared beta for the industry to an asset beta (ungeared beta) for the industry, and then
- use this asset beta (ungeared beta) and the CAPM to establish the cost of equity in an ungeared company.

Normal DCF techniques are used to establish the expected cash flows for the project. Having established a cost of equity for an ungeared company, the expected project cash flows are discounted at this cost of equity to obtain the base case NPV.

Example

A company operating in the insurance industry is considering whether to diversify by investing in a project in the transport industry.

The company has a gearing ratio of 30% debt and 70% equity, and its equity beta is 0.940. Its debt capital is risk-free.

The transport industry has an average equity beta of 1.362, and firms in the transport industry on average have a gearing ratio of 40% debt to 60% equity.

The risk-free rate of return is 5.3% and the expected market return is 8.3%.

The rate of taxation on profits is 23%.

The cash flows of the project after tax will be:

Year 0	$(600,000)
Years 1–3	$250,000

Required
Calculate the base case NPV.

a

Answer

The all-equity beta for the transport industry is calculated by un-gearing the equity beta for the transport industry.

$$\beta_A = 1.362 \times \frac{60}{60 + 40\,(1 - 0.23)}$$

$\beta_A = 0.90$.

Using the CAPM, we can now calculate the cost of an all-equity financed company in the transport industry:

5.3% + 0.90 (8.3% - 5.3%) = 8.0%.

This cost of capital should be used to discount the project cash flows, to obtain the base case NPV.

Year	Cash flow	Discount factor at 8%	PV
	$		$
0	(600,000)	1.000	(600,000)
1 – 3	250,000	2.577	644,250
Base case NPV			**+ 44,250**

5.4 PV of other costs

Other costs are the costs arising a consequence of the project, but not directly related to the project cash flows. Typically, these costs include the costs of raising new equity to finance the project, or the costs of obtaining debt finance.

Issue costs might be an allowable expense for tax purposes. When they are tax-allowable, the PV of issue costs must allow for the reduction in tax payments that will occur. The PV of the issue costs is therefore net of the present value of any tax relief on the costs.

Unless you are given other information, you should assume that the PV of other costs is calculated using the **risk-free cost of capital as the discount rate**.

Examination hint

If a company plans to raise new capital to finance a project, it will want to raise enough capital to finance the project after paying the issue costs. For example, suppose that a company intends to issue new equity to raise $20 million and issue costs are 5% of the amount raised. The company needs $20 million after paying the issue costs, and presumably the issue costs will be paid for out of the proceeds from raising the finance.

$20 million is therefore 95% (100% – 5%) of the capital to be raised.

The capital to be raised = $20 million /0.95 = $21,052,632.

This means that the issue costs will be $1,052,632.

Since the finance will be raised at the beginning of the project, the PV of the issue costs for the equity is $1,052,632, minus the PV of the tax relief on the issue costs.

Example

Assume that in the previous example, the investment of $600,000 would be financed by $400,000 of new equity and $200,000 of new debt.

Issue costs are 5% of the funds raised for equity and 2% of the funds raised for debt capital.

The risk-free cost of capital is 5.3%. The rate of taxation on profits is 23%. Issue costs are allowable for tax purposes.

Required
Calculate the PV of the issue costs for financing the project. Assume that tax is paid in the year following the year in which the taxable profit occurs.

Answer

The finance required is:

- Equity: $400,000 after issue costs and $400,000/0.95 = $421,053 before issue costs.
- Debt: $200,000 after issue costs and $200,000/0.98 = $204,082 before issue costs

Issue costs before tax:		$
Equity	$400,000 × 5/95	21,053
Debt	$200,000 × 2/98	4,081
Total issue costs		25,134

The PV of issue costs is calculated using the risk-free rate of 5.3% as the discount rate. There is tax relief on the issue costs, which will be received one year in arrears.

Year	**Item**	**Cash flow**	**Discount factor at 5.3%**	**PV**
		$		$
0	Issue costs	(25,134)	1.000	(25,134)
1	Tax saved at 23%	5,781	1/(1.053)	5,490
PV of issue costs				(19,644)

5.5 Present value of the tax shield (PV of the tax relief on interest costs)

When a new project is financed wholly or partly with new debt finance, there will be tax relief on the interest. The PV of these tax benefits should be included in the APV of the project.

The PV of the tax relief on interest is calculated by:

- calculating the interest costs in each year
- calculating the savings in taxation arising as a consequence, for each year of the project
- discounting these savings in taxation to a present value, using the pre-tax (before-tax) rate of interest on the debt as the discount rate.

Calculating interest payments

The amount of interest costs in each year will depend on the terms of repayment of the debt capital.

- If the debt finance is repaid in full at the end of the term of the borrowing, the interest cost is calculated simply as:

  Amount borrowed × Interest rate on the loan or the bonds
- If the loan is an amortising loan, and the debt is repaid gradually over the term of the loan, you will need to work out:
  - the annual payment on the loan, principal repayment + interest, and
  - separate this total annual payment into the principal repayment and the interest payment.

This separation of interest charges and the loan principal repayment is necessary because the tax relief applies to the interest payments only and not to the repayment of the loan principal.

Example

In the previous example, suppose that the company obtains borrows $204,081 in the form of a three-year amortising loan at 5.3% interest.

The annuity factor for years 1 – 3 at 5.3% is 2.708.

The rate of taxation is 23% and tax is payable in the year following the profit to which the tax relates.

Required
Calculate the PV of the interest tax shield.

Answer

The annual payments on the amortising loan can be calculated using the annuity factor for Years 1 – 3 at 5.3%, which is the cost of borrowing:

$$\frac{\text{Amount borrowed}}{\text{Annuity factor at 5.3\%, Years 1 - 3}} = \frac{\$204{,}081}{2.708} = \$75{,}362$$

The interest costs each year are calculated on the amount of the loan principal still unpaid at the beginning of the year. The amount of principal repaid each year is the difference between the total annual payment and the interest charge. In this example, the figures are calculated as follows:

Year	Loan principal unpaid	Interest at 5.3%	Loan principal repaid	
	$	$		$
1	204,081	10,816	(75,362 – 10,816)	64,546
	(64,546)			
2	139,535	7,395	(75,362 – 7,395)	67,967
	(67,967)			
3	71,568	3,793	(75,362 – 3,793)	71,569
	(71,569)			
	(1)	(rounding error)		

Having calculated the interest payments on the debt finance, we can now calculate the tax relief on the interest payments, and the PV of this tax relief.

Year	Item		Cash flow	Discount factor at 5.3%	PV
			$		$
2	Tax relief on Year 1 interest	(23% × 10,816)	2,488	1/(1.053)2	2,244
3	Tax relief on Year 2 interest	(23% × 7,395)	1,701	1/(1.053)3	1,456
4	Tax relief on Year 3 interest	(23% × 3,793)	872	1/(1.053)4	709
PV of tax shield					4,409

5.6 Summary of the APV method

Taking the three previous examples together, the APV of the investment project would be calculated as follows:

		$
	Base case NPV	44,250
-	PV of other costs	(19,644)
+	PV of tax relief on interest	4,409
=	APV	29,015

The APV of the project is positive; therefore on financial considerations (but ignoring the project risk) the project is worthwhile and should be undertaken.

5.7 Reasons for using the APV method

The APV method might be used in preference to adjusting the weighted average cost of capital (WACC) of the company using the Modigliani-Miller formulas. This is for several reasons.

- The APV method does not rely on assumptions about the new WACC of the firm if the project is undertaken.

- The APV method allows for the specific tax relief on the borrowing to finance the project, and does not assume that the debt will be perpetual debt.
- The APV method allows for other costs, such as the costs of raising new finance (issue costs).

It might be argued that APV is therefore the best method of estimating the effect of a new investment on the value of the business entity, and the wealth of its shareholders.

5.8 Comparison of NPV and APV methods

The NPV method of project evaluation and the APV method provide different valuations for proposed capital investment projects. It is possible that one method might indicate that a project is acceptable financially, whereas the other method indicates that the project is not viable.

The NPV and the base case NPV are calculated using the same cash flows, except that the cash flows for the base case NPV should exclude 'other costs' such as financing costs, whereas these are included in the calculation of an NPV.

Example

A company is considering whether to invest in setting up a new business. The cost of the investment would be $9 million. The project would be financed by raising $4.5 million of new equity finance and the same amount of new debt finance. The $9 million would be used to purchase assets for $8 million. There would be an investment of $700,000 in working capital, and issue costs would be $200,000 for the equity and $100,000 for the debt finance.

The purchased assets would attract capital allowances in the form of a 25% annual writing down allowance on a reducing balance basis.

The pre-tax operating cash flows from the investment are expected to be as follows:

Year	Pre-tax operating cash flows
	$000
1	1,800
2	2,100
3	2,400
4	2,700

Tax on profits is at the rate of 30%. Assume that tax payments occur in the same year as the profit or benefit to which they relate.

At the end of Year 4, the intention is to sell off the business as a continuing operation, and the expected receipts from the sale, net of tax, are S3.60 million.

The following information is also relevant:

(1) The investment will alter the company's gearing to 80% equity and 20% debt capital.

(2) The equity beta for the project is 1.25.

(3) The debt finance for the project will be the same as for the company's other debt, which is 7% before tax.

(4) The issue costs of raising the new equity and debt finance would not be allowable for tax purposes.

(5) The risk-free rate of return is 5% and the market return is 9%.

Required

(a) Calculate the NPV of the project.

(b) Calculate the APV of the project.

Answer

Workings: Capital allowances and tax relief

Year	Written down value	Capital allowance 25%	Tax relief 30%
	$000	$000	$000
	8,000		
1	(2,000)	2,000	600
	6,000		
2	(1,500)	1,500	450
	4,500		
3	(1,125)	1,125	338
	3,375		
4	(844)	844	253

There is no balancing charge, because it is assumed that the disposal value at the end of year 4, net of tax, includes the estimated tax effect of the disposal of the business.

Net present value

Cost of equity K_E = 5% + 1.25 (9 – 5)% = 10%.
WACC = [80% × 10%] + [20% × 7% × (1 – 0.30)] = 8.98%, say 9%.

Year	0	1	2	3	4
	$000	$000	$000	$000	$000
Investment	(9,000)				
Sale value					3,600
Operating cash flow		1,800	2,100	2,400	2,700
Tax (30%)		(540)	(630)	(720)	(810)
Tax relief (workings)		600	450	338	253
Net cash flow	(9,000)	1,860	1,920	2,018	5,743
Discount factor 9%	1.000	0.917	0.842	0.772	0.708
Present value	(9,000)	1,706	1,617	1,558	4,066

NPV = – $53,000

Adjusted present value

The project will be financed 50% with equity and 50% with debt capital.

Asset beta = 1.25 × 4,500/[4,500 + (4,500 × 0.70)] = 0.7353.

Cost of ungeared equity K_{EU} = 5% + 0.7353(9 – 5)% = 7.94%, say 8%.

The cash flows for discounting are the same as for the NPV method, with the exception that issue costs should be removed. These are $300,000 in Year 0.

Year	0	1	2	3	4
	$000	$000	$000	$000	$000
Net cash flow	(8,700)	1,860	1,920	2,018	5,743
Discount factor 8%	1.000	0.926	0.857	0.794	0.735
Present value	(8,700)	1,722	1,645	1,602	4,221

Base case NPV = + $490,000

Other costs

There is no tax relief on the issue costs, so the PV of issue costs (all in Year 0) is $300,000.

PV of the tax shield

It is assumed that interest costs each year will be $4,500,000 × 7% = $315,000.
Tax relief on these interest costs at 30% will be $94,500 per year for 4 years.
This tax relief should be discounted at 7%.
PV of tax relief on interest = $94,500 × 3.387 = $320,000.

Summary

		$000
	Base case NPV	490
-	PV of other costs	(300)
+	PV of tax relief on interest	320
=	APV	+ 510

The APV is + $510,000, indicating that the project should be undertaken, whereas the NPV is negative, indicating that it should not be undertaken.

In this particular example, the APV and NPV methods give conflicting recommendations.

Impact of different finance methods on the financial statements

- Debt or equity
- Including the investment

6 Impact of different finance methods on the financial statements

This section contains examples to demonstrate how you might assess the impact of different financing methods on the financial statements of a company.

6.1 Debt or equity

Example:

A company wishes to raise $100,000 either through issuing shares or by borrowing at 10% per annum, on the first day of the next accounting period.

The before column represents the forecast draft financial statements as at the end of the next accounting period.

The impact on the forecast, of raising equity or issuing debt is as follows. (Note that the following figures do not yet show the results of the investment of the amount raised and ignore taxation).

	Before	After (equity issue)	After (debt issue)
	$000	$000	$000
Non-current assets	300,000	300,000	300,000
Current assets	500,000	600,000	590,000
	800,000	900,000	890,000
Share capital of $1 each **(1)**	50,000	150,000	50,000
Retained earnings			
brought forward	280,000	280,000	280,000
profit for the year	80,000	80,000	70,000
	360,000	360,000	350,000
	410,000	510,000	400,000
Non-current liabilities **(2)**	90,000	90,000	190,000
Capital employed **(3)**	500,000	600,000	590,000
Current liabilities	300,000	300,000	300,000
	800,000	900,000	890,000

	Before	After (equity issue)	After (debt issue)
	$000	$000	$000
Profit before interest and tax **(4)**	100,000	100,000	100,000
Interest	(20,000)	(20,000)	(30,000)
Profit for the year **(5)**	80,000	80,000	70,000
ROCE ((**4** ÷ **3**) × 100)	20.0%	16.67	16.9%
EPS (**5** ÷ **1**)	$1.60	$0.53	$1.40
Gearing ((**2** ÷ **3**) × 100)	18.0%	15.0%	32.2%

Commentary

ROCE (calculated as profit before interest and tax divided by long-term capital employed) is lower in each case. This is simply due to the cash raised leading to an increase in capital employed. The forecast capital employed at the year-end if debt were to be issued is $10,000 lower than that for equity. This is due to the interest that would have to be paid on the debt.

Remember that the example has ignored the impact of investing the $100,000 raised. Companies do not raise cash without a reason. The $100,000 would earn a return which would push ROCE upward but this is ignored in the example.

EPS is lower in each case but much more so for the equity issue. For the equity issue this is because the same amount of profit is shared between a greater number of shares. For the debt issue, there is slight fall due to the interest payment reducing the profit. Again, remember that the numbers ignore the positive impact of the investment.

Gearing would fall due to the equity issue because there would be more equity but the same amount of debt. Gearing increases due to the debt issue for the opposite reason.

6.2 Including the investment

Example

A company wishes to raise $100,000 either through issuing shares or by borrowing at 10% per annum, on the first day of the next accounting period.

The cash is to be invested in an asset that will provide a 30% return per annum.

The impact on the forecast, of raising equity or issuing debt is as follows:

	Before	After (equity issue)	After (debt issue)
	$000	$000	$000
Non-current assets	300,000	400,000	400,000
Current assets	500,000	530,000	520,000
	800,000	930,000	920,000
Share capital of $1 each **(1)**	50,000	150,000	50,000
Retained earnings			
brought forward	280,000	280,000	280,000
profit for the year	80,000	110,000	100,000
	360,000	390,000	380,000
	410,000	540,000	430,000
Non-current liabilities **(2)**	90,000	90,000	190,000
Capital employed **(3)**	500,000	630,000	620,000
Current liabilities	300,000	300,000	300,000
	800,000	930,000	920,000

	Before	After (equity issue)	After (debt issue)
Profit before interest and tax **(4)**	100,000	130,000	130,000
Interest	(20,000)	(20,000)	(30,000)
Profit for the year **(5)**	80,000	110,000	100,000
ROCE ((**4** ÷ **3**) × 100)	20.0%	20.6%	21.0%
EPS (**5** ÷ **1**)	$1.60	$0.73	$2.00
Gearing ((**2** ÷ **3**) × 100)	18.0%	14.3%	30.6%

Commentary

ROCE is higher in each case. Capital employed has increased and this would tend to lower ROCE. The capital employed if debt is raised would be lower due to the need to pay interest and this lowers the asset base.

The investment is expected to generate a 30% return. This is higher than the existing 20% return earned before the investment is made. The impact of the higher return is bigger than that of the increased investment in each case causing ROCE to increase.

EPS is lowered by the equity issue. The earnings are increased by the investment but that figure is spread over a greater number of shares, and overall, the dilutive effect of the greater number of shares has outweighed the gain from the investment, supressing EPS.

For the debt issue, there is an increase. The increase return from the new investment is greater than the extra interest paid to finance it. The number of shares has not changed so EPS has increased.

Gearing would fall due to the equity issue because there would more equity but the same amount of debt. Gearing increases due to the debt issue for the opposite reason. The increased profit is added to equity in each case and this also has the effect of lowering gearing.

CHAPTER 12

Valuation and free cash flows

Contents

Valuation of equity

- The need for a valuation
- Valuation methods
- Valuation based on asset values
- Valuation based on earnings and P/E ratio
- Dividend valuation model

1 Valuation of equity

1.1 The need for a valuation

All valuation methods are based on estimates and assumptions.

Valuation methods can be used to decide on an offer price in a mergers and acquisitions scenario, or may be used to justify an offer price. The final price is often agreed through negotiation, and the management of the bidding company must use judgement in deciding how high a price they might be willing to pay. The only 'correct' valuation is the price that the bidder makes and the shareholders in the target company accept.

1.2 Valuation methods

Each method produces a different valuation, but each valuation can provide useful information and help with deciding what the offer price should be. You should be prepared to use each of the different valuation methods, and then discuss the assumptions and estimates on which the valuation is based. You might also be required to compare the different valuations produced by each method, and then recommend (with reasons) a valuation that you consider appropriate as a basis for making an offer to the target company shareholders.

There are several approaches to making a valuation of the shares in a company:

- Asset based valuation which as the name suggests are based on the asset value of the target company.
- Market-based valuations, using estimates of future earnings or dividends
- Cash-flow based valuations, using discounted cash flow of expected future returns from the acquisition. The expected value added (EVA) model is another form of cash flow-based model but this is covered in a later chapter.

1.3 Valuation based on asset values

Disposal value

The minimum value of a target company is the value of its net assets. (Net assets are the value of the company's total assets minus its liabilities.) If net assets can be valued according to the disposal value of the assets, this would indicate the amount that could be obtained for the shareholders of the company in the event that the company is liquidated and its assets sold off.

However the net disposal value (or 'break-up' value) of the target company's assets is usually irrelevant, unless asset value is higher than the value of the business as a going concern. A target company is usually acquired with the intention of continuing its business operations, and the value of assets in a going concern should be higher than their break-up value.

In a takeover bid, it is also impractical to estimate the disposal value of the target company's assets, except perhaps as a very approximate estimate.

Book value

In practice, a minimum valuation for a target company might be based on the book value of its assets. The minimum value of the equity would then be the book value of the assets minus the book value of the liabilities.

Some assets might be under-valued, but where non-current assets are re-valued regularly book value might be sufficient for an asset-based valuation without the need for further adjustments.

If you are required to make an asset-based valuation in your examination, you should be prepared to consider some adjustments to the valuation of certain assets, where information in the question indicates that the valuation of certain assets (particularly intangible assets) might be too high or too low.

A valuation based on the book value of net assets should be considered a minimum valuation, and not one that the target company shareholders are likely to accept. An offer price would have to be in excess of book value ('book value plus') for the bid to have any chance of success.

Example

The following information is available about a private company, Company Z.

	$000
Tangible non-current assets	250
Intangible non-current assets	75
Current assets	60
	385
Ordinary shares of $1	50
Revaluation reserve	80
Retained profits	145
	275
Bank loans	90
Current liabilities	20
	385

Required

Provide an asset-based valuation of the shares in Company Z.

Answer

The book value of the net assets is $275,000 or $5.50 per share. However, this valuation is based on the assumption that the tangible non-current assets are suitably valued, and that $75,000 represent a realistic value for the intangible non-current assets.

It is therefore unlikely that the target company shareholders will accept an offer below $5.50 per share, and the offer will almost certainly need to be higher than $5.50 if the takeover is to succeed.

Valuations based on other valuation methods should be compared with the asset-based valuation. There should be some concern (for the bidding company) if a valuation based on expected earnings, dividends or cash flows is lower than the asset-based valuation.

1.4 Valuation based on earnings and P/E ratio

A simple method of estimating a value for a company in the absence of a stock market value is to use earnings per share and a price-earning ratio:

Value = EPS × Estimated P/E ratio.

The problem with this valuation method for a private company is that a suitable estimate must be obtained for both EPS and the P/E ratio.

- The EPS might be the EPS of the target company in the previous year, an average EPS for a number of recent years or a forecast of EPS in a future year. Any of these estimates for EPS could be used.

- Since a private company does not have a market value for its shares, the shares do not have a P/E ratio. A P/E ratio must therefore be selected by looking at the P/E ratio for similar companies whose shares are traded on a stock market. The P/E ratio selected might be based on the average P/E ratio of a number of similar companies whose shares are traded on a stock market, for which a current P/E ratio is therefore available.

However, shares in public companies should be worth more than shares in an identical private company, because they are more 'liquid'. They can be sold on the stock market at any time, whereas shares in a private company cannot be sold at all unless a willing private buyer can be found.

Since shares in a quoted company ought to have a higher price than an identical private company, the P/E ratio of a quoted company should also be higher than the P/E ratio applied to a valuation of the private company's shares.

For example, if a quoted company has a P/E ratio of 11.5 times, the P/E ratio used to value shares in a similar private company in the same industry should be less than 11.5. Unfortunately, there is no reliable method of deciding how much lower than 11.5 a suitable P/E ratio should be.

Another problem with selecting a suitable P/E ratio is that it might not be possible to identify quoted companies that are very similar to a private company. Some quoted companies might operate in the same industry, and might even be competitors of the private company in some markets. However, a comparable quoted company is likely to be larger than the private company, and might well operate in a wider range of markets and in different geographical markets.

Example

The EPS of a private company, ABC Company, was \$2.50 last year and is expected to rise to \$2.80 next year. Similar companies whose shares are quoted on the stock market have P/E ratios ranging from 10.0 to 15.6. The average P/E ratio of these companies is 12.5.

A valuation of the company might be to take the prospective EPS and apply the average P/E ratio for similar companies:

Valuation = \$2.80 × 12.5 = \$35.00 per share.

An alternative evaluation might be to take the actual EPS last year and apply the lowest P/E ratio of any other similar stock market company, reduced by, say, 10% to allow for the fact that ABC Company is a private company and does not have a stock market quotation.

Valuation = \$2.80 × (90% × 10) = \$25.20.

Here, a P/E ratio of 9 (90% × 10) has been used in the valuation.

Another valuation might be to use the EPS for last year and a P/E ratio of 9. This would give a share value of \$2.50 × 9 = \$22.50.

By making different assumptions, the earnings-based valuation method has provided valuations in a wide range of $22.50 to $35. From this example, it might be apparent that the P/E ratio valuation method has a number of weaknesses:

- It is based on subjective opinions about what EPS figure and what P/E ratio figure to use.
- It is not an objective or scientific valuation method.
- It is based on accounting measures (EPS) and not cash flows. However, the value of an investment such as an investment in shares is derived from the cash that the investment is expected to provide to the investor (shareholder).

The valuation can be compared with valuations using other valuation methods.

1.5 Dividend valuation model

The dividend valuation model is a more objective and cash-based approach to the valuation of shares. It is based on the view that the value of a share to shareholders is the value of all the future dividends that they expect to receive from the shares in the future.

If the fair value of a share represents the value of all expected future dividends, this value can be estimated by discounting expected future dividends to a present value.

All expected **future dividends 'in perpetuity'** may be discounted to a present value at the **shareholders' cost of capital**. The shareholders' cost of capital is the return on investment that shareholders expect to receive from their shares in the company.

The usual assumption in the dividend valuation model is that the annual dividend will grow in the future. A valuation for shares in a company can therefore be obtained by making a forecast of what the future rate of dividend growth each year will be.

A simplifying assumption is that the dividends will grow at a constant annual percentage rate.

If it is assumed that the company will pay an annual dividend that grows by a constant percentage amount every year into the foreseeable future, the present value of those dividends, and so the value of the shares, is:

$$P_0 = \frac{D_1}{K_e - g}$$

Where:

P_0 is the current value of the share ex dividend
D_1 is the expected amount of the annual cash dividend in **one year's time** (next year)
K_e is the shareholders' cost of capital expressed as a proportion (so 9% = 0.09, etc)
g is the expected annual growth rate in dividends expressed as a proportion (3% = 0.03 etc)

This is the valuation of the share ex dividend. Note that this valuation formula is based on the assumptions that:

- the dividend is paid annually, and
- the dividend for the current year has just been paid.

Note on the cost of shareholder equity

To use the dividend valuation we need an estimate of the cost of equity capital. When the bidding company is a quoted company, it could use its own cost of equity to make the valuation. Estimating the cost of a company's equity is described in the chapter on the cost of capital.

If the bidding company is also a private company, an estimate of the cost of equity is required. This might be obtained from estimates of the cost of equity of similar quoted companies.

Example

A company has just paid an annual dividend of $0.48. Dividends are expected to grow by 4% each year into the foreseeable future. The shareholders' cost of capital is 12%.

Using the dividend valuation model, the expected value of the share (ex dividend) is:

$$P_0 = \frac{0.48\,(1.04)}{0.12 - 0.04} = \$6.24$$

This provides a useful guide to a potential buyer of the shares, to suggest what the valuation of the shares should be.

If there is no expected growth in annual dividends, and the company is expected to pay a constant annual dividend in the future, the share valuation would have been $4.00. Because the annual dividend is expected to increase every year, the valuation is much higher.

Using the dividend growth model, the fair value of shares changes with:

- changes in expected future dividends (for example, changes in the expected annual growth rate in dividends), or
- changes in the shareholders' required rate of return (the equity cost of capital).

Example

In the previous example, if the expected growth rate in annual dividends falls from 4% to 3%, the valuation of the shares will fall to:

$$P_0 = \frac{\$0.48\,(1.03)}{(0.12 - 0.03)} = \$5.49$$

Change in the annual rate of dividend growth

The dividend growth model can also be used to value shares when the expected growth rate in dividends is expected to change.

Example

A company has just paid an annual dividend of \$0.63. This dividend is expected to remain constant for two more years, but from Year 3 it is expected to grow by 3% each year into the foreseeable future. The cost of shareholders' funds is 10%.

The expected value of the shares (ex dividend) **at the end of Year 2** can be calculated using the dividend growth model:

$$P_2 = \frac{0.63\,(1.03)}{0.10 - 0.03} = \$9.27$$

The expected current value of the share is:

- this valuation at the end of Year 2 discounted to a Year 0 value,
- plus the present value of the expected dividends at the end of Year 1 and Year 2.

Year			**Discount factor at 10%**	
		\$		\$
1	Dividend	0.63	0.909	0.57
2	Dividend	0.63	0.826	0.52
2	End of Year 2 value	9.27	0.826	7.66
	Share value			8.75

Gordon's growth model

Dividend growth can be achieved by retaining some profits (retained earnings) for reinvestment in the business. Reinvested earnings should provide extra profits in the future, so that higher dividends can be paid. When a company retains a proportion of its earnings each year, the expected annual future growth rate in dividends can be estimated using the formula:

$$g = br$$

Where:

g = annual growth rate in dividends in perpetuity
b = proportion of earnings retained (for reinvestment in the business)
r = the shareholders' required return on capital, which is also assumed to be the rate of return that the company will make on its investments of retained earnings.

Example

A company has just achieved annual earnings per share of $0.50, of which 60% has been paid in dividends and 40% has been reinvested as retained earnings. The company is expected to retain 60% of its earnings every year and pay out the rest as dividends. The return on investment achieved by the company is expected to be 10% per annum.

The anticipated annual growth in dividends = 40% × 10% = 4% or 0.04.

Using the dividend growth model, the expected value per share is:

$$P_0 = \frac{0.30\,(1.04)}{0.10 - 0.04} = \$5.20$$

Advantages and disadvantages of the dividend valuation models

The dividend valuation models provide a present value of expected future dividends that is based on future cash flows (dividends) for a shareholder. It is therefore a form of cash flow based model as well as a market-based model of valuation.

The main weakness of the dividend growth model for the valuation of shares in an acquisition is that the bidding company hopes to win control of the target company. When it obtains control, it will decide the dividend policy of the acquired company. It might decide to increase or reduce the dividend payout ratio (as a percentage of earnings). This would affect the expected dividend growth rate.

It can also be argued that a more appropriate method of valuation should be one based on the total cash flows of the acquired company, not just the dividends that will be remitted to the parent company.

Cash flow-based company valuations are described in the next three sections of this chapter.

Cash flow models

- Valuation of a business using DCF
- The advantages of a cash flow basis for business valuation
- Net present value method

2 Cash flow models

2.1 Valuation of a business using DCF

DCF can be used to estimate a present value of the future profitability of a company. Management might want to know the present value of expected profits of a business in future years. One reason for wanting this information is to enable management to put a current value on the business, possibly in order to:

- decide how much to offer for a target company in a takeover bid, or
- decide whether to accept or reject a takeover offer from another company.

The value of a business can be estimated by discounting expected future cash flows from the business over a number of years into the future. The cash flows that should be used for discounting are the expected **free cash flows** of the business. Forecasts of free cash flows might include growth (inflation) assumptions that are dealt with in the usual way.

2.2 The advantages of a cash flow basis for business valuation

There are several strong arguments in favour of a cash flow approach to valuation.

- Cash flows earned by a business are much more closely correlated to value and shareholder wealth than accounting profits. Valuations should therefore be based on expectations of future cash flows rather than expectations of profit or accounting return on investment.
- Returns on an investment, such as the acquisition of another company, must be sufficient to cover the costs of the finance used to make the acquisition. This includes the cost of equity finance as well as the cost of any debt finance. It is therefore appropriate to assess the value future cash flows from an acquisition in terms of whether they provide a return in excess of the total cost of financing.

A key point to note is that if the purchase price for an acquisition exceeds the value of the returns that will be obtained from the acquisition, allowing for the acquirer's cost of capital, the acquisition will destroy value. The value of the acquisition will be less than the acquirer pays for it.

This is a strong argument for suggesting that businesses should be valued on the basis of expected future cash flows and the cost of capital.

2.3 Net present value method

The net present value method is straightforward. The valuation of a company or a business should be calculated as the net present value of expected future cash flows from the business, discounted at an appropriate cost of capital.

The following steps are required to apply the NPV valuation method.

- Estimate the relevant incremental cash flows from the business to be acquired.
- Discount these cash flows at an appropriate cost of capital that reflects the risk of the investment.
- The maximum price that should be paid for the business is the present value (or net present value) of these future expected cash flows.

The NPV method might be appropriate where the future cash flows from an acquired business will be affected by the acquisition. For example, the acquirer might have plans to invest extra capital in the acquired business after the acquisition has taken place. This additional investment will affect future cash flows, and so should affect the valuation.

Example

QX Company is considering the acquisition of an operating division from a multinational company. If it acquires the division, it will invest an additional $12 million immediately to modernise equipment.

It has been estimated that the annual after-tax cash flows after the acquisition and additional investment will be as follows:

Year	$ million
1	6
2	8
3	10
4	8
5 onwards (per year)	4

An appropriate after-tax cost of capital for valuing the acquisition is 8%.

Required
Estimate the maximum amount that QX Company should be prepared to pay to acquire the operating division from the multinational company.

a

Answer

Year	Cash flow	Discount factor	PV
	$ million	8%	$ million
0	(12)	1.000	(12.000)
1	6	0.926	5.556
2	8	0.857	6.856
3	10	0.794	7.940
4	8	0.735	5.880
5 onwards (per year)	4	9.188	36.752
			50.984

Working:

Discount factor at 8%	
In perpetuity (1/0.08)	12.500
Years 1 – 4	3.312
Year 5 in perpetuity	9.188

The maximum price to pay for the operating division is about $51 million.

e

Example

Company WY is considering the acquisition of another company, Company BN. Company BN has 4 million shares in issue.

After the acquisition Company WY intends to invest a further $6 million for the purchase of new operating assets in Company B. It is expected that annual cash flows for equity will be $1.0 million in the first year following the acquisition, and that these will increase by 8% each year for the next four years, after which the rate of growth in annual cash flows will fall to 3%.

The cost of capital is 10%.

Required

Calculate a valuation of the equity capital of Company BN.

a

Answer

Year	Cash flow	Discount factor at 10%	Present value
	$000		$000
0	(6,000)	1.000	(6,000)
1	1,000	0.909	909
2	1,080	0.826	892
3	1,166	0.751	876
4	1,260	0.683	861
5	1,360	0.621	845
6 onwards	20,615	0.621	12,802
Valuation			+ 11,185

A valuation based on the projected cash flows is $11.185 million or about $4.10 per share for the 4 million shares.

Workings

After Year 5 the annual rate of growth in cash flows falls to 3%, so the cash flow in Year 6 (in $000) will be 1,401.

The valuation of $1,401,000 in Year 6, rising by 3% in perpetuity, can be calculated using the dividend growth model formula. The end of Year 5 present value of these cash flows is:

$$\text{PV in \$000} = \frac{1{,}401(1.03)}{(0.10 - 0.03)}$$

= (in $000) 20,615.

This is an end-of-Year 5 discounted value, which needs to be converted to a present value using the Year 5 discount rate.

Note on the method of calculation used in this example

Make sure that you understand the technique for valuation of annual cash flows from a year in the future, where the cash flows are expected to grow by a constant percentage amount each year in perpetuity. This use of the Gordon's growth model for an NPV valuation or shareholder value added valuation could well feature n an examination question.

Free cash flow

- What is free cash flow
- Free cash flow for the firm
- Calculating free cash flow for the firm
- Free cash flow to equity
- Valuation using free cash flows

3 Free cash flow

3.1 What is free cash flow?

Free cash flow is the amount of cash generated by a company or business during a specified period of time (say one year) minus the cash payments that the company or business is obliged to make. Essential payments include taxation payments and capital expenditure to replace ageing non-current assets ('replacement' capital expenditure).

Free cash flow can be defined more specifically as:

- free cash flow to the firm; or
- free cash flow to equity.

Free cash flow can be estimated for future periods and be used in valuation.

Free cash flows for equity might be used in the valuation of the share capital of a company; whereas free cash flow for the firm would be used for the valuation of the entire business, equity plus debt capital.

3.2 Free cash flow to the firm

Free cash flow to the firm is the amount of free cash flow generated by the business as a whole, regardless of the source of finance. It is therefore calculated without deducting interest payments as an essential cash payment.

There are differing views about whether capital expenditure for expanding the business is an essential cash payment.

- One view is that only replacement capital expenditure should be deducted as essential cash payments.
- A different view is that replacement capital expenditure and capital expenditure to grow the business internally (organically) should both be deducted in calculating free cash flows, but that capital spending on acquisitions and cash received from business disposals should be excluded.
- A third view is that all capital expenditure (net of proceeds from disposals) should be included in the calculation of free cash flow.

There is no 'correct' answer. However, free cash flow is the amount of cash that management can decide how to use.

- If it is assumed that expanding the business is a free decision by management, only replacement capital expenditure should be deducted in calculating free cash flow.
- On the other hand, if it is assumed that capital expenditure to pay for expansion of the business is necessary to grow operating cash flows in future years, a better definition of free cash flow would be one where both replacement capital expenditure and capital expenditure to pay for growth and expansion are deducted.

3.3 Calculating free cash flow to the firm

Free cash flow to the firm is used to calculate the total value of a business.

There are two methods of calculating free cash flow to the firm, although they are closely connected.

Method 1

This method starts with operating profit (EBIT) and makes adjustments to that figure as follows to arrive at a free cash flow figure.

Method 1	
Earnings before interest and tax (EBIT)	X
Less tax on EBIT	(X)
Add back: Depreciation (and any other non-cash expenditures)	X
	X
Less: Working capital increases	(X)
Plus: Working capital decreases	X
	X
Less: Replacement capital expenditure	(X)
Free cash flow to the firm	**X**

Method 2

This method starts with cash flow from operations. This could be as given in the statement of cash flows or constructed from first principles.

Method 2	
Cash flow from operations	X
Less:	
Tax payments on profit	(X)
Replacement capital expenditure	(X)
Free cash flow to the firm	**X**

3.4 Free cash flow to equity

Free cash flow to equity is the amount of free cash flow after deduction of interest payments).

Free cash flow to the firm	X
Minus: Interest payments	(X)
Equals: Free cash flow to equity	X

Free cash flow to equity is used to calculate the value of equity of a business.

Free cash flow to equity is the amount that is theoretically available for the payment of dividends though, in practice, only a part of this figure is paid.

3.5 Valuation using free cash flows

The typical approach to performing a business valuation using free cash flows involves dividing the company's future into two periods:

- the explicit forecast period (the next few years for which it is possible to calculate free cash flows with reasonable confidence); and
- the implicit forecast period or terminal value period.

The explicit forecast period is the next few years. The free cash flow in each of these years can be calculated by applying assumptions about growth rates, margins tax rates and so on. Typically the growth rate is expected to vary over this period and ends when the growth rate is expected to become (or at least assumed to become) constant.

The length of the explicit forecast period varies depending on the company, industry and situation. However, this is largely at the discretion of the person carrying out the calculation.

The implicit forecast period is all periods after the time horizon set to define the explicit forecast period. The cash flows in each year after the time horizon are modelled assuming a constant growth rate. The present value of all cash flows that relate to the implicit interest rate period can be represented as a single figure (terminal value) at the end of the explicit forecast period.

The value of the firm is calculated as:

Present value of free cash flow to the firm in the explicit period	X
Terminal value (present value of free cash flows to the firm in the implicit period)	X
Value of the firm	X

Note that the value of equity could be calculated as:

Value of the firm	X
Value of debt	(X)
Value of the equity	X

Example

The following information is available about the cash flows of a potential takeover target

Current annual sales: $10 million

Competitive advantage period: 5 years

Cost of capital: 10%

Other value driver information:

Year	**1**	**2**	**3**	**4**	**5**	**After year 5 (annual)**
	%	%	%	%	%	%
Sales growth (%)	8	7	6	5	4	0
Operating profit margin (% of sales)	20	20	18	15	15	10
Tax rate (%)	30	30	30	30	30	30
Incremental fixed capital investment (as a % of growth in sales)	5	5	4	4	2	0
Incremental working capital investment (as a % of growth in sales)	20	20	15	15	10	0

Annual depreciation charges are $4 million. It is assumed that fixed capital replacement cost is equal to depreciation.

The company has investments with a market value of $2 million and the total value of its debt liabilities is $4.5 million.

Required: Calculate the value of the firm and hence the value of the equity.

Answer

Year	1	2	3	4	5	6 onwards
	$m	$m	$m	$m	$m	$m
Increase in sales **(W1)**	0.80	0.76	0.69	0.61	0.52	0
Sales	10.80	11.56	12.25	12.86	13.38	13.38
Operating profit margin	20%	20%	18%	15%	15%	10%
Operating profit	2.16	2.31	2.21	1.93	2.01	1.34
Tax rate @ 30%	(0.65)	(0.69)	(0.66)	(0.58)	(0.60)	(0.40)
Operating profit after tax	1.51	1.62	1.55	1.35	1.41	0.94
Depreciation	4.00	4.00	4.00	4.00	4.00	4.00
Operating cash flow	5.51	5.62	5.55	5.35	5.41	4.94
Replacement FCI (= Dep^n)	(4.00)	(4.00)	(4.00)	(4.00)	(4.00)	(4.00)
Incremental FCI **(W1)**	(0.04)	(0.04)	(0.03)	(0.02)	(0.01)	0
Incremental WCI **(W2)**	(0.16)	(0.15)	(0.10)	(0.09)	(0.05)	0
Free cash flow	1.31	1.43	1.42	1.24	1.35	0.94
Discount factor at 10% **(W3)**	0.909	0.826	0.751	0.683	0.621	6.209
PV of free cash flow	1.19	1.18	1.07	0.85	0.84	5.84

Total PV of free cash flows: $10.97m

The value of the operational assets is $10.97 million, say $11.0 million.

	$m
Valuation of operational assets	11.0
Value of non-operational assets	2.0
Total value of all assets	13.0
Less: Value of debt	(4.5)
Equals: Value of equity	8.5

Workings:

W1 Increase in sales and incremental FCI

	1	2	3	4	5	6
Sales for the year	10.80	11.56	12.25	12.86	13.38	13.38
Sales in previous year	10.00	10.80	11.56	12.25	12.86	13.38
Incremental sales	**0.8**	**0.76**	**0.69**	**0.61**	**0.52**	**nil**
Incremental FCI rate	5%	5%	4%	4%	2%	0
Incremental FCI	0.04	0.04	0.03	0.02	0.01	nil

W1 Incremental WCI

	1	2	3	4	5	6
Incremental sales	0.8	0.76	0.69	0.61	0.52	nil
Incremental FCI rate	20%	20%	15%	15%	10%	0
	0.16	0.15	0.10	0.09	0.05	nil

W3 Discount factor for year 6 to infinity

Discount factor at 10%	
In perpetuity (1/0.10)	10.000
Years 1 – 5	3.791
Year 6 in perpetuity	6.209

Different questions will ask you to apply different growth assumptions and different time horizons for the explicit forecast period.

Applications of the Black-Scholes option pricing model

4 Applications of the Black-Scholes option pricing model

4.1 Introduction

The Black-Scholes option pricing model can be used to value equity and to also to help assess default risk of debt.

These applications are based on the idea that when a company borrows money the shareholders acquire a call option and a put option written by the lenders, on the underlying assets of the business, with an exercise price equal to the face value of the debt.

Corporate bonds must be serviced with a higher rate of interest than government bonds. Government bonds are often considered to be risk free (or of very low risk though this depends on the country) whereas corporate bonds carry credit risk. Therefore, lenders require a higher rate of return for lending to corporates than they would for lending to countries.

There is another way of looking at this. Governments do not have an option to default (though it does happen occasionally). When a firm borrows money it has an option to default on that loan. The option to default must be paid for so corporate rates of interest are higher than the rates available on government borrowing.

Call option

When a firm borrows money, in effect the lender acquires the firm's assets and the shareholders acquire an option to buy them back by paying off the debt. They have a call option on the assets with an exercise price being the face value of the debt.

This implies that if the debt is repaid the shareholders can take the full value of the assets of the business.

At the exercise date (date of redemption of the date):

- If the value of the assets is worth more than the face value of the debt (the exercise price) the shareholders will exercise the option by paying the debt.
- If the value of the assets is worth less than the face value of the debt (the exercise price) the shareholders will allow the option to lapse. They can do this by walking away and allowing the company to slip into bankruptcy.

Put option

If the firm's assets are worth less than face value of the debt the shareholders will not exercise the call option. They can walk away from the investment. The lenders will be left with a situation where they will not receive the face value of the debt but will receive the firm's assets instead. In other words, when a company borrows money the shareholders acquire a put option on the assets of the firm. The exercise of this put option is the face value of the debt. (They exercise the option by walking away from the company thus forcing the lender to take the assets instead of the redemption proceeds).

4.2 BSOP and equity valuation

Formulae for the Black-Scholes model are given in the formula sheet in the examination. They are repeated hear for your convenience.

$$c = P_a N(d_1) - P_e N(d_2) e^{-rt}$$

where

$$d_1 = \frac{\ln(P_a / P_e) + (r + 0.5s^2)t}{s\sqrt{t}}$$

$$d_2 = d_1 - s\sqrt{t}$$

Proxies must be used for the variables in the above equations:

	Basic model	This application
c	the value of the call option	the value of equity
P_a	the price of the underlying item	the fair value of the total assets (less current liabilities) of the firm – the total value of the firm
P_e	the exercise price of the option	the face value of debt It is assumed that the debt is zero coupon. If this is not the case the exercise price is determined by calculating the value of an equivalent zero coupon bond with the same yield and term to maturity
t	time to expiry of the option (in years)	period of time before the debt is due for redemption
s	volatility	standard deviation of the value of the firm's assets

Other variables are as before:

e = the constant e.

r = the risk-free interest rate

Example

A firm has assets less current liabilities of \$100m. This figure varies with a standard deviation of 0.4.

The face value of the outstanding debt is \$80m. This debt is zero coupon and is to be paid in 5 years' time.

The risk free rate is 5%

Required:

Calculate the value of equity.

Answer

Step 1. List the variables

P_a = \$100m
P_e = \$80m
r = 5% (= 0.05)
t = 5 years to expiry
s = 0.40

Step 2. Calculate d_1

$$d_1 = \frac{\ln(^{Pa}/_{Pe}) + (r + 0.5s^2)t}{s\sqrt{t}}$$

$$d_1 = \frac{\ln(^{100}/_{80}) + [0.05 + (0.5 \times 0.40^2)]\,5}{0.4\sqrt{5}}$$

$$d_1 = \frac{\ln(1.25) + [0.05 + 0.08]\,5}{0.8944}$$

$$d_1 = \frac{0.2231 + 0.65}{0.8944}$$

$$\mathbf{d_1} = \frac{0.8731}{0.8944} = \mathbf{0.9762\ (say\ 0.976)}$$

Step 2. Calculate d_2

$d_2 = d_1 - s\sqrt{t}$

$d_2 = 0.9762 - 0.4\ \sqrt{5}$

$d_2 = 0.9762 - 0.8944$

d_2 = 0.0818 (say 0.082)

Step 3. Obtain values for $N(d_1)$ and $N(d_2)$

$N(d_1)$.

When $d_1 = 0.976$ the corresponding value in the normal distribution table is 0.3355.

The value of d_1 is positive, so add 0.50.

$N(d_1) = 0.3355 + 0.50 = 0.8355$.

$N(d_2)$.

When $d_2 = 0.082$, the corresponding value in the normal distribution table is 0.0326.

The value of d_2 is positive, so add 0.50.

$N(d_2) = 0.0326 + 0.50 = 0.5326$.

Step 4. Calculate the option price (for a call option)

$c = P_a N(d_1) - P_e N(d_2) e^{-rt}$

Tip – calculate the value of e^{-rt} first

$rt = (0.05)(5) = 0.25$

$e^{-0.25} = 1/e^{0.25}$

$e^{0.25} = 1.284$

Therefore $1/e^{0.25} = 0.7788$

$$\text{Option price} = P_s N(d_1) - P_e N(d_2) e^{-rt}$$
$$= 100(0.8355) - 80\ (0.5326)\ (0.7788)$$
$$= 83.55 - 33.183 = \mathbf{50.37}$$

Conclusion: The value of equity is $50.37m.

4.3 BSOP model and equity valuation – firms in financial distress

The option has no intrinsic value when the value of the assets is less than the face value of the debt. This does not mean the equity is worthless. Out of the value options still have value which reflects the possibility that the option will move into the money in the future.

Example

A firm has assets less current liabilities of $50m. This figure varies with a standard deviation of 0.4.

The face value of the outstanding debt is $80m. This debt is zero coupon and is to be paid in 5 years' time.

The risk free rate is 5%

Required:

Calculate the value of equity.

a

Answer

Step 1. List the variables

P_a = \$50m
P_e = \$80m
r = 5% (= 0.05)
t = 5 years to expiry
s = 0.40

Step 2. Calculate d_1

$$d_1 = \frac{\ln(^{Pa}/_{Pe}) + (r + 0.5s^2)t}{s\sqrt{t}}$$

$$d_1 = \frac{\ln(^{50}/_{80}) + [0.05 + (0.5 \times 0.40^2)]\,5}{0.4\sqrt{5}}$$

$$d_1 = \frac{\ln(0.625) + [0.05 + 0.08]\,5}{0.8944}$$

$$d_1 = \frac{-0.47 + 0.65}{0.8944}$$

$$\mathbf{d_1} = \frac{0.18}{0.8944} = \mathbf{0.2012\ (say\ 0.2)}$$

Step 2. Calculate d_2

$d_2 = d_1 - s\sqrt{t}$

$d_2 = 0.2 - 0.4\ \sqrt{5}$

$d_2 = 0.2 - 0.8944$

$d_2 = -0.6944$ (say -0.69)

Step 3. Obtain values for $N(d_1)$ and $N(d_2)$

$N(d_1)$.

When $d_1 = 0.2$ the corresponding value in the normal distribution table is 0.0793.
The value of d_1 is positive, so add 0.50.
$N(d_1) = 0.0793 + 0.50 = 0.5793$.

$N(d_2)$.

When $d_2 = -0.69$, the corresponding value in the normal distribution table is 0.2549.
The value of d_2 is negative, so subtract 0.2549 from 0.50.
$N(d_2) = 0.50 - 0.2549 = 0.2451$

Step 4. Calculate the option price (for a call option)

$c = P_a N(d_1) - P_e N(d_2) e^{-rt}$

$$\text{Option price} = P_s N(d_1) - P_e N(d_2) e^{-rt}$$
$$= 50(0.5793) - 80\ (0.2451)\ (0.7788)$$
$$= 28.97 - 15.27 = 13.7$$

Conclusion: The value of equity is $13.7m.

The equity in the firm still has substantial value because of the option characteristics of the equity. This explains why the equity of insolvent firms might still have value. The volatility of the asset base and the time until the debt has to be repaid means that there is a chance that the option will go into the money if the company continues to trade (though note that company law might forbid this in some cases).

4.4 BSOP model and debt – debt characteristics

Returning to the example used in section 2.2.

Example

A firm has assets less current liabilities of $100m. This figure varies with a standard deviation of 0.4.

The face value of the outstanding debt is $80m. This debt is zero coupon and is to be paid in 5 years' time.

The risk free rate is 5%

This led to the following inputs and outputs from the BSOP model

BSOP model inputs

P_a	=	$100m
P_e	=	$80m
r	=	5% (= 0.05)
t	=	5 years to expiry
s	=	0.40

BSOP model outputs

d_1	=	0.976	$N(d_1)$	=	0.8355
d_2	=	0.082	$N(d_2)$	=	0.5326

$c = \$50.37m$

$e^{-rt} = 0.7788$

Required: Calculate the value of the debt, the interest rate carried by that debt and the credit spread on that debt.

Value of the debt

The total market value of the firm = Value of equity + Value of debt

$100m = $50.37m + Value of the debt

Value of debt = $100m – $50.37m = $49.63m

Interest rate on the debt

The fair value of the debt is linked to its face value through the interest rate.

Fair value $(1 + i)^n$ = face value (the amount paid on redemption)

$\Rightarrow$ \$49.63m $(1 + i)^5$ = \$80m

$\Rightarrow i = \sqrt[5]{80/49.63} - 1 = 10\%$

Credit spread on the debt

The risk free interest rate is 5% this implies a credit spread of 5% (10% – 5%).

4.5 BSOP model and debt – default

An earlier chapter explained that credit risk reflects the expected loss from a loan. The expected loss is a function of the loss given default (LDG) and the probability of default (p(d)). This is a simple expected value calculation.

The loss given default is the amount that could be lost if a lender defaults. It is not necessarily the amount of the loan as the lender might hold some form of collateral or the borrower may be able to pay a percentage of the amount owed.

The BSOP model can be used to provide information in this area.

Probability of default

The value of $N(d_2)$ is the probability that a call option will be in the money at the exercise date.

Therefore the probability that it will not be in the money is: $1 - N(d_2)$

Example

Returning to the example in an earlier section.

A firm has assets less current liabilities of \$100m. This figure varies with a standard deviation of 0.4.

The face value of the outstanding debt is \$80m. This debt is zero coupon and is to be paid in 5 years' time.

The risk free rate is 5%.

This led to the following inputs and outputs from the BSOP model.

BSOP model inputs			BSOP model outputs					
P_a	=	\$100m	d_1	=	0.976	$N(d_1)$	=	0.8355
P_e	=	\$80m	d_2	=	0.082	$N(d_2)$	=	0.5326
r	=	5% (= 0.05)						
t	=	5 years to expiry				c = \$50.37m		
s	=	0.40				e^{-rt} = 0.7788		

Required: Calculate the probability of default.

a

Answer

Probability of default = 1 – N(d2) = 1 – 0.5326 = 0.4674 or 46.74%

Expected loss

When a firm borrows cash the shareholders are given a put option on the firm's assets, written by the lenders with an exercise price equal to the face value of the debt. The ability to walk away at the date of redemption of the debt if the asset value is less than the face value of the debt has a value to the shareholders. This value is provided by the lender. It is the expected loss on the debt.

The value of the put option (expected loss from the lenders' view) can be calculated using put-call parity as explained in an earlier chapter.

The relationship is repeated here for your convenience.

Value of put	+	Current market price of underlying item	=	Value of call	+	Present value of the exercise price.

This can be rearranged to:

Value of put	=	Value of call	+	Present value of the exercise price.	–	Current market price of underlying item

Note that the present value of the exercise price must be calculated using continuous discounting. The discount factor is found using e^{-rt}. This was covered in an earlier chapter.

e

Example

A firm has assets less current liabilities of $100m. This figure varies with a standard deviation of 0.4.

The face value of the outstanding debt is $80m. This debt is zero coupon and is to be paid in 5 years' time.

The risk free rate is 5%.

This led to the following inputs and outputs from the BSOP model.

BSOP model inputs			**BSOP model outputs**					
P_a	=	$100m	d_1	=	0.976	$N(d_1)$	=	0.8355
P_e	=	$80m	d_2	=	0.082	$N(d_2)$	=	0.5326
r	=	5% (= 0.05)						
t	=	5 years to expiry				c = $50.37m		
s	=	0.40				e^{-rt} = 0.7788		

Required: Calculate the value of the put option on the assets (the expected loss).

Answer

Value of put	=	Value of call	+	Present value of the exercise price..	–	Current market price of underlying item
	=	\$50.37m	+	(\$80m × 0.7788)	–	\$100m
	=	\$50.37m	+	\$62.3m	–	\$100m
	=	**\$12.67m**				

Loss given default

This can be calculated from the previous numbers by rearranging the following expression for expected loss:

= Loss given default × Probability of default

This can be rearranged to:

$$\text{Loss given default} = \frac{\text{Expected loss}}{\text{Probability of default}}$$

Example

Using data from the previous examples.

$$\text{Loss given default} = \frac{\text{Expected loss}}{\text{Probability of default}}$$

$$\text{Loss given default} = \frac{\$12.67\text{m}}{0.4674} = \$27.12\text{m}$$

CHAPTER 13

International investment and financing decisions

Contents

Factors affecting foreign investment decisions

- Factors restricting foreign investment
- Exchange rate risk (currency risk)

1 Factors affecting foreign investment decisions

1.1 Factors restricting foreign investment

International companies invest in other countries because they hope to make a good financial return from their investment, and attractive opportunities might exist in other countries. Developing countries might be particularly attractive for foreign investment because these countries might be expected to achieve considerable economic growth in the future.

However, investments by private companies in developing countries might be restricted for several reasons.

- The country might not have an infrastructure of transport and communication systems to support commerce and trade. International companies might be reluctant to invest in capital projects in companies where the road network is inadequate for transporting heavy goods or large quantities of goods.
- The general standard of education of the local population might be low. International companies might need its employees to have certain basic skills, and if standards of education are low, these skills might not exist (and might be difficult to create with training programmes).
- There is always a **political risk**, that the government of the country will take measures against foreign investors. For example, there have been examples in the past of governments forcing foreign companies to sell their assets to domestic companies, or taking a business into state ownership. A foreign government might also impose measures such as restrictions on foreign currency dealings or the imposition of withholding tax on payments of dividends and interest to foreign companies.
- There is a **general economic risk** that the economy of a developing country will not develop as well as expected. It might be difficult for a foreign company to make a good return on an investment in a country with a weak economy.

Companies considering a major capital investment in another country also need to consider:

- the exchange rate risk
- the risk of exchange controls and similar cash flow restrictions
- taxation on remittances to the parent company's country.

1.2 Exchange rate risk (currency risk)

Exchange rate risk, also called FX risk and currency risk, is the financial risk from the possibility (or probability) that foreign currency exchange rates will change. The risk is greater when a foreign exchange rate is volatile, and moves by fairly large amounts over time, often both up and down.

Three aspects to exchange rate risk are:

- transaction risk;
- translation risk;
- economic risk.

Transaction risk

Transaction risk affects any company that receives income or makes payments in a foreign currency. It is the risk that when a quantity of foreign currency will be received or paid at a time in the future, the exchange rate might move between 'now' and the time that receipt or payment of the currency will occur. As a consequence of the exchange rate movement the amount of money received or paid in the company's own currency (domestic currency) will be less or more than originally expected.

Exchange rates can move favourably as well as adversely, but the main concern for risk management is with the possibility and consequences of an adverse exchange rate movement.

Example

A UK company has bought goods from a foreign supplier and must pay $700,000 for them in three months' time. The current exchange rate is £1 = $2, and the company therefore expects to pay £350,000 in three months.

If the exchange rate changes so that after three months it is £1 = $1.75, and the company has done nothing to hedge its currency exposure (hedging is described in a later chapter), it will have to pay £400,000 to acquire the dollars to pay the supplier. Due to the exposure to currency transaction risk and the adverse movement in the exchange rate, the UK company has to pay £50,000 more than originally expected.

Transaction risks can affect international companies investing in another country in two ways:

- the foreign investment might purchase goods from other countries, or sell goods to other countries, and so will be exposed continually to transaction risks on its trading
- more significant for the purpose of the examination, the multinational parent company will require its foreign subsidiary to remit the profits from the venture to the parent, in the form of interest or dividends. Transaction exposures exist over the entire life on the capital investment project, because the interest payments or dividend payments from the foreign investment must be converted

into the parent company's own currency. Changes in the exchange rate will affect the amount of dividends that the parent company receives in its own currency.

Translation risk

Translation risk is a financial reporting risk for companies with foreign investments. For the purpose of preparing consolidated financial accounts, the financial statements of foreign subsidiaries must be translated into the reporting currency of the parent multinational. Changes in the exchange rate create gains or losses on translation, which affect the reported results of the group.

For example, suppose that a foreign subsidiary has net assets of 20 million francs at the beginning of a financial year for its parent company, whose domestic currency is dollars. The exchange rate is $1 = 4 francs at the beginning of the year and $1 = 5 francs at the end of the year.

Due to the adverse movement in the exchange rate during the year, the net investment at the beginning of the year, which had a value on translation of $5 million, will only be included in the consolidated balance sheet at a value of $4 million at the end of the year, a fall in value on translation of $1 million.

International companies may therefore wish to consider the consequences of translation risk for their reported consolidated statements.

Economic risk

Economic risk refers to the long-term movement in exchange rates caused by changes in the competitiveness of a country. This in turn affects the competitiveness of companies based in that country.

Economic risk is the risk that fluctuations in foreign exchange rates will change the present value of an investor's cash flows in a country.

For example, over the long term the euro might increase in value against the US dollar. If this happens, goods produced and paid for in US dollars will become cheaper relative to goods produced and paid for in euros. US companies will therefore become more competitive in terms of price, relative to companies in the Eurozone, because of the exchange rate movement.

Economic risk can be assessed through consideration of economic outlooks for the country and region under consideration.

It can be reduced by:

- matching foreign currency investments with liabilities in the same currency so that a loss on the investment is offset by a gain on the liability (or vice versa);
- strong due diligence procedures; or
- diversification of operations across several countries.

Estimating exchange rates and the impact of exchange rate movements on investment decisions

2 Estimating exchange rates and the impact of exchange rate movements on investment decisions

2.1 Estimating future 'spot' exchange rates

A company might wish to estimate future 'spot' exchange rates in order to carry out a capital investment appraisal of a proposed foreign investment, where:

- the cash flows will be in a foreign currency, but
- at some stage in the life of the project the cash will be converted into cash flows in the currency of the investing parent company.

An estimate of a future spot rate is a forecast of what the exchange rate might be at a future date, sometimes several years ahead.

(Confusion can arise because an estimate of a future spot rate is not the same as a forward exchange rate that can be obtained in the foreign exchange markets. Forward exchange rates for forward exchange contracts are described in a later chapter.)

There are two related methods of estimating future spot exchange rates:

- purchasing power parity theory
- interest rate parity theory.

Remember, however, that spot exchange rates move up and down continually, and any forecast of what the spot rate will be can only be an approximate estimate of what the average exchange rate for a future period will be.

2.2 Purchasing power parity theory

Purchasing power parity (PPP) theory states that the spot rates between two currencies will change over time in relation to the rate of inflation in the countries from which the currencies originate.

When the rate of inflation is higher in Country A than in Country B, the currency of Country A will fall in value against the currency of Country B.

The relationship is represented in the following formula which is provided to you in the exam.

$$S_1 = S_0 \times \frac{1 + h_c}{1 + h_b}$$

where:

S_1 = Estimated spot rate at end of period

S_0 = Current spot rate

h_c = period inflation rate in the variable currency

h_b = period inflation rate in the base currency

The base currency is the currency for which there is 1 unit in the quoted exchange rate, and the variable currency is the currency whose value is expressed as a number of units in value per 1 unit of the base currency.

For example in the exchange rate £1 = $1.90, the pound sterling is the base currency and the dollar is the variable currency.

This means that the base and variable currency vary depending on whether the foreign currency quote is direct or indirect (see chapter 17). The formula can be written as follows to show this, however these version are not given to you in the exam.

If quotes are direct

$$S_T = S_0 \times \frac{1 + i_d}{1 + i_f}$$

If quotes are indirect

$$S_T = S_0 \times \frac{1 + i_f}{1 + i_d}$$

where:

S_t = Estimated spot rate at end of period

S_0 = Current spot rate

i_f = period inflation rate in foreign currency

i_d = period inflation rate in domestic currency

The formula provides the exchange rate required for DCF analysis of international investments.

Example

The current exchange rate for euro/British pound (£/€1) is 0.6750.

A UK company wishes to evaluate a proposed capital investment in Germany. The investment will be for five years, and a large proportion of the project cash flows will be in euros.

The company needs to forecast what the euro/British pound spot rate will be each year for the full project period. It has been estimated that inflation in the UK will be 3% each year.

It has also been estimated that inflation in the euro zone will be 1.5% each year.

The spot exchange rates at the end of each year can be estimated using PPP theory, as follows. (The variable currency in this example is the British pound, since €1 = £0.6750).

The easiest way of forecasting the rate for each year is to:

- apply the formula to the spot rate to find the rate in one year's time; and then
- apply the formula to the rate in one year's time to find the rate in two years' time and so on as follows:

Year		Forecast rate
0	Spot (actual) rate	0.6750
1	0.6750 × 1.03/1.015	0.6850
2	0.6850 × 1.03/1.015	0.6951
3	0.6951 × 1.03/1.015	0.7054
4	0.7054 × 1.03/1.015	0.7158
5	0.7158 × 1.03/1.015	0.7264

Alternatively each forecast rate can be constructed from the current spot rate as follows:

Year		Forecast rate
0	Actual rate	0.6750
1	0.6750 × (1.03)/(1.015)	0.6850
2	$0.6750 \times (1.03)^2/(1.015)^2$	0.6951
3	$0.6750 \times (1.03)^3/(1.015)^3$	0.7054
4	$0.6750 \times (1.03)^4/(1.015)^4$	0.7158
5	$0.6750 \times (1.03)^5/(1.015)^5$	0.7264

In the above example, the forecast inflation rates were constant for each year. This might not always be the case.

Example

The current exchange rate for euro/British pound (£/€1) is 0.6750.

A UK company wishes to evaluate a proposed capital investment in Germany. The investment will be for five years, and a large proportion of the project cash flows will be in euros.

The company needs to forecast what the euro/British pound spot rate will be each year for the full project period. It has been estimated that inflation in the UK will be 3% each year UK for years 1 to 4 and 5% in year 5.

It has also been estimated that inflation in the euro zone will be 1.5% each year for three years, and 2% in each of years 4 and 5.

The spot exchange rates at the end of each year can be estimated using PPP theory, as follows. (The variable currency in this example is the British pound, since €1 = £0.6750).

Year		Forecast rate
0	Actual rate	0.6750
1	0.6750 × 1.03/1.015	0.6850
2	0.6850 × 1.03/1.015	0.6951
3	0.6951 × 1.03/1.015	0.7054
4	0.7054 × 1.03/1.02	0.7123
5	0.7123 × 1.05/1.02	0.7332

or

Year		Forecast rate
0	Actual rate	0.6750
1	$0.6750 \times (1.03)/(1.015)$	0.6850
2	$0.6750 \times (1.03)^2/(1.015)^2$	0.6951
3	$0.6750 \times (1.03)^3/(1.015)^3$	0.7054
4	$0.6750 \times (1.03)^4/[(1.015)^3)(1.02)]$	0.7123
5	$0.6750 \times [(1.03)^4(1.05)]/[(1.015)^3(1.02)^2]$	0.7332

2.3 International Fisher effect

Fisher argued that investors in all countries expect the same real rate of return after allowing for inflation. Therefore, the difference in interest rates between two countries could be explained by differences in the rates of inflation in those countries.

$$1 + r_{home} = 1 + r_{overseas} \times \frac{1 + i_f}{1 + i_d}$$

where:

r_{home} = domestic interest rate

$r_{overseas}$ = foreign interest rate

i_f = period inflation rate in foreign currency

i_d = period inflation rate in domestic currency

This formula is not provided in the exam. However, it is very useful because it allows a discount rate in one currency to be adjusted for differential inflation to find a discount rate in another currency.

2.4 Interest rate parity theory

Interest rate parity theory can be derived from the International Fisher effect and PPP.

Interest rate parity theory is based on the assumption that exchange rates will adjust to eliminate differences in interest rates between countries.

It is used to derive forward rates from spot rates by adjusting the spot rate by the interest rate differential.

The relationship is represented in the following formula which is provided to you in the exam.

$$F_0 = S_0 \times \frac{1 + i_c}{1 + i_b}$$

where:

F_1 = Forward rate

S_0 = Current spot rate

i_c = period interest rate in the variable currency

i_b = period interest rate in the base currency

This formula is similar to the PPP theory formula, except that the forecast annual interest rate is used instead of the annual forecast rate of inflation.

Once again, the formula can be written as follows to show this, however these version are not given to you in the exam.

If quotes are direct

$$F_0 = S_0 \times \frac{1 + i_d}{1 + i_f}$$

If quotes are indirect

$$F_0 = S_0 \times \frac{1 + i_f}{1 + i_d}$$

where:

F_0 = Estimated spot rate at end of period

S_0 = Current spot rate

i_f = period interest rate in foreign currency

i_d = period interest rate in domestic currency

In circumstance of market perfection the forward rate derived from interest rate parity would be the same as the forecast spot rate derived from purchasing power parity. Therefore, the forward rates can also be used as a proxy for the forecast spot rates in DCF calculation. (However, note that in practice there is poor correlation between forward rates and future spot rates).

e

Example

The current exchange rate for British pound against the euro (€/£1) is 1.4815.

The forecast annual interest rate for the British pound is 5% in each year.

The forecast annual interest rate for the euro is 2.5% in each year.

Required: Estimate a spot rate (€/£1) at the end of each year for years 1 – 4.

a

Answer

Year		**Forecast rate**
0	Actual rate	1.4815
1	1.4815 × 1.025/1.05	1.4462
2	1.4462 × 1.025/1.05	1.4118
3	1.4118 × 1.025/1.05	1.3782
4	1.3782 × 1.025/1.05	1.3454

or

Year		**Forecast rate**
0	Actual rate	1.4815
1	1.4815 × 1.025/1.05	1.4462
2	$1.4815 \times 1.025^2/1.05^2$	1.4118
3	$1.4815 \times 1.025^3/1.05^3$	1.3782
4	$1.4815 \times 1.025^4/1.05^4$	1.3454

In the above example, the forecast interest rates were not expected to change. This might not always be the case.

Example

The current exchange rate for British pound against the euro (€/£1) is 1.4815. The forecast annual interest rate for the British pound is 5% in years 1 and 2 and 6% in years 3 and 4.

The forecast annual interest rate for the euro is 2.5% in year 1 and 3% in each of years 2 – 4.

Required: Estimate a spot rate (€/£1) at the end of each year for years 1 – 4.

Answer

Year		Forecast rate
0	Actual rate	1.4815
1	1.4815 × 1.025/1.05	1.4462
2	1.4462 × 1.03/1.05	1.4187
3	1.4187 × 1.03/1.06	1.3785
4	1.3782 × 1.03/1.06	1.3395

Year		Forecast rate
0	Actual rate	1.4815
1	$1.4815 \times (1.025)/(1.05)$	1.4462
2	$1.4815 \times [(1.025)(1.03)]/(1.05)^2$	1.4187
3	$1.4815 \times [(1.025)(1.03)^2]/[(1.05)^2(1.06)]$	1.3785
4	$1.4815 \times [(1.025)(1.03)^3]/[(1.05)^2)(1.06)^2]$	1.3395

2.5 Impact of changes in exchange rate

Expected changes in an exchange rate can have a significant effect on the financial viability of an international investment project.

Example

A company is considering a four-year investment in another country, where it will establish a subsidiary. The subsidiary will remit all its profits each year to the parent company, and no additional tax will be paid by the parent company in its own country on the profits and dividends of its foreign subsidiary.

The investment will cost $230,000 in Year 0, and expected after-tax profits of the subsidiary (all distributable) are as follows:

Year	000 pesetas
1	200
2	400
3	500
4	300

The current exchange rate is $1 = 4 pesetas. The cost of capital for evaluating all aspects of the project is 15%.

The expected rate of inflation in the parent company's country and Peseta-land is as follows:

Year	Forecast annual inflation	
	Dollar-land	Peseta-land
1	2%	5%
2	3%	6%
3	3%	8%
4	2%	5%

Required

(a) Calculate the expected NPV of the project if changes in the exchange rate are ignored.

(b) Calculate the NPV of the project allowing for expected changes in the exchange rate.

a

Answer

(a) **Ignoring changes in the exchange rate**

Year	Pesetas cash flow	Exchange rate (Pesatas 000)	Cash flow ($000)	Discount rate 15%	PV ($000)
0			(225)	1.000	(230.0)
1	200	4.0	50	0.870	43.5
2	400	4.0	100	0.756	75.6
3	500	4.0	125	0.658	82.3
4	300	4.0	75	0.572	42.9
				NPV	+ 14.3

(b) **Allowing for changes in the exchange rate**

Year		Estimated exchange rate
1	$4.0 \times (1.05)/(1.02)$	4.12
2	$4.0 \times (1.05)(1.06)/(1.02)(1.03)$	4.24
3	$4.0 \times (1.05)(1.06)(1.08)/(1.02)(1.03)^2$	4.44
4	$4.0 \times (1.05)^2(1.06)(1.08)/(1.02)^2(1.03)^2$	4.57

Year	Pesetas cash flow	Exchange rate (Pesatas 000)	Cash flow ($000)	Discount rate 15%	PV ($000)
0			(225)	1.000	(230.0)
1	200	4.12	48.5	0.870	42.2
2	400	4.24	94.3	0.756	71.3
3	500	4.44	112.6	0.658	74.1
4	300	4.57	65.6	0.572	37.5
				NPV	(4.9)

In this example, the project will not achieve a return of 15% and its NPV is negative, because of the expected movement in the exchange rate during the project period.

International DCF appraisal

- Features of a foreign country investment appraisal
- Taxation and international investment
- Foreign investment decisions using DCF
- Market imperfections

3 International DCF appraisal

3.1 Features of a foreign country investment appraisal

An examination question might ask you to evaluate a proposed capital investment in a foreign country, possibly a developing country where the risks of investment are comparatively high due to a weak local currency and the risk of exchange controls.

Comments on cash flows

- All cash flows must be modelled in the usual way. This might include the need to take into account transaction costs (say for currency conversion), tax flows abroad and at home, the effect of subsidies and so on.
- Post tax cash flows of the investing company might need to take account of double tax relief.
- Estimated cash flows take account of expected inflation rates. (The inflated cash flows should be discounted at the money cost of capital.)
- Most of the cash flows for the foreign investment will be in the currency of the foreign country, although some cash flows might be in the currency of the parent company. Therefore, a key element of a question will be the need to translate cash flows using estimated exchange rates.
- There might be restrictions on the amount of payments that can be made from the foreign country, due to exchange control restrictions. This means that the cash profits from the project might not be payable immediately in full as dividends to the investing company.

Comments on the discount rate

- You might be required to establish a **cost of capital for evaluating the project**, possibly using the CAPM and a beta factor for the project.
- It might be necessary to convert a discount rate in one country into the equivalent rate that would be suitable in another. The International Fisher Effect equation can be used to do this.

3.2 Taxation and international investment

Taxation affects investment decisions, and it is necessary to estimate the tax payments for a proposed capital investment project in another country. Taxation is considered in more detail in a later chapter, with respect to international or multinational companies. Briefly, however, there are two important aspects to tax on the profits and distributions of foreign subsidiaries.

- **Withholding tax**. Some countries levy a withholding tax on interest or dividends paid by companies to foreign investors, including foreign parent companies. Withholding tax is additional tax, reducing the net cash flows for the parent company from its foreign subsidiary.
- **Double taxation agreements**. Many countries have double taxation agreements with each other. The purpose of a double taxation agreement is to prevent punitive taxation by taxing profits twice, once in each country. A double taxation agreement allows an international company to set off the tax payable in its own country on the profits of or income received from a foreign subsidiary, against the tax already paid by the subsidiary in its own country. The effect of double taxation agreements is to help to make international investments more attractive by avoiding excessive and punitive tax on the pre-tax returns that the investments make.

Example

An international company pays tax on its worldwide profits in its own country at the rate of 25%.

It has a subsidiary in a foreign country where the rate of tax on profits is only 12%, but dividends paid to a foreign investor are subject to additional withholding tax of 10%. This is 10% of the cash paid as dividends.

The parent company intends to remit as much as possible from its foreign subsidiary in the form of dividends.

The foreign subsidiary makes a profit before tax of 1,000,000 dinars.

(The exchange rate is $1 = 1 dinar and has been fixed at this rate for a long time.)

There is a double taxation agreement between the two countries.

Dividend paid by subsidiary

	Dinar
Profit before tax	1,000,000
Tax at 12%	(120,000)
Gross dividend (before withholding tax)	880,000
Withholding tax (10%)	(80,000)
Cash dividend (100%)	800,000

Parent company's cash flow

	$
Dividend (800,000 dinar @ $1 = 1 dinar)	800,000
Tax at 25%	250,000
Less: Double tax relief (the tax suffered abroad on the profits) = (120,000 + 80,000 dinar) @ $1 = 1 dinar	(200,000)
Tax payable	(50,000)
Post tax income from the subsidiary	750,000

3.3 Foreign investment decisions using DCF

There are two methods for calculating the NPV of an overseas project.

Method 1

Prepare the foreign currency cash flow forecast for the project.

Discount the foreign currency flows using a discount rate appropriate to projects in the foreign country in that currency.

Convert the resulting NPV to the domestic currency at the spot exchange rate.

Adjust this amount for any other amounts paid or received in the home currency.

Method 2

Prepare the foreign currency cash flow forecast for the project.

Convert the project cash flows into the domestic currency using expected future exchange rates.

Discount these at the domestic discount rate to give a domestic currency NPV.

Adjust this amount for any other amounts paid or received in the home currency.

Comment

In conditions of capital market perfection the two methods would result in the same domestic currency NPV. This is because the future spot rates would be linked to the current spot rates by the differential interest rates and inflation rates inherent in the discount rate.

Future spot rates might be found using interest rate parity, purchasing power parity or the international Fisher effect.

Example

A company is considering an investment in another country, by setting up a foreign subsidiary. The investment would cost 20 million foreign currency units (CUs).

The company will also have to spend $200,000 in its own country at the start of the project on legal fees and set-up costs.

At current prices, the cash flows from the project in the other country are expected to be as follows, before allowing for tax:

Year	CUs (million)
0	(20.0)
1	8.0
2	10.0
3	8.0

Taxation in the foreign country is at 50%, and is payable in the year following the year in which the taxable profits occur.

In addition, in Year 1 of the project, the foreign government will refund 50% of the cost of the investment as a tax allowance. This will be refunded in the form of a cash payment to the subsidiary.

The tax rate in the company's own country is 30% and is payable in the period in which the related expense is incurred.

The expected rate of inflation in the company's own country over the next three years is expected to be 6% each year.

The rate of inflation in the foreign country is expected to be 10% each year.

The foreign equity beta for the new project is 1.80.

The company is all-equity financed, and would finance the new project with equity.

The risk-free rate of return is 10% and the market return is 15%, in the foreign country.

The current rate of exchange is $1 = 4 Currency Units.

Required

Calculate the NPV of the investment, and recommend whether it should be undertaken.

a

Answer

Method 1: Calculate NPV in foreign currency and then translate at the spot rate

The following cash flow estimates are all in millions of CUs:

Year	0	1	2	3	4
Cash flows before inflation	(20.00)	8.00	10.00	8.00	
Cash flows after inflation at 10%	(20.00)	8.80	12.10	10.65	
Tax at 50%		10.00	(4.40)	(6.05)	(5.33)
Net cash flows	(20.00)	18.80	7.70	4.60	(5.33)
Discount factor (19%) **(W1)**	1.000	0.840	0.706	0.593	0.499
	(20.00)	15.79	5.44	2.73	(2.66)
NPV (CUs m)	1.30				
Exchange rate	÷4.0				
NPV ($m)	0.33				
Set up costs ($m)	(0.20)				
Tax relief on set up costs ($m)	0.06				
Project NPV ($m)	0.19				

Conclusion: The investment has a positive NPV and should be undertaken.

Working: Discount rate

The project is all-equity financed. The cost of capital for the project can therefore be calculated directly from the CAPM, using a beta factor of 1.80.

Cost of equity = 10% + 1.80 (15% – 10%) = 19%.

Method 2: Translate cash flows into domestic currency and then discount using domestic discount rate

Year	0	1	2	3	4
Cash flows before inflation	(20.00)	8.00	10.00	8.00	
Cash flows after inflation at 10%	(20.00)	8.80	12.10	10.65	
Tax at 50%		10.00	(4.40)	(6.05)	(5.33)
Net cash flows	(20.00)	18.80	7.70	4.60	(5.33)
Exchange rates **(W1)**	4.00	4.15	4.31	4.47	4.64
	(5.00)	4.53	1.79	1.03	(1.15)
Discount factor (14.7%) **(W2)**	1.000	0.872	0.760	0.663	0.578
	(5.00)	3.95	1.36	0.68	(0.66)
NPV ($m)	0.33				
Set up costs ($m)	(0.20)				
Tax relief on set up costs ($m)	0.06				
Project NPV ($m)	0.19				

Workings

W1 Exchange rates (using PPP)

Year		Forecast rate
0	Spot (actual) rate	4.00
1	4.00 × 1.10/1.06	4.15
2	4.15 × 1.10/1.06	4.31
3	4.31 × 1.10/1.06	4.47
4	4.47 × 1.10/1.06	4.64

W2 Discount rate (using International Fisher effect)

1.19 x 1.06/1.10 = 0.1467 or 14.7%

3.4 Market imperfections

The previous section explained two approaches that could be used in foreign currency DCF. Each approach would give the same answer in circumstances of market perfection.

However, this would not be the case if there were market imperfections. Market perfection does not exist in reality (though markets can be very efficient).

Exchange controls

Example exchange controls are an important market imperfection.

Exchange controls are actions by a government that:

- restrict or prevent the ability of its own nationals to buy foreign currency in order to make payments to foreign suppliers
- restrict or prohibit the payment of interest or dividends to foreign investors, including payments from subsidiary companies to their foreign parent
- restrict the flow (payments) of capital out of the country.

The impact of exchange controls can be illustrated using the same example as that used previously.

Example

A company is considering an investment in another country, by setting up a foreign subsidiary. The investment would cost 20 million foreign currency units (CUs).

The company will also have to spend $200,000 in its own country at the start of the project on legal fees and set-up costs.

At current prices, the cash flows from the project in the other country are expected to be as follows, before allowing for tax:

Year	CUs (million)
0	(20.0)
1	8.0
2	10.0
3	8.0

Taxation in the foreign country is at 50%, and is payable in the year following the year in which the taxable profits occur.

In addition, in Year 1 of the project, the foreign government will refund 50% of the cost of the investment as a tax allowance. This will be refunded in the form of a cash payment to the subsidiary.

The tax rate in the company's own country is 30% and is payable in the period in which the related expense is incurred.

The expected rate of inflation in the company's own country over the next three years is expected to be 6% each year.

The rate of inflation in the foreign country is expected to be 10% each year.

The foreign equity beta for the new project is 1.80.

The company is all-equity financed, and would finance the new project with equity.

The risk-free rate of return is 10% and the market return is 15%, in the foreign country.

Due to foreign exchange control regulations, the company will not be permitted to withdraw its surplus cash from the country in dividends until the end of Year 3. At the end of Year 3, the dividends paid from the foreign subsidiary to the parent company will be the total cash profits from the project, less the net tax payments.

The current rate of exchange is $1 = 4 Currency Units.

Required

Calculate the NPV of the investment, and recommend whether it should be undertaken.

Answer

Method 1: Calculate NPV in foreign currency and then translate at the spot rate

The exchange controls have no impact on this answer. It is the same as before and gives an NPV of $0.19m.

Method 2: Translate cash flows into domestic currency and then discount using domestic discount rate

Year	0	1	2	3	4
Cash flows before inflation	(20.00)	8.00	10.00	8.00	
Cash flows after inflation at 10%	(20.00)	8.80	12.10	10.65	
Tax at 50%		10.00	(4.40)	(6.05)	(5.33)
Net cash flows	(20.00)	18.80	7.70	4.60	(5.33)
Net cash inflow (CUs)				25.77	
Exchange rate **(W1)**	4.00			4.47	
Cash flows ($)					
Remittance from overseas				5.76	
Initial investment	(5.00)				
Set up costs	(0.2)				
Tax relief on set up cots	0.06				
Net cash flows ($)	(5.14)			5.76	
Discount factor (14.7%) **(W2)**	1.000			0.663	
Present values	(5.14)			3.81	
NPV (domestic currency)	(1.33)				

Workings

W1 Exchange rates (using PPP)

Year		Forecast rate
0	Spot (actual) rate	4.00
1	4.00 × 1.10/1.06	4.15
2	4.15 × 1.10/1.06	4.31
3	4.31 × 1.10/1.06	4.47

W2 Discount rate (using International Fisher effect)

1.19 x 1.06/1.10 = 0.1467 or 14.7%

The NPV is negative; therefore the project should not be undertaken.

The negative NPV has been caused by:

- the delay until Year 3 in being able to repatriate the investment profits in the form of dividend payments; coupled with
- the falling value of the foreign currency against the dollar between Year 0 and Year 3.

International sources of finance

- Possible sources
- Currency borrowing to reduce the currency risk in capital investments
- Local capital markets for borrowing

4 International sources of finance

4.1 Possible sources

An important aspect of financial management is the choice of methods of financing for a company's assets. Companies use a variety of sources of finance and the aim should be to achieve an efficient capital structure that provides:

- a suitable balance between short-term and long-term funding;
- adequate working capital; and
- a suitable balance between equity and debt capital in the long-term capital structure.

International capital investment can be funded with debt or equity or a mixture of the two raises at home, in the same country of the overseas investment or in a third country. factors that must be considered when choosing a source of finance include:

- amount needed;
- costs associated with the finance;
- term – how long is the finance available for;
- flexibility – is it raise more or repay the funds with little effort;
- repayment – when will the amount raised need to be repaid if at all;
- the impact of the finance on the financial statements.

4.2 Currency borrowing to reduce the currency risk in capital investments

International capital investment is similar in many respects to capital investment in a company's own country, although there are some extra risks. As explained earlier, a major additional risk is the currency risk. Changes in the value of a foreign currency relative to the investing company's currency could have a significant effect on a project NPV.

One way of reducing currency risk is to borrow in the currency of the investment to finance some or all of a proposed international project. Borrowing in the currency of the investment reduces risk in two ways.

- **It reduces the translation risk**. By borrowing in the currency of the investment, the parent company is able to match assets in a foreign currency with liabilities in the same currency. To the extent that the assets and liabilities are matched in value, any movement in the exchange rate will have an equal effect on the translated value of the assets and liabilities. For example, if a company invests in a project costing 20 million foreign currency units, and borrows 20 million foreign currency units to finance the project, assets and liabilities in the foreign currency are matched, and translation risk is eliminated.

- **It also reduces the transaction risk**. This is because when a company borrows in a foreign currency, it must pay interest and repay the loan in the same currency. It will use cash flows from the project to make the payments. In doing so, it is able to match some of its receipts in the foreign currency with payments in the same currency. To the extent that receipts and payments in the same foreign currency can be matched, transaction risk is eliminated

4.3 Local capital markets for borrowing

The ability of a company to borrow in the currency of an international investment depends on:

- whether there is a large and active local capital market, and
- if there is a large capital market for the foreign currency, whether the company is able to borrow in that market.

An international company might be able to borrow in the local currency from a bank, possibly through its foreign subsidiary. It is much less likely that the foreign country will have a well-developed corporate bond market for issuing bonds in the local currency. The international bond markets are also inappropriate for borrowing in any currency except the major international currencies (mostly the US dollar and the euro).

CHAPTER 14

Mergers and acquisitions

Contents

Mergers and takeovers: strategic and regulatory issues

1 Mergers and takeovers: strategic and regulatory issues

1.1 Introduction to mergers and acquisitions

The distinction between acquisitions and mergers

A company with a growth strategy might seek to grow by means of a merger or acquisition. Mergers and acquisitions involve the amalgamation of two companies.

- Typically, one company acquires the other and becomes the parent company. The second company becomes a subsidiary within the group.
- Occasionally, a new parent company might be created, and the two merging companies become subsidiaries of the new parent company.

A merger is an amalgamation of two companies of approximately equal size. In a takeover, a larger company usually acquires a majority of the share capital in a smaller 'target' company. In practice, business combinations are usually an acquisition of one company by another.

However the financial management issues are broadly the same for mergers as for acquisitions.

The objective of a merger or takeover

The objective of a takeover should be consistent with the overall objectives of the company making the takeover, which should be to increase the wealth of its shareholders. Similarly, the objective of a merger should be to satisfy the objectives of both companies – to increase the wealth of the shareholders of both companies. It is not always obvious, however, how a merger or takeover might add value and create wealth for shareholders.

More specifically, the purpose of an acquisition or a merger is to grow the company. In an acquisition, the acquiring company takes over the business of the target company – its net assets, its other resources, its sales and markets and (hopefully) its profits.

1.2 Arguments for and against the use of acquisitions and mergers as a means of expansion

Alternatives to acquisitions

A company that is pursuing an expansion strategy might consider alternative expansion strategies. The main alternatives are:

- growth through internal development of the business
- growth by means of a joint venture.

A comparison of growth by acquisition and internal growth

Growth by acquisition has several advantages when compared to growth through internal development,.

- By far the most important advantage of an acquisition is that growth is achieved much more quickly. By making an acquisition, a company immediately gets bigger. If the target for acquisition has been selected well, the company should be able to move towards its strategic goals more quickly than if it tried to grow internally.
- It is often argued that when a target company is acquired, it should be possible to achieve 'synergies' and add value by increasing the combined profits of the two companies. Synergy is explained in more detail later.
- When a company is trying to grow its business in another country, acquisition might be better than internal growth, because the company will acquire skilled employees who already understand the business, the country, its laws and culture and its language.
- Unless a company acquires available target businesses, its competitors might acquire them instead and the strategic threat from the enlarged competitor might increase.

There are several reasons, however, why growth through internal development might be preferred to growth by acquisition.

- There is a high risk that the price paid for an acquisition will be too high, and the financial return from buying an over-valued company will be low.
- Many acquisitions are failures. This means that an acquisition strategy is a high-risk strategy. The reasons why acquisitions often fail are explained later.
- With a strategy of internal growth, the company's management should be able to plan and control the development of the business more effectively, because the practical problems associated with acquisitions do not arise. The practical problems include difficulties with employees in the acquired company and the management time needed to combine the systems of the two companies after the acquisition.
- An acquisition is not usually 'ideal' and there will be some features of the target company that the acquirer might not want to buy. After the acquisition, the acquiring company might want to sell off unwanted parts of the business. This can be a time-consuming process, and the prices obtained from selling off these operations and assets might be low.

A comparison of growth by acquisition and growth by joint venture

An opportunity might arise to grow the business by forming a joint venture with one or more other entities. Growth through joint ventures has some advantages over growth through acquisition.

- When a company wants to enter the market in a foreign country, there might be a risk that an acquisition will create a hostile response from the government of the country concerned and from the customers of the target company. There might even be legal restrictions on the maximum percentage of shares in a domestic company that a foreign investor is allowed to acquire. These difficulties might be avoided by setting up a joint venture with a local company.
- Joint ventures should involve a lower capital investment, because the setup costs will be shared with the joint venture partner. The business risks and (in a foreign country) political risks are also shared.
- A joint venture partner might bring skills and expertise to the venture that the company does not have. The companies in a joint venture might therefore complement each other, and improve the prospects for success of the venture.

Joint ventures also have disadvantages, compared with an acquisition.

- The joint venture partners might have different strategic objectives, and might want different end-results from the business venture. This might eventually lead to a conflict of interests and disagreement between the partners.
- With an acquisition, the acquirer obtains management control of the target business. In a joint venture, control is shared with the other partner or partners.
- At some stage in the future, it is likely that one joint venture partner will want to buy-out the other, if the venture is a success. For the company selling its share of the business to the other partner, the joint venture will not have been successful in achieving long-term growth in the business, only a short-term financial return.

1.3 Evaluation of an acquisition proposal

Before deciding whether or not to try to acquire a proposed target, an assessment should be carried out to judge whether the proposed target would be an acquisition that result in the company achieving a strategic objective.

Johnson and Scholes proposed a model for judging proposed strategies. This model can be used to evaluate proposed acquisitions.

The model suggests that any strategy (which would include a merger or acquisition) should be evaluated for its:

- suitability;
- feasibility; and
- acceptability.

Suitability:

A strategy is suitable if it would achieve the strategic objective for which it is intended.

An acquisition should enhance shareholder value. The overriding objective of enhancing shareholder value is pursued through strategic decisions, for example acquiring a company in order to increase market share.

Suitability must be evaluated in terms of how the acquisition will help the company achieve its objectives.

These might include

- increased market share in order to achieve economies of scale;
- entry to a new market either in terms of physical location or product range;
- removal of a competitor;
- securing supply of crucial raw material through the purchase of a supplier; or
- acquiring know how.

The above list is by no means exhaustive. A question will explain what the company is trying to do. Your answer should explain whether the acquisition will deliver the required outcome. In other words, does it address the strategic requirements, given the circumstances and the situation?

Feasibility:

Feasibility – cash, regulatory approval/ time scale/ management structure

The feasibility of a strategy is concerned with whether it will work. A strategy is feasible if it can be implemented successfully.

Questions to consider when assessing feasibility include:

- Is there sufficient finance for the acquisition?
- Will the proposed acquisition meet regulatory problems?
- Does the company have sufficient management skill and expertise to integrate the new business?
- Are there any other specific integration issues?
- Can the company meet any regulatory timescales for conducting the offer?

Acceptability

The acceptability of a strategy is concerned with whether it will be acceptable to key stakeholders. If it is not acceptable to a key stakeholder, that stakeholder will oppose the strategy.

Management should then consider whether a strategy that is not acceptable to a key stakeholder should be undertaken or not.

There are several aspects of 'acceptability'.

- Shareholders will not regard an acquisition as acceptable if the expected returns on investment are too low, or if the risk is too high in relation to the expected return.
- Shareholders might prefer the cash being used to make the acquisition to be paid as a dividend instead.
- Shareholders may not regard an acquisition as acceptable if it reduces the share price of the company.
- Shareholders may not accept risk diversification as a reason for an acquisition because they already hold well diversified portfolios.
- Shareholders might regard an acquisition as unacceptable if they will be expected to provide a large amount of additional investment finance.
- Any stakeholder group might consider an acquisition unacceptable if they regard it as unethical.
- Employees might consider an acquisition to be unacceptable if it will lead to unemployment or changes in working conditions.
- Employees might consider an acquisition to be unacceptable if it will reduce profitability with an adverse effect on bonus schemes.
- Lenders might consider an acquisition to be unacceptable if it increases the gearing of the company.
- A regulatory authority might object to the acquisition if it reduces competition in a market.

1.4 Criteria for choosing an acquisition target

The choice of acquisition targets might be based on any of the following criteria:

- Strategic aims and objectives.
- Cost and relative size.
- Opportunity and availability.
- Potential synergies.

These are discussed further below:

Strategic aims and objectives

An acquisition target is usually selected because acquiring the target would help the acquiring company to achieve its strategic targets. For example, a company might be seeking to grow the business by expanding its product range for its existing markets, or moving into new geographical markets. Acquiring a suitable business would enable a company to expand its product range or move into new geographical markets. Some companies have pursued a strategy of buying up a large number of small companies in a fragmented market, with the intention of becoming the largest company and market leader.

Cost and relative size

Although there are occasional examples of small companies acquiring much larger ones in a 'reverse takeover', target companies are usually selected because they are affordable.

Opportunity and availability

In many cases, targets for acquisition are selected because of circumstances. An opportunity to acquire a particular company might arise, and the acquiring company might decide to take the opportunity whilst it is available.

Potential synergy

Synergy is sometimes called the '2 + 2 = 5' effect. It is the concept that the combined sum of two separate entities after a merger or acquisition will be worth more than their sum as two separate entities.

1.5 Synergy

Acquisition targets might possibly be selected because they provide an opportunity to increase total profits through improvements in efficiency. One reason for the success of private equity funds in acquiring target companies has been their ability to achieve additional efficiencies and economies that the previous company management had been unable to do. A strategy of private equity funds might be to look for target companies that they consider under-valued, with the intention of improving their operations and creating extra value.

When two separate entities come together into a single entity, opportunities might arise for increasing profits.

Synergies might be divided into three categories:

- Revenue synergies
- Cost synergies
- Financial synergies.

Revenue synergies

Revenue synergies are increases in total sales revenue following a merger or acquisition, by increasing total combined market share. For example, if Company A has annual sales revenue of $500 million acquires Company B which has annual sales revenue of $200 million, the combined revenue of the two companies after the merger might be, say, $750 million.

It is unusual for revenue synergies to occur, but they might occur in the following circumstances:

- The acquisition or merger creates an enlarged company that is able to promote its brand more effectively, and market share increases because customers are attracted by the new brand image.
- The acquisition or merger creates an enlarged company that is able to bid for large contracts, such as contracts to supply the government, which the two companies were unable to do before they combined due to their smaller size.

Cost synergies

Cost synergies are reductions in costs as a consequence of a merger or takeover. They might arise because it is possible to improve efficiency. For example, it might be possible to reduce the size and cost of administrative departments by combining the administrative functions of the two companies. It is not unusual for takeovers to result in staff redundancies, partly for this reason.

Cost synergies might also be possible by combining other activities, such as combining warehouse facilities.

Experience has shown, however, that companies often have difficulty in achieving planned cost synergies after a takeover, because combining the activities of the two companies after the takeover is often a long and complex process.

Financial synergies

A larger (combined) company or group might be able to raise finance in a cheaper way. The enlarged company might have access to financial markets, such as the bond market, that the two individuals companies could not access before the takeover, due to their smaller size.

The larger company might also be seen as a lower credit risk, so that it is able to borrow from banks at a lower rate of interest.

1.6 The high failure rate of acquisitions

Many acquisitions fail, and do not provide the value for shareholders that was expected when the acquisition was made. There are several reasons for failure.

- The purchase price paid for an acquisition is often too high.
- The expected synergies do not occur.
- There are serious problems with integrating the acquired company into the new group.
  - Employees in the acquired company might find it difficult to accept the different culture of the acquiring company, and a new set of policies and procedures. The loss of staff might be high, and valuable knowledge and expertise might be lost.

  - There might be problems with establishing effective management control in the acquired company. Control systems might have to be reviewed and changed.

- Senior management in the acquiring company might not give the acquired company sufficient time and attention to make the acquisition operationally and financially successful.
- Competitors might react to an acquisition with a new competitive strategy of their own. Increased competition might drive down the profits for all participants in the market.

1.7 Reverse takeovers

Reverse takeovers sometimes occur in acquisitions where the purchase price is paid in new shares issued by the acquirer.

A reverse takeover is a transaction in which an entity acquires another entity and the shareholders of the acquired entity end up with control of the combined entity.

Example

Before the transaction

X Plc has 10,000 ordinary shares in issue.

Y Ltd also has 10,000 ordinary shares in issue.

The transaction

X Plc buys the entire share capital of Y Ltd and pays for them by issuing 30,000 new ordinary shares to the owners of Y.

After the transaction

X Plc owns 100% of Y Ltd.

The original owners of Y Ltd own 75% (30,000 shares out of 40,000 shares) of the combined entity.

X Plc is the legal acquirer but in effect Y Ltd has taken over X Plc (because its original owners now control it).

Uses

A reverse takeover can be used by a private company to become publicly traded without going through an initial public offering. In the example above, Y Ltd is now part of a publically traded entity.

The legal acquirer (X Plc above) is often described as a shell company.

Benefits

The benefits to the reverse acquirer (Y Ltd) above are those associated with being a traded entity without the costs and delay of going through an IPO process..

- The shares now held by the original owners of the legal subsidiary are more liquid and that should make them more valuable.

- The company has greater access to capital markets.
- The company is better able to use share option schemes to incentivise its directors and other employees.
- The shares can be used to acquire other companies.

Valuation for mergers and acquisitions

- The need for a valuation
- Factors to consider in pricing a takeover bid
- Valuation methods
- Estimating earnings growth
- Types of acquisition

2 Valuation for mergers and acquisitions

2.1 The need for a valuation

Valuation and the offer price are key issues in a merger or acquisition. When a merger is negotiated, the two companies need to reach agreement on the valuation of shares in each company for the purpose of deciding the terms of the merger. In a takeover:

- the acquiring company needs to decide what price it is prepared to offer for the target company
- the directors of the target company need to decide whether the offer is acceptable and whether it should be recommended to the shareholder, and
- the shareholders in the target company need to decide whether they are willing to accept the offer made for their shares.

The target company might be a public company whose shares are already quoted on a stock market. In such cases the current share price is a useful guide to valuation, but a bidder will not succeed unless the offer price is higher than the current market price. Without a higher offer, the shareholders in the target company have no reason to accept and agree to sell their shares to the bidder.

When the target company is a private company, there is no market price that can act as a benchmark or guide to an offer price.

In bidding for both public and private companies, the acquiring company therefore needs to make estimates of the value of the target company, in order to decide what price it might be prepared to offer. The price should be sufficiently high to win acceptance from the target company shareholders, but not so high that the bidding company pays too much. When an acquisition is over-priced, the return on the investment will be low and the acquiring company will lose value for its shareholders.

It is not usual to make a bid to buy the debt capital or the preference shares of a target company. A valuation is required for the equity shares in the target company, and not a valuation for the company as a whole.

Valuation is an art, not a science

It is important to remember that the valuation of companies for the purpose of a merger or acquisition is not a science. Although there are valuation methods, these are all based on estimates and assumptions.

Valuation methods can be used to decide on an offer price, or may be used to justify an offer price. However, the final price is often agreed through negotiation, and the management of the bidding company must use judgement in deciding how high a price they might be willing to pay. The only 'correct' valuation is the price that the bidder makes and the shareholders in the target company accept.

A company preparing to make a takeover bid should consider several valuation methods and compare the different valuations they produce. Judgement should then be used to arrive at a price that should be offered for the target company shares.

Overvaluation

An acquisition might be overvalued (this is often found to be the case with hindsight). The wealth of the shareholders is reduced when too much is paid for an acquisition.

The main causes of overvaluation are:

- failure to realise expected synergies; or
- underestimating the costs of integrating the company

Another issue is that a buying company must pay a bid premium to encourage the owners of a quoted company to sell. The share price of a potential quoted target often rises in anticipation of a bid as speculators buy shares in expectation that the acquirer will pay a bid premium. This leads to a transfer of wealth from the owners of the buying company to the owners of this selling company. This is often reflected in a fall of the bidders share price.

2.2 Factors to consider in pricing a takeover bid

When a company is considering a takeover bid for another company, there a several important factors to consider before deciding what offer price might be appropriate. These include:

- Potential synergies (see earlier)
- Risk exposure;
- Real options;
- Financing;
- Valuation assumptions;

Risk exposure

An acquisition or merger might alter the exposure to market risk, and either increase or reduce the asset beta of the enlarged company. Before masking a takeover bid, or deciding on a suitable offer price, the company making the acquisition should consider what changes might happen to its risk exposures, and how significant they might be.

Real options

An acquisition might create real options to expand operations or re-deploy at some time in the future. Real options are described in another chapter.

Briefly, a real option is an option to take a course of action at some time in the future, often depending on how the business develops. If an acquisition creates a real option, such as an option to expand into a new geographical market at some time in the future, this option has some value.

Financing

An acquisition often requires substantial financing, and the acquiring company needs to consider how it might be able to raise the finance.

It might be difficult to raise new debt finance to acquire a highly-geared target company (depending on conditions in the debt markets) when the acquiring company is also highly-geared.

Using retained earnings to finance acquisitions might have implications for dividend policy.

Valuation assumptions

In a takeover process, separate valuations for the target company are made by the company making the takeover bid and the directors of the target company. Shareholders in both companies might also have their own views on valuation.

Valuations are based on assumptions, but many assumptions are based on judgements rather than 'hard evidence'. Estimates might be unreliable, such as estimates of the growth rate in future profits or free cash flows of the target company.

To allow for negotiations on price, the directors of the company making the takeover bid should consider an initial offer price and a price that they might be willing to go up to.

The directors of the target company should consider whether to reject an initial offer from the bidding company, but then consider the minimum price they would be willing to agree to and recommend to their shareholders.

2.3 Valuation methods

You might be required in your examination to use several methods for valuation of a target company. Each method will produce a different valuation, but each valuation can provide useful information and help with deciding what the offer price should be. You should be prepared to use each of the different valuation methods, and then discuss the assumptions and estimates on which the valuation is based. You might also be required to compare the different valuations produced by each method, and then recommend (with reasons) a valuation that you consider appropriate as a basis for making an offer to the target company shareholders.

There are several approaches to making a valuation of the shares in a company:

- A valuation based on the net asset value of the target company.
- Market-based valuations, using estimates of future earnings or dividends

- Cash-flow based valuations, using discounted cash flow of expected future returns from the acquisition
- A valuation based on an expected value added (EVA) model: this is another form of cash flow-based model.

Many of these were covered in chapter 12.

2.4 Estimating earnings growth

A question on valuation might need the calculation of the forecast growth rate of earnings. This could be obtained from internal sources or from external sources.

Internal sources

The growth rate can be estimated from internal sources in one of two ways:

- extrapolation of historical growth; and
- Gordon's growth model

Extrapolation of historical growth

This is based on the idea that the shareholders' expectations will be based on what has been experienced in the past.

An average rate of growth is estimated by taking the geometric mean of growth rates in recent years.

$$\text{Geometric growth rate} = \sqrt{\frac{\text{value at end of period of n years}}{\text{value at start}}}$$

Where:

n = number of terms in the series (e.g. years of growth)

Example: Extrapolation of historical growth

The earnings of a company has been as follows over the last five years:

Year	Earnings
20X1	100
20X2	110
20X3	120
20X4	134
20X5	148

The average rate is calculated as follows:

$$g = \sqrt[4]{\frac{148}{100}} - 1 = 0.103 \text{ or } 10.3\%$$

Gordon's growth model (the earnings retention valuation model

Growth is achieved by retaining profits (retained earnings) for reinvestment in the business.

When a company retains a proportion of its earnings each year, the expected annual future growth rate can be estimated using the formula:

$$g = br$$

Where:

g = annual growth rate in dividends in perpetuity

b = proportion of earnings retained (for reinvestment in the business)

r = rate of return that the company will make on its investments

Example

A company has just achieved annual earnings $500,000.

The company is expected to retain 60% of its earnings every year and pay out the rest as dividends.

The company's return on capital employed is 10%.

The anticipated annual growth in dividends = br = 60% × 10% = 6%

You might have to derive the figures for the percentage of earnings retained and return on capital employed from extracts of financial statements provided in a question.

Growth rate from external sources

A growth rate might also be obtainable from business information services or from industry analysts.

2.5 Types of acquisition

Risk profile

Acquisitions might impact the risk profile of the acquiring company. There are two aspects to the risk profile:

- Financial risk: the financial risk of the acquiring company might change because of a change in financial gearing due to the method used to finance the acquisition. For example, if gearing increases because the acquisition is financed largely by debt capital, the financial risk of the company will increase as a consequence of the acquisition.
- Business risk. The target company might operate in an industry or market sector where the business risk is very different from the business risk profile of the acquiring company. When this happens, the business risk profile of the company will change as a result of the acquisition.

Categorising acquisitions

Acquisitions can be categorised in terms of their impact on risk profile and this in turn can influence the valuation techniques used.

Effect on risk profile	Appropriate valuation method
None. Acquisitions that impact neither the acquiring company's exposure to financial risk nor to business risk	Asset based valuations Market-based valuations (dividends or earnings) Cash flow models (using free cash flows). As there is no change in the risk profile the company's current cost of capital can be used in valuations.
Acquisitions that affect the acquiring company's exposure to financial risk but not to business risk.	Adjusted present value model.
Acquisitions that affect the acquiring company's exposure to both financial risk and business risk.	Iterative valuation procedures.

Many of the methods used to value businesses have already been covered in chapter 12.

Other valuation approaches

- APV method of assessing a company valuation
- The iterative method of equity valuation
- Valuation of high-growth start-up companies

3 Other valuation approaches

3.1 APV method of assessing a company valuation

The APV method estimates the base case value (the value as if the company were all equity financed) and adds the PV of the financing side effects to that value to arrive at the total market value of the entity.

Example

X Plc is currently financed by 75% equity and 25% debt capital.

The equity beta of the company's shares is 1.10.

The debt capital is considered risk-free.

Tax on profits is at the rate of 30%. The market rate of return is 9.5%.

X Plc is considering a takeover bid for Y Plc and believes that Y Plc's owners will accept a bid of $15m.

X Plc would finance the acquisition entirely with irredeemable debt at the risk-free rate of 6%.

The costs of the acquisition would be $2.5 million with tax relief on all the costs received one year later.

The acquisition of Y Plc will increase the post-tax operating profits by $2 million per year in perpetuity.

Required:
Use an APV approach to recommend whether the acquisition of Y Plc is worth $15m.

Answer

	$m
Base case PV of future inflows ($2 million/0.09 **(W2)**)	22.22
Acquisition costs	(2.50)
Tax relief on acquisition costs ($2.5m × 30% × $^{1}/_{1.06}$)	0.70
Tax relief on the interest (6% × $15m × 30% × $^{1}/_{0.06}$)	4.50
Acquisition price	(15.00)
APV	9.92

The APV is positive, indicating that the acquisition is worthwhile at a purchase cost of $15 million.

Workings

(1) Ungeared beta: $\beta_{EU} = 1.10 \times 75/[75 + 25(1 - 0.30)] = 0.81$

(2) Cost of equity = 6% + 0.81(9.5 – 6.0)% = 8.8%, say 9%.

3.2 The iterative method of equity valuation

Another approach to obtaining a valuation for the equity of a company can be used where the target company is in a different industry sector and it is not certain what the cost of equity and cost of capital should be used for the valuation. The valuation method is independent of how the acquisition will be financed.

The method is 'iterative', which means that the same method is used to make a large number of repeated valuations until a 'steady state' is reached, and each successive valuation produces amended firm and equity values.

There are a number of ways of performing an iterative valuation. One method is as follows;

Step 1	Calculate the asset beta (ungeared beta) for each separate entity. The asset betas might be given or might need to be calculated from the equity betas)
Step 2	Calculate the asset beta (ungeared beta) for the combined entity using the pre-acquisition market values of each entity as weighting
Step 3	Calculate the equity beta (geared beta) for the combined entity using the combined debt and equity figures including the amount borrowed to finance the acquisition.
Step 4	Calculate the cost of equity using the CAPM equation.
Step 5	Calculate WACC
Step 6	Discount cash flows to find total market value of the new firm.
Step 7	Find market value of equity by deducting market value of debt from the total market value of the firm.

The problem: Steps 3 to 5 are based on a debt to equity ratio that results in WACC that is used to arrive at a market value. This then results into a new debt to equity ratio. The debt to equity ratio used to arrive at a value does not exist once the companies actually combine. This is because the debt to equity ratios used so far have been based on those input to the combined entity but these fail to take account that the impact of the combination has on the figures.

This is a circular problem. We need a WACC to find market value but that market value indicates that the WACC used was incorrect.

The solution to this problem is to use the new debt to equity ratios found at step 7 and re-perform steps 3 onwards. This iterative process can be carried out many times until a steady state (or insignificant difference) remains.

It is hard to see how this could be examined as the iteration might require many repetitions which would be too time consuming for an exam. However, the syllabus does require an understanding of this so the following example shows a single iteration.

Example

X Plc has offered \$300m to buy Y Plc. The acquisition will be financed with debt. X Plc can borrow at the risk free rate.

The following information is relevant.

Market values:	X Plc	Y Plc
Equity	300	200
Debt	50	50
	350	250
Equity β	1.34	2.35
Rf	5%	
Rm	8%	
Tax rate	30%	

The following cash flow forecasts have been made for each entity together with expected synergies

t	X Plc	Y Plc	Synergies
1	40	5	15
2	50	5	17
3	60	5	20
4	70	5	24
5	80	5	30
6 (Terminal value)	420	40	115

Required: Calculate the value of the combined entity's equity to the first iteration.

Answer

Step 1: Calculate the asset beta of each entity

	X Plc	**Y Plc**
$\beta_a = \beta_e(V_e/V_e + V_d(1 - T))$	= 1.34(300/300 + 50(0.7)	= 2.35(200/200 + 50(0.7)
	= 1.2	= 2

Step 2: Calculate the asset beta of the combined entity

Market values:	X Plc	Y Plc	Combined
Equity	300	200	500
Debt	50	50	100
	350	250	600

$$\beta a \text{ (combined)} = \beta_{a\,X\,Plc}\,(V_{X\,Plc}/V_{combined}) + \beta_{a\,Y\,Plc}\,(V_{Y\,Plc}/V_{combined})$$

$$\beta a \text{ (combined)} = 1.2(350/600) + 2(250/600)$$

$$\beta a \text{ (combined)} = 0.7 + 0.83 = 1.53$$

Step 3: Calculate the equity beta of the combined entity (including new gearing)

Market values:	Combined
Equity	500
Debt (100 + 300)	400
	900

$\beta_a = \beta_e(V_e/V_e + V_d(1 - T))$ $\quad$ $1.53 = \beta_e(500/500 + 400(0.7))$

$\beta_e = 2.39$

Step 4: Calculate cost of equity

$k_e = R_f + \beta(R_m - R_f)$ $\quad$ $k_e = 5\% + 2.39(8\% - 5\%) = 12.17\%$

Step 5: Calculate WACC

$$WACC = (Ve/Ve + Vd)\ ke + (Vd/Ve + Vd)\ Kd\ (1 - T)$$

$$WACC = (500/900)\ 12.17\% + (400/900)\ 5\%(0.7)$$

$$WACC = 6.76\% + 1.555\% = 8.32\%$$

Step 6: Discount the combined entity cash flows at the WACC

t		Cash flows	Discount factor (8.32%)	Present values
1	(60 + 15 + 15)	90	0.923	83.09
2	(67 + 15 + 17)	99	0.852	84.38
3	(75 + 15 + 20)	110	0.787	86.55
4	(90 + 15 + 24)	129	0.726	93.70
5	(105 + 15 + 30)	150	0.671	100.59
6	(500 + 100 + 115)	715	0.619	442.64
				890.95

Market value of the new combined entity= $890.95m

Step 7: Market value of equity of combined entity

	$m
Total market value	890.95
Market value of debt	(400.00)
Market value of equity	490.95

Iteration 1

Repeat steps 3 to 7 using the above information.

Step 3: Calculate the equity beta of the combined entity

$\beta_a = \beta_e(V_e/V_e + V_d(1 - T))$ $\quad$ $1.53 = \beta_e(490.95/490.95 + 400(0.7))$

$\beta_e = 2.41$

Step 4: Calculate cost of equity

$k_e = R_f + \beta(R_m - R_f)$ $\quad$ $k_e = 5\% + 2.41(8\% - 5\%) = 12.23\%$

Step 5: Calculate WACC

$$WACC = (Ve/Ve + Vd)\ ke + (Vd/Ve + Vd)\ Kd\ (1 - T)$$

$$WACC = (490.95/890.95)\ 12.23\% + (400/890.95)\ 5\%(0.7)$$

$$WACC = 6.74\% + 1.57\% = 8.31\%$$

Step 6: Discount the combined entity cash flows at the WACC

t		Cash flows	Discount factor (8.31%)	Present values
1	(60 + 15 + 15)	90	0.923	83.10
2	(67 + 15 + 17)	99	0.852	84.40
3	(75 + 15 + 20)	110	0.787	86.58
4	(90 + 15 + 24)	129	0.727	93.75
5	(105 + 15 + 30)	150	0.671	100.65
6	(500 + 100 + 115)	715	0.620	442.96
				891.43

Market value of the new combined entity= $891.43m

Step 7: Market value of equity of combined entity

	$m
Total market value	891.43
Market value of debt	(400.00)
Market value of equity	491.43

In this case there is little difference between the values after the first iteration. The conclusion from this is that the original WACC was a reasonable estimate of the cost of capital of the combined entity. This may not be the case in other examples where the market value might have changed significantly after the first iteration. In that case it would have been necessary to repeat until there was no significant difference between the market value of equity found in the last and penultimate iterations.

3.3 Valuation of high-growth start-up companies

The techniques already described in this chapter can be used for any sort of company valuation. However, a particular problem arises in the case of high-growth companies that are being set up, or have recently been set up. Valuations might be needed by venture capital organisations that have been asked to invest capital in the business.

The special features of high-growth start-up companies are as follows:

- The risk of failure of the business is high. Venture capital investors might allow for a high failure rate when they make their investment decisions.
- Estimates of cash flows will be subject to enormous uncertainty, and might be little better than a guess.
- The company's equity will have no value for a venture capitalist until an 'exit route' is available, and the venture capitalist is able to sell the shares, either in a stock market flotation or in a trade sale of the company to another more established company in the industry.

A venture capitalist might therefore be more interested in the exit valuation at the end of the investment period, rather than estimates of cash flows in the intervening years. An estimated exit valuation might be discounted to a present value, so that the venture capitalist can assess how much it might be willing to invest in the company.

The company's management need to prepare a robust business plan, to give a venture capitalist some reassurance that the business risks with the start-up business can be managed successfully.

Regulatory framework and processes

- Regulation of takeovers
- Regulation in the EU
- Regulation in the UK
- Competition law
- Defences against a hostile takeover
- Will shareholders in the target company accept an offer for their shares?

4 Regulatory framework and processes

4.1 Regulation of takeovers

The regulatory framework for mergers and acquisitions varies between countries.

There are two broad categories of regulation

	Shareholder model (market based model)	**Stakeholder model**
Where originated	US, UK and Commonwealth countries	Mainland Europe
Aim	Protection of shareholders	Protection of broad range of stakeholders stakeholders including shareholders, employees, creditors and society at large
Foundation	Case law and voluntary codes (though sometimes with legal backing)	Statute
Predicated on	Wide share ownership	Narrow share ownership

4.2 Regulation in the EU

The EU Takeovers Directive was issued in 2002 as a component of the EU Financial Services Action Plan and Directive became effective in 2006.

It set out minimum rules to cover the regulation of takeovers of companies whose shares are traded on regulated markets with the aim of achieving harmonisation and convergence of the regulatory systems in EU member states.

The requirements in the directives were drawn from many of those found in the UK City Code on Takeovers

Key requirements of the directive include the following:

- mandatory-bid rule;
- equal treatment of shareholders;

- squeeze-out rule and sell-out rights;
- board neutrality; and
- the break-through rule

The mandatory-bid rule

A bidder that has purchased a specified percentage of shares must offer to buy the remaining shares at a price no lower than the highest price paid for shares already acquired.

This protects minority shareholders and allows them to sell their shares at a fair price when the profile of the ownership of the company has changed.

The threshold reached before the mandatory bid rule applies varies from country to country. In the UK it is specified by the City Code for Takeovers and Mergers and is at 30%.

The principle of equal treatment

Once control has been achieved, a bidder must offer to buy shares from the minority shareholders on the same terms as those under which control was achieved.

Squeeze-out and sell-out rights

A bidder that has purchased a specified percentage of shares has the right to force the minority shareholders to sell their shares, thus, squeezing them out of the company.

The squeeze-out thresholds vary from country to country and are:

- 80% in Ireland;
- 90% in the UK; and
- 95% in Belgium, France, Germany and the Netherlands.

Sell-out rights

A bidder that has purchased a specified percentage of shares can be forced to buy the remaining shares off the minority shareholders.

Board neutrality

Several measures are designed to prevent management acting in their own interests at the expense of the interests of the shareholders. For example, a board is not allowed to use certain defences (e.g. poison pill defence) against a takeover without obtaining shareholder approval.

The break-through rule

This enables a bidder with a specified proportion of the company's equity to break-through the company's multiple voting rights and exercise control as if one share-one vote existed.

4.3 Regulation in the UK

Panel on Takeovers and Mergers

The Panel on Takeovers and Mergers (the "Panel") is an independent body made up of representatives from UK financial institutions and professional associations with key members currently appointed by the Bank of England.

It was established in 1968 and its main functions are:

- to issue and administer the City Code on Takeovers and Mergers (the "Code"); and
- to supervise and regulate takeovers and other matters to which the Code applies in accordance with the rules set out in the Code.

It has been designated as the supervisory authority to carry out certain regulatory functions in relation to takeovers pursuant to the EU Takeover Directive.

Its statutory functions are set out in the Companies' Act 2006 (CA2006) which also contains other rules relevant to the conduct of takeovers.

The City Code on Takeovers and Mergers

The City Code on Takeovers and Mergers (known as the City Code) was introduced as a voluntary code in 1968. It applies to any offer where the target or offeree is a listed or unlisted public company resident in the UK.

Although described as voluntary, it was mandatory in practice as the stock exchanges insisted on compliance as one of its conditions of membership.

Compliance with the code is no longer voluntary following the enactment of legislation to comply with the EU Takeovers Directive.

The aims of the code are as follows:

- to ensure that shareholders in an offeree company are treated fairly and are not denied an opportunity to decide on the merits of a takeover and
- that shareholders in the offeree company of the same class are afforded equivalent treatment by an offeror.

The Code also provides an orderly framework within which takeovers are conducted.

In addition, it is designed to promote, in conjunction with other regulatory regimes, the integrity of the financial markets.

The City Code: General principles

The City Code is divided into general principles and detailed rules which must be observed by persons involved in a merger or takeover transaction. The principles of the City Code are the following.

- All the shareholders of the target company must be treated in the same way
- Shareholders must be provided with sufficient information and given sufficient time to make a decision.

- If the board advises the shareholders it must give its views on the effects of the implementation of the bid on employment, conditions of employment and the locations of the company's places of business.'
- The directors of the target company must act in the interest of the company as a whole and not deny the holders of securities the opportunity to decide on the merits of the bid.
- All parties must do everything to prevent the creation of a false market in the shares of the target company. The term "false market" refers to a distortion of the market such that it does not fairly reflect the value of shares, perhaps through a deliberate action of one of the parties to the bid. For example, the directors of a target company could issue false information about the company with the aim of driving up the share price.
- An offerer can only announce a bid when it knows that the terms of the bid can be fulfilled (i.e. the offered price can be paid).
- An offer must proceed without undue delay so that a bid does not hinder a target company in the conduct of its affairs for longer than is reasonable.

The City Code: Bidding

The Takeover Code sets out rules that a bidding company must follow.

Acceptance condition

An offeror sets a threshold for the minimum number of acceptances for a bid to be successful (the acceptance condition). For example, the offeror could specify that a bid will only be considered successful if it is able to acquire 90% of the shares of a target. If it were to acquire only 75% of the shares it is not bound to buy these and it can withdraw its offer. The City Code allows any threshold from 50% upwards but the usual threshold is 90%

Market purchases

A bidding company is allowed to buy shares in the target company in the stock market, but once a certain proportion of the total number of shares in issue has been purchased it must make a formal offer for all of the remaining shares in the target company.

This rule prevents a buying company from acquiring a target company by stealth, through the purchase of a controlling interest in the shares by means of stock market purchases. It also ensures that the shareholders in the target company are treated equally by the bidder.

Key thresholds

Holding	Significance
30%	City code definition of control. Offeror must make mandatory bid for the rest of the shares on the same terms as those held.
90%	Offeror can force minority to sell (squeeze out rights. Minority can force offeror to buy their shares (sell-out rights)

4.4 Competition law

Most countries have some form of competition law to protect the interests of the consumer or general public. The purpose of competition law is to prevent any company from acquiring such a large share of the market by means of a merger or acquisition that it will be able to exert a strong influence over:

- prices;
- output; or
- other market conditions.

An ability to 'control' the market could be against the public interest and unfair to consumers.

The Competition and Markets Authority (CMA)

In the UK, a proposed acquisition that might give the acquirer undue influence over the market can be referred to a government-appointed ***Competition and Markets Authority*** (formerly called the Competition Commission and the Monopolies and Mergers Commission) for investigation.

The CMA has the power to prohibit an acquisition, or to allow an acquisition to go ahead only on condition that the acquirer complies with certain conditions that would reduce its market influence.

For example, if one company that operates a chain of supermarkets proposes to acquire a rival company, the acquisition might be referred to the CMA. The CMA might allow the acquisition to go ahead only on condition that the acquirer agrees to dispose of certain stores operated by the target company. Any decision of the CMA is subject to appeal to Competition Appeal Tribunal.

An acquisition might be referred to the CMA subject to several tests:

- **The turnover test:** The CMA will not usually conduct an investigation if the subject of the takeover bid has revenue of less than £70 million.
- **The share of supply test:** The CMA will not usually conduct an investigation unless the combined entity supplies 25% of goods or services of a particular type following the merger.
- **The substantial lessening of competition test:** Even if the above thresholds are met, the CMA will conduct an investigation only if the merger results in a substantial lessening of competition.

The European Union

Mergers fall within the exclusive jurisdiction of the European Union where the following two criteria are met as a result of the merger:

- The combined entity has worldwide turnover of more than €5 billion per annum; and
- European Union turnover of more than €250 million per annum

The European Union will block a merger if it has an adverse effect on competition.

4.5 Defences against a hostile takeover bid

In a friendly takeover bid, the company wanting to make the acquisition makes a bid that the board of the target company will recommend to their shareholders. In this situation, the target company will allow the acquirer access to its accounts, records and management information, so that the acquirer is able to carry out 'due diligence' and satisfy themselves that they are offering a fair price for the business.

A hostile bid occurs when the board of the target company rejects a takeover offer and refuses to recommend it to the shareholders.

A hostile takeover bid is risky, because the bidder has to make the offer for the target company's shares without the benefit of management information about the company (for example, management accounting information about current financial performance). If the takeover bid is 'friendly' and welcomed by the board of directors of the target company, confidential information will probably be made available to the bidder.

The directors of a target company have several defences against a takeover bid. These vary between countries. In the UK, the terms of the offer for the company's shares must be given to the company's shareholders, who are then free to decide whether or not to accept the offer for their shares. If enough shareholders accept the offer, the bid will be successful.

The most important defence against a hostile takeover (in the UK) is to persuade the shareholders to reject the bid. There are several ways in which this might be done. In each case, the directors of the company must deal honestly with the shareholders, and should not give them information that is incorrect or misleading.

Methods of persuading the shareholders to reject a bid include the following:

- Announcing that the company expects to increase its profits substantially in the future; therefore the offer price from the bidder is too low.
- Announcing an intention to return a large amount of equity to the shareholders in the near future, in the form of an increased dividend or a share buy-back; therefore the offer price from the bidder is too low.
- Explaining the future strategy of the board of directors for increasing the company's profits in the future.

When it is uncertain whether shareholders will be persuaded to reject the offer, other methods of defence in the UK are:

- To try to get the takeover referred to the Competition Commission, which has the power to prevent a takeover if it is likely to affect competition adversely in the industry, for example by creating a monopoly company in the industry.
- To find a '**white knight**'. A white knight is another company that is prepared to make its own takeover bid for the company, at a higher price or on better terms.

4.6 Will shareholders in the target company accept an offer for their shares?

A company making a takeover bid wants to win sufficient acceptances from shareholders in the target company that it acquires full control of the company. The willingness of shareholders to accept a bid for their shares will depend on several factors:

- the offer price: share price valuations are explained in the following sections of this chapter
- the purchase consideration – cash, debt capital or shares in the bidding company: the significance of the purchase consideration is explained later
- job security: when the directors, managers and employees of the target company are major shareholders, job security might be relevant. These shareholders might reject an offer if they are concerned about their job security after a takeover.
- alternative options: there might be the possibility of a rival and more attractive offer.

Financing acquisitions and mergers

- Purchase consideration
- All-share consideration
- Cash or debt finance in the purchase consideration

5 Financing acquisitions and mergers

5.1 Purchase consideration

In a merger, one company might acquire the other company by issuing new shares. The shareholders in the other company exchange their shares for the new shares in the first company. For example, if company A and company B merge, company A might issue new shares in exchange for the shares in company B. The company B shareholders therefore become shareholders in the enlarged company A.

Similarly, a takeover might be paid for by issuing new shares to the shareholders in the target company, who will then become shareholders in the buying company after the takeover.

e

Example

Company X makes a successful bid to acquire the shares in company Y. Company Y consists of 500,000 shares of $1 each. Company X offers 3 new shares for every 2 shares in company Y. Company X therefore issues 750,000 new shares to purchase the shares in company Y and the company Y shareholders become shareholders of company X. If the shares of company X are valued at $4 each before and after the takeover, the takeover price is $3,000,000 (750,000 shares × $4).

Instead of making an acquisition by exchanging shares, a company might pay for some or all of the acquisition:

- in cash (which it might obtain by borrowing)
- by issuing debt securities in exchange for some of the shares in the target company

In the example above for example, company X might have acquired the shares in company Y for $3 million by paying $2 million in cash and $2 of redeemable loan stock for every 1 share in company Y.

Cash to finance a takeover bid might be obtained from existing cash resources, or by issuing new shares to other investors, or by borrowing.

The purchase consideration – both the total purchase price for a takeover and the nature of the purchase consideration (shares, cash or debt securities) – are usually subject to negotiation in a friendly takeover.

- In a friendly takeover, the directors of the target company negotiate terms that they then recommend to their shareholders for acceptance.
- In a hostile takeover, the bidding company makes an offer to the shareholders in the target company, without the co-operation of the board of directors of the target company. With a hostile takeover bid, the bid is much more likely to succeed if it is an all-cash offer, because the shareholders in the target company might not want to retain any investment in the acquiring company.

5.2 All-share consideration

When a takeover is financed by issuing new shares as the purchase consideration, either the shareholders in the buying company or the shareholders in the target company will gain value at the expense of the shareholders in the other company.

Example

Company A and company B are companies whose shares are traded on a stock market. Company A makes profits after tax of $800,000 each year and company B makes after-tax profits of $400,000. Both companies have 1 million shares in issue. Company A shares are valued on a price/earnings multiple of 10 and company B shares are valued on a P/E multiple of 9 ($3.60 per share).

Suppose that company A makes an offer of $4.40 per share for company B, valuing company B at $4.4 million. This values the company on a P/E ratio of 11.

Its own shares are valued at $8 each (EPS $0.80 × P/E ratio 10). If company A makes an all-share offer, it would therefore propose to issue 550,000 new shares to the shareholders in company B ($4.4 million/$8 per share). The terms of its offer would therefore be 11 new shares in company A for every 20 shares in company B.

If the offer is accepted by the shareholders of company B, company A would consist of 1,550,000 shares after the takeover. The combined after-tax profits of the company might be $1.2 million ($800,000 + $400,000), which is the sum of the profits of the individual companies before the takeover.

Does the takeover create wealth for the shareholders of company A?

The answer depends on what happens to the share price of company X after the takeover. Unless there is an increase in the P/E ratio, or an increase in the profits of the combined companies, a takeover will destroy value for the shareholders of the company making the takeover when all of the following conditions apply:

- The purchase consideration is all shares.
- The purchase price is on a higher P/E multiple than the P/E ratio of the company making the takeover.
- There is no increase in the combined profits of the two companies after the takeover.

In this example, if the P/E ratio of the company after the takeover is 10, the total value of the company will be $12 million ($1.2 million × 10), which is $7.74 per share ($12 million/1,550,000 shares).

The former shareholders in the two separate companies will therefore lose or gain value in their investment, as follows:

Shares owned by	Number of shares	Value at $7.74	Investment value before the takeover	(Loss)/gain in value
		$m	$m	$m
Original shareholders in A	1,000,000	7.74	8.00	(0.26)
Former shareholders of B	550,000	4.26	3.60	0.66
		12.00	11.60	

There has been some increase in value in the combined company, because the earnings of company B are now valued on a higher P/E multiple. However, all the benefits are enjoyed by the former shareholders in company B. The original shareholders in company A have suffered a loss in value due to the takeover.

All-share consideration: the effect of synergy

If there is synergy, and total annual earnings and cash profits increase, the total value of the businesses should be expected to increase, adding value for the shareholders.

In the example above, suppose that after the acquisition of company B by company A, there are benefits from economies of scale and total annual earnings increase by $200,000 to $1,400,000. Suppose also that the P/E ratio of the enlarged company A is 10. The total value of company A will now be $1.4 million × 10 = $14 million. The price per share will be $9.03.

The former shareholders in the two separate companies will therefore gain value in their investment, as follows:

Shares owned by	Number of shares	Value at $9.03	Value before takeover	Gain in value
		$m	$m	$m
Original shareholders in A	1,000,000	9.03	8.00	1.03
Former shareholders of B	550,000	4.97	3.60	1.37
		14.00	11.60	

Because of the synergy and growth in combined earnings (or cash profits), shareholders in both companies benefit from the takeover.

5.3 Cash or debt finance in the purchase consideration

Another way of providing extra value for shareholders in a takeover might be to pay for the acquisition in whole or in part with either cash (financed by borrowing) or debt securities. The benefit of paying in these ways is that there is tax relief on the interest cost.

The target company's shareholders might want to be paid in cash; therefore offering to buy the target company's shares for cash (financed by new debt) could be attractive to those shareholders, who will be cashing in their investment by accepting the takeover offer.

Example

Returning to the previous example, suppose that a takeover price of $4,400,000 is agreed for company B, and that this purchase price is paid all in cash, with the money obtained from a bank loan at 8% interest.

The rate of tax is 25%, and after the takeover there is no synergy. The company's shares continue to be valued on a P/E multiple of 10.

The company's earnings and value after the takeover can be calculated as follows:

	$	$
Profits of 'old' company A		800,000
Profits of 'old' company B		400,000
		1,200,000
Interest on debt ($4.4 million × 8%)	(352,000)	
Less tax relief at 25%	88,000	
Net cost of interest		(264,000)
Annual earnings after the takeover		936,000

Value of company A shares	**$**
After the takeover ($936,000 × 10)	9,360,000
Before the takeover	8,000,000
Gain to company A shareholders	1,360,000

Company A will now be geared, and its cost of capital might therefore change. If so, the P/E ratio would no longer be 10. Even so, financing a takeover with debt capital can add to the wealth of the shareholders because of the tax relief on debt interest.

CHAPTER 15

Corporate reconstruction and reorganisation

Contents

Capital reconstructions

- Definition of a reconstruction
- The purpose of a reconstruction
- The problems with a reconstruction scheme
- Examination questions on reconstructions
- Market reaction to schemes of reconstruction

1 Capital reconstructions

1.1 Definition of a reconstruction

A capital reconstruction is a major reorganisation of the capital structure of a company. When a reconstruction occurs, the reason is usually because the company is in financial difficulties. For example, its Z score might indicate that it is in danger of financial collapse. It is more probable however that cash flow projections, and possibly profit projections, indicate that the company cannot avoid financial collapse and liquidation unless urgent action is taken to 'reconstruct' the company's finances.

A reconstruction might involve:

- the injection of new cash
- the conversion of debt capital into equity; and
- possibly the conversion of equity shares from one form to another.

Existing equity shareholders might be required to relinquish all their shares and accept a much smaller quantity of new shares in the reconstructed company. The majority of the new shares on the reconstructed company might be held by lending banks or bond investors, who agree to exchange their loans or bonds for new shares in the reconstructed company. Reconstructions are likely to be subject to regulation by company law.

1.2 The purpose of a reconstruction

The purpose of a capital reconstruction is to find a way of allowing the company to continue in business, and avoid insolvency and liquidation. A reconstruction is therefore only worth considering:

- if it is likely to be more beneficial to all the parties concerned than a liquidation of the company (and the sale of its assets), and
- the reconstructed company has a good chance of surviving and restoring itself to profitability.

A reconstruction will benefit all the parties if it is likely to result in them getting more cash or more value from the reconstruction than from an enforced liquidation of the company.

For example, the effect of a reconstruction scheme might be to:

- reduce the total debt of the company (because some debt capital might be exchanged for new equity); and
- defer the repayment obligations for other debt capital.

This reduction in total debt and deferral of interest payments and principal repayments might allow the company to make a profit and achieve positive cash flows. If the company is able to recover, it should be able to pay back its outstanding debts and also create value (in the share price) for the former lenders who are now equity shareholders.

The parties who must agree to a reconstruction therefore include all the creditors of the company (or a sufficient number of them, in accordance with the requirements of national company law) and the shareholders.

1.3 The problems with a reconstruction scheme

There are some major problems with arranging a capital reconstruction. These are:

- finding a reconstruction arrangement that will benefit all the parties; and
- obtaining the approval of the stakeholders.

The scheme will affect the rights of the various stakeholders in the entity. In most jurisdictions the regulatory environment within which the entity operates will have mechanisms to protect the rights of each class of interested party.

In short they are often given a right of veto. As a result each party has to be persuaded into acceptance of the scheme.

Typically the protective mechanisms will include some or all of the following:

- court approval,
- the scheme must be approved by a specified majority (eg 75%) of each stakeholder group,
- the scheme must be authorised within the constitution of the entity.

Each of the parties involved in a reconstruction (banks who are lending money, bondholders, unpaid trade creditors and the shareholders) need to believe that the reconstruction offers them the prospect of more cash or more value than a liquidation of the company. Each of the parties will therefore compare what they will probably receive:

- if the construction scheme is agreed; and
- if the scheme is rejected and liquidation occurs.

Example

A company has 1 million shares of $1 in issue, $5 million in 6% bonds and trade creditors of $200,000. The company is in severe financial difficulties and unless a reconstruction scheme is agreed, the company will be liquidated.

The bondholders would expect to receive $0.40 in the $1 in a liquidation, and the trade creditors and equity shareholders would receive nothing.

The following reconstruction scheme might be proposed:

- The company cancels its existing equity shares and issues, say, 10 million new shares of $0.05 each.
- The bondholders are offered 9.9 million of these shares in exchange for their bonds.
- The remaining 100,000 shares might be offered to the existing equity shareholders, in a 1 for 10 exchange. The shareholders will surrender their $1 shares in the company and receive one new share of $0.05 each for every 10 of their $1 shares.
- A bank might agree to provide a loan to the newly-reconstructed company.
- The trade creditors might be offered $0.30 in the $1 in full settlement of the unpaid debts.

This scheme might be agreed, but only if the following conditions are met:

- The company will expect to be profitable and to have positive cash flows as a result of the new structure.
- The bondholders believe they will gain more from accepting equity in the company than forcing a liquidation to receive $0.40 in the $1.
- The trade creditors and equity shareholders also agree.
- The reconstruction complies with the requirements of company law.

1.4 Examination questions on reconstructions

Company law on reconstructions varies between countries, and it is therefore unlikely that you will be expected to demonstrate a detailed understanding of the law. However, you should be aware that some legal process and approval for a proposed scheme of reconstruction might be required.

Capital reconstruction proposals can be fairly complex, so it is unlikely that in your examination you will be required to devise and recommend a detailed scheme of reconstruction for a particular company.

However an examination question might give you some details about a company that is in financial difficulties, and give details of a reconstruction scheme that has been proposed. You might then be asked to comment on the proposed scheme.

To answer this type of question, you should consider three aspects to the proposal.

Step 1

The first step is to make sure that you understand what the capital of the reconstructed company will be.

- How many shares will be in issue and who will own them?
- How much debt capital will the company have, and what will be the rate of interest payable on the debt?

Step 2

Having established what the new capital structure will be, you should make a financial analysis to decide whether the company is likely to become profitable and have positive cash flows after the reconstruction has occurred.

If the company is unlikely to survive in its reconstructed form, the reconstruction proposal should not be supported or recommended.

Step 3

If you consider that the company will return to profits and positive cash flows if the reconstruction occurs, you should then look at each of the investor groups in the company.

If any investor group is unlikely to benefit from the reconstruction, it will not support the reconstruction proposals. For each investor group – ordinary shareholders, preference shareholders, bondholders and banks – you should consider what will happen to them:

- if there is no reconstruction
- if the company is reconstructed.

The position faced by stakeholders if the scheme does not proceed is found by calculating the amount of cash that would be available and then distributing it on the basis specified in the regulatory environment within which the entity operates.

Typically stakeholders would share in the following order.

- Holders of fixed charge
- Holders of floating charge
- Unsecured creditors
- Preference share holders
- Ordinary shareholders

Example

X Plc's products have experienced reliability problems and competition has caused a 40% fall in sales in the last 2 years.

The company's managers are confident that the technical problems can be overcome, but this will require an investment of $2.25 million for new automated equipment and quality monitoring machinery.

X Plc's bank, Y Bank Plc, is concerned about the company's recent performance, and a new debt or equity issue on the stock market is not possible.

Without the new investment X Plc is unlikely to be competitive, and might not survive the next financial year.

With the new investment, profits before interest and tax are forecast to be at least $750,000 per year for at least five years from 2016.

X Plc plc: Summarised statement of financial position as at 30 September 2015

	$'000	
Land and buildings	1,500	
Plant and machinery (net)	2,100	
		3,600
Current assets		
Inventories	1,340	
Receivables	1,090	
Cash at bank and in hand	35	
Total current assets		2,465
Total assets		6,065
Capital and reserves		
Share capital ($1 ords)	1,000	
Share premium	945	
Revenue reserves	(240)	
Total shareholders' funds		1,705
Non-current liabilities		
Term loan (from Y Bank Plc)	800	
9% debenture 2028	500	
8% convertible debenture 2020	1,000	
10% loan stock 2023	500	
		2,800
Current liabilities		
Overdraft	620	
Other creditors	940	
		1,560
Total capital and liabilities		6,065

Notes

(1) The 9% straight debenture is secured by a fixed charge on the company's main factory building, the convertible debenture and term loan by a floating charge on fixed assets. The loan stock and overdraft are unsecured.

(2) The land and buildings are believed to have a realisable value 20% less than their net book value.

(3) Inventories would be sold at 50% of their book value if the company ceased trading.

(4) The new equipment would result in redundancies with an immediate after tax cost of $500,000. If the company were to be liquidated after tax redundancy payments would total $1 million. Redundancy payments may be assumed to rank before unsecured creditors.

(5) Obsolete machinery with a net book value of $800,000 will be sold for $300,000 irrespective of whether or not the new investment takes place. The remainder of the plant and machinery could be disposed of at net book value. All disposal values are after tax.

(6) The overdraft currently costs 10% per year and the bank term loan 12% per year.

X Plc's finance director has proposed the following reconstruction scheme after consultation with a venture capital company.

(i) Existing shareholders are to be offered 28 cents per share to redeem their shares, which would then be cancelled.

(ii) The venture capital will pay $1 million for 700,000 new 25 cents ordinary shares.

(iii) The company's directors have agreed to 500,000 new 25 cents ordinary shares at a price of $1.50 per share.

(iv) The convertible debenture is to be replaced by new ordinary shares (par value 25 cents), with 60 ordinary shares for every $100 nominal value loan stock.

(v) The term loan is to be renegotiated with the bank and the total amount of the loan increased to $2 million. This would have an expected interest charge of 13% per annum. A floating charge on fixed assets would be offered on the overdraft.

(vi) All other long-term loans would remain unchanged.

Required:

Evaluate whether or not the suggested scheme of reconstruction is likely to succeed.

Answer

Understanding the scheme

You might not have time to do this in an exam question but the best way to understand the scheme is to reconstruct the statement of financial position incorporating the scheme requirements. However, as a minimum, you will need to construct workings for key balances after a scheme is executed including creditors, share capital, cash, bank overdraft etc.

	Before		**4**	**5**	**i**	**ii**	**iii**	**iv**	**v**	**After**
	$'000									$'000
Land and buildings	1,500									1,500
Plant and machinery	2,100	2,250		(800)						3,550
	3,600									5,050
Current assets										
Inventories	1,340									1,340
Receivables	1,090									1,090
Cash at bank and in hand	35	(2,250)	(500)	300	(280)	1,000	750		1,000	255
	2,465									2,685
Total assets	6,065									7,735
Capital and reserves										
Share capital ($1 ords)	1,000				(1,000)	175	125	150		450
Share premium	945				(945)	825	625	850		2,300
Revenue reserves	(240)		(500)	(500)	1,665					425
	1,705									3,175
Non-current liabilities										
Term loan (from Y Bank Plc)	800								1,200	2,000
9% debenture	500									500
8% convertible debenture	1,000							(1,000)		nil
10% loan stock	500									500
	2,800									3,000
Current liabilities										
Overdraft	620									620
Other creditors	940									940
	1,560									1,560
Total capital and liabilities	6,065									7,735

New share distribution

Shareholder	**Number**	**Price per share**	**Amount subscribed**	**% held**
Venture capitalist	700,000	1.43	1,000,000	39
Directors	500,000	1.50	750,000	28
The convertible debenture	600,000	1.67	1,000,000	33
	1,800,000			100

It is also useful to construct workings to show key performance indicators (e.g. interest cover, eps) that you might refer to when performing the appriasl of the scheme.

Interest payments of the reconstructed entity

	Balance $000	Rate	Annual interest $000
Secured			
9% debenture	500	9%	45
Bank term loan	2,000	13%	260
Overdraft	620	10%	62
	3,120		367
Unsecured			
10% loan stock	500	10%	50
	4,560		417

Performance measures

	$000
Profit	750
Bank term loan	(417)
	333
Tax (30%)	(100)
	233
Interest cover (750:417)	1.8
EPS (233/1,800)	12.9c

Appraisal of the scheme

Cash position of stakeholders without the scheme

If the reconstruction does not take place it is possible that the company will be forced into receivership during the next year or soon afterwards as losses are likely to continue without the new investment.

If the company was to go into receivership, the expected realisable value of assets would be:

	Secured $'000	Secured $'000	Unsecured $'000	Total $'000
Cash available				
Land and buildings (80% × 1,000)	1,200			1,200
Plant and machinery (300 + (2,100 – 800))		1,600		1,600
Inventories (50% × 1,340)			670	670
Receivables			1,090	1,090
Cash			35	35
Total cash available	1,200	1,600	1,795	4,595
Secured creditors				
9% debenture (fixed charge)	(500)			(500)
Available for floating charge holders	700	1,600		3,095
8% convertible debenture	(700)	(300)		(1,000)
Bank term loan	nil	800		(800)
Available for other creditors	nil	500	1,795	2,295
Redundancy payments	1,000			(1,000)
Available for unsecured creditors				1,295
Unsecured creditors				
10% loan stock	*500			314
Overdraft	*620			390
Other creditors	*940			591
	2,060		maximum	(1,295)
Available for the shareholders				nil

*Unsecured creditors will only receive approximately 63 cents in the dollar (1,295/2,060).

Availability of security after adoption of the scheme

		$000
Cash available		
Land and buildings (80% × 1,000)		1,200
9% debenture (fixed charge)		(500)
Available for floating charge holders		700
Plant and machinery ((2,100 – 800) + 2,250*)		3,550
Available for floating charge holders		4,250
Bank term loan	2,000	
Bank overdraft	620	
Total floating charge		2,620

Therefore, the charges are all well covered.

Positions of stakeholders with or without the scheme

Ordinary shareholders:

If the company fails the shareholders receive nothing.

The scheme offers the shareholders $280,000.

The scheme is likely to be accepted by the shareholders.

Y Bank Plc:

Bank overdraft:

If the company fails Y Bank Plc will receive approximately $390,000 which is 63% of the overdraft due.

With the scheme Y Bank Plc will benefit from enhanced security on the overdraft meaning that it will become 100% recoverable.

Term loan

If the company fails Y Bank Plc will receive full repayment of the $800,000 term loan.

The scheme requires Y Bank Plc to lend a further $1·2 million term loan at an additional 1% interest rate.

The interest cover on the loan is quite low at 1.8.This might not be not be satisfactory to the bank.

However, there appears to be ample security for the loan so the bank should accept the scheme.

Debenture holders

The debenture holders are likely to receive full repayment with or without the scheme.

However, they may take the opportunity presented by their ability to prevent the scheme to ask for some form of incentive, for example the addition of warrants to the debenture, in order to agree to the reconstruction.

The debenture holders should accept the scheme.

10% Loan stock holders

If the company fails the 10% loan stock holders receive only 63% of their loan ($314,000 out of a total $500,000).

If they accept the scheme they stand a much better chance of full repayment of their loan.

The 10% loan stock holders should accept the scheme.

Convertible debenture holders

If the company fails the convertible debenture holders will receive full repayment of the $1,000,000 loan.

They are being asked to exchange certain repayment of $1,000,000 for ordinary shares at an effective price of $1.67 per share. This alone might lead them to reject the offer. In addition, the share price is higher than that being asked of the directors ($1.50) and the venture capitalist ($1.43).

The convertible debenture holders would reject the scheme.

Other creditors

Other creditors are in a similar position to the unsecured loan stock holders, and would stand a much better chance of full repayment of their loan after the reconstruction. Other creditors are likely to agree to the reconstruction.

Note: There is no need to appraise the scheme from the point of view of the venture capital company or the directors as they have approved the scheme already.

1.5 Market reaction to schemes of reconstruction

The markets usually react positively to schemes of reconstruction.

A scheme is a sign that management are dealing with the important issues facing the company. Furthermore, the agreement to the scheme by the providers of capital is often taken as a positive sign. After all, they would not have agreed to the reconstruction unless they believed that the company will recover.

Business reorganisation

- Unbundling
- Demergers
- Divestments
- Management buyouts and management buy-ins
- Share buy-back (share repurchase scheme)
- Going private

2 Business reorganisation

2.1 Unbundling

A capital reconstruction (as explained in the previous section of this chapter) is one type of business reorganisation.

Another type of business organisation is a portfolio reorganisation. This involves changing the mix of investments or assets held in the business portfolio. In this sense "business portfolio" refers to the collection of different businesses and assets owned by an entity. In the case of an entity being a group the portfolio might represent the subsidiaries of the group.

A strategy that involves the disposal of significant assets (including production lines, divisions etc.) or businesses is known as unbundling.

A portfolio reorganisation normally occurs as a result of a business strategy decision, such as:

- Divestment: selling off a non-core part of the group's business operations
- Demerger: dividing two divisions of a company into two entirely separate and independent companies.

Unbundling usually occurs as a result of a strategic decision rather than in response to financial difficulties.

2.2 Demergers

A demerger is the splitting up of a group of companies into two (or more) separate and independent companies. Often, the group in a demerger is a conglomerate, consisting of widely-different businesses.

For example, some years ago in the UK, there was a demerger of chemicals company ICI from pharmaceuticals company Zeneca. In 2007 Cadbury Schweppes proposed either to demerge its confectionery division (Cadbury) and soft drinks division (Schweppes) into independent companies, or to sell off its soft drinks division as part of a strategic review.

The shareholders in the company before the demerger receive shares in both demerged companies. They can choose to hold all the shares, and be a shareholder in both companies. Alternatively, they can sell their shares in one of the companies and remain a shareholder in just one of the demerged companies. (They could also sell their shares in both companies.)

If the company before the demerger has debt capital, it will have to negotiate with its banks or representatives of its bondholders, to agree which of the demerged companies should take on the debt obligations.

The nature of a demerger is illustrated in the following diagram

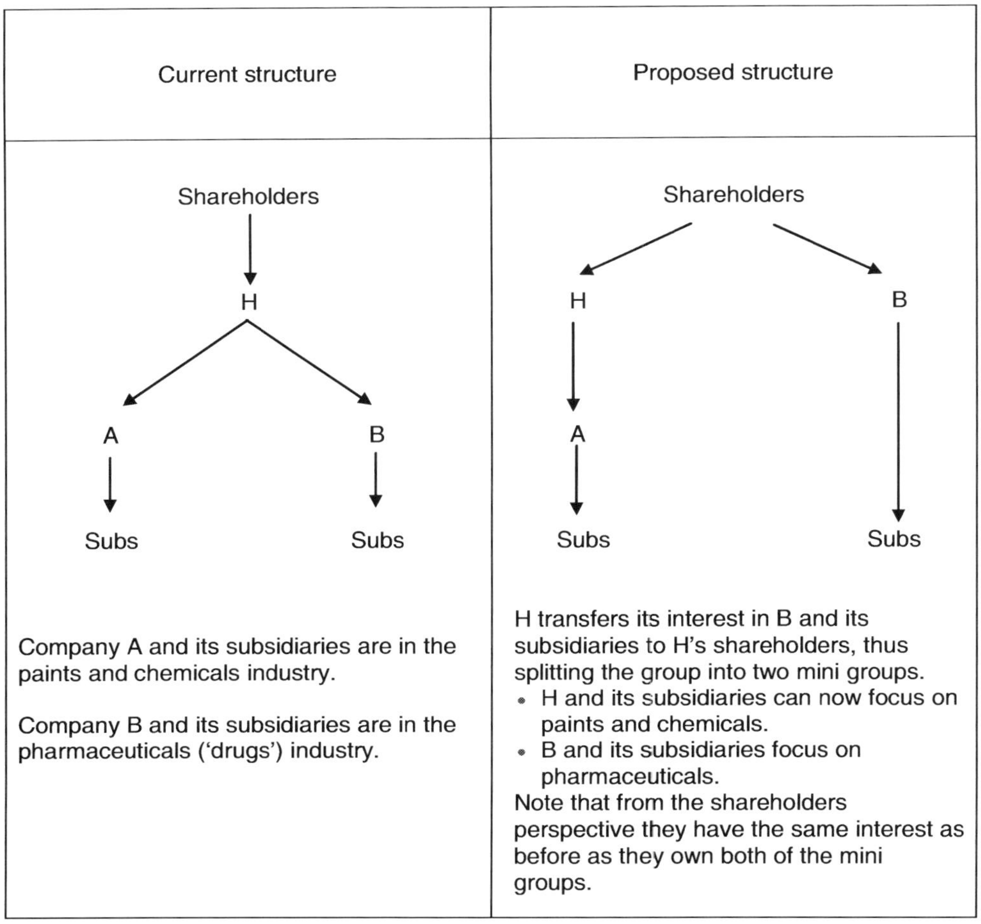

Purpose of a demerger

A demerger requires the consent of the company's shareholders, and the purpose of the demerger should be in the best interests of the shareholders. This means that a demerger is only justified if it is expected to increase the total wealth of the shareholders.

The reasons that may be put forward for a demerger are as follows:

- A conglomerate group of different businesses is often valued at less than the sum of the value of its separate businesses, if these were independent. This is because stock market investors often prefer 'specialised' businesses to conglomerates. Therefore, the demerger is expected to release shareholder value.
- 'Specialised' businesses can focus on their core competencies.
- Specialised businesses can develop their own strategies for the future and are more likely to be successful if they can decide their strategies independently.

- There might be some savings in head office costs, no longer incurred after the demerger.

2.3 Divestments

A divestment is the sale of a business by a company to an external purchaser (or external purchasers). The business that is sold might be a subsidiary company or a sub-group of subsidiary companies within the overall group.

Examples of divestments would be:

- the sale of a business to another company
- the sale of a business to a management team, in a management buy-out (MBO): the management team, often supported by venture capital finance, become the shareholders of the divested company
- the sale of a business to external buyers who become the management team as well as the shareholders (a management buy-in).

The company making the divestment should try to ensure that it obtains a satisfactory price for the subsidiary or division. The buyers should try to ensure that they pay a reasonable price and that the purchase is financed in the best way possible.

In contrast to a demerger, where the shareholders of the original company become shareholders in both demerged companies, a divestment (or 'spin-off') involves the sale of the ownership of a business.

The purchase consideration for a divestment:

- normally consists mainly or entirely of cash
- although the selling company might retain an equity interest, and continue to hold a proportion of the shares.

Purpose of divestments

A divestment can have any of the following purposes:

- to raise cash for the company, when it needs additional funding or has liquidity difficulties
- to get rid of a loss-making business
- because the company receives a very attractive offer price for selling the business
- for strategic reasons, for example, exiting a particular industry so that management can concentrate on the remaining businesses .

The strategic reason most commonly suggested for making a divestment is because the company is selling off a 'non-core' business. The company has a competitive advantage over rivals in businesses where it has 'core competencies', and it should therefore concentrate on these areas of business. In principle, the divestment should allow the company to invest all its resources in those parts of the business where it can make the greatest profits. This will benefit the shareholders.

2.4 Management buyouts and management buy-ins

Management buyouts and management buy-ins are divestments for the company selling the business, but business ventures for the management team that buys it.

With a management buyout, the purchasers of the divested business include a team of managers who work for the subsidiary or division that is being sold off, and these managers will run the business (as entrepreneurs) after they have bought it.

A management buy-in involves the purchase of a divested business by an external management team, which run the business (as entrepreneurs) after they have bought it.

With both management buyouts and management buy-ins, it is usually the case that the management team do not have sufficient capital of their own to afford the business they are trying to buy, and they have to rely on the support of venture capital finance.

The structure of venture capital finance

A **venture capital firm** might be willing to provide capital support to a management buyout or a management buy-in if it believes that:

- the management team have a robust and realistic business plan for the company
- the management team appear to have the capabilities to make the company a success
- the management team makes a significant capital contribution to the purchase of the business, so that they have a strong financial motive for making the business a success
- the financial returns appear satisfactory, allowing for the high business risk in the project.

Venture capital firms expect a high return on their investments, because a proportion of them are not successful and the investment risk is high.

The financing of a management buyout or management buy-in might be as follows:

- The individual managers in the management team agree to subscribe some of their own money to buy shares in the company they are buying. (If the MBO or MBI involves setting up a new company, the managers agree to buy a quantity of shares in the new company.)
- The venture capital firm also buys a quantity of equity shares, so that the proportions of shares owned by the management team and by the venture capital firm are in a satisfactory balance. The venture capital firm will want an equity stake in the company, but will not want its stake to be so large that there is no incentive or motivation for the management team to make the company a success.

- The venture capital firm will provide additional finance, possibly in the form of redeemable preference shares or unsecured lending. The intention should be that as the company grows and becomes more profitable and cash-rich, it will be able to redeem the preference shares or loan.
- The venture capital firm often negotiates additional loans, possibly secured bank loans, to bring the total capital available up to the amount needed to buy the company.
- The management team may be given an incentive scheme (such as a share option scheme) that will allow them to take more equity if the company is successful.

An MBO or MBI cannot go ahead unless enough capital is provided to purchase the business, and the expected profits from the business must be sufficient to meet the costs of debt interest and preference share dividends, and achieve a profit for the equity shareholders.

Benefits of an MBO

The costs of an MBO may be less than for other forms of disposal such as selling the assets of the company or selling the company to a third party.

An MBO may be the quickest method in raising funds compared to the other methods.

There would be less resistance from the managers and employees, making the process smoother and easier to accomplish.

The parent may retain a better relationship and beneficial links with company sold and may be able to purchase or sell goods and services to it.

It may be able to get a better price for the company. The current management and employees possibly have the best knowledge of the company and are able to make it successful. Therefore they may be willing to pay more for it.

It may increase a parent's reputation among its internal stakeholders such as the management and employees. It may also increase its reputation with external stakeholders and the markets if it manages the disposal successfully and efficiently.

2.5 Share buy-back (share repurchase scheme)

A share buy-back is the purchase by a company of some of its own equity shares, which are then cancelled.

- The shares might be purchased in the stock market at the current market price.
- Alternatively, the company might offer to buy back a quantity of shares at a fixed price from shareholders willing to sell them. Or the company might invite its shareholders to submit bids for the price at which they would be willing to sell a quantity of their shares to the company. When the company invites tenders from its shareholders in this way, it will buy back shares from the shareholders submitting the lowest prices for selling their shares.

Share repurchases are carried out as a part of a planned programme, which requires the prior consent of the shareholders, and which must treat all the equity shareholders fairly (for example, by giving them all an opportunity to sell back some of their shares).

After a share buy-back, the company will have fewer shares in issue.

Purpose of a share buy-back

A share buy-back might be appropriate when the company has a large amount of surplus cash, and cannot find enough new investment opportunities for investing the money. Instead of holding the cash (and earning a low rate of interest), it would benefit shareholders if the cash is paid back to them.

An alternative to a share buy-back is a special dividend payment. A dividend would be paid to all the shareholders, and so all the shareholders would receive some cash. However, the company might wish to avoid giving the impression that higher dividends will continue to be paid in the future.

There might be a tax advantage for shareholders in selling back shares rather than receiving a higher dividend.

By reducing the number of shares in issue, the cash profits per share and earning per share after the buy-back should be higher, and the market value of the remaining shares should therefore increase. A share buy-back should therefore be expected to increase the wealth of the remaining shareholders.

Increasing the company's financial gearing

Another reason for a share buy-back is to increase the company's gearing. The company may borrow debt capital and use the money to buy back and cancel some of its shares. Replacing equity with low-cost debt may reduce the WACC and increase the value per share of the remaining shares.

2.6 Going private

A 'public company' might 'go private'. The public company must be a company whose shares are traded on a stock market. When it goes private, it abandons its stock market status and it shares are no longer traded on the market.

Going private usually involves a major change in the share ownership of the company. When its shares are traded on a stock market, the majority of the shares are probably held by institutional investors. When the company 'goes private', the shares are normally acquired by either:

- a small number of former managers in the company and venture capital organisations, or
- a private equity organisation.

Typically, the chairman or chief executive officer of the company, who might be a significant shareholder, decides to withdraw the company from the stock market. He seeks financial support from venture capitalists and banks, and makes an offer to the existing shareholders to buy their shares. The existing shareholders must be offered a sufficiently high price for their shares, to persuade them to sell.

Reasons for going private

When a company goes private, the reasons may be as follows:

- The company is obtaining no benefit from its stock market status. For example:
  - the company might not want to use the stock market to raise new equity capital
  - investors might be unwilling to support a new share issue, so that the company is unable to obtain new funding from the stock market
  - the company either does not want to issue new equity to finance takeovers, or is unable to persuade the shareholders of target companies to accept its shares as the purchase consideration for a takeover.
- The chairman or chief executive officer, who is also a major shareholder, might think that the shares are under-valued. By taking the company private and acquiring more of the shares, he will expect to increase his own wealth.

When a significant number of companies revert to private status and give up their stock market status, this would be an indication that the stock market is not acting efficiently in providing capital to companies and that having a stock market status does not help to increase share values.

Private equity

Private equity organisations specialise in buying companies, often companies that are not as successful as they should be.

- The private equity firm has a fund for buying companies, and often borrows from banks to obtain large quantities of additional debt finance.
- A company acquired by a private equity firm may be a public company whose shares are traded on a stock market. If so, the private equity firm will buy the

company and 'take it private'. This means that the company's shares are withdrawn from trading on the stock market, and the shares are 'de-listed'.

A new management team is appointed to run the company. These managers are usually offered large incentives to make the company successful. This is the key to a successful private equity venture: the acquired company must be changed from an under-performing company to a company with much more value.

In addition, the purchased company might have valuable assets such as land and buildings that the new owners use to raise more capital. For example, property might be sold and leased back or used as collateral for additional borrowing.

If the company is successful, the private equity firm may decide to 'cash in' its investment. One way of doing this is to re-list the shares and re-launch the company on the stock market. When the company is re-launched on the market, the private equity firm will sell its shares to other investors.

Private equity firms have been particularly successful in recent years. Some of this success has been due to the low cost of borrowing. A large proportion of the purchase price of target companies has been paid for with debt capital, on which the interest rate has been fairly low (and there is tax relief on the interest payments).

CHAPTER 16

The treasury function

Contents

The treasury function

- Role of the treasury function
- Cash flow forecasting and cash management
- Financing long-term and short-term investments
- Financial risk management
- Centralised or decentralised?

1 The treasury function

1.1 Role of the treasury function

In many large organisations, there is a treasury function or treasury department. The role of the treasury department consists mainly of:

- managing the liquidity and cash flows of the organisation
- managing the foreign exchange positions and cash flows
- helping to obtain finance for the organisation
- managing the exposures to financial risk, by hedging currency exposures, interest rate exposures and other risk exposures.

1.2 Cash flow forecasting and cash management

Cash flow forecasting is an important aspect of treasury management. A company must have enough cash (or access to borrowing, such as a bank overdraft facility) to meet its payment obligations. Cash forecasts are therefore made and revised regularly, to establish whether the organisation expects to have a cash surplus or to be short of cash.

- If a cash deficit is forecast, measures should be taken to ensure that cash will be available. It might be necessary to ask a bank for more finance. Some expenditure might be deferred. Alternatively, measures might be taken to speed up receipts from customers.
- If a cash surplus is forecast, the treasury department will consider how the surplus funds should be used. For example, if the surplus is expected to be temporary, how long will the surplus last and what is the most profitable method of investing the money (without risk) for that period?

Short-term cash forecasts can be prepared using receipts and payments cash budgets. Longer-term cash forecasts can be made by preparing an expected cash flow statement for the forecast period.

Cash management

A centralised treasury department is able to manage the cash position of the group as a whole. It can manage total cash receipts, total cash payments and total net cash balances.

One technique for doing this is to pool bank accounts. All the bank accounts throughout the group for a particular currency might be pooled. At the end of each day, the balances in each account are transferred to a centralised cash account. (The cash is 'pooled'). The cash deficits in some accounts and cash surpluses in other accounts are therefore netted. In this way, the company can avoid interest charges on accounts that are in deficit, and transfer cash between accounts as required.

Pooling and netting of cash flows therefore improves cash management. However, for pooling and netting to be effective, the cash has to be managed by a central treasury department.

1.3 Financing long-term and short-term investments

A company must be able to finance its planned long-term and short-term investments (including any proposed takeovers). Preference share capital is rare, and the options available to companies are therefore as follows:

- For long-term investments, there should be long-term finance. Long-term finance is either equity or debt. Bank loans might be classified as long-term debt, provided that it is a fixed loan or a revolving credit facility for several years. However, bank loans are typically for up to about seven years
- Short-term investments might be defined as working capital assets. Inventory and receivables should normally be financed by a combination of long-term finance and short-term liabilities (such as trade payables).

Sources of equity

For many companies, the main source of new equity finance is retained profits. Profits are retained and reinvested to finance new investments and further growth. Occasionally, a company might wish to raise extra capital by issuing new shares for cash. However, it is difficult for a small company to raise new finance in this way if its shares are not traded on a stock market and it has only a small number of individual shareholders.

A company whose shares are traded on the stock market might wish to issue new shares for cash. In some countries (such as the UK), it is a legal requirement for companies issuing new shares for cash to offer the shares to the existing shareholders in proportion to their existing shareholding. (The shareholders might agree to waive this right in certain circumstances and within certain limits).

A company will only be able to issue new shares for cash in this way if it has the confidence and support of its shareholders and other institutions in the stock market.

In a takeover bid, the shareholders in the target company might be offered new shares in the bidding company as the purchase consideration.

In some cases, a company whose shares are not traded on the stock market might be able to raise new capital by issuing shares, when the new equity finance is provided by specialist 'venture capital' organisations.

Sources of debt

For most companies, the main source of debt capital is their bank or banks. Large companies, however, are able to raise debt capital by issuing bonds in the bond markets.

Sources of short-term finance

Companies obtain short-term finance mainly from trade credit and bank lending. Large companies might have access to other sources of short-term borrowing, such as:

- commercial paper programmes (CP), or
- bankers' acceptance facilities (BA acceptances).

Trade finance

When the company needs finance to support its foreign trade, the treasury function might be responsible for arranging the financing.

1.4 Financial risk management

The treasury department is usually responsible for the management of financial risk. The main financial risks facing companies are:

- foreign exchange risk or currency risk
- interest rate risk
- credit risk
- market risk, where companies hold large quantities of market securities (such as shares and bonds) as assets. Market risk is the risk of an adverse movement in the market price of these assets.

Foreign exchange risk and interest rate risk are described in later chapters (although translation risk and transaction risk have been described in the context of overseas capital investment, in an earlier chapter.)

Credit risk

Credit risk is the risk that a debt will not be paid and will become a bad debt, or that a customer will make debt payments later than scheduled. Credit control and credit risk management are aspects of day-to-day financial management, and you should already be familiar with credit management and debt collection systems.

Companies that borrow from banks are a credit risk to the bank, and a function of the treasury department in large companies might be to monitor the perceived credit risk of the company. Large companies might have a formal credit rating from one of the credit rating agencies (such as Moody's and Standard & Poor's). The cost of borrowing for these companies depends on their credit rating.

- Banks will charge a higher 'spread' over the risk-free rate on loans to companies with a lower credit rating.
- If a company wants to issue new bonds, the interest payable on the bonds will depend on the credit rating attached to them.

The treasury management of a company that has debt with a credit rating might therefore be required to monitor the rating and maintain a dialogue with the credit rating agencies.

The link between credit ratings spreads over the risk-free rate and the cost of borrowing has been explained in the earlier chapter on the cost of capital.

1.5 Centralised or decentralised?

Advantages of a centralised treasury function

A centralised treasury department should be able to evaluate the financing requirements of the group as a whole and may be able to negotiate better rates when borrowing.

Experts and resources within one location would reduce duplication costs.

The department could operate as an internal bank and undertake matching of funds. Therefore, it could transfer funds from subsidiaries which have spare cash resources to ones which need them, avoiding the costs of going into the external market to raise funds.

The department may be able to undertake multilateral internal netting and thereby reduce costs related to hedging activity.

Many hedging techniques are quite sophisticated and require a certain level of expertise. The concentration of experts and resources within one central department may result in a more effective decision-making environment and higher quality risk monitoring and control.

A centralised department would prevent subsidiaries from taking positions in potentially disastrous derivative exposures.

A centralised treasury frees up management time at the subsidiaries.

Advantages of a decentralised treasury function

Each subsidiary company may be better placed to take local regulations, custom and practice into consideration.

Granting autonomy to subsidiaries on how they undertake their own fund management may result in increased motivation and effort from the subsidiary's senior management and thereby increase future income.

Subsidiary companies which have access to their own funds may be able to respond to opportunities quicker and establish competitive advantage more effectively.

The money markets

- Definition of the money markets
- Purpose of the money markets
- The inter-bank market

The subject matter of this section has been removed from the syllabus. However, this section has been retained for your convenience as it is now assumed knowledge from F9.

2 The money markets

2.1 Definition of the money markets

The money markets are wholesale markets for dealing in short-term lending and borrowing and for trading short-dated financial instruments.

- 'Wholesale' markets are markets for large-value transactions.
- Short-dated financial instruments are financial instruments that have one year or less to maturity when they are issued. They include Treasury bills, bills of exchange, commercial paper and certificates of deposit (CDs). The repo market, which is one of the money markets, also deals in short-dated bonds (bonds with a short time remaining to maturity) as well as other money market securities.

The main money markets are:

- the inter-bank market and
- the repo market.

There are international money markets for all the main currencies. For example, London is a major money market centre which operates large money markets in US dollars, euros, yen, Swiss francs and Canadian dollars as well as sterling.

2.2 Purpose of the money markets

The main purpose of the money markets is to provide:

- short-term liquidity to entities needing money, and
- short-term investment opportunities for entities with surplus liquidity.

Banks are the most active participants in the money markets, but some large companies also have direct access to the markets. Smaller companies and individuals might be offered an opportunity by their bank to borrow or lend at money market interest rates, and their access to the money markets is made through the bank. This means that companies are able to borrow or deposit money short-term in the money markets through their bank. When they participate through their bank, they can borrow or lend much smaller amounts of money than the normal size of money market transaction.

Money markets also provide ready access to short-term borrowing and lending opportunities in foreign currency. This is important for companies involved in international trade that need short-term finance for transactions involving a foreign currency.

2.3 The inter-bank market

The inter-bank market is a market for borrowing and lending large amounts of money for a short-term, often 'overnight' (for one day) but possibly up to one year. As the name of the market indicates, it is mainly a market for borrowing or lending between banks, but as explained earlier, companies are able to participate directly or through their bank. (When they participate through their bank, they can borrow or lend much smaller quantities of money.)

Interest rates in the inter-bank market vary according to:

- the duration of the loan, and
- the credit rating or credit status of the borrowing bank.

Banks with a very high credit rating are able to borrow at lower rates than banks with a lower credit rating.

The interest rates charged to top-quality banks are monitored. In London for example, a number of banks report their borrowing rates to the British Bankers Association (BBA) each day, and the BBA uses these rates to determine the average borrowing rates for top-rated banks.

LIBOR

The BBA publishes these rates as the BBA London Inter-Bank Offered Rate or LIBOR. LIBOR (also written as Libor) is an important rate in the London markets, because it provides a guideline on interest rates to banks and it is also used as a benchmark interest rate in some derivatives markets. (Derivatives are explained later.)

The financial press publishes LIBOR rates, which might be presented as follows:

Market interest rates

18th July	**Overnight**	**Month**	**Three months**	**Six months**	**One year**
US$ Libor	5.30375	5.32000	5.36000	5.40906	5.50594
Euro Libor	4.09063	4.11463	4.14250	4.28488	4.52538
£ Libor	5.60625	5.67125	5.84875	6.00250	6.26000
Swiss Fr Libor	2.39000	2.42000	2.48833	2.65083	2.91250
Yen Libor	0.61250	0.64250	0.74563	0.84938	0.99750
Canada Libor	4.34833	4.32167	4.46000	4.64000	4.89833

LIBOR can be regarded as a risk-free money market rate. The money market yield curve is normally upward-sloping, but this is not always the case, and a yield curve may be downward sloping along all or a part of its length.

Only a few LIBOR rates are published in the financial press, and it is possible to borrow or lend for any money market period.

Money market rates are shown as annual rates of interest. The actual amount of interest payable on a money market loan, or receivable on a money market deposit, depends on the term of the loan or deposit as well as the interest rate.

There are specific rules for the calculation of money market interest, but for the purpose of your examination, you can assume that the interest payable or receivable is the annual interest rate multiplied by the number of months of the loan or deposit and divided by 12. Here are some examples.

- For a three-month loan of $1,000,000 when three-month LIBOR is 5.36%, the interest rate is (5.36% × 3/12) 1.34% and the interest payable is $13,400.
- For a six-month deposit of €1,000,000 when six month LIBOR is 4.28488%, the interest rate is 2.14244% and interest receivable will be €21,424.40.

Only top-rated banks are able to borrow at LIBOR. Other banks and companies borrow at a 'spread' above LIBOR or earn interest on deposits at a rate below LIBOR. For example a company might be able to borrow at LIBOR plus 0.5% (plus 50 basis points), and if one-month LIBOR is 6.125%, it is able to borrow for one month at 6.625%.

Note on base rates

Not all companies borrow from their bank at a rate of interest based on LIBOR. Many companies, especially smaller companies, might pay a rate of interest on an overdraft or variable rate loan at an interest rate linked to the bank's base rate. For example a company might borrow at base rate plus 2%. A base rate is an 'administered rate' which means that it is set by the lending bank and is not directly related to market rates of interest.

Changes in money market interest rates

Money market interest rates can change rapidly, in response to market conditions and prospects for the economy. However, in the United States, the European Union and the UK, the biggest influence on LIBOR rates is the central bank. The central bank is able to raise or lower the money market interest rate for its dealings with commercial banks, and it uses interest rates to try to influence the state of the economy (and in particular the rate of inflation). If the central bank in the UK raises its interest rate by 0.25% for example, banks will immediately increase their LIBOR rates by the same amount.

CHAPTER 17

Foreign exchange risk and currency risk management

Contents

Foreign exchange risk

1 Foreign exchange risk

1.1 The need for foreign exchange

Many companies make foreign exchange transactions with their banks. The need for foreign exchange arises from international trade and international investment.

- A company buying goods from another country might be required to pay in a foreign currency, such as the domestic currency of the supplier. It must therefore obtain the foreign currency to make the payment.
- A company selling goods abroad might price the goods in the buyer's domestic currency, or in another currency such as US dollars. When the customer pays in the foreign currency, the company might sell the currency received in exchange for its own domestic currency
- A company investing abroad might need to obtain foreign currency to acquire or to make the investment.

If a company in Australia wants to buy goods from a supplier in Germany, and the purchase price is in euros, the Australian company has to buy euros from its bank in order to make the payment to the supplier.

Similarly, if a company in The UK sells goods to a customer in Africa, and the price is paid in US dollars, the company will probably sell the dollars it has received to its bank, in exchange for sterling. (Alternatively, the company could keep the dollars in a US dollar bank account, if it has one.) The company in Africa would also need to buy dollars from a bank in order to pay the UK supplier.

Many foreign currencies can be bought and sold freely in the foreign exchange markets (FX markets), which are operated world-wide by banks. On the other hand, some currencies do not have a liquid market, and foreign companies might be reluctant to accept payment in those currencies.

1.2 Currency transaction exposures

Transactions in foreign currency give rise to currency transaction exposures. Transaction exposures were explained in the earlier chapter in international investment.

A transaction exposure occurs when a payment of a foreign currency is required at a future date, or when a receipt of a payment in a foreign currency will occur at a future date. An exposure to risk occurs because the exchange rate could move adversely between 'now' and the time that the currency payment or receipt happens, with the result that either:

- it costs more to buy the foreign currency to make the currency payment, or
- there is less income when a currency payment is received and the currency is converted into domestic currency by selling it to a bank.

Currency transaction exposures can be analysed according to when the currency payment or receipt is expected to happen, and exposures can be measured in each foreign currency. An exposure is simply:

- the amount of payments that will be made in the currency, and
- the amount of the currency that will be received.

If payments and receipts of the same currency are expected at the same time, the net exposure is the difference between the expected receipt and the expected payment.

1.3 Exchange rates and volatility

Banks quote exchange rates at which they are willing to buy and sell currencies in the FX markets.

Exchange rates are quoted as a number of units of one currency (the variable currency) in exchange for one unit of the other currency (the base currency). As described earlier, the quote might be a direct quote (as used in most countries) or as an indirect quote (as used in the UK).

Exchange rates can be very volatile. This means that exchange rates can move up or down by large amounts, within a fairly short period of time.

For example, since the euro was created in 1999, when its value was about €1 = $1.20, the exchange rate has ranged between about €1 = $0.75 to about €1 = $1.35.

Exchange rate volatility creates foreign exchange risk for anyone involved in buying, selling, borrowing or investing foreign currency.

Foreign currency risk can be classified into three types. These are:

- Translation risk;
- Economic risk; and
- Transaction risk

1.4 Translation risk

Translation risk arises in international companies with foreign subsidiaries. Income statements and statements of financial position (balance sheets) will be denominated in the local currency of the subsidiary and, on consolidation, will be translated into the currency of the holding company. On translation of financial statements from one currency to another, losses or gains arise due to exchange rate movements.

Translation risk is therefore the risk of losses (or gains) arising on the translation of the financial statements of a foreign subsidiary into the currency of the parent company, for the purpose of preparing consolidated accounts.

1.5 Economic risk

Economic risk refers to the long-term movement in exchange rates caused by changes in the competitiveness of a country.

For example, over the long term the euro might increase in value against the US dollar. If this happens, goods produced and paid for in US dollars will become cheaper relative to goods produced and paid for in euros. US companies will therefore become more competitive in terms of price, relative to companies in the Eurozone, because of the exchange rate movement.

Economic risk, in the context of foreign exchange, is therefore the risk that a company might choose to locate its operations in a country whose currency gains in value over time against the currencies of its competitors in world markets. The consequence of an increase in the value of the domestic currency is a loss of competitiveness.

1.6 Transaction risk

Transaction risk is the foreign exchange risk that arises in transactions between two parties:

- where the normal transaction currency of each party is different, and
- when the transaction involves a future receipt/payment between the two parties.

Transaction risk is the risk that, for any future transaction in a foreign currency, the amount received or paid in domestic currency might be different from the amount originally expected because of movements in the exchange rate between the date of the initial transaction and the date of settlement (payment/receipt).

For example, transaction risk will arise when a UK company buys goods from a Chinese supplier when the price is in US dollars, and payment is required three months after the date of the purchase.

- For the UK buyer, there is a risk that the US dollar will increase in value against the British pound in the three months before settlement is required. If the dollar strengthens in value, the cost in pounds of obtaining the dollars to pay the supplier will be higher than originally expected.
- For the Chinese supplier, there is a risk that the US dollar will fall in value against the Chinese Renminbi in the three months before settlement. If the dollar

falls in value, the dollar receipts will learn less in Renminbi that originally expected when the sale was made.

Volatile exchange rates increase transaction risk. Transaction risk can disrupt international trade, and make businesses more reluctant to trade internationally, because losses arising from adverse movements in an exchange rate reduce the profit on sales transactions, or increase costs of purchases. The transaction loss might even offset the amount of normal trading profit.

Example: Transaction risk

1 January

A Japanese company sells goods to a UK buyer for £100,000.

The exchange rate is ¥190/$1. Therefore, the Japanese company expects to receive ¥ 19,000,000.

The UK buyer is allowed three months' credit.

31 March

The Japanese company receives £100,000 from the UK buyer.

The exchange rate is ¥180/$1.

Therefore, the Japanese company receives ¥18,000,000.

This is ¥1,000,000 less than expected when the transaction was entered into. (The company has made an exchange loss of ¥1,000,000).

This example illustrates several points about transaction risk.

- Currency risk arises from exposure to the consequences of a rise or fall in an exchange rate. Here, the Japanese company was exposed to the risk of a fall in the value of the UK pound.
- Transaction risk arises only when the settlement of the transaction (and receipt/payment) will occur at a future date.
- Exchange difference only occurs in the above circumstances when there is a movement in the exchange rate (which almost always happens to a greater or lesser degree).
- An exposure lasts for a period of time. Here, the exposure lasts from when the goods were sold on credit until the time that the customer eventually pays.

Currency risk is a two-way risk, and exposure to risk can lead to either losses or gains from movements in an exchange rate. In the above example, the exchange rate could have moved the other way.

Example: Transaction risk

1 January

A Japanese company sells sugar to a UK buyer for £100,000.

The exchange rate is ¥190/$1. Therefore, the Japanese company expects to receive ¥19,000,000.

The UK buyer is allowed three months' credit.

31 March

The Japanese company receives £100,000 from the UK buyer.

The exchange rate is ¥200/$1.

Therefore, the Japanese company receives ¥20,000,000.

This is ¥1,000,000 more than expected when the transaction was entered into. (The company has made an exchange gain of ¥1,000,000).

Thus the exchange rate can have a big impact on the final outcome of the transaction. The Japanese company above was presumably happy to sell its goods for £100,000 or ¥19,000,000. However, the value of the transaction could fluctuate a great deal.

Example: Transaction risk: impact on final receipt

Referring to the numbers in the previous examples.

	¥	¥
Original sale value in yen	19,000,000	19,000,000
Exchange difference on settlement		
Rate = 180/$1: Exchange loss	(1,000,000)	
Rate = 200/$1: Exchange gain		1,000,000
Final receipt	18,000,000	20,000,000

Trading profits for companies engaged in foreign trade can be significantly affected by currency movements. When exchange rates are volatile and unpredictable, the gain or loss on currency exchange could possibly be even bigger than the expected gross profit from the transaction.

Example: Transaction risk: impact on final margin

Referring to the numbers in the previous examples.

Suppose the Japanese company operated on a 10% margin.

	¥	¥
Original sale value in yen	19,000,000	19,000,000
10% margin	1,900,000	1,900,000
Exchange difference on settlement		
Rate = 180/$1: Exchange loss	(1,000,000)	
Rate = 200/$1: Exchange gain		1,000,000
Final profit	900,000	2,900,000

As illustrated, risk is two way. Transaction risk means that a company could be worse off (downside risk) or better off (upside risk) depending on the way the exchange rates move.

Companies often use methods to remove or reduce the volatility (risk). This is described as hedging. There are a variety of hedging techniques that can be used.

Most hedging techniques result in the company missing out on exchange gains in order to protect themselves from exchange losses. Some people find this surprising at first but a trading company exists to produce its goods and sell them at what it believes to be an acceptable margin. Hedging techniques protect the margin by locking out volatility.

1.7 Summary

Translation risk does not affect the cash flows of a group of companies. It is a risk of non-cash ('paper') losses or gains in preparing consolidated financial statements.

Transaction risk does affect cash flows, because movements in exchange rates affect the amount of cash received in domestic currency, or the amount paid in domestic currency, for at least one of the two parties to the transaction.

Economic risk is a strategic risk, affecting the competitiveness of a business entity over the longer term

The FX markets: spot rates

- Bid and offer rates
- Spot rates
- Quoting exchange rates
- Cross rates

2 The FX markets: spot rates

You need to understand how currencies are bought and sold in the FX markets. This section of the chapter explains the basic 'rules' for buying and selling currency.

2.1 Bid and offer prices

You need to calculate the cash flows in a foreign currency exchange transaction. If so, you might be given one figure for the current exchange rate between two currencies. In practice, banks quote two rates: a bid rate and an offer rate.

- The bid rate is the rate at which the bank will buy the base currency.
- The offer rate is the rate at which the bank will sell the base currency.

Most exchange rates are quoted to four decimal places.

It is easy to get confused about which exchange rate should be applied to a particular transaction. The basic rule to remember is that the bank will use the rate that is more favourable to itself and less favourable to the customer.

Example

A UK company needs $10,000 to pay a US supplier. The bank's current rates for sterling/US dollar (US$/£1) are 1.9850 – 1.9855.

The British pound is the base currency, since the rate is quoted as £1 = £X.

The company needs to buy US dollars in exchange for British pounds, in order to pay the US supplier. The bank is selling dollars and receiving British pounds in exchange. It will apply a rate of 1.9850 to the currency transaction with the company, because 1.9850 will give it more British pounds than the rate of 1.9855. The cost of buying the dollars is therefore £5,037.78 ($10,000/1.9850).

Example

The same UK company receives US$15,000 from a customer, and it wants to convert these dollar receipts into British pounds. The exchange rate is 1.9850 – 1.9855.

The bank will buy dollars at 1.9855, and so the company will receive £7,554.77 (15,000/1.9855) in exchange for the dollars.

Taking this transaction and the previous example together, the UK company's cash flows in British pounds from the two transactions would be as follows:

	£
Buy $10,000 at 1.9850: pay	(5,037.78)
Sell $15,000 at 1.9855: receive	7,554.77
Net receipts	2,516.99

It would be more sensible for the company to pay the S10,000 to the US supplier out of the $15,000 it receives from its customer. That would leave it needing to sell just US$5,000 at 1.9855. The receipts in British pounds would then be £2,518.26 ($5,000/1.9855).

Example

(a) A French company has received Aus$7,000 from a customer in Australia. The current exchange rate for the euro and the Australian dollar (Aus$/€1) is 1.5230 – 1.5240.

How much will the company receive in euros for selling the Australian dollars?

(b) An Australian company needs to buy €12,000 to pay a Spanish supplier. The exchange rate is the same as above. How much will it cost the company to obtain the euros that it needs?

Answer

(a) The bank is buying Australian dollars and selling euros. It will offer the rate more favourable to itself, which is 1.5240. The company will receive $7,000/ 1.5240 = €4,593.18.

(b) The Australian company needs to buy euros, and the bank will charge the rate most favourable to itself. To buy €12,000, the Australian company will have to pay 12,000 × 1.5240 = Aus$18,288.

2.2 Spot rates

In the FX markets, banks trade currencies both spot and forward. A spot transaction is a transaction for the sale of one currency in exchange for another, for 'immediate' settlement. 'Immediate' settlement in practice usually means after two working days, so that if a company makes a spot transaction with a bank on a Monday, the actual exchange of currencies will happen on Wednesday, two working days later. For the purpose of the examination, however, you can treat spot transactions as transactions for immediate settlement.

Although currency can be bought and sold 'spot', spot transactions cannot be used to 'hedge' a currency exposure and foreign exchange risk.

2.3 Quoting exchange rates

The exchange rate is the price of one currency in terms of another, that is, the number of units of one currency that could be bought with one unit of another currency. Please note that 'price' refers to the price of the foreign currency that is being sold.

There are two methods of quoting exchange rates. The method used varies from country to country and, in some countries from currency to currency. The two methods are direct quotes and indirect quotes.

Direct quotes

This is the number of units of the domestic currency that will be exchanged for one unit of a foreign currency.

An example of a direct quote is between yen and GBP. ¥200 can be exchanged for £1, usually expressed as ¥200/£1.

Indirect quotes

This is the number of units of foreign currency that will be traded for 1 unit of the domestic currency. In London, for example, the exchange rate quotation between pounds and yen is normally expressed as a number of yen that can be purchased or sold for a pound. For example, ¥200 per £1 and expressed as £1/¥200.

This is an example of indirect quote and is also known as a reverse quote.

Comment

Note that a direct quote of one currency is the indirect quote of the other.

Example: Direct and indirect

¥200/£1 is a direct quote of the yen price of a pound (as would be used in Japan).

£1/¥200 is an indirect quote of the pound price of a yen (as would be used in the UK).

2.4 Cross rates

The exchange rate for two currencies might be derived as a cross rate. This means that they are not traded directly on the FX markets, but are both traded through the US dollar.

For example, if the exchange rate for the US dollar against the Hong Kong dollar (USD/HKD) is 8.1000 and the rate for the US dollar against the Canadian dollar (USD/CAD) is 1.2475, the cross rate for the Hong Kong dollar against the Canadian dollar (CAD/HKD) is 8.1000/1.2475, which is C$1 = HK$6.4930.

e

Example

The three-month forward rate for the US dollar against the Swiss franc is 1.2166 (US$1 = SwFr1.2166). The three-month forward rate for the US dollar against the British pound is £1 = US$1.8610.

What is the three-month forward rate for the Swiss franc against the British pound (quoting the pound as the base currency)?

a

Answer

US$1 = SwFr 1.2166

£1 = 1.8610

Therefore £1 = 1.2166 × 1.8610 = SwFr 2.2641.

Hedging exposure to foreign exchange risk

- The purpose of hedging risk
- Methods of hedging exposures to foreign exchange risk
- Matching receipts and payments
- Netting

3 Hedging exposure to foreign exchange risk

3.1 The purpose of hedging risk

The purpose of hedging an exposure to risk is to eliminate or reduce the possibility that actual events will turn out worse than expected. The purpose of hedging an exposure to currency risk is to remove (or reduce) the possibility that a future transaction involving a foreign currency will have to be made at a less favourable exchange rate than expected.

Exchange rates can move up or down, and spot rates could move favourably as well as adversely. However, many companies prefer to hedge their currency risks by fixing an exchange rate now for a future transaction, even if this means that it will not be able to benefit from any favourable movement in the exchange rate.

3.2 Methods of hedging exposures to foreign exchange risk

The most important methods of hedging exposures to currency risk, which you will be expected to know for the examination, are:

- matching receipts and payments
- netting receipts and expenditure (or netting assets and liabilities)
- forward exchange contracts (described earlier)
- creating a money market hedge
- currency futures (described later)
- currency options (described later)
- currency swaps.

3.3 Matching receipts and payments

This involves matching foreign currency receipts and payments in order to reduce transaction risk.

When a company expects to have future cash receipts in a foreign currency and future cash payments in the same currency at about the same time, it can use the receipts to make some or all of the payments. To the extent that future receipts match future payments, the foreign exchange risk is eliminated. Movements in the spot exchange rate will affect the netted receipts and payments equally. The loss from the adverse movement affecting the cash receipts or payments will be offset by the gain from the favourable movement affecting the cash payments or receipts.

Example

A UK company expects to receive US$400,000 in two months' time and to make payments of $600,000, also in two months.

To hedge its currency exposures, the company can net $400,000 of receipts and payments, leaving a net exposure of just $200,000 in payments. This exposure might be hedged with a forward exchange contract.

3.4 Netting

Netting can be applied to cash flows in a foreign currency or to assets and liabilities denominated in a foreign currency. It is a process which involves netting credit balances against debit balances so that only the net amount is transferred or left outstanding.

The aim of netting is to save transaction costs by reducing the size of foreign currency transfer.

Bilateral netting

This involves only two parties. The parties might be within a group or simply trading partners.

Each party owes the other money and a net cash transfer is made to satisfy the obligation. Amounts might have to be translated into a common currency in order to determine the size of the transfer.

Example

X Plc is a UK company with two subsidiaries, A Inc based in the USA and B SA based in France.

A Inc owes B SA €400,000.

B SA owes A Inc $500,000.

The exchange rate is €1 = $1.1.

X Plc requires the settlement to be dollars.

Therefore, A owes B $440,000 (€400,000 @ $1.1 = €1), but B owes A $500,000.

Therefore, B pays $60,000 to A.

Multilateral netting

Multilateral netting involves more than two parties. It is used by groups with subsidiaries based in several countries. The process involves a series of possible payments backwards and forwards between group members into a simple net payment. This can seem quite complicated at first sight so is best explained with an example.

Example

X Plc is a large multinational company based in the UK.

It has 3 subsidiaries; A Inc is based in the USA, B Gmbh is based in the Eurozone and C Co is based in Japan.

The following cash flows are due to be paid in two weeks' time.

Owed by	Owed to	Amounts
X Plc	A Inc	US$ 9 million
X Plc	B Gmbh	EU€ 2 million
C Co	B Gmbh	EU€ 3 million
C Co	A Inc	US$ 1.8 million
B Gmbh	A Inc	US$ 2 million
B Gmbh	X Plc	EU€ 5 million
A Inc	C Co	JPY 500 million
A Inc	X Plc	US$D 4 million

X Plc uses multilateral netting in GBP.

The following exchange rates are to be used:

US$/£1	$1.5
EU€/£1	€1.35
JPY /£1	JPY 140

The net payments and receipts are calculated as follows:

Step 1: List the payments and translate them into the currency to be used for netting. (You could do this on the question paper)

Owed by	Owed to	Amounts	Rate	Amount in £
X Plc	A Inc	US$ 9 million	1.5	6000.0
X Plc	B Gmbh	EU€ 2 million	1.35	1481.5
C Co	B Gmbh	EU€ 3 million	1.35	2222.2
C Co	A Inc	US$ 1.8 million	1.5	1200.0
B Gmbh	A Inc	US$ 2 million	1.5	1333.3
B Gmbh	X Plc	EU€ 5 million	1.35	3703.7
A Inc	C Co	JPY 500 million	140	3571.4
A Inc	X Plc	US$D 4 million	1.5	2666.7

Step 2: Construct a table with the paying companies in row 1 and the receiving companies in column 1.

Receipts to	Payments from: X Plc	A Inc	B Gmbh	C Co
X Plc		2,666.7	3,703.7	
A Inc	6,000.0		1,333.3	1,200.0
B Gmbh	1,481.5			2,222.2
C Co		3,571.4		

Step 3: Add down to find the total payments by each entity

Receipts to	Payments from: X Plc	A Inc	B Gmbh	C Co
X Plc		2,666.7	3,703.7	
A Inc	6,000.0		1,333.3	1,200.0
B Gmbh	1,481.5			2,222.2
C Co		3,571.4		
Payments	(7,481.5)	(6,238.1)	(5,037.0)	(3,422.2)

Step 4: Add across to find the total receipts to each entity

Receipts to	Payments from: X Plc	A Inc	B Gmbh	C Co	Receipts
X Plc		2,666.7	3,703.7		6,370.4
A Inc	6,000.0		1,333.3	1,200.0	8,533.3
B Gmbh	1,481.5			2,222.2	3,703.7
C Co		3,571.4			3,571.4
Payments	(7,481.5)	(6,238.1)	(5,037.0)	(3,422.2)	22,178.8

Step 5: Compare the receipts and payments to find the net flows

Receipts to	Payments from: X Plc	A Inc	B Gmbh	C Co	Receipts
X Plc		2,666.7	3,703.7		6,370.4
A Inc	6,000.0		1,333.3	1,200.0	8,533.3
B Gmbh	1,481.5			2,222.2	3,703.7
C Co		3,571.4			3,571.4
Payments	(7,481.5)	(6,238.1)	(5,037.0)	(3,422.2)	22,178.8
Receipts	6,370.4	8,533.3	3,703.7	3,571.4	
Net flows	(1,111.1)	2,295.2	(1,333.3)	149.2	

Step 6: Show the payments and receipts and the parties involved.

This has been set out as a matrix below but you would not need to use this format for this stage. X Plc would have to arrange for X Plc and B Gmbh to pay £2,444.4 (1.111.11 + 1,333.3) to A Inc and C Co who are owed £2,444.4 (2.295.2 + 149.2). This could be done in several ways as follows:

Receipts	Payments from: X Plc	A Inc	B Gmbh	C Co	Receipts
X Plc					
A Inc	1,111.1		1,184.1		2,295.2
B Gmbh					
C Co			149.2		149.2
	(1,111.1)		(1,333.3)		2,444.4

Alternatively:

Receipts	Payments from: X Plc	A Inc	B Gmbh	C Co	Receipts
X Plc					
A Inc	961.9		1,333.3		2,295.2
B Gmbh					
C Co	149.2				149.2
	(1,111.1)		(1,333.3)		2,444.4

Management of barriers to remittance

Governments may place restrictions on remittances that can be paid overseas. This would prevent a foreign owner from extracting the profit made in a regime.

The restriction may or may not be linked to exchange controls.

If the restriction is not linked to exchange controls the following methods might be used to get around the barriers.

- Profit of the restricted subsidiary can be reduced by the parent making charges for management fees, royalties or central overhead allocation. These charges would take the place of the dividend.
- The parent could increase transfer prices to reduce profit. The increased transfer prices would take the place of the dividend.
- The parent could instruct the subsidiary to make a loan to the parent (in the amount of the dividend).
- The parent could set up a back to back parallel loan. This would involve the subsidiary making a loan to an entity in its own country and the parent receiving an equivalent amount from a party related to that entity but based outside the country. This would also be an effective way of avoiding exchange restrictions.

Note that the government that has imposed the restrictions might well have other regulations in place to prevent companies circumventing the rules in the ways described.

Forward FX contracts and forward rates

- Forward rates
- Forward contracts
- Premiums and discounts
- Forward contracts and hedging exposure to FX risk

4 Forward FX contracts and forward rates

4.1 Forward rates

Banks trade in foreign currencies both for immediate delivery (either to or from the bank) at the spot rate or for future delivery (either to or from the bank) at a forward rate.

The forward rate is the rate at which a bank is willing to trade in foreign currency at a pre-agreed date.

Banks are able to quote forward exchange rates for currencies because of the money markets (short-term borrowing and lending markets). Forward exchange rates differ from spot rates because of the interest rate differences between the two currencies.

Forward rates are calculated by applying the interest rate differential to the spot rate using the interest rate parity equation. This was demonstrated earlier in this chapter.

A forward rate could be a stronger or weaker rate than the spot rate depending on whether the interest rate on the variable currency is higher or lower than the interest rate on the base currency.

- When the forward rate is stronger than the spot rate the foreign currency is said to be trading at a premium to the spot rate.
- When the forward rate is weaker than the spot rate the foreign currency is said to be trading at a discount to the spot rate.

Trading in foreign currency at the forward rate is through forward exchange contracts. These are a very powerful risk management tool as they allow companies to lock in future exchange rates.

For example, a Japanese company can arrange a forward contract 'now' to sell a quantity of US dollars in exchange for British pounds in three months' time, at a rate of exchange that is agreed 'now'. This means that it knows exactly how many pounds it will receive.

4.2 Forward contracts

A forward exchange contract is a contract entered into 'now' for settlement at an agreed future date (or at any time between two agreed future dates).

It is a contract between a customer and a bank for the purchase or sale of:

- a specified amount; of
- a specified foreign currency;
- for delivery at a specified future date
- at a specified rate

The customer specifies the amount of foreign currency and the date and the bank specifies the rate at which it is willing to deal.

A bank will arrange a forward contract for settlement at any future date, but commonly-quoted forward rates are for settlement in one month, three months, six months and possibly one year.

Forward exchange transactions are available in all the major traded currencies of the world, although settlement dates of more than one year forward are very unusual in any currencies except the most heavily-traded currencies such as the dollar-euro.

4.3 Premiums and discounts

Forward rates are derived from current spot rates and interest rate differences between currencies but it is common practice to quote forward rates as adjustments to the spot rate.

The adjustment might be:

- a premium (designated pm) where the future rate is stronger than the spot rate; or
- a discount (designated dis) where the future rate is weaker than the spot rate.

The nature of the adjustment to the spot rate to achieve the strengthening or weakening of the foreign currency depends on whether the quotes are direct or indirect.

	Forward rate at a premium to spot	**Forward rate at a discount**
Direct quotes	Add premium	Deduct premium
Indirect quotes	Deduct a discount	Add discount

Example: Forward rate premiums and discounts (direct quote)

The following examples show how the forward rate is calculated and then how it is presented as an adjustment to the spot rate.

The example shows the foreign currency trading at a discount and at a premium.

	Foreign currency trading at a premium	Foreign currency trading at a discount
Spot rate	¥150/$1	¥150/$1
Japanese interest rate	10%	5%
US interest rate	5%	10%
Forward rates calculated as:		
$F = S \times \frac{1 + i_d}{1 + i_f}$	$F = 150 \times \frac{1.1}{1.05}$	$F = 150 \times \frac{1.05}{1.1}$
	F = ¥157.14/$1	F = ¥143.18/$1
Forward rates published as:	¥	¥
Spot	150.00	150.00
Premium	7.14	
Discount		(6.82)
Forward rate	157.14	143.18

The next example shows the situation for a currency quoted indirectly and adds in further complications.

The first of these is that forward rates (shown as adjustment to spot) are quoted as spreads just like the spot rate. The correct rate to use depends on whether the foreign currency is being bought or sold.

The second complication is that the adjustments might be given in units which are a different order of magnitude for some quotes. For example, the adjustment to an indirect quote of dollars may be given in cents.

Example:

A UK company expects to receive US$75,000 in six months from a US customer and it wishes to hedge the exposure to currency risk by arranging a forward contract.

The following rates are available (US$/£1):

GBP/USD			
Spot (£1=)	1.7530	-	1.7540
Six months forward	240	-	231 pm

The dollar is quoted forward at a premium. The premium is shown in 'points' of price, so that 240 – 231 means 0.0240 – 0.0231.

The bank will apply the rate that is more favourable to itself. (If you need to work out which rate is more favourable, use the spot rates to do this).

The company will be selling US dollars in exchange for pounds, and the higher rate will be used (the offer rate).

Spot rate	1.7540
Forward points (deduct premium)	(0.0231)
Forward rate	1.7309

The company can use a forward contract to fix its future income from the US dollars at £43,330.06 (75,000/1.7309).

Forward rates do not predict future spot rates

A one-year forward rate of £1 = $1.9660 does not mean that the spot rate of exchange will be $1.9660 in one year's time. Forward rates do not attempt to predict what future spot rates will be. A forward rate represents the comparative investment value of the two currencies between 'now' and the settlement date for the forward contract.

However, the interest rate parity formula for predicting future exchange rates is also used to predict forward exchange rates. With this theory it is assumed that the forward rate does predict what the future spot rate will be. The interest rate parity formula was explained in the earlier chapter on international capital investment.

4.4 Forward contracts and hedging exposure to FX risk

For companies, forward FX contracts can be used to hedge an exposure to currency risk (transaction risk). Currency risk will arise, for example, when a company expects to receive a quantity of a foreign currency in several months' time, which it will sell in exchange for its own domestic currency. If it plans to sell the foreign currency in a spot transaction, until it receives the currency, it is exposed to the risk that the exchange rate will move adversely and the currency will fall in value and be worth less than its current value.

For example, suppose that an Italian company expects to receive 5 million Japanese yen in three months' time, and the current exchange rate for euros against the yen (yen/€ 1) is 135.00. At this rate, the Italian company would be able to exchange the yen for €37,037 (5 million/135.0).

- However, there is a risk that the yen will fall in value during the three months, during which the company has an FX risk exposure arising from its future yen income. If the yen fell in value and after three months the spot rate is 150.00, the yen income would be worth only €33,333.
- On the other hand, if the yen strengthened in value, say to 120.00 spot after three months, the income would be worth €41,667.

Although foreign exchange rates can move favourably as well as adversely, companies engaged in international trade usually prefer to avoid exposure to currency risk. They can 'hedge' currency exposures by arranging forward contracts to buy or sell currency. By fixing the exchange rate 'now' for a future currency purchase or sale transaction, the uncertainty or risk in the exchange rate is eliminated.

Example

A British company needs to pay a German supplier €50,000 in three months' time. A bank quotes the following forward rates for three months (€/£1): 1.4820 – 1.4830.

If the company arranges a forward contract to buy the euros in exchange for British pounds, the forward rate will be 1.4820. This is the rate that is more favourable to the bank, because it will receive more pounds in exchange for the euros. The cost to the company of obtaining €50,000 in three months' time is £33,738.19 (50,000/1.4820).

Advantages of forward contracts

Forward contracts are easy to set up and are available between a large number of currencies.

The can be tailor made to meet a company's requirements with respect to currencies, amount and delivery date.

Hedging with forward contracts is very effective. A forward contract eliminates the risk of an adverse movement in the exchange rate and allows a company to make financial plans (such as cash budgets) with greater certainty

The amount of cash to be paid or received is known in advance with certainty. In the example above, the company knows exactly how much it will have to pay in British pounds in three months' time.

Disadvantages of forward contracts

Hedging an exposure to currency risk with a forward contract gives protection against adverse exchange rate movements, but prevents the company from taking advantage of any favourable movement in the spot rate.

The contract is for delivery so a user must be ready to buy or sell the agreed amount at the delivery date. In the above example, the company has a contractual obligation to carry out the terms of the agreement and buy the euros at 1.4820 at the settlement date. If the spot rate at this date is more favourable, say 1.6000, the company cannot choose to ignore the forward contract and buy euros at the spot rate.

A forward contract may not be available for the currencies needed.

There is a cost involved as users bear the spread between the buy rates and the sell rates.

Money market hedge

- Definition of a money market hedge
- Constructing a hedge for a future currency receipt
- Constructing a hedge for a future currency payment
- Advantages and disadvantages

5 Money market hedge

5.1 Definition of a money market hedge

A money market hedge is another method of creating a hedge against an exposure to currency risk. Instead of hedging with a forward exchange contract, a company can create a hedge by borrowing or lending short-term in the international money markets, to fix an effective exchange rate 'now' for a future currency transaction.

5.2 Constructing a hedge for a future currency receipt

A company might expect to receive an amount of foreign currency at a future date, which it intends to exchange into its domestic currency. It wants to hedge its exposure to currency risk.

One way of hedging the risk is to make a forward exchange contract with a bank, in which it sells the future foreign currency receipts to the bank in exchange for domestic currency, at an exchange rate fixed 'now' by the forward contract.

Another way of hedging the risk is to establish a money market hedge. The money market hedge works by arranging a lending or borrowing transaction now, with a settlement date the same as the date when the future currency receipt or currency payment will occur. In the case of a hedge for a future receipt of foreign currency, it needs to borrow 'now' in the foreign currency, so that when the currency receipt actually occurs, it will be sufficient to pay the amount borrowed 'now' plus interest.

- To create a money market hedge, the company should borrow an amount of the currency immediately, for repayment at the same time that the future currency income will be received. The income in the currency will be used to repay the loan with interest. The amount borrowed should therefore, together with the accumulated interest for the borrowing period, equal the amount of the future currency income.
- Having borrowed the quantity of currency, the company should exchange it immediately (spot) for its domestic currency.
- The domestic currency obtained in this way can be used in the company's business. However, for examination purposes, you might be expected to assume that the domestic currency will be invested or deposited for the same period as the currency loan.
- At the end of the loan period, when the company uses its currency income to repay the currency loan, the deposit plus accumulated interest is an equivalent

amount in domestic currency. This can be used to calculate an effective forward interest rate for the hedge of the currency exposure.

A numerical example might help to clarify this technique.

Example

A UK company expects to receive a payment of US$800,000 in three months' time. It wants to hedge this exposure to currency risk using a money market hedge.

Spot three-month interest rates currently available in the money markets are:

	Deposits	Borrowing
US dollar	4.125%	4.250%
British pound	6.500%	6.625%

The spot exchange rate (US/£1) is 1.7770 – 1.7780.

Step 1

The UK company will be receiving US dollars in three months' time. It should therefore borrow US dollars for three months. The borrowing rate will be 4.25% (the higher of the two quoted rates). This is an annual rate, and in answering an examination question, you should calculate the rate for the interest period as an appropriate fraction of the annual rate. Here, the interest for three months will be 4.25% × 3/12 = 1.0625% or 0.010625.

The borrowed dollars plus accumulated interest after three months needs to be $800,000, therefore the amount of dollars borrowed should be:

$$\frac{\text{Final amount}}{(1+\text{interest rate for the period})} = \frac{\$800,000}{1.010625} = \$791,589$$

Step 2

The company should sell the borrowed $791,589 in exchange for British pounds. The appropriate spot rate is 1.7780. The company will receive £445,213.

We now assume that this will be placed on deposit for three months. The interest rate on deposits for sterling is 6.500%. This is an annual rate, and the interest for three months is assumed to be 6.5% × 3/12 = 1.625% or 0.01625.

After three months, the deposit plus accumulated interest will be £445,213 × 1.01625 = £452,448.

Step 3

At the end of three months, the company will receive US$800,000. Its three-month loan will mature, and the $800,000 is used to pay back the loan plus interest. The company has £452,448 from its deposit (its short-term investment in British pounds).

The money market hedge has therefore fixed an effective exchange rate for the dollar receipts, which is calculated as $800,000/£452,448. This gives an effective three-month forward rate of £1 = $1.7682.

5.3 Constructing a hedge for a future currency payment

To create a money market hedge for a future currency payment, a similar approach is required. To hedge a future payment in currency, a company should deposit an amount of the currency 'now' in the money market, so that the amount deposited plus interest will be sufficient to make the currency payment at the future date.

- A company with an obligation to make a payment in foreign currency at a future date should therefore buy a quantity of the currency now and place it on deposit until the payment is due to be made. The amount of currency placed on deposit, plus the accumulated interest, should equal the amount of the future payment.
- Buying the currency now spot will cost money. For the examination, it should usually be assumed that the company has to borrow in domestic currency to buy the foreign currency spot, and that the length of the loan period is the same as the deposit period for the foreign currency.
- At the end of the deposit period, the foreign currency deposit plus interest is used to make the currency payment. The domestic currency loan has accumulated interest, and the total amount now payable to settle the loan can be used to calculate the effective interest rate for the currency transaction.

Again, an example might help to clarify the method.

Example

Suppose that a UK company is expecting to pay a supplier US$500,000 in six months' time, and it wants to fix an effective exchange rate for this transaction with a money market hedge.

Spot six-month interest rates currently available in the money markets are as follows:

	Deposits	Borrowing
US dollar	4.125%	4.250%
British pound	6.500%	6.625%

The spot exchange rate (US$/£1) is 1.7770 – 1.7780.

Step 1

The company should deposit US dollars for six months. The deposit rate will be 4.125% (the lower of the two quoted rates). This is an annual rate, and in an examination the rate for the interest period is calculated as an appropriate fraction of the annual rate. Here, the interest for six months will be 4.125% × 6/12 = 2.0625% or 0.020625.

The dollars placed on deposit plus accumulated interest after six months needs to be \$500,000, therefore the amount of dollars placed on deposit for six months should be:

$$\frac{\text{Final amount}}{(1+\text{interest rate for the period})} = \frac{\$500{,}000}{1.020625} = \$489.896$$

Step 2

These dollars should be bought with British pounds. The appropriate spot rate is 1.7770. The company will therefore pay £275,687 to obtain the dollars.

We now assume that this money has to be borrowed for a six-month loan period. The interest rate on deposits for sterling is 6.625%. This is an annual rate, and the interest for six months will be 6.625% × 6/12 = 3.3125% or 0.033125.

After three months, the loan plus accumulated interest will be £275,687 × 1.033125 = £284,819.

Step 3

At the end of six months, the US deposit plus interest is used to make the payment of \$500,000. The sterling loan is repayable with interest, and the amount payable can be used to calculate an effective exchange rate for the money market hedge.

The effective exchange rate is therefore £1 = \$1.7555 (\$500,000/£284,819)

Conclusion: forward exchange contracts and money market hedges

In practice, a money market hedge should result in an effective exchange rate similar to the forward exchange rate. In the examination, however, one method of hedging might well result in a more favourable exchange rate than the other.

An examination question might give you a set of exchange rates and interest rates for two currencies, and details of a transaction that creates a currency risk exposure. The question might then ask you to compare a forward exchange contract with a money market hedge, and recommend which method of hedging is better.

You might also be required to compare a money market hedge with other methods of currency hedging, such as currency options and currency futures. These are explained in later chapters.

5.4 Advantages and disadvantages

Advantages of money market hedges

They are an effective hedge.

They allow expected forward receipts to be converted into current cash flows.

Disadvantages of money market hedges

Setting up a money market hedge is a more complicated process and requires a greater level of expertise than using forwards.

Money market hedging is not available to hedge risks between all currencies. Forward contracts can hedge a wider range of currencies than money market hedges.

Money market hedging is only suitable for relatively large sums.

Synthetic agreements for forward exchange (SAFEs)

- The nature of SAFEs
- The purpose of SAFEs

6 Synthetic agreements for forward exchange (SAFEs)

6.1 The nature of SAFEs

In a normal forward exchange contract, the two parties to the transaction agree to exchange a quantity of one currency for a quantity of a second currency, at a fixed rate of exchange. At settlement, an exchange of the two currencies takes place.

A synthetic agreement for forward exchange (SAFE) is a forward contract for the exchange of a notional amount of principal in the two currencies. They are similar to FRAs which are also contracts on a notional amount of principal. Like FRAs, SAFEs are settled by an exchange of cash based on movements in the exchange rate since the contract was made. (This type of contract, which is cash-settled on the basis of movements in prices or rate, is called a **contract for difference**.)

There are two types of SAFE:

- **Non-deliverable forwards** or NDFs. These are contracts that are cash-settled on the basis of movements in both the spot rate of exchange and also the size of the forward premium or discount. NDFs are also called **FX forwards**.
- **Exchange rate agreements** or ERAs. These contracts are cash-settled on the basis of movements in the size of the forward premium or discount only.

6.2 The purpose of SAFEs

SAFEs were created originally by banks in response to rules on capital adequacy. These international rules, known as the Basel rules, require banks to maintain a minimum amount of capital against their exposures to potential losses from credit risk and market risk. 'Traditional' forward contracts require more capital than SAFEs.

SAFEs are now used as a substitute for traditional forward contracts in currency markets where the currencies are not freely-convertible or easily-convertible. In these currency markets, the settlement of traditional forward contracts would be difficult and often impractical.

SAFEs therefore enable a company to obtain a hedge against currency risk where the currency is not freely convertible. For example when capital controls and exchange restrictions on a currency are imposed by the government, the currency markets might trade non-deliverable forwards (NDFs) to allow companies to hedge exposures (or take exposures) in the currency. The cash settlement of the SAFE is often in a different currency that is freely tradable, such as the US dollar.

A problem with SAFEs for currencies that are not freely convertible is that banks might have difficulty in hedging their own foreign currency exposures in these currencies, and they might compensate themselves for this risk by setting much wider spreads between the forward buying and selling rates for these contracts.

CHAPTER

18

Interest rate risk. Hedging with FRAs and swaps

Contents

The nature of interest rate risk

- The effect of a change in interest rates
- Interest rate volatility and interest rate risk
- Short-term and long-term interest rates
- Money market interest rates: LIBOR

1 The nature of interest rate risk

1.1 The effect of a change in interest rates

Interest rates can move up or down, although economists are often able to predict the direction of future movements. A movement in interest rates can affect companies in either a positive or a negative way.

- If a company has borrowed at a variable rate of interest, it will have to pay higher interest costs if the interest rate goes up, and lower interest costs if the rate goes down.
- If a company has borrowed at a fixed rate of interest, for example by issuing bonds, it will continue to pay the same rate of interest even if market interest rates go down. However, competitors who have borrowed at a variable rate of interest, or competitors who decide to issue fixed rate bonds after the rate has fallen, will gain a competitive advantage.
- An investor in fixed rate bonds who expects to sell the bonds before their maturity will also be affected by a change in interest rates. A rise in interest yields will result in a fall in the price of existing fixed rate bonds. A fall in the market interest rate will send bond prices up.

Changes in interest rates are particularly significant for organisations that deal in financial assets and liabilities, such as banks and investment institutions. However, they can also be very important for other companies that borrow extensively, and have fixed rate or floating rate debts totalling hundreds of millions of dollars.

For example, if a company has borrowed $500 million from a syndicate of banks at a variable rate of interest, an increase in the annual interest rate of just 0.25% will result in higher interest costs of $1,250,000 each year.

1.2 Interest rate volatility and interest rate risk

Interest rate risk is particularly high when:

- interest rate changes are frequent (and sometimes large), and
- it is uncertain whether the next movement in rates will be up or down.

In other words, interest rate risk increases with interest rate volatility. Volatility is likely to be higher when expected inflation rates are high than when expected inflation rates are low.

1.3 Short-term and long-term interest rates

A distinction is made between:

- short-term interest rates, which are money market interest rates
- long-term interest rates, which are bond yields.

Volatility in short-term rates affects short-term lending and borrowing, and also all variable rate lending, such as bank loans. Volatility in longer-term rates affects bond investors.

Note that yields on a corporate bond are affected by:

- interest rates for risk-free bonds (domestic government bonds)
- changes in the perceived credit risk of the bond issuer.

For example, suppose that a company's bonds which have been rated AA by a credit rating organisation are now downgraded to a rating of A+. The yield on the bond will increase to reflect the lower credit rating, and the market price of the bonds will fall. However, the increase in the bond yield is due to a credit risk factor rather than to interest rate risk.

1.4 Money market interest rates: LIBOR

Short-term interest rates for borrowers are set at a margin above the base rate or official rate of the lending bank, or at a margin above a money market rate. The money markets are markets for wholesale borrowing and lending short-term, for periods ranging from overnight up to about 12 months. ('Wholesale' means borrowing and lending in large amounts.)

Each major financial centre has a money market and a 'benchmark' rate that the participants in the market use. In London, the benchmark rate of interest is the London Interbank Offered Rate or LIBOR.

- There are LIBOR rates for each maturity of lending, such as seven-day LIBOR, one-month LIBOR, three-month LIBOR and so on.
- London is a major international money market centre, and there are LIBOR rates in the major currencies as well as in sterling. For example, there is a US dollar LIBOR and a Swiss franc LIBOR. There is also a euro LIBOR, but the commonly-used benchmark rate for the euro is a rate called the **euribor rate.**
- In Paris, there are PIBOR rates; in Frankfurt there are FIBOR rates; and so on.

A company borrowing British pounds from a bank at a floating rate of interest might pay interest at a margin above LIBOR. For example, if interest is payable every six months, a borrower might pay interest at 1.50% above the six-month sterling LIBOR rate.

(**Basis points**: 1% = 100 basis points, and in the money market, interest rates may be stated as a number of basis points above LIBOR. So LIBOR plus 1.50% might be stated as 150 basis points above LIBOR.)

When a company borrows at a variable rate of interest, it pays interest at the end of each interest period, which might be each month, or every three months, or every six months, and so on. The rate of interest payable for the period is decided by reference to the benchmark rate, such as three-month LIBOR, at the **beginning** of the interest period. As LIBOR rises or falls, the interest payable in each interest period also goes up or down.

Calculating the interest

There are rules in the money markets about how interest should be calculated. The rules differ between currencies. For example:

- Interest on a sterling money market loan is calculated as:

  Loan principal × Annual interest rate × (Number of days in the loan period/365)

- Interest on a US dollar money market loan is calculated as:

  Loan principal × Annual interest rate × (Number of days in the loan period/360)

For your examination, you will normally be able to make the assumption that interest is calculated as:

Loan principal × Annual interest rate × (Number of months in the loan period/12).

Hedging interest rate risk: FRAs

- Hedging methods
- Forward rate agreements (FRAs)
- The features of an FRA agreement
- How an FRA works

2 Hedging interest rate risk: FRAs

2.1 Hedging methods

Some organisations might wish to hedge their exposures to interest rate risk. They might also want to take advantage, if possible, from any favourable movements in interest rates. There are several ways in which risks can be hedged and opportunities to benefit from interest rate changes can be exploited.

The methods that you need to understand and might be required to use in your examination are:

- forward rate agreements or FRAs
- interest rate swaps
- interest rate options (described in a later chapter)
- interest rate futures (described in a later chapter)

All these methods can be used to deal with the possibility that 'spot' rates of money market interest will change, or current yields on bonds will change, and will be different at some time in the future.

2.2 Forward rate agreements (FRAs)

A forward rate agreement (FRA) is a forward contract for an interest rate. FRAs are negotiated 'over-the-counter' with a bank. In some respects, an FRA is similar to a forward exchange rate. It is a contract arranged 'now' that fixes the rate of interest for a future loan or deposit period starting at some time in the future. For example, an FRA can be used to fix the interest rate on a six-month loan starting in three months' time.

Banks are able to quote forward rates for interest rates because there is a large and active money market, and banks are able to borrow and deposit funds short-term. As a result, if a bank can borrow for nine months at one rate of interest and deposit funds for three months at another rate of interest, it can work out a rate to quote to a customer that wants to borrow between the end of month 3 and the end of month 9. A 'forward rate' can be fixed now that will guarantee the bank a profit on the transaction.

Example

A bank can borrow dollars for nine months at 5% and can deposit dollar funds for three months at 4.75%. Suppose that it borrows $1 million for nine months and places them on deposit for three months.

- After nine months, it will have to repay $1 million + ($1 million × 5% × 9/12) = $1,037,500. The interest payable is $37,500.
- After three months, its dollar deposit will grow to $1 million + ($1 million × 4.75% × 3/12 = $1,011,875. The interest received is $11,875.
- To break even by lending to a customer from the end of month 3 to the end of month 9 (six months), the bank would need to earn interest of $25,625 ($37,500 – $11,875).
- The (annual) interest rate on the month 6-month lending would therefore have to be: $\frac{25,625}{1,011,875} \times \frac{12}{6} \times 100\% = 5.06\%$

This is not what banks would do in practice, but the example is intended to show that banks are able to use spot money market rates (which are rates for borrowing or depositing funds 'now') to derive interest rates for a future interest period, knowing that they will make a suitable return.

2.3 The features of an FRA agreement

An FRA, like a forward exchange contract, is a binding agreement between a bank and a customer. It is an agreement that fixes an interest rate 'now' for a future interest period.

- An FRA for an interest period starting at the end of month 3 and lasting until the end of month 9 is a 3v9 FRA or a 3/9 FRA.
- Similarly, an FRA for a three-month period starting at the end of month 2 is a 2v5 FRA or a 2/5 FRA.

An FRA is an agreement that fixes a forward interest rate on a notional amount of money.

Buying and selling FRAs

FRAs are bought and sold.

- If a company wishes to fix an interest rate (cost) for a future borrowing period, it buys an FRA. In other words, **buying an FRA fixes a forward rate for short-term borrowing.**
- If a company wishes to fix an interest rate (income) for a future deposit period, it sells an FRA.. Selling an FRA fixes a forward rate for a short-term deposit.

The counterparty bank sells an FRA to a buyer and buys an FRA from a seller.

FRA rates

A bank trading in FRAs will publish indicative rates. For example, prices for sterling FRAs might be quoted as follows:

3 v 6	5.27 – 5.23
4 v 7	5.32 – 5.28
5 v 8	5.39 – 5.34
9 v 12	5.63 – 5.56
3 v 9	5.40 – 5.36
4 v 10	5.45 – 5.41
6 v 12	5.50 – 5.45

A bank will always apply the rate that is more favourable to itself. For example, a company wanting to fix the interest cost with a 6 v 12 FRA, using the rates in the table above, would be quoted a rate of 5.50% for the FRA.

Notional loans and deposits

A forward exchange contract for currency is an agreement to buy and sell currency at a future date, when there will be an exchange of currencies between the two parties. An FRA is different. It is not an actual agreement to take out a loan or to make a deposit. An FRA is an agreement on a notional loan or deposit, not an actual loan or deposit. The size of the notional amount of principal (the notional loan or deposit) is specified in the FRA agreement.

2.4 How an FRA works

An FRA works by comparing the fixed rate of interest in the FRA agreement with a benchmark rate of interest, such as LIBOR. The comparison takes place at the beginning of the notional interest period for the FRA.

- If the FRA rate is higher than the benchmark rate (LIBOR), the buyer of the FRA must make a payment to the seller of the FRA, in settlement of the contract
- If the FRA rate is lower than the benchmark rate (LIBOR), the buyer of the FRA receives a payment from the seller of the FRA, in settlement of the contract.

The amount of the payment is calculated from the difference between the FRA rate and the benchmark rate (LIBOR rate), applied to the notional principal amount for the FRA and calculated for the length of the interest period in the agreement.

Example

Suppose that a company knows that it will need to borrow £5 million in three months' time for a period of six months. (Alternatively, suppose that a company has a floating rate loan of £5 million, with interest payable every six months, and the next interest period due to start in three months' time.)

The company can hedge its exposure to the risk of a rise in the six-month interest rate by buying a 3 v 9 FRA for a notional principal amount of £5 million. If the bank's FRA rates for 3 v 9 FRAs are 5.40 – 5.36, the rate applied to the agreement will be 5.40%. The benchmark rate of interest, or '**reference rate**', will be the six-month sterling LIBOR rate.

Settlement of the FRA

Suppose that at the end of month 3, six-month LIBOR is 6.25%. The FRA rate is lower; therefore the FRA rate is settled by a payment from the bank to the buyer of the FRA.

- The difference between the FRA rate and LIBOR is 0.85%. The payment to settle the FRA will therefore be based on an interest difference of: 0.85% × £5 million × 6/12 = £21,250.
- The actual payment will be less than this, because the FRA is settled immediately, at the beginning of the notional interest period, and not at the end of the period. The £21,250 is therefore discounted from an end-of-interest period value to a start-of-interest period value, using the reference rate of interest as the discount rate. This PV is the amount received in settlement of the FRA.

Suppose that at the end of month 3, six-month LIBOR is 4.75%. The FRA rate (5.40%) is higher than the spot rate. Therefore the FRA rate is settled by a payment from the buyer of the FRA to the bank. The difference between the FRA rate and LIBOR is 0.65%.

- The payment to settle the FRA will therefore be based on this interest rate difference: 0.65% × £5 million × 6/12 = £16,250.
- Again, because the payment is at the beginning of the interest period and not at the end of the period, the £16,250 should be discounted to a present value at the reference rate of interest. This PV is the amount of the payment in settlement of the FRA.

How an FRA fixes a forward interest rate

Continuing the example, the company will presumably want to borrow £5 million for six months from the end of month 3. It will do so by arranging an ordinary short-term loan with a bank. The interest rate on the loan might be set at LIBOR + 1%.

- Suppose that at the end of month 3, six-month LIBOR is 6.25%. The company will therefore borrow for six months at 7.25%. It will receive a payment from the FRA of 0.85%, so that the net cost of borrowing will be 6.40% (7.25% – 0.85%). This net effective interest rate is equal to the FRA rate of 5.40% + 1%. The company has therefore been able to fix LIBOR at 5.40% with the FRA.
- Suppose that at the end of month 3, six-month LIBOR is 4.75%. The company will therefore borrow for six months at 5.75%. However, it must also make a payment of 0.65% to settle the FRA, bringing the total cost of borrowing for the six months to 6.40% (5.75% + 0.65%). Again, this total effective rate is equal to the FRA rate of 5.40% + 1% and the FRA has therefore fixed the effective LIBOR rate at 5.40%.

Conclusion: using an FRA to hedge an interest rate risk exposure

An FRA, like a forward exchange rate, therefore fixes an interest rate in advance.

- An FRA can therefore be used by a borrower to hedge an exposure to a future increase in the spot interest rate, or to protect a depositor against a future fall in the interest rate.
- However, the user of an FRA cannot benefit from any favourable movement in the interest rate, because the FRA fixes the rate and is a binding contract.

Example

A company has forecast that due to an expected cash shortage, it will need to borrow $20 million for three months in two months' time. A bank quotes the following rates for FRAs:

2 v 3	3.61 – 3.59
2 v 5	3.67 – 3.63
3 v 5	3.68 – 3.65

Required

What would be the FRA agreement with the bank, and what rate would apply to the agreement?

If the company can borrow at LIBOR + 50 basis points, what will be its effective rate of borrowing for the three months if US dollar LIBOR is 4.50% at the start of the notional interest period for the FRA?

Answer

The company needs a 2v5 FRA.

It needs to borrow; therefore the bank will quote the higher rate, 3.67.

In three months' time on the fixing data, if US dollar LIBOR is 4.50% the bank will pay the equivalent of (4.50% - 3.67%) = 0.83%.

	%
Three-month borrowing rate (4.50% + 50 basis points	5.00
Less: settlement received in FRA agreement	(0.83)
Effective borrowing rate	4.17

The effective borrowing rate is the same as the FRA rate of 3.67% plus the 50 basis points borrowing margin that the company is required to pay on the money it borrows: 3.67% + 0.50% = 4.17%.

Interest rate swaps

- The features of an interest rate swap
- Swap rates
- The effect of a coupon swap

3 Interest rate swaps

3.1 The features of an interest rate swap

An interest rate swap is an agreement between two parties, such as a company and a bank that deals in swaps, for a period of time that is usually several years. Swaps are therefore usually **long-term** agreements on interest rates.

In a swap agreement, the parties agree to exchange 'interest payments' on a notional amount of principal, at agreed dates throughout the term of the agreement.

The interest rate payments that are exchanged in a 'coupon swap' are as follows:

- One party to the swap pays a fixed rate (the swap rate).
- The other party pays interest at a reference rate or benchmark rate for the interest period, such as LIBOR.

The purpose of an interest rate swap is often to:

- swap a variable rate of interest payment (or receipt) into a fixed interest rate payment (or receipt)
- swap a fixed rate of interest payment (or receipt) into a variable rate of interest payment (or receipt).

e

Example: 'plain-vanilla-swap'

For example, a company might arrange a four-year swap with a bank, for which the notional principal amount is $20 million and:

- the company pays interest every six months at a fixed rate of, say, 4.25%
- the bank pays interest every six months at the six-month LIBOR rate for the period.

Since both parties pay interest every six months, if the payment dates coincide, the swap payments will simply be settled by a net payment for the difference in rates from one party to the other.

Over the life of the four-year swap, there will therefore be eight exchanges of interest payments. However, in an interest rate swap, there is no exchange of principal. The interest relates to a notional amount of principal, not an actual asset or liability.

- If the six-month LIBOR rate for one of the periods is, say, 5.00%, the exchange of payments would be settled by a payment from the bank to the company of 0.75% interest (5.00% – 4.25%) on $20 million for six months.
- If the six-month LIBOR rate for one of the periods is, say, 3.00%, the exchange of payments would be settled by a payment from the company to the bank of 1.25% interest (4.25% - 3.00%) on $20 million for six months.

The payments in a plain vanilla swap are at the end of each notional interest period, therefore the amounts payable are not discounted (unlike an FRA).

3.2 Swap rates

Swap rates are the fixed rates that will be used by a bank in a coupon swap agreement. Swap rates might be quoted as follows:

US dollar **Term**	**Bid**	**Ask**
Years	%	%
1 year	4.03	4.06
2 years	4.17	4.20
3 years	4.29	4.32
4 years	4.63	4.66
5 years	4.91	4.94
6 years	5.14	5.17
7 years	5.33	5.36
10 years	5.73	5.76
15 years	6.16	6.19
20 years	6.35	6.38

These rates might be for a swap against three-month US dollar LIBOR. The lower rate (the bid rate) is the rate that the bank would pay in a swap. The higher rate (the ask rate) is the fixed rate that the bank would receive in a swap. Banks dealing in swaps make a profit or 'turn' from the difference between the bid and ask rates. Swap rates for the major international currencies are quoted for terms of up to 30 years.

3.3 The effect of a coupon swap

In a coupon swap, one party pays a fixed rate of interest and the other pays 'the floating', which is the variable reference rate of interest, such as six-month LIBOR. For a company with a loan or bonds in issue, the effect of arranging a swap can therefore be:

- to swap from fixed rate interest liabilities to floating rate liabilities, or
- to swap from floating rate liabilities to fixed rate liabilities.

Example

A company has a bank loan of £10 million on which it pays variable rate interest at LIBOR + 1%. The loan has five more years to maturity. The company is worried about the risk that interest rates will soon rise, and it wants to set a limit on its interest costs.

It might therefore arrange a five-year swap with a bank, with interest rates to coincide with the interest payments on its bank loan.

The bank might quote rates of 5.34 – 5.39 for a five-year swap in sterling.

The company will receive the floating rate in the swap, to offset the floating rate payments on its bank loan. It will pay the fixed rate, and the rate will therefore be 5.39%.

The swap therefore alters the net interest payments for the company as follows:

	%
Loan payments	(LIBOR + 1)
Swap	
Receive the floating	LIBOR
Pay the fixed	(5.39)
Net interest cost	(6.39)

The company had a floating rate liability of LIBOR + 1%, and has now changed this into a net fixed interest liability of 6.39%.

On each interest payment date, the company will pay LIBOR + 1% in interest on its bank loan, and under the swap agreement will receive or pay the difference between LIBOR for the period and the fixed rate of 5.39%.

You might see that an interest rate coupon swap is similar in concept to an FRA, but is for a longer period of time and covers more than one interest period.

The company might subsequently change its mind. For example, after two years, it might decide that it wants a floating rate liability again. If so, it can go back to a floating rate liability by arranging with the bank to cancel the swap and agreeing a cancellation payment (for the value of the swap at the date of cancellation).

Example

A company has 5% bonds in issue with a nominal value of 40 million euros. The bonds have ten more years to maturity. The company wants to exchange its fixed rate liability for a floating rate liability in euros. A bank quotes the following rate for a ten-year swap: 4.22 – 4.25.

By arranging a swap, what will be the effective interest cost for the company?

a

Answer

	%
Cost of the bonds	(5.00)
Swap	
Receive the fixed	4.22
Pay the floating	(LIBOR)
Net interest cost	(LIBOR + 0.78)

Using interest rate swaps
■ Swapping interest rate liabilities
■ Obtaining fixed rate liabilities
■ Credit arbitrage

4 Using interest rate swaps

Interest rate swaps are used to manage interest rates on liabilities (and assets, in the case of investment institutions and banks). They can therefore be a method of hedging exposures to interest rate risk.

4.1 Swapping interest rate liabilities

Some large companies use interest rate swaps to manage their net interest liabilities (in each currency). For example, a company that borrows extensively, through a combination of bank loans and bond issues, might have a policy that:

- 25% of its debts should be at a fixed rate
- 25% of its debt should be at a floating rate, and
- the remaining 50% may be at a fixed or floating rate, or a mixture of fixed and floating, depending on the judgement of the finance director or treasury department.

The company might then use interest rate swaps to alter its net liabilities, within the company's policy guidelines, between fixed rate and floating rate. It might move towards more floating rate liabilities if interest rates are expected to fall, and towards fixed rate liabilities when interest rates are expected to rise.

The advantage of using swaps is that a company can alter its net liabilities from fixed to floating rate or floating to fixed rate, without having to alter or re-negotiate its actual loans or bond issues. For example, a company with fixed rate bonds can swap from fixed to floating rate liabilities with a swap, without having to redeem the bonds early and negotiate a floating rate loan with a bank.

4.2 Obtaining fixed rate liabilities

Many companies are unable to obtain fixed rate debt. Fixed rate interest liabilities come from issuing bonds. Medium-term bank loans are invariably at a floating rate. If a company is too small to issue bonds, or does not have the credit status to issue bonds, it must borrow from banks to obtain debt finance.

If a company wants fixed rate liabilities, but can only borrow from a bank, it can obtain a loan at a floating rate and swap into a fixed rate net liability.

Example

A company borrows from its bank for five years at LIBOR plus 150 basis points. It wants its interest rate liabilities to be fixed, so it makes a five-year swap transaction with a bank, in which it pays a fixed rate of 5.8% and receives LIBOR.

As a result of the swap, the company's net interest obligations are fixed at 7.3%.

	%
Loan payments	(LIBOR + 1.50)
Swap	
Receive the floating	LIBOR
Pay the fixed	(5.80)
Net interest cost	(7.30)

4.3 Credit arbitrage

At one time, swaps were sometimes used to obtain a lower interest rate on borrowing. This was possible because swaps banks were able to identify opportunities for 'credit arbitrage'. These opportunities arose because of anomalies in the rates of interest at which different companies could borrow.

When an opportunity for credit arbitrage exists, one of the following situations will occur:

Situation 1

Two companies want to borrow. They can both borrow at either a fixed rate or a floating rate. Company A has to pay a higher rate of interest than Company B. However, the difference in borrowing costs between the two companies is less for fixed rate borrowing than for variable rate borrowing.

For example:

	Fixed rate borrowing cost	Variable rate borrowing cost
Company A	7.25%	LIBOR + 1.5%
Company B	6.50%	LIBOR + 0.5%
Difference	0.75%	1.0%

Credit arbitrage is possible using an interest rate swap if Company A wants to borrow at a variable rate of interest and Company B wants to borrow at a fixed rate.

Situation 2

Two companies want to borrow. They can both borrow at either a fixed rate or a floating rate. Company C has to pay a higher rate of interest than Company D. However, the difference in borrowing costs between the two companies is more for fixed rate borrowing than for variable rate borrowing.

For example:

	Fixed rate borrowing cost	Variable rate borrowing cost
Company C	7.75%	LIBOR + 1.5%
Company D	6.50%	LIBOR + 0.5%
Difference	1.25%	1.0%

Credit arbitrage is possible using an interest rate swap if Company C wants to borrow at a fixed rate of interest and Company B wants to borrow at a variable rate.

Example

A bank is aware that two companies can borrow at the following rates:

	Fixed	Floating
Company A	5.50%	LIBOR + 0.50%
Company B	6.40%	LIBOR + 1%

Company A wants to borrow at a floating rate, and can do so at LIBOR + 0.50%. Company B wants to borrow at a fixed rate, and can do so at 6.40%. However, an opportunity for credit arbitrage exists, because company A can borrow at a fixed rate 0.90% less than company B, but at a floating rate only 0.50% less than company B. The opportunity for credit arbitrage totals 0.40% (0.90% - 0.50%).

A bank might therefore propose the following arrangement:

- Company A should borrow at a fixed rate, by issuing bonds at 5.50%. Company B should borrow at a floating rate, by obtaining a bank loan at LIBOR + 1%.
- Company A should enter into a swap with the bank in which it receives 5.20% fixed and pays LIBOR.
- Company B should enter into a swap with the bank in which it pays 5.25% fixed and receives LIBOR.

The net interest cost of each company would be as follows:

	Company A	Company B
	%	%
Borrowing cost	(5.50)	(LIBOR + 1)
Swap		
Receive	5.20	LIBOR
Pay	(LIBOR)	(5.25)
Net cost	(LIBOR + 0.30)	(6.25)

Company A reduces its net borrowing cost by 0.20% below the cost of borrowing directly at a floating rate, and company B reduces its fixed rate cost by 0.15% below the cost of issuing bonds at 6.40%. The bank makes a profit of 0.05% from the difference between its fixed rates in the swap for receiving (5.25% from company B) and paying (5.20% to company A).

Interest rate forwards from yield curves

- Calculation of forward rates
- Interest rate forwards and SWAP valuation

5 Interest rate forwards from yield curves

Yield curves were covered in chapter 9. That chapter also explained how yield curves could be used to place a value on a bond and how a yield curve could be derived from information about bonds of a same risk class but of different maturities.

This session explains how the spot yield curve can be used to calculate forward rates of interest for use in constructing FRAs and in swap valuation.

5.1 Calculation of forward rates

This is best explained using an example.

Example

The annual spot yield curve for bonds of a given risk class are as follows:

Maturity	Yield
One year	3.0%
Two years	3.6%
Three years	4.3%
Four years	5.1%
Five years	5.8%

A company whose bonds were in this risk class would have to pay interest at 3.0% for a one year loan, 3.6% for a two year loan and so on.

A company that wanted a two year loan might consider an alternative course of action. It could borrow an amount for one year and then borrow the same amount at the end of year 1 (beginning of year 2). The second amount would pay off the first loan in effect rolling it over into the second year.

A company that wished to do this would not know what interest rate it would face in one year's time but it would be able to lock a rate in with a 12v24 FRA. Common sense suggests that at the start date a bank would not offer deals where a two year loan was more favourable or less favourable than a one year loan followed by a fixed forward rate. This "equality" can be used to calculate the forward rate as:

12v24 FRA

Interest on a two year loan	=	**Interest on a one year loan followed by locked in rate (r) for year two**

The 12v24 FRA rate (r) is calculated from the spot yield curve as follows:

$1.036^2 = (1.03)(1+r)$

$1.036^2/1.03 = 1 + r$

$r = 0.042$ or 4.2%

A similar approach can be used to calculate the 24v36, 36v48 and 48v60 FRA rates

24v36 FRA

Interest on a three year loan	=	**Interest on a two year loan followed by locked in rate (r) for year three**

The 24v36 FRA rate (r) is calculated from the spot yield curve as follows:

$1.043^3 = (1.036)^2(1+r)$

$1.043^3/1.036^2 = 1 + r$

$r = 0.057$ or 5.7%

36v48 FRA

Interest on a four year loan	=	**Interest on a three year loan followed by locked in rate (r) for year four**

The 36v48 FRA rate (r) is calculated from the spot yield curve as follows:

$1.051^4 = (1.043)^3(1+r)$

$1.051^4/1.043^3 = 1 + r$

$r = 0.0754$ or 7.5%

48v60 FRA

Interest on a five year loan	=	**Interest on a four year loan followed by locked in rate (r) for year five**

The 48v60 FRA rate (r) is calculated from the spot yield curve as follows:

$1.058^5 = (1.051)^4(1+r)$

$1.058^5/1.051^4 = 1 + r$

$r = 0.0865$ or 8.7%

Summary

Maturity	**Yield**	**Forward rates**
One year	3.0%	3.0% (= spot)
Two years	3.6%	4.2%
Three years	4.3%	5.7%
Four years	5.1%	7.5%
Five years	5.8%	8.7%

5.1 Interest rate forwards and swap valuation

Any swap offered will be based on the yield curves appropriate to a company's debt.

The swap will be priced so that at the start of the SWAP the expected cash inflows to the company and outflows from the company will net to zero.

This is best explained using an example.

Example

A company has variable rate debt of $100m repayable in 5 years.

It wishes to enter into variable to fixed interest swap.

The bank has offered to enter into a swap with the company under which it will pay the company variable rate less 40 basis points (0.4%). In return the company will make a fixed rate payment to the bank.

A bank has compiled a yield curve for the company's bonds and derived forward rates from these as follows:

Maturity	Yield	Forward rates
1 year	3.0%	3.0%
2 years	3.6%	4.2%
3 years	4.3%	5.7%
4 years	5.1%	7.5%
5 years	5.8%	8.7%

Required

Calculate the fixed rate that the bank will charge.

Answer

				Expectation at start of SWAP	
Maturity	Yield	Forward rates	Basis adjustment	Variable rate paid by bank to company	Cash flow paid to company
1 year	3.0%	3.0%	0.4%	2.6%	$2.6m
2 years	3.6%	4.2%	0.4%	3.8%	$3.8m
3 years	4.3%	5.7%	0.4%	5.3%	$5.3m
4 years	5.1%	7.5%	0.4%	7.1%	$7.1m
5 years	5.8%	8.7%	0.4%	8.3%	$8.3m

Present value of the variable rate receipts expected from the SWAP

Year	Cash flow	Discount factor	PV ($m)
1	$2.6m	1/1.03 = 0.971	2.52
2	$3.8m	$1/1.036^2 = 0.932$	3.54
3	$5.3m	$1/1.043^3 = 0.881$	4.67
4	$7.1m	$1/1.051^4 = 0.820$	5.82
5	$8.3m	$1/1.058^5 = 0.754$	6.26
			22.81

Let x be the fixed rate cash flow to the bank. The present value of these flows is given by the following:

Year	Cash flow ($m)	Discount factor	PV ($m)
1	x	1/1.03 = 0.971	0.971x
2	x	$1/1.036^2 = 0.932$	0.932x
3	x	$1/1.043^3 = 0.881$	0.881x
4	x	$1/1.051^4 = 0.820$	0.820x
5	x	$1/1.058^5 = 0.754$	0.754x
			4.358x

The swap will be priced so that at the start of the SWAP the expected cash inflows to the company and outflows from the company will net to zero. (Worth repeating)!

Therefore:

$4.358x = 22.81$

$x = \$5.23m$

The fixed rate charged = $5.23m/$100m or 5.23%

Currency swaps

- The nature of currency swaps
- Reasons for using currency swaps
- FX swaps

6 Currency swaps

6.1 The nature of currency swaps

Interest rate swaps are swaps in the same currency, usually between a fixed rate and a floating rate of interest, with interest calculated on a notional amount of principal. Currency swaps are similar, but with some significant differences:

- The swap is between two different currencies. One party pays interest on an amount of principal in one currency. The other party pays interest on an equivalent amount of principal in a different currency.
- The interest rates that are swapped need not be a fixed rate in exchange for a floating rate. A currency swap can be between a fixed rate in one currency and a (different) fixed rate in the other currency.
- There is an actual exchange of principal. There must be an exchange of principal at the end of the swap, at a rate of exchange that is fixed at the beginning of the swap. (There might also be an actual exchange of principal at the beginning of the swap, but this is not usual.)

Example

A UK company has taken an opportunity to borrow US$180 million in the bond markets, by issuing a seven-year bond. However, it wants to have its interest liabilities in sterling, not dollars. It might therefore arrange a seven-year currency swap in which the agreed exchange rate is £1 = US$1.80.

- For the seven years of the swap, the UK company will receive fixed rate interest in US dollars from the swap counterparty. The interest received on each interest payment date will be interest for the period at the agreed swap rate for US dollars, on $180 million.
- The UK company will pay interest in the swap on £100 million, also at a fixed rate agreed in the swap.
- The interest received in US dollars can be used to meet the dollar interest liabilities on the bonds. This leaves the company with net interest obligations in sterling.
- At the end of the swap, there is an exchange of principal. The UK company will receive US$180 million from the swap counterparty and in exchange must pay £100 million. It will use the US$180 million to redeem the dollar bonds.

The effects of the currency swap may be summarised as follows:

	Interest	**Principal payments (end of the swap)**
Bonds	Pay dollars	Pay dollars ($180 million)
Currency swap	Receive dollars	Receive dollars ($180 million)
	Pay sterling	Pay sterling
Net effect	Pay sterling	Pay sterling

The effect of the currency swap has therefore been to borrow in one currency, but swap the interest and loan principal repayment liabilities into a different currency.

Currency swaps are therefore used to hedge long-term currency risk.

6.2 Reasons for using currency swaps

As the previous example shows, currency swaps can be used to swap interest payment and principal repayments from one currency into another, and so are a method of hedging long-term currency risk exposures.

Companies can use currency swaps to borrow at a favourable interest rate in the international loans or bonds markets, and swap their liabilities into a currency of their preference. This could enable them to borrow more cheaply than borrowing directly in the currency of their preference.

If the currency swap involves an exchange of interest at a fixed rate in one currency for a floating rate in the other currency, the swap can also be used to hedge interest rate risk.

However, currency swaps are far less common than interest rate swaps. Interest rate swaps are used extensively in the financial markets, particularly by banks and other financial institutions.

6.3 FX swaps

An FX swap is similar to a currency swap, but with one important difference.

- In a currency swap, the two swap counterparties exchange a series of interest payments in the two currencies over the life of the swap.
- In an FX swap, there is no exchange of interest payments. There is an exchange of principal at the start of the swap and a re-exchange at the end of the swap, but there are no cash flows during the term of the swap.

The reason for having FX swaps is that a company might find it difficult to raise debt in a particular currency. For example, a company might want to issue bonds in a currency for which the bond market is illiquid and not popular with investors. The company might want to issue bonds to obtain a liability in the currency for the purpose of hedging its currency exposures.

To create its liability in the currency, the company might:

- Issue bonds in another currency, such as US dollars
- Arrange an FX swap for the immediate exchange of the dollars for the other currency. The company would then have a liability to repay the currency at the end of the term of the swap.

CHAPTER 19

Futures and hedging with futures

Contents

Financial futures

- The nature of futures contracts
- Commodity futures and financial futures
- Futures exchanges
- Settlement dates
- Futures prices

1 Financial futures

1.1 The nature of futures contracts

A future is forward contract for the purchase or sale of a standard quantity of an item, for settlement or delivery at a specified future date. It is therefore a contract to buy or sell a quantity of an item at a future settlement date, at a price agreed 'now'. Futures contracts have some special features.

- They are standardised contracts. Every futures contract for the purchase/sale of a particular item is identical to every other futures contract for the same item, with the only exception that their settlement dates/delivery dates may differ.
- They are traded on an exchange, rather than negotiated 'over-the-counter'.

1.2 Commodity futures and financial futures

Commodity futures are futures contracts for the sale and purchase of standard quantities of standard commodities, such as wheat, oil, copper, gold, rubber, soya beans, coffee, cotton, sugar, and so on.

Financial futures are futures contracts for the sale and purchase of a financial item, such as a quantity of currency, a notional portfolio of shares, a quantity of notional government bonds, a notional three-month deposit, and so on. There are currency futures, short-term interest rate futures, bond futures and stock index futures.

1.3 Futures exchanges

Futures are traded on futures exchanges. Each futures exchange has its own particular futures contracts. Only in a few cases do two futures exchanges compete for business by offering trading in similar futures contracts.

The major futures exchanges include the Chicago Board of Trade (CBOT) and Chicago Mercantile Exchange (CME), Eurex and LIFFE.

1.4 Settlement dates

Futures are traded on a futures exchange for just four settlement dates each year. These are usually in March, June, September and December. Futures are therefore referred to by their settlement date, such as March Eurodollar futures or September S&P500 futures.

The actual settlement date for contracts in each month is specified by the futures exchange. In examination questions it is normally assumed (for simplicity) that contract settlement dates are at the end of the month.

1.5 Futures prices

The price for futures is the price at which buyers and sellers agree to make a transaction with each other.

Dealing in futures contracts continues throughout the trading day on the futures exchange, and the prices at which futures are bought and sold vary with each transaction. However, the exchange authorities receive information about the prices of transactions that have been made, and up-to-the minute price information is published to the market. Buyers and sellers of futures are therefore aware of what current market prices are.

The role of the futures exchange

- Counterparty to all trades
- Margin

2 The role of the futures exchange

The futures exchange regulates the market that it provides. It establishes rules of conduct and provides the systems in which trading can take place. In addition, the exchange provides security to the market by virtually eliminating credit risk for its participants.

2.1 Counterparty to all trades

An important feature of trading on a futures exchange is that when a buyer and seller agree a transaction in futures and report the transaction to the exchange, the exchange takes on the role of counterparty to the buyer and the seller in the transaction. This means for example that if X makes a transaction to sell 20 December currency futures to Y:

- the futures exchange will become the buyer of 20 December futures from X and
- the exchange will also become the seller of 20 December futures to Y.

Both X and Y have a contract with the exchange, and not a contract with each other. X is therefore not relying on the good credit standing of Y to honour the contract, and Y is not relying on the good credit standing of X. They both rely on the credit standing of the exchange itself. Since the credit status of the exchange is high, the credit risk is minimised.

The exchange protects itself against credit risk from participants in the exchange, by means of a system of margin payments. Margin payments are explained below.

(Note: Strictly speaking, the exchange itself is not the counterparty to every transaction. The exchange is represented by a clearing house, that acts as counterparty to every transaction. For the LIFFE futures exchange in London, for example, the clearing house is the London Clearing House or LCH).

2.2 Margin

After someone has bought or sold futures at an agreed price, the market price of the futures will move up or down. The buyer or seller of the futures will make a gain or a loss on the futures position, depending on whether the market price has moved favourably or adversely. If the price moves adversely by a large amount, a person might have a large loss on his futures position. A problem for the futures exchange is how to prevent someone with a large loss from refusing to settle the contract and pay for the loss. This problem is overcome by a requirement for every position in futures to be covered by a cash deposit with the exchange. This cash deposit is called a margin.

- When two parties agree to the sale/purchase of a quantity of futures, both parties are required to pay a cash deposit, called an **initial margin**, to cover the risk of short-term losses on their position.
- If a position goes into loss because the market price moves adversely, the exchange will call for an additional cash payment of **variation margin** to cover the loss.

In this way, all loss positions have been covered by cash payments, and there is no credit risk for the exchange from non-payment of losses by the buyers or sellers of futures contracts.

Example

A company arranges to buy futures on coffee at a contract price of $2,000 per tonne. Having bought the futures, it must pay a deposit or initial margin to the futures exchange. The seller of the coffee futures must also pay initial margin.

If the 'spot' price of coffee then falls, and the price of coffee futures falls too, the company will be making a loss on its futures position. To cover these losses, the exchange will ask the company to pay an additional variation margin.

Margin protects the futures exchange against bad debt risk from buyers or sellers of futures who makes losses on their position.

Open positions and closing positions

- Open positions: long and short positions
- Settlement
- Closing positions

3 Open positions and closing positions

3.1 Open positions: long and short positions

When a person has bought futures without previously having sold any, he establishes a **long position** in the futures. A long position in futures therefore represents an undertaking to buy a quantity of futures at a future date. For example, if a company buys 10 March US dollar-euro currency futures, it is 'long' 10 March futures.

It is possible to sell futures without having any (in other words, without having a long position). A position in which a person has sold futures, without previously buying them, has a **short position**. For example, someone can sell 100 September S&P500 Index futures, without already 'owning' 100 futures or even without owning an equivalent quantity of shares in companies in the S&P500 Index.

Short and long positions are both **open positions** in futures, and at any time, the total amount of long positions is always equal to the total of short positions. This is because the number of futures contracts sold and the number purchased must be equal.

3.2 Settlement

Someone with an open position in futures can keep the position open until the futures contract reaches its settlement date. At settlement, the holder of a long position will require the futures exchange to settle the contract for the purchase of the underlying items in the futures contract. Similarly, at settlement the holder of a short position will be required to make the sale of the underlying item to the futures exchange.

Some futures contracts are cash-settled, and some are settled by physical delivery. For example, short-term interest futures are always cash settled, whereas bond futures are settled by the actual delivery of a quantity of bonds from the seller to the buyer.

3.3 Closing positions

Open positions are not usually kept open until settlement, and so only a few futures contracts are actually settled at their settlement date. Instead, positions are usually closed before settlement.

- The holder of a long position can close the position by selling an equal number of the futures, for the same settlement date, before the settlement date. For example, a long position in 30 June Eurodollar futures can be closed at any time before settlement in June by selling 30 June Eurodollar futures.
- The holder of a short position can close the position by buying an equal quantity of the futures, at any time before settlement. For example, a short position of 25 September FTSE100 futures can be closed at any time before settlement in September by buying 25 September FTSE100 futures.

When a long position is closed, the original buying price and the selling price to close the position will be different, and there will be an overall gain or loss from the difference between the buying and selling prices. Similarly, when a short position is closed, the original selling price and the buying price to close the position will be different, and there will be an overall gain or loss from the difference between the selling and buying prices.

Dealing in futures therefore results in gains or losses on the futures position, which arise because of movements in the market price of the futures.

Example

A company wants to hedge a currency transaction exposure. The exposure relates to a transaction that will occur in November, and the company needs to sell 20 euro currency futures. There are futures with settlement dates in September and December, but not November.

It should therefore sell futures for the next settlement date after the expected transaction, which in this example is December. Suppose the company sells 20 futures at a rate of 1.3500 ($1.3500 = €1).

In November when the transaction occurs, the company should close its position. It opened the position by selling 20 December futures, and it should close the position by buying 20 December futures. There will be a cash profit or loss on closing the position.

The company will use the spot market for the transaction in euros. The gain or loss on the futures position, taken with the spot price, will result in a net exchange rate close to (but probably not equal to) the rate of 1.3500 that was obtained in the futures contract.

This will be illustrated in more detail later.

Ticks and tick values

- Ticks
- The value of a tick

4 Ticks and tick values

4.1 Ticks

A tick is the minimum price movement for a futures contract. For example:

- US dollar-euro currency futures are contracts for €125,000 in exchange for US dollars. They are priced at the EUR/USD rate ($ per €1), and the size of a tick is US$0.0001.
- Short-term interest futures are priced up to a theoretical maximum of 99.9999 and each tick is 0.0001 in price. A tick represents an interest rate of 0.01% per annum.
- Stock index futures are priced in terms of the stock index itself. For example, DAX Index futures might be priced at 8200 or the Hang Seng Index futures at 21750. Price movements are in units of the index itself.

4.2 The value of a tick

Since every futures contract is for a standard quantity of the underlying item, each movement in price of one tick has the same value, representing a gain or loss to a buyer and a corresponding loss or gain to a seller. For example:

- The value of one tick for a US dollar-euro currency future (€125,000 in exchange for US dollars) is: 125,000 euros × $0.0001 per euro = $12.50.

  This can be proved easily. If the price of the contract is $1.2000, the cost of 125,000 would be $150,000. If the exchange rate rises by one tick to $1.2001, the cost of €125,000 would be $150,012.50. This upward price movement would represent a gain of $12.50 to someone with a short position in the futures and a loss to the holder of a long position.
- A Eurodollar future is a short-term interest future representing a three-month deposit of US$1,000,000. The value of one tick for a Eurodollar future is therefore: $1,000,000 × 3/12 × 0.0001 = $25.
- For stock index futures, each one tick of price has a fixed value. The value of a tick for FTSE100 futures, for example, is £10.

Example

Tick values can be used to calculate the gain or loss on a futures position. For example, suppose that a company buys 20 June Eurodollar futures at 9650 and sells 20 June futures later at 9672 to close the position. There is a gain of 0.0022 ticks on each contract, the value of each tick is $25, and the total gain is therefore:

20 contracts × 22 ticks × $25 per tick = $11,000.

Basis and basis risk

- Basis
- Basis risk

5 Basis and basis risk

5.1 Basis

The futures price for an item is never the same as the spot market price or current market price, except at settlement date for the contract. For example, a company might sell September sterling/US dollar futures in April at a price of 1.9800 when the current spot exchange rate is 1.9600. The difference of 0.0200 or 200 points is called '**basis**'.

As a futures contract moves towards settlement, the basis should gradually reduce in size, until it is nil at settlement date. If the basis is not nil at settlement, dealers in the market would be able to make an instant guaranteed profit by:

- buying or selling in the futures market, and simultaneously
- selling or buying in the cash market (spot market).

However, most futures positions are closed before settlement. When a futures position is closed, there will still be some basis, and the futures price and the current spot market price will be different.

For your examination, you might be required to estimate what the basis should be when a position is closed. To do this, we have to make the simplified assumption that the basis will reduce in a straight line from the time the futures position is opened to 0 at settlement date. Using this assumption, we can estimate the expected basis at the intended date for closing the position.

Example

A company sells September sterling/US dollar futures at the end of April at a price of 1.9800 when the current spot exchange rate is 1.9600. There are exactly five months to settlement date, assuming the settlement date for the September futures contract is at the end of that month. The company expects to close the position at the end of July, after three months.

The basis is 200 at the end of April. Assuming that basis falls to zero at a steady rate, it should be expected to fall by 200 between the end of April and the end of September, which is by 40 each month. (This is the total basis of 200 points divided by 5 months.) At the end of July, after three months, basis should have fallen by 120, and the expected basis when the position is closed in July would therefore be 80 (200 – 120). We would therefore estimate that the futures price will be higher than the spot rate by 80.

(The futures price will be higher than the spot rate because it was higher when the futures were originally sold and the short position in the futures was established.)

5.2 Basis risk

In practice, basis does not fall at an even rate.

Basis risk is the risk that when a futures position is closed, the size of the actual basis will be different from the expectation of what the basis should be. In the example above, when the position in September currency futures is closed in July, the futures price might be 1.9790 and the current spot price might be 1.9740, giving a basis of 50. This is less than the expected basis of 80 that was estimated when the futures position was opened, by a difference of 30.

The significance of basis is explained later.

Hedging risk exposures with futures

- Creating a hedge with futures
- Imperfect hedges
- Basis and imperfect hedging

6 Hedging risk exposures with futures

6.1 Creating a hedge with futures

Futures can be used to hedge a short-term exposure to currency risk, interest rate risk or market risk for share prices. They can hedge short-term exposures only, because virtually all futures trading is in contracts with a settlement date within the next 12 months.

The concept of hedging with futures is to create a position in futures that is the opposite of the exposure that is being hedged. By creating an opposite position in futures:

- any loss on the position that is being hedged will be matched by a gain on the futures position
- however, any gain on the position that is being hedged will be matched by a loss on the futures position.

A useful rule to remember is that:

- a **long position in futures** will gain from an increase in the futures price and lose from a fall in the price
- a **short position in futures** will gain from a fall in the futures price and lose from a rise in the price.

The settlement date for the futures must be later than the date of the transaction that is being hedged. For example, if a company is hedging a position in interest rates for the euro, and intends to close the position in August, it should open a position in September futures. If it opened a position in June futures, the futures would reach settlement in June, and the position would no longer be hedged.

Example

A US company expects to receive 2,000,000 euros from a customer in April, in four months' time, and it wishes to hedge the exposure with currency futures. On receipt of the euros in April, the company will exchange them into US dollars. The company's exposure is to a fall in the value of the euro.

Each US dollar/euro currency future is for €125,000. The US company will want to sell euros in exchange for US dollars, therefore it will sell June futures to hedge its position. It will sell 16 contracts (which is €2,000,000/€125,000 per contract).

If the euro falls in value against the US dollar, the value of the €2,000,000 receivable will fall. However, the price of the futures will also fall and since the company has a short position in the futures, it will gain from the fall in price. The gain on the futures position will offset the fall in value in the dollars.

6.2 Imperfect hedges

With futures, it is not usually possible to hedge a position exactly. Futures are contracts for a standard quantity of an underlying item, whereas the position for which the hedge is required might not be an exact multiple of the value of a futures contract.

Example

A French company expects to receive US$1,200,000 in July, in three months' time, and it wants to hedge its exposure with currency futures. It will exchange the dollar income in July for euros, and so will be selling dollars and buying euros. Its exposure is therefore to a fall in the value of the dollar.

A futures contract is for 125,000 euros. It will create a hedge with futures by purchasing September futures. We need to calculate the equivalent value of $1,200,000 in euros. Suppose the company can buy September futures at 1.2350 ($1.2350 per €1).

- This represents 971,660 euros (US$1,200,000/1.2350).
- 971,660 euros is equivalent to 7.8 contracts (€971,660/€125,000 per contract).

The company cannot buy a fraction of a future, and so must buy 7 or 8 contracts. If it buys 7 contracts, it will be hedging €875,000 and if it buys 8 contracts, it will be hedging €1,000,000. In both cases, the hedge is imperfect.

In this example, the company will probably buy 8 contracts, because 7.8 is nearer 8 than 7.

Having bought futures to create a long position, the company will gain from a rise in the futures price (a rise in the exchange rate, which means a weaker dollar). This will offset the fall in the value of the future dollar income of $1,200,000 due to a fall in the value of the dollar.

Note on buying or selling futures as a hedge

You need to understand how a hedge is created, by buying or by selling futures. The basic principle is that the futures position that provides a hedge against the risk must be the 'opposite' of the underlying position, so that a loss on the underlying position will be offset by a gain on the futures position (and a gain on the underlying position results in a loss on the futures position).

In this example, the company will receive US dollars. This is the underlying position. The risk is that dollars will fall in value against the euro. The hedge is created by paying US dollars in the futures contracts, which is the opposite of the underlying position. Paying US dollars means receiving/buying euros, so the hedge is constructed by purchasing dollar/euro futures.

6.3 Basis and imperfect hedging

A hedge with futures is also imperfect because of basis and basis risk. When a hedge is created with futures, the current spot price will differ from the futures price by the basis. Over time, since basis falls towards 0, changes in the futures price will be larger than changes in the current spot market price. This means that the hedge created by the futures position will not provide a gain or loss that matches exactly the loss or gain on the transaction or position that is being hedged.

The effect of basis on hedging is described in more detail later.

Hedging with currency futures: the approach summarised

You might find the following guidelines useful in deciding how to create a hedge with currency futures:

Step		**Comment**
1	Identify the underlying transaction that you are trying to hedge.	Does the company need to buy a quantity of a currency at the future date or sell a quantity of a currency? Which currency will the company need to buy or sell?
2	What is the currency risk in the underlying transaction?	Will the company have to pay more if a currency goes up in value, or if it goes down in value? Or will it receive less if a currency goes up in value or down in value? It is useful to think of the currency in which the futures are denominated.
3	Work out a futures position that creates a profit if there is a 'loss' on the underlying transaction.	What futures position is needed so that if a loss is incurred on the underlying transaction because of an adverse exchange rate movement, a profit will be made on the futures position? Or what futures position is needed so that if less income is obtained from the underlying transaction because of an adverse exchange rate movement, a profit will be made on the futures position?

Currency futures

- Features of currency futures
- Advantages and disadvantages of hedging with currency futures
- Hedging currency exposures with futures

7 Currency futures

7.1 Features of currency futures

Currency futures are contracts for the purchase/sale of a standard quantity of one currency in exchange for a second currency. Futures contracts are priced at the exchange rate for the transaction.

Most currency futures are contracts for the major international currencies. For example:

Currency future (CME)	Amount
US dollar – euro	EUR 125,000
US dollar – yen	12.5 million yen
US dollar – British pound	£62,500
US dollar – Swiss franc	SFr125,000
US dollar – Canadian dollar	C$100,000

An examination question on currency futures should tell you the size of each futures contract.

7.2 Hedging currency exposures with futures

The principles of hedging with futures have been explained already. However, several examples will be used to illustrate how hedging works. Study each example carefully: they get progressively more difficult.

Example: perfect hedge, no basis

It is July. A US company must pay 750,000 euros to a Spanish supplier in November, and wishes to hedge its currency exposure with currency futures. In this example, it is assumed that there is no basis, and the futures price and the current spot market exchange rate are always equal. The price of December futures in July is 1.2100 ($1.2100 per €1). The value of a tick is $12.50. (This is €125,000 × $0.0001 per $1.)

The exposure is to the risk of a rise in the value or cost of the euro between July and November. The underlying position is that the US company will pay euros in November. So to create a futures hedge against the risk of a rise in the cost of the euro, it should buy euro currency futures. If the cost of the euro goes up, the company will have to pay more to obtain the 750,000 euros, but this higher cost will be offset by a gain on the futures position.

This logic can be set out in the three-step approach described earlier, as follows:

Step		Comment
1	Identify the underlying transaction that you are trying to hedge.	The US company will be paying 750,000 euros
2	What is the currency risk in the underlying transaction?	The cost of obtaining the euros will go up. The cost/value of the euro will rise against the dollar.
3	Work out a futures position that creates a profit if there is a 'loss' on the underlying transaction.	If a loss will be incurred on the underlying transaction if the value of the euro goes up, the futures position should create a profit if the value of the euro goes up. So buy euro currency futures, since a profit will be made if the value of the euro goes up and the futures can be sold at a higher price.

The US company should therefore buy 6 December contracts (€750,000/€125,000 per contract) at a price of 1.2100. The company is therefore 'long' 6 December contracts.

Suppose the spot exchange rate in November when the US company must make the payment in euros is 1.2240. The cost of buying the euros has gone up.

The long' futures position is closed by selling 6 December contracts at 1.2240, because in this example the futures price is also 1.2240. The position is closed at a profit, as follows:

Open futures position: buy at	1.2100
Close position: sell at	1.2240
Gain	0.0140

Gain = 140 ticks per contract at $12.50 per tick.

Total gain on futures position = 6 contracts × 140 ticks × $12.50 = $10,500.

The US company has to pay US1.2240 to obtain the euros to make the payment in November, but the net cost is calculated by taking the cost of the spot transaction and the gain or loss on the futures position.

	$
Spot market: buy €750,000 at 1.2240	918,000
Less gain on futures position	(10,500)
Net cost of €750,000	907,500

The net cost is $907,500, so the effective exchange rate secured by futures hedge = US$907,500/€750,000

= US$1.2100/€1.

This is the spot rate and the futures price at the time the position was opened.

Conclusion

With a perfect hedge and no basis, futures can therefore fix the effective exchange rate at the spot rate when the hedge was created. However, in practice, the hedge is likely to be imperfect and there is basis.

Example: imperfect hedge but no basis

It is June. A UK company expects to receive US$1,000,000 from a customer in August, and wishes to hedge its currency exposure with currency futures. In this example, it is assumed that there is no basis, and the futures price and the current spot market exchange rate are always equal. The price of September futures in June is 1.8200. The value of one tick is $6.25.

The exposure is to the risk of a fall in the value of the US dollar between June and August. The company will receive US dollars. It can create a hedge with futures by selling dollars and buying British pounds. The UK company should therefore buy the currency futures, which are denominated in British pounds.

This logic can be set out in the three-step approach described earlier, as follows:

Step		Comment
1	Identify the underlying transaction that you are trying to hedge.	The UK company will be receiving $1 million.
2	What is the currency risk in the underlying transaction?	The value of the dollar will fall and the income will be worth less in sterling. Futures are denominated in sterling, so it is better to state that the risk is that the value of sterling will increase.
3	Work out a futures position that creates a profit if there is a 'loss' on the underlying transaction.	If a loss will be incurred on the underlying transaction if the value of sterling goes up, the futures position should create a profit if the value of sterling goes up. So buy sterling currency futures, since a profit will be made if the value of sterling goes up and the futures can be sold at a higher price.

At a rate of 1.8200, the sterling equivalent of $1,000,000 is £549,451. Each futures contract is for £62,500, therefore the company would want to buy 8.79 contracts. The company will probably decide to buy 9 contracts, although the hedge is imperfect.

Suppose that in August when the dollars are received, the dollar has actually strengthened in value and the exchange rate is 1.7800 (and the futures price is also 1.7800). The company will sell the $1,000,000 and close its futures position. The position for the company is as follows:

Open futures position: buy at	1.8200
Close position: sell at	1.7800
Loss	0.0400

Loss = 400 ticks per contract at $6.25 per tick.

Total loss on futures position = 9 contracts × 400 ticks × $6.25 = $22,500.

	$
Received from customer	1,000,000
Loss on futures	(22,500)
Net receipt in dollars	977,500
Sell dollars at 1.7800 (spot rate)	
Income in British pounds	£549,157

Effective exchange rate secured by futures hedge = US$1,000,000/£549,157 = $1.8210/£1.

This is close to the spot rate and futures price at the time the position was opened. Ignoring basis, the futures hedge has therefore fixed the effective exchange rate close to the spot rate and futures price when the hedge was created. However, in this example, the exchange rate moved favourably, and the gain from the increase in value of the dollar income was offset by a loss on the futures position.

e

Example: imperfect hedge and basis

A Netherlands company expects to pay US$1,200,000 to a US supplier in late November. It is now late July, and the current spot exchange rate is €1 = $1.2200. The current spot price for December dollar-euro currency futures is $1.2170. The company wants to hedge its exposure with currency futures.

The logic of establishing a hedge with currency futures can be set out in the three-step approach described earlier, as follows.

Step		**Comment**
1	Identify the underlying transaction that you are trying to hedge.	The European company will be paying $1.2 million.
2	What is the currency risk in the underlying transaction?	The cost/value of the dollar will increase and the cost in euros will rise. Futures are denominated in euros, so it is better to state that the risk is that the value of the euro will fall.

Step		Comment
3	Work out a futures position that creates a profit if there is a 'loss' on the underlying transaction.	If a loss will be incurred on the underlying transaction if the euro falls in value, the futures position should create a profit if the value of the euro falls. So sell euro currency futures, since a profit will be made if the value of the euro falls and the futures position can be closed by buying euro futures at a lower price than the futures were originally sold.

The company will sell futures to create a 'short position' to hedge the currency risk.

- The equivalent value of $1,200,000 at the current futures price is 986,031 euros ($1,200,000/1.2170).
- The number of contracts required is therefore 7.9 contracts (€986,031/€125,000 per contract).
- The company will probably create the hedge with 8 contracts (by selling 8 December futures).

In this example, the basis is 30 points in July (1.2200 – 1.2170). The December futures contract reaches settlement in five months' time, therefore basis should fall by 6 points each month (30 basis points/5 months). By the end of November, four months later, the basis should therefore have fallen by 24 points, from 30 to 6.

Suppose that in November when the dollars are paid, the spot rate has moved to 1.2040 and the futures price is 1.2030. (The actual basis is 10.) The company will close its futures position.

Open futures position: sell at	1.2170
Close position: buy at	1.2030
Loss	0.0140

Gain = 140 ticks per contract at $12.50 per tick.

Total gain on futures position = 8 contracts × 140 ticks × $12.50 = $14,000.

	$
Payment to customer	1,200,000
Gain on futures	(14,000)
Dollars to be purchased spot	1,186,000
Buy dollars at 1.2040 spot	
Cost in euros	€985,050

Effective exchange rate secured by futures hedge = US$1,200,000/€985,050 = US$1.2182/€1.

This is fairly close to the spot rate and futures price at the time the position was opened. In this example, the expected basis in November was 6 points and the actual basis was 10 points, and the gain on the futures position was therefore 4 points or ticks per contract more than expected. This has affected the value of the hedge by 8 contracts × 4 ticks × $12.50 = $400.

7.3 Advantages and disadvantages of hedging with currency futures

Advantages of hedging with currency futures

Low transaction costs.

Rates are set by the market and do not depend on financial strength of the user.

There is no default risk as the contract is with the market.

Future hedges are flexible with respect to the date of the hedged transaction because profit or loss can be taken at any on the contracts by closing out the contract on the market.

Disadvantages of hedging with currency futures

Hedging with futures is a more complicated process than using forward contracts or money market hedges.

The user must open an account with the exchange and deposit margin with the market.

Hedging with futures is only available for hedging a limited number of currencies.

Hedging with futures is only available for amounts of fixed size so the hedged risk may not be fully covered.

Short-term interest rate futures (STIRs)

- Features of short-term interest rate futures
- Hedging short-term interest rate exposures with STIRs
- Hedging examples

8 Short-term interest rate futures (STIRs)

8.1 Features of short-term interest rate futures

A short-term interest rate future (STIR) is a contract for the purchase and sale of a notional deposit, usually a three-month bank deposit. An examination question should give you the contract size for any STIR and the length of the deposit period. The most commonly-traded STIRs include the following:

Contract	Underlying amount = three-month deposit of:	Tick value (0.0001 of price)
Eurodollar	US$1,000,000	$25
Euribor	€1,000,000	€25
Short sterling	£500,000	£12.50

Prices

The futures price for STIRs is the annual interest rate. However, the rate is deducted from 100, which means that:

- A rate of 4% per year is indicated by a futures price of 96.0000 (100 – 4)
- A rate of 5.2175% is indicated by a futures price of 94.7825
- A price of 93.5618 represents an annual interest rate for the three-month deposit of 6.4382%.

A reason for pricing STIRs in this way is that:

- when interest rates go up, the value of a future will fall, and
- when interest rates fall, the price of the future will rise.

In this way, prices for STIRs move in the same way as cash market prices for bonds and other interest products.

8.2 Hedging short-term interest rate exposures with STIRs

STIRs can be used to hedge exposures to the risk of a rise or fall in short-term interest rates. Using short-term interest rate futures is similar to using currency futures to hedge a currency exposure. However, the following rules need to be applied.

- If the aim is to hedge against the risk of an increase in the short-term interest rate, the hedge is created by **selling futures**. If the interest rate does go up, futures prices will fall, and there will be a profit on the short position in STIRs
- If the aim is to hedge the risk of a fall in the short-term interest rate, the hedge is created by **buying futures**.

Short-term interest rate futures are futures for three-month deposits. If a company wishes to hedge an interest rate risk for a different interest period, such as two months, four months or six months, the number of futures to create the hedge should be adjusted by a factor: (Interest period to be hedged/3 months).

Example 1: number of futures for the hedge

It is now the end of October. A company expects to borrow $5 million for six months from February, in four months' time and is concerned about the risk of a rise in the eurodollar interest rate. It decides to hedge the exposure with eurodollar futures. Each eurodollar future is for a three-month deposit of $1,000,000.

The company will hedge the position by selling March futures. The number of contracts required for the hedge for a six-month loan is:

$$\frac{\$5,000,000}{\$1,000,000 \text{ per contract}} \times \frac{6 \text{ months}}{3 \text{ months}} = 10 \text{ contracts}$$

If changes in the three-month interest rate and changes in the six-month interest rate are similar during the period that the hedge is in place, hedging with three-month STIRs will be an effective method of hedging exposures to movements in the six-month interest rate.

Example 2: number of futures for the hedge

It is now the end of July. A company expects to borrow £10.5 million for two months from the end of October, in three months' time and is concerned about the risk of a rise in the sterling interest rate. It decides to hedge the exposure with sterling futures. Each future is for a three-month deposit of £500,000.

The company will hedge the position by selling November futures. The number of contracts required for the hedge for a two-month loan is:

$$\frac{\$10,500,000}{£500,000 \text{percontract}} \times \frac{2\text{months}}{3\text{months}} = 14\text{contracts}$$

8.3 Hedging examples

Example: perfect hedge, no basis

A company will need to borrow 8 million euros from the end of May. It is now January. The company is concerned about the risk of a rise in the euribor rate (the benchmark interest rate for the euro) and it wishes to hedge its position with futures. The current spot euribor rate is 3.50% (for both three months and six months) and the current June euribor futures price is the same, 96.50.

The value of 1 tick for a euribor futures contract is €25 (€1,000,000 × 0.0001 × 3/12).

Required

(a) How should the company hedge its interest rate exposure if it plans to borrow the 8 million euros for (1) three months or (2) six months.

(b) Suppose that in May when the company borrows the 8 million euros, the three-month and six-month spot euribor rate is 4.25% and the June futures price is the same, 95.75 (100 – 4.25). Calculate the effective annual interest rate that the company has secured with its futures hedge if it borrows the 8 million euros for (1) three months or (2) six months.

Answer

The exposure is to the risk of a rise in the euribor rate. Therefore the company should:

- sell 8 June euribor futures (€8,000,000/€1,000,000 per contract) if it is hedging a three-month loan exposure, and
- sell 16 June contracts (8 contracts × 6 months/3 months) if it is hedging a six-month loan exposure.

In May, the futures position will be closed. The selling price is 95.75.

Open futures position: sell at	96.50
Close position: buy at	95.75
Gain	00.75

Gain = 75 ticks per contract at €25 per tick.

Total gain on futures position:

(a) Hedging the three-month rate = 8 contracts × 75 ticks × €25 = €15,000.

(b) Hedging the six-month rate = 16 contracts × 75 ticks × €25 = €30,000.

The company will borrow 8 million euros at 4.25%.

	(a) Hedging the three-month rate	**(b) Hedging the six-month rate**
	€	€
Interest cost: €8 million × 3/12 × 4.25%	85,000	
Interest cost: €8 million × 6/12 × 4.25%		170,000
Less gain on futures position	(15,000)	(30,000)
Net effective cost	70,000	140,000

The net effective cost can be converted into an effective annual interest rate that has been achieved by the hedge with futures.

(a) Net effective interest rate for hedge of three-month rate =

$$\left(\frac{70{,}000}{8{,}000{,}000}\right)\times\frac{12}{3}=0.035 \text{ or } 3.50\%.$$

(b) Net effective interest rate for hedge of six-month rate =

$$\left(\frac{140{,}000}{8{,}000{,}000}\right)\times\frac{12}{6}=0.035 \text{ or } 3.50\%.$$

Given a perfect hedge and no basis, the hedge fixes the effective interest rate at the interest rate when the futures position was opened.

e

Example: imperfect hedge and no basis

A UK company will need to borrow £4.75 million for three months from the beginning of September. It is now April. The company is concerned about the risk of a rise in the LIBOR rate and wishes to hedge its position with futures. The current spot three-month LIBOR 5.45% and the current futures price is the same, 94.55.

Required

How should a hedge for the interest rate exposure be created, and what will be the effective interest rate for the loan from September if the spot LIBOR rate is 5.14% in early September and the September futures price is the same, 94.86?

The value of one tick for a 'short sterling' future is £12.50 (£500,000 × 0.0001 × 3/12).

a

Answer

The exposure is to the risk of a rise in the LIBOR rate; therefore the company should sell September short sterling futures. The number of contracts to sell is 9.5 contracts (£4.75 million/£500,000 per contract).. The company should sell either 9 or 10 futures, but the hedge will be imperfect. In this example, the company sells 10 September contracts.

The selling price in April is 94.55. In early September, the futures position will be closed.

Open futures position: sell at	94.55
Close position: buy at	94.86
Loss	00.31

Loss = 31 ticks per contract at £12.50 per tick.

Total loss on futures position = 10 contracts × 31 ticks × £12.50 = £3,875

The company will borrow £4.75 million for three months at 5.14%.

	£
Interest cost: £4.75 million × 3/12 × 5.14%	61,037.50
ADD: loss on futures position	3,875.00
Total effective cost	64,912.50

Effective interest rate for hedge of three-month rate

$$= \left(\frac{64,912.50}{4,750,000}\right) \times \frac{12}{3}$$

= 0.0547 or 5.47%

Given an imperfect hedge and no basis, the hedge fixes the effective interest rate at a rate close to the interest rate when the futures position was opened (5.45%).

Example: perfect hedge and basis

A company will need to borrow US$20 million for three months from the end of October. It is now the end of June. The company is concerned about the risk of a rise in the US$ LIBOR rate and wishes to hedge its position with futures. The current spot three-month US$ LIBOR is 4.30% and the current December eurodollar futures price is 96.30.

The value of 1 tick for a Eurodollar future is $25.

Required

How should a hedge for the interest rate exposure be created, and what will be the effective interest rate for the loan from October if the spot US$ LIBOR rate is 4.10% and the December futures price at this date is 96.06?

Answer

The exposure is to the risk of a rise in the US$ LIBOR rate; therefore the company should sell December Eurodollar futures. The number of contracts to sell is $20 million/$1,000,000 per contract = 20 contracts.

The selling price at the end of June is 96.30. The current spot three-month interest rate is 4.30%, equivalent to 95.70. The basis is therefore 60 points. This should be expected to reduce in size by 10 points each month in the six months between the end of June and the end of December when the futures reach their settlement date. By the end of October when the futures position is closed 4 months later, the expected basis should be 20 points. (This is 60 points minus (4 months × 10 points per month.)

At the end of October, the futures position will be closed.

Open futures position: sell at	96.30
Close position: buy at	96.06
Gain	00.24

Gain = 24 ticks per contract at $25 per tick.

Total gain on futures position = 20 contracts × 24 ticks × $25 = $12,000.

The company will borrow $20 million for three months at 4.10%.

	$
Interest cost: $20 million × 3/12 × 4.10%	205,000
Less: Gain on futures position	(12,000)
Net effective cost	193,000

Effective interest rate for hedge of three-month rate = $\left(\frac{193{,}000}{20\text{ million}}\right) \times \frac{12}{3}$

= 0.0386 or 3.86%.

At the end of October, the actual basis is 16 points, because the spot three-month rate is 4.10% (95.90) and the futures price is 96.06. (96.06 – 95.90 = 0.16 or 16 points).

The value of 16 points or ticks on the futures position would be 20 contracts × 16 ticks × $25 = $8,000. This represents an effective interest rate on borrowing $20 million for three months of [($8,000/$20 million) × (12/3) =] 0.0016 or 0.16%. This is the difference between the effective interest rate secured by the futures position and the interest rate in the futures contract when the position was opened in June (3.70%).

Conclusion

The effectiveness of a hedge is reduced when the hedge is imperfect and because of basis and basis risk.

Example: perfect hedge and basis

A company will need to borrow £60 million for four months from the end of April. It is now the end of November. The company is concerned about the risk of a rise in the LIBOR rate and wishes to hedge its position with futures. The current spot three-month LIBOR is 5.50% and the current June sterling interest rate futures price is 94.85. The company is able to borrow at LIBOR + 0.75%.

One tick is 0.01% and the value of a tick is £6.25. The nominal three-month deposit in a sterling futures contract is £500,000.

Required

(a) How should a hedge for the interest rate exposure be created?

(b) What will be the expected effective interest rate for the loan from the end of April? The expected basis at the close-out date should be estimated, but basis risk should be ignored for the purpose of this example.

(c) What will be the actual effective cost of borrowing the £60 million at the end of April if LIBOR at that time is 5.75%?

a

Answer

(a) The exposure is to the risk of a rise in the LIBOR rate; therefore the company should sell June futures. The number of contracts to sell is:

$$\frac{\text{£60 million}}{\text{£500,000 per contract}} \times \frac{\text{4 months}}{\text{3 months}} = \text{160 contracts}$$

The company should sell 160 June STIRs at 94.85, which 'fixes' the interest rate at 5.15% for the end of June.

(b) Basis at the end of November is the difference between the futures price (94.85) and the LIBOR spot rate (5.5% or 94.50). Basis is therefore 35 points (94.85 – 94.50).

There are seven months from the end of November to settlement of the futures contract at the end of June, so basis is expected to fall at the rate of 5 basis points (0.05) per month. By the end of April when the futures position will be closed, expected basis is 0.10 (2 months × 0.05) and the futures price is expected to be higher by the spot rate by this amount.

Selling the futures contracts therefore 'fixes' the LIBOR interest rate at a rate close to 5.25% for the end of April (the 5.15% in the futures price plus the expected basis of 0.10%).

Since the company can borrow at LIBOR + 0.75% the total effective borrowing rate for the four months that the company hopes to 'lock in' with the futures – given no basis risk – is 5.25% + 0.75% = 6.00%.

(c) If the spot LIBOR rate at the end of April is 5.75% or 94.25, the expected futures price will be 94.35 (10 basis points higher, given no basis risk).

The futures position will be closed as follows:

	%
November: sell at	94.85
April: buy to close at	94.35
Profit	0.50

Profit per contract = (0.50/0.005 per tick) × £6.25 per tick = £625.

Profit on 160 contracts = £625 × 160 = £100,000.

The company will borrow £60 million for 4 months at an interest rate of 6.50% (LIBOR + 0.75%).

The interest cost of the loan will be £60 million × 6.50% × 4/12 = £1,300,000.

	£
Interest cost of loan	1,300,000
Gain on futures position	(100,000)
Net borrowing cost	1,200,000

The effective net interest cost is £1,290,000. On a loan of £60 million for four months, this represents an effective interest rate of:

$$\frac{£1,200,000}{£60 \text{ million}} \times \frac{12}{4} = 6.00\%$$

This actual effective borrowing rate of 6.00% is the same as the expected effective borrowing rate calculated in part (b).

CHAPTER 20

Hedging with options

Contents

Hedging with options

- Main features of hedging with options
- Creating a hedge

1 Hedging with options

1.1 Main features of hedging with options

Financial options can be used to hedge exposures to the risk of adverse movements in exchange rates, interest rates, bond prices and share prices. Hedging with options differs from hedging with forward contracts, money market hedges, FRAs and futures, in several important ways.

- The hedge has a cost. A hedge should normally be created by buying options rather than selling/writing options, and the option buyer must pay the premium to obtain the options to create the hedge.
- An option does not have to be exercised. It will only be exercised if it is in-the-money. If it is out-of-the-money, the option holder will let the option lapse and buy or sell the underlying item in the cash market, at the more favourable market price. This means that an option holder can use the options as a protection against adverse movements in the market rate, but can take advantage of any favourable movement in the market rate.

Example

An investor holds 5,000 shares in another company, XYZ, which have a current market price of $6.00. The investor will want to sell the shares in a few months' time, in April, but not before then. He is concerned that the share price might fall between now and April, but is also aware of the possibility that it could rise.

The investor can hedge the exposure to market risk (share price risk) by purchasing a put option on 5,000 shares in XYZ, for expiry in April. Suppose the strike price of the option is $6.00, so that the option is at-the-money when written.

- If the share price falls below $6.00 before April, say to $5.50, the investor can exercise the option and sell at the strike price of $6.00.
- On the other hand, if the share price rises above $6.00, say to $7.00, he can let the option lapse and sell the shares at the market price of $7.00.

1.2 Creating a hedge

The **rule for creating a hedge with options** is as follows:

- To hedge against the risk of a rise in the price of the underlying item, buy call options
- To hedge against the risk of a fall in the price of the underlying item, buy put options

Currency options

- Features of currency options
- Hedging with currency options
- Gains or losses on options and the effective exchange rate
- Imperfect hedges
- Traded options versus OTC (over the counter) options

2 Currency options

2.1 Features of currency options

The main features of currency options have already been described.

- A currency option gives its holder the right to buy (call option) or sell (put option) a quantity of one currency in exchange for another, on or before a specified date, at a fixed rate of exchange (the strike rate for the option).
- Currency options can be purchased over-the-counter or on an exchange. Examination questions are more likely to feature exchange-traded options than OTC options. Currency options are traded on some exchanges, notably the Philadelphia Stock Exchange, and options on currency futures are traded on the CME exchange in Chicago.
- Traded currency options are for a standard quantity of one currency in exchange for another currency, and strike prices are quoted as exchange rates. The premiums are normally quoted as an amount in one currency per unit of the other currency. For example, traded options on currency futures for US$ - £ are for £62,500 and are priced in US cents per £1.

2.2 Hedging with currency options

The rules for using exchange-traded currency options to hedge an exposure to currency risk are as follows:

- Establish what the exposure is. The company will have a future intention or obligation to buy or sell a quantity of currency in exchange for another. Establish whether the currency will be bought or sold, how much will be bought or sold, and when.
- Decide whether a call option or a put option is required to hedge the exposure.
- Decide on the strike price for the option. For exchange-traded options, there will normally be a small range of strike prices to choose from.
- Calculate how many option contracts must be purchased to create the hedge.

Example

A US company expects to pay 1 million euros to a supplier in Belgium. It is now November and the payment is due in March. The company wants to use currency options to hedge the exposure. Each currency option is for 125,000 euros.

The company will need to buy euros to make the payment to the supplier; therefore it wants to hedge against the risk of a rise in the value of the euro (= a fall in the value of the dollar). The company should therefore buy call options.

We shall suppose that the company chooses a strike price of 1.2400 (US$/€1) for the options, and that the premium for a March call option at this strike price is 3.43 US cents per euro.

The company should buy 8 call option contracts (€1,000,000/€125,000 per contract). The cost of the premium will be $34,300 (1,000,000 × $0.0343).

2.3 Gains or losses on options and the effective exchange rate

The effective exchange rate that is obtained from a hedge with options on currency futures depends on what happens when the settlement date arrives, and whether the option is exercised or not.

The following example illustrates this point:

Example

Continuing the previous example, a US company expects to pay €1 million at the end of March and buys 8 call options on March euro currency futures at a strike price of 1.2400.

We can look at the position of the US company if the spot exchange rate (US$/€1) in March is:

(a) $1.2000

(b) $1.2200

(c) $1.2500

(d) $1.2800

(e) $1.3000

a

Answer

The call option will be exercised if the futures price at the end of March is over 1.2400. At the end of March when the futures contract reaches settlement, the futures settlement price should be the current spot exchange rate.

	Spot rate at expiry				
	1.2000 Do not exercise	**1.2200 Do not exercise**	**1.2500 Exercise**	**1.2800 Exercise**	**1.3000 Exercise**
	$	$	$	$	$
Cost of buying €1 million	1,200,000	1,220,000	1,240,000	1,240,000	1,240,000
Cost of premium	34,300	34,300	34,300	34,300	34,300
Total cost	1,234,300	1,254,300	1,274,300	1,274,300	1,274,300
Effective exchange rate	$1.2343	$1.2543	$1.2743	$1.2743	$1.2743

The hedge has enabled the company to fix a maximum effective exchange rate of $1.2743 for buying the euros, but at the same time allowing the company to obtain a lower effective exchange rate if the spot price is below the strike price, and the option is not exercised.

2.4 Imperfect hedges

When a hedge is created with exchange-traded currency options, the hedge is often imperfect, for reasons similar to those already explained for hedging with futures. When a hedge with exchange-traded currency options is imperfect, and the options are exercised, the un-hedged or over-hedged amount of currency should be bought for sold in the spot currency market, at the spot rate, at the same time that the options are exercised.

e

Example: imperfect hedge

A company in Belgium expects to pay US$2 million to a supplier in Arabia. It is now November and the payment is due in March. The current spot rate is 1.2100. The company wants to use currency options to hedge the exposure. Each currency option is for 125,000 euros and the value of 1 tick (0.0001) is $12.50.

The company will need to buy US dollars and sell euros to make the payment to the supplier; therefore it wants to hedge against the risk of a rise in the value of the dollar and a fall in the value of the euro. Since the contracts are for euros, the company should therefore buy put options.

We shall suppose that the company chooses a strike price of $1.2200 = €1 for the options, and that the premium for a March put option at this strike price is 2.75 US cents per euro.

- At a strike price of $1.2200, $2,000,000 is the equivalent of 1,639,344 euros.
- To hedge 1,639,344 euros, the company needs to buy 13.1 put options (1,639,344 euros/125,000 euros per contract).

The company will probably buy 13 put options. The cost of the premium will be 13 contracts × 125,000 × $0.0275 = $44,687.50. The company will buy these dollars spot at $1.2100, and so the cost of buying the options (in euros) will be €36,931.82.

(a) **The spot exchange rate moves in the option holder's favour**

Suppose that the exchange rate moves in the time to expiry such that the company does not want to exercise the options to sell futures at 1.2200 because the euro is worth more than 1.2200. In this example, suppose that the spot rate in March when the dollars must be paid is $1.2500 = €1. The company will let the option lapse and purchase the dollars spot at $1.2500. The effective exchange rate is as follows:

	€
Purchase $2,000,000 at $1.2500	1,600,000.00
Cost of option premium	36,931.82
Total cost	1,636,931.82
Effective exchange rate for $2 million ($2 million/€1,636,931.82)	$1.2218 = €1

(b) **The spot exchange rate moves adversely**

Suppose that the exchange rate moves in the time to expiry such that the company wants to exercise the options. In this example, suppose that the spot rate in March when the dollars must be paid is $1.1800 = €1. The company will exercise the option to sell the 13 futures contracts at $1.2200.

	$
November: sell options at	1.2200
March: close by buying at	1.1800
Profit per contract	0.0400

Profit on futures position = 13 contracts × 400 ticks × $12.50 per tick = $65,000

	$
Payment to be made in $	2,000,000
Gain on futures	(65,000)
Dollars to be purchased at the spot rate	1,935,000

	€
Cost of buying $1,935,000 spot at 1.1800	1,639,830.51
Original cost of option premium	36,931.82
Total cost	1,676,762.33
Effective exchange rate for $2 million ($2 million/€1,676,762.33)	$1.1928 = €1

2.5 Traded options versus OTC (over the counter) options

Options might be traded on a market. These options are standardised with respect to size (e.g. the number of units of currency upon which an option is taken) and other factors. The market offers to sell standardised puts and calls and the standardisation allows the options to be priced on the market.

OTC options are personal contracts between the writer and the buyer of the option.

Each of these has advantages over the other depending on circumstances.

Advantages and disadvantages of traded options

Advantages

Traded options can be sold on the market at any time.

Traded options are usually American options. This means that they can be exercised over a period rather than at a point in time. This makes them more flexible in situations where there is uncertainty over the date of a hedged transaction.

Disadvantage

Traded options are of a standard size. Therefore, it may not be possible to hedge the full amount of the transaction. A company would have to enter into too few or too many options, choosing whether to be under or over hedged.

Advantages of OTC options

OTC options can be agreed for a longer period than traded options thus providing flexibility and protection against currency movements in the longer term.

OTC options are tailored specifically for a particular transaction, ensuring maximum protection from currency movements.

Disadvantage

OTC options might carry greater credit risk than traded options because the contract is with a single entity rather than the market.

Premiums on OTC options can be larger than those on traded options.

Interest rate options

- Features of interest rate options
- Types of interest rate option
- Borrowers' options
- Lenders' options
- Swaptions

3 Interest rate options

3.1 Features of interest rate options

An interest rate option is an option on a notional loan or deposit (or an option on an interest rate future), where the loan or deposit period begins:

- on the expiry date for the option for a European-style option, or
- on or before the expiry date for the option, for an American-style option.

The option guarantees a maximum or a minimum rate of interest for the option holder, and interest rate options are therefore sometimes called **interest rate guarantees** or **IRGs**.

- A call option guarantees a maximum rate of interest.
- A put option guarantees a minimum rate of interest.

The maximum or minimum rate of interest guaranteed by the option is the strike rate for the option, in comparison with an agreed benchmark rate of interest, such as LIBOR or euribor.

An interest rate option is for a notional loan or deposit. If it is exercised, an actual loan or deposit is not created. Instead, the option is 'cash-settled' by a payment from the writer of the option to the option holder.

3.2 Types of interest rate option

Many interest rate options are arranged over-the-counter (OTC). These include:

- borrowers' options and lenders' options
- caps, floors and collars.

Options on interest rate futures are traded on the futures exchanges where the interest rate futures are also traded.

3.3 Borrowers' options

A borrower's option guarantees a maximum borrowing rate for the option holder. The strike rate for the option is compared with an agreed reference rate or benchmark interest rate, such as LIBOR.

- It the reference rate of interest is higher than the strike rate when the option reaches expiry, the option will be exercised. The option writer must make a payment to the option holder for the difference between the actual interest rate (reference rate) and the strike rate for the option.
- It the reference rate of interest is lower than the strike rate when the option reaches expiry, the option holder will let the option lapse.

The premium for the option might be expressed either:

- as an actual percentage of the notional principal amount, or
- as an annual rate of interest on the notional principal amount.

A borrower's option can be used to fix a maximum effective borrowing rate for a future short-term loan, but allow the option holder to benefit from any fall in the interest rate up to the expiry date for the option.

Example

A company intends to borrow US$10 million in four months' time for a period of three months, but is concerned about the volatility of the US dollar LIBOR rate. The three-month US$ LIBOR rate is currently 3.75%, but might go up or down in the next four months. The company therefore takes out a borrower's option with a strike rate of 4% for a notional three-month loan of US$10 million. The expiry date is in four months' time. The option premium is the equivalent of 0.5% per annum of the notional principal. For simplicity, we shall suppose that the company is able to borrow at the US dollar LIBOR rate.

(a) If the three-month US dollar LIBOR rate is higher than the option strike rate at expiry, the option will be exercised. If the three-month LIBOR rate is 6%, the company will exercise the option, and the option writer will pay the option holder an amount equal to the difference between the strike rate for the option (4%) and the reference rate (6%). The payment will be based on 2% of $10 million for three months. (This payment is discounted because a borrower's option is settled at the beginning of the notional interest period, and not at the end of the interest period).

(b) If the three-month US dollar LIBOR rate is lower than the option strike rate at expiry, the option will not be exercised. For example, if the LIBOR rate after four months is 3%, the option will not be exercised and will lapse.

These possible outcomes are summarised in the table below, assuming (for the purpose of illustration) a spot LIBOR rate at the option expiry date of (a) 6% and (b) 3%.

	LIBOR rate at expiry	
	6%	3%
	Exercise the option	Do not exercise
	%	%
Borrow for three months at	6.00	3.00
Receive from option writer	(2.00)	-
Cost of option premium	0.50	0.50
Effective interest cost (% annual rate)	4.50	3.50

If the borrower can borrow at the reference rate of interest, a borrower's option sets the maximum borrowing cost at the strike rate plus the option premium cost.

3.4 Lenders' options

A lender's option guarantees a minimum deposit rate (savings rate) for the option holder. In all other respects, it is similar to a borrower's option. The strike rate for the option is compared with an agreed reference rate or benchmark interest rate, such as LIBOR.

- It the reference rate of interest is lower than the strike rate when the option reaches expiry, the option will be exercised. The option writer must make a payment to the option holder for the difference between the actual interest rate (reference rate) and the strike rate for the option.
- It the reference rate of interest is higher than the strike rate when the option reaches expiry, the option holder will let the option lapse.

3.5 Swaptions

A swaption is an option on a swap. It gives its holder the right, but not the obligation, to enter into a swap agreement at a future date, on terms that are fixed now.

Swaptions are not commonly used, particularly by companies, because of the cost of the option premium.

Caps, floors and collars

- Caps
- Floors
- Collars
- Zero cost collars
- Creating a short-term collar with options on interest rate futures

4 Caps, floors and collars

Borrowers' and lenders' options are options for one interest period only. Companies that borrow might seek to hedge their interest rate risk for a number of consecutive interest periods. For example, a company borrowing from a bank might have a five-year loan with interest payable every six months, at a variable rate of interest. The loan would therefore have ten consecutive interest periods, with the interest rate fixed for just the first six-month period. The company might want to hedge its exposure to the risk of a high interest rate in the next nine interest periods.

Caps, floors and collars are OTC interest rate options that allow a company to hold interest rate options for a series of consecutive interest periods, instead of having to arrange a number of separate single-period borrowers' or lenders' options.

4.1 Caps

An interest rate cap is a borrower's option on a series of consecutive interest periods. For example, a company might buy a cap fixing the maximum six-month LIBOR rate at the strike rate for the option, for nine consecutive interest periods, each expiring at six-monthly intervals.

e

Example

A company borrows £8 million for five years from a bank at a variable rate of interest, with interest payable every six months at six-month LIBOR plus 0.50%. The LIBOR rate for the first six months of the loan is 5%, therefore the company pays interest for this first six months at 5.5%.

If the company wants to hedge the risk of a rise in the LIBOR rate for the next nine interest periods, it can arrange a cap for a notional principal amount of £8 million. It might select a strike rate of 5%. Alternatively, it might select a strike rate of 6%, because the premium would be cheaper.

Suppose the strike rate for the cap is 5%, for the next nine interest periods. The exercise dates for the cap can be arranged to coincide with the start of each six-month interest period for the loan. The cap will fix the maximum effective rate of interest on the loan for the next none periods.

- The cap fixes the maximum effective LIBOR rate at 5%.
- The company will borrow at an effective maximum rate of 5.5% (strike rate + 0.50%).
- However, the company has to pay the premium for the cap. This might be 1% per year of the notional principal amount. The cost of the premium would make the total maximum effective rate 6.50% per year.

For each notional interest period of the cap, the cap operates in a very similar way to a borrower's option.

- If the reference rate of interest for the interest period (LIBOR or euribor) is higher than the strike rate for the cap, the writer of the option must make a payment to the option holder for the difference.
- If the reference rate of interest for the interest period is lower than the strike rate for the cap, the option in the cap will not be exercised.

e

Example

Returning to the previous example, suppose that the six-month LIBOR rates at the first five exercise dates in the cap are as follows:

2nd interest period, Year 1 (1)	LIBOR = 4.0%
1st interest period, Year 2 (2)	LIBOR = 4.5%
2nd interest period, Year 2 (3)	LIBOR = 5.25%
1st interest period, Year 3 (4)	LIBOR = 5.75%
2nd interest period, Year 3 (5)	LIBOR = 6.0%

The strike rate for the cap is 5%. The outcome for each interest period will be as follows:

Interest period/ expiry date	LIBOR		Borrow at LIBOR + 0.50%	Receipt from cap	Net interest rate
(1)	4.0%	Do not exercise	4.50%	-	4.50%
(2)	4.5%	Do not exercise	5.00%	-	5.00%
(3)	5.25%	Exercise	5.75%	(0.25)%	5.50%
(4)	5.75%	Exercise	6.25%	(0.75)%	5.50%
(5)	6.0%	Exercise	6.50%	(1.00)%	5.50%

The cap therefore sets an effective interest rate of 5.50% (the strike rate + 0.50%) and also allows the option holder to benefit from a lower LIBOR rate, by choosing not to exercise the option when this rate is more favourable than the strike rate for the option. However, the effective interest rates are actually higher than in the table above, because the cost of the option premium needs to be added.

With interest rate caps (and also with floors and collars), the **payment by the option writer** when a cap is exercised is **at the end of the notional interest** period, not when the option is exercised. The payment is therefore not discounted. In the example above, the payment by the option writer for the fifth expiry date would be:

(6.00 – 5.00) % × £8 million × 6/12 = £40,000. This would be made at the end of the six-month interest period.

4.2 Floors

Interest rate floors are similar to caps, except that they are a series of successive lenders' options. They can be used to fix a minimum interest rate for a series of interest rate periods.

4.3 Collars

A major disadvantage of caps and floors is the high cost of the premiums. A company might want to hedge its exposure to the risk of a rise or fall in an interest rate for a number of consecutive interest periods, but might not want to pay the cost of the premium for the cap or the floor.

This can be done by arranging an interest rate collar.

- As an **alternative to a cap**, a company can arrange a collar in which it:
  - buys a cap at one strike rate, and simultaneously
  - sells a floor at a different, lower strike rate.

  The effect of this collar is to fix a maximum interest cost through the mechanism of the cap, but also to fix a minimum interest cost through the mechanism of the floor.

  The cost of the cap premium and the income from the sale of the floor are the net premium cost for the collar.

  Collar premium = Cap premium cost – Floor premium income.

- Similarly, as an **alternative to a floor**, a company can arrange a collar in which it:
  - buys a floor at one strike rate, and simultaneously
  - sells a cap at a different, higher strike rate.

  The effect of this collar is to fix a minimum interest income through the mechanism of the floor, but also to fix a maximum interest income through the mechanism of the cap.

  The cost of the floor premium and the income from the sale of the cap are the net premium cost for the collar.

  Collar premium = Floor premium cost – Cap premium income.

  A collar therefore has the effect of fixing the reference rate of interest between a high and a low limit.

4.4 Zero cost collars

Even the cost of a collar can be quite high. However, it might be possible to arrange a zero cost collar. This is collar for which the premium is zero.
For example, if a collar consists of buying a cap and selling a floor, the premium value of the cap and the premium value of the floor would be equal, leaving no premium to pay for the collar.

When a zero cost collar is possible – and it is by no means always possible to arrange a collar for no cost – the strike rate for the cap and the strike rate for the collar will be very close to each other, if not the same. In effect, this would fix the interest period at a single rate for the full term of the collar, or would restrict the range between maximum and minimum interest rate to a very narrow limit.

4.5 Creating a short-term collar with options on interest rate futures

An interest rate collar can be created with options on interest rate futures.

You need to remember that an interest rate future is a contract on a notional interest-earning deposit.

To create a collar with options on interest rate futures to fix a maximum and a minimum cost of borrowing, you should:

- Buy put options on interest rate futures for the maximum interest rate in the collar. If the spot interest rises above this put option rate and the futures price therefore falls below it, the options will be exercised to sell the futures at the exercise price and make a profit from closing the futures position.
- Sell call options on interest rate futures for the minimum interest rate in the collar. If the spot interest falls below the call option rate and the futures price therefore rises above it, the call option holder will exercise option on the futures at the exercise price. The company must buy the futures at that price and make a loss on the futures position.
- The net cost of the collar is the premium paid for the put options minus the premium received from selling the call options.

Example

It is now the end of March and the spot LIBOR rate is. A company needs to borrow $120 million at the end of July for 2 months. It can borrow at LIBOR plus 1% and it wants to create an interest rate collar so that its effective borrowing cost will be within the range 5% to 6%.

Futures on three-month dollars are for $1 million each.

Current option prices are as follows, at the end of March. Premiums are shown as annual % rates. A three-month dollar short-term interest rate future is for a deposit of $1,000,000.

	CALLS		PUTS	
Expiry:	**Jun**	**Sep**	**Jun**	**Sep**
Strike price:				
9500	0.225	0.305	0.165	0.215
9600	0.025	0.080	0.490	0.750

Required

(a) Explain how the collar should be created and how many options contracts should be used.

(b) Calculate the premium cost of the collar.

(c) Calculate the effective cost of borrowing the $120 million if the LIBOR rate at the end of July is 6% and he futures price at this date is also 6%. (In other words, basis is ignored for the purpose of this question.)

a

Answer

(a) The borrowing period will begin at the end of July, therefore options on September futures should be used.

The company borrows at LIBOR plus 1% and wants the collar to establish an effective borrowing range of 5% to 6%. This means that the collar needs to establish a borrowing range for LIBOR of 4% to 5%, with a maximum LIBOR cost of 5% and a minimum LIBOR cost of 4%.

The company should therefore buy put options at the 5% interest rate of 9500 and sell call options at the 4% rate of 96.00.

The company intends to borrow $120 million for 2 months; therefore the number of option contracts is:

[$120 million/$1 million per future] × [2 months/3 months] = 80 contracts.

(b)

	Premium % per year
Cost of September put options at 9500	0.215
Income from September call options at 9600	0.080
Net cost of collar	0.135

The cost of the premium in $ is:
80 contracts × $1 million × 0.135% × 3/12 = $27,000.

(c) At the end of July if the spot LIBOR rate is 6%, the company will borrow $120 million for two months at 7%.

The put options on dollar interest rate futures will also be exercised at 9500, and if the futures price is 6% (9400), there will be a profit of 100 ticks (9600 – 9500) on closing the futures position.

The profit on the futures will be: 80 contracts × 100 ticks × $25 = $200,000.

The net effective cost of borrowing is therefore as follows:

	$
Interest on $120 million for 2 months at 7%	1,400,000
Gain on futures	(200,000)
Cost of collar	27,000
Total effective cost	1,227,000

This represents an effective interest rate of:

$$\frac{\$1,227,000}{\$120 \text{ million}} \times \frac{12 \text{ months}}{2 \text{ months}} = 0.6135 \text{ or } 6.135\%$$

This is the maximum borrowing cost established by the collar (6%) plus the cost of the premium (0.135%, see earlier calculation).

Delta hedging

- Delta defined
- Constructing a delta hedge for a call options exposure
- Constructing a delta hedge for a put options exposure
- The Greeks

5 Delta hedging

Buying call options or put options is a method of hedging financial risk. Options are a zero-sum game, and to the extent that an option holder is protected against risk, the option writer is exposed to risk. For banks and other institutions that write options, their own exposure to risk from writing options can be hedged with a delta hedge.

5.1 Delta defined

The delta of an option is defined as the change in the price of an option in proportion to the change in the value of the underlying item.

$$\text{Delta} = \frac{\text{Change in value of the option}}{\text{Change in market value of underlying item}}$$

For example, in the case of an option on a company's shares, if the share price goes up by $1, the option price will go up if it is a call option or down if it is a put option. However, the change in the price of the option will not exceed $1. The value of an option delta is therefore in the range – 1 to + 1.

- A **call option** that is **deeply in-the-money** has a delta close to + 1
- A **put option** that is **deeply in-the-money** has a delta close to – 1.
- An **option that is deeply out-of-the-money** has a delta close to 0.
- An **option that is at-the-money** has a delta close to + 0.5 (call option) or – 0.50 (put option).

Delta is always positive for calls and negative for puts.

Even though delta will be a number between 0.0 and 1.0 for a long call (and/or short put) and 0.0 and –1.0 for a long put (and/or short call), these numbers are commonly presented as a percentage of the total number of shares represented by the option contract(s). This is convenient because the option will (instantaneously) behave like the number of shares indicated by the delta.

For example, if an American call option on XYZ has a delta of 0.25(=25%), it will gain or lose value just like 25 of 100 shares of XYZ as the price changes for small price movements.

The value of an option's delta can be calculated. It is related the value of $N(-d_1)$ or $N(d_1)$ in the Black-Scholes option pricing model.

The Black-Scholes option pricing model was covered in an earlier chapter. The formulae are repeated here for you convenience.

$c = P_a\,N(d_1) - P_e\,N(d_2)\,e^{-rt}$

where

$$d_1 = \frac{\ln(P_a / P_e) + (r + 0.5s^2)t}{s\sqrt{t}}$$

$d_2 = d_1 - s\sqrt{t}$

c = Price of the call option (call option value)
P_a = the price of the underlying item, such as the current share price (stock option) or current exchange rate (currency option)
$N(d_1)$ = the probability in a normal distribution that the value is less than d_1 standard deviations above the mean. (This is explained later. $N(d_2)$ is also explained later.
P_e = the exercise price or strike rate for the option
e = the constant e. You will need a calculator that calculates values to the power of e.
r = the risk-free interest rate (as an annual rate: for example, 5% = 0.05)
t = time to expiry of the option, in years. For example, if the option has three months to expiry, t = 0.25.
s = standard deviation of the value/returns of the underlying item. This should be the annual volatility, for consistency with the values of r and t.

5.2 Constructing a delta hedge for a call options exposure

A bank that writes a large number of options has an option portfolio. It might want to create a hedge for its exposure to adverse price movements.

- An option portfolio is said to be delta neutral when its delta is 0.
- A bank that writes call options can create an option position that is delta neutral by purchasing a quantity of the underlying item. For example, a bank that has written call options on the shares of XYZ Company can hedge the position by holding some shares in XYZ.
- If the value of the underlying shares goes up, the value of the call options will also go up. The bank will incur a loss on its options position, because it has written options. However, it makes a gain on the rise in the value of the underlying shares.
- A delta neutral position will exist when the rise in the value of the options (= benefit to the option holders and loss for the option writer) is matched by an equal rise in the value of the shares held by the option writer (bank). This will leave the bank with neither a loss nor a gain.

The number of shares that a call option writer should hold to create a delta hedge = [Quantity of the underlying item on which there are options] × [Option delta.]

For example if the delta value for call options on 1,000,000 shares of XYZ Company at an exercise price of $15 is 0.45, a delta hedge will be created by holding 450,000 of the shares (1,000,000 × 0.45).

Calculating delta for call options

The value of delta for a position in call options is the value of $N(d_1)$ in the Black-Scholes model formulae:

Amount of underlying item to be hedged × $N(d_1)$ = Amount of underlying to hold as a hedge

Example

A UK bank is writing currency call options on €200 million in exchange for British pounds. The value of delta of the options is 0.5326, measured as $N(d_1)$.

In order for the bank to be certain that it will not make a loss, it could hedge its options position by holding a quantity of euros.

The quantity of euros that it would need to hold to create a hedge is €200 million × 0.5326 = €106.52 million.

Example

In principle, the same formula can be used to calculate how many at-the-money call options it would be necessary to hold to eliminate exchange rate risk entirely.

For example, suppose that a UK company needs to buy €100 million in three months time and wants to use currency call options to create a hedge that would eliminate the exchange rate risk entirely. At-the-money call options on euros have a delta value of 0.5326. Each option is for €100,000.

Re-arranging the previous formula, we can calculate the amount of euros for which at-the-money call options should be purchased is:

€100 million/ $N(d_1)$
= €100 million/0.5326
= €187.758 million.
Since each option contract is for €100,000, this would mean buying 1,878 contracts.

Any increase in the value of the euro would mean that the cost of buying the €100 million at the option exercise date would increase, but this 'loss' would be offset entirely by a gain on the call options position.

In practice however, creating a hedge with options that eliminates the risk entirely is very expensive, because of the cost of the options. In this example, if the company did decide to use options to create a hedge, the number of options that it would buy is likely to be €100 million/€100,000 per contract = 1,000 contracts.

5.3 Constructing a delta hedge for a put options exposure

A similar technique can be applied to calculate a hedge position for a writer of put options. The difference is that if a bank writes put options, it will incur a loss on the options position if the price of the underlying item falls.

To create a hedge, it therefore needs to be 'short' in the underlying item. It could do this by borrowing the underlying item in the case of shares, or selling the item forward if it is currency.

For example if the delta value for put options on 1,000,000 shares of XYZ Company at an exercise price of $15 is – 0.27, a delta hedge will be created by borrowing 270,000 of the shares (1,000,000 × 0.27), and the settlement date for returning the borrowed shares should be the same as the expiry date for the option..

Calculating delta for put options

The value of delta for a position in put options is the value of $N(-d_1)$ in the Black-Scholes model formulae:

Amount of underlying item to be hedged × $N(-d_1)$ = Amount of underlying to hold as a hedge

Example

A UK bank is writing currency put options on €50 million in exchange for British pounds. The value of delta of the options is 0.4674, measured as $N(-d_1)$.

In order for the bank to be certain that it will not make a loss, it could hedge its options position by selling forward a quantity of euros, for settlement on the same date as the expiry date for the options.

The quantity of euros that it would need to sell forward to create a hedge is €50 million × 0.4674 = €23.37 million.

Example

In principle, the same formula can be used to calculate how many at-the-money put options it would be necessary to hold to eliminate exchange rate risk entirely.

For example, suppose that a UK company will receive €20 million in three months time and wants to use currency put options to create a hedge that would eliminate the exchange rate risk entirely. At-the-money put options on euros have a delta value of 0.4764 ($N(-d_1)$). Each option is for €100,000.

Re-arranging the previous formula, we can calculate the amount of euros for which at-the-money call options should be purchased is:

€20 million/ $N(-d_1)$

= €20 million/0.4764

= €41,981,528.

Since each option is for €100,000 this would mean having to buy 420 put option contracts.

As stated earlier, creating a hedge with options that eliminates the risk entirely is very expensive, because of the cost of the options. In this example, if the company did decide to use options to create a hedge, the number of options that it would buy is likely to be €20 million/€100,000 per contract = 200 contracts.

5.4 The Greeks

You might come across the term 'the Greeks'. Organisations that deal in options calculate a variety of option ratios for establishing and monitoring their option positions. These ratios are called 'the Greeks', because they are all designated by a Greek letter (though strangely there is not Greek letter "vega")

Delta (Δ)

Delta has already been explained. It is the change in the price of an option (in money value) for a given change in the price of the underlying item.

The value of delta changes as the price of the underlying item changes. For example, if the market price of a share rises, the delta value of a call option on the shares will increase.

The delta value of an option may also be seen as a probability estimate that the option will expire in-the-money. For example, a deeply in-the-money option has a delta close to + 1 (call option) or – 1 (put option) and the probability estimate that it will expire in the money is therefore close to 100%.

A deeply out-of the-money option has a delta close to 0, and the probability that it will expire in-the-money is therefore close to 0%.

For an at-the-money option, the probability that it will expire in the money is about 50%.

Gamma (Γ)

The gamma for an option is the ratio of the change in the delta of an option for a given change in the value of the underlying item. For example, it is the change in the delta of a share option for an increase or decrease of $0.01 in the share price.

The value of gamma for an option is very low as the certainty increases that the option will expire in-the-money or out-of-the-money.

The value of gamma increases with uncertainty as to whether the option will expire in-the-money or out of-the-money.

Vega (v)

Vega measures the ratio of the change in the option price for a 1% change in the volatility of the underlying item. If volatility in the underlying item increases, vega increases.

Vega is typically expressed as the amount of money, per underlying share the option's value will gain or lose as volatility rises or falls by 1%.

Vega can be an important Greek to monitor for an option trader, especially in volatile markets since some of the value of option strategies can be particularly sensitive to changes in volatility.

Rho ())

Rho is a measure of the sensitivity of the option price to interest rate changes.

	Impact on option price	
	Calls	**Puts**
Interest rate rises	Increase	Decrease
Interest rate falls	Decrease	Increase

Except under extreme circumstances, the value of an option is least sensitive to changes in the risk-free-interest rates. For this reason, rho is the least used of the first-order Greeks.

Theta (\)

Theta is a measure of the sensitivity of the option price to the remaining time to expiry of the option.

The theta value indicates how much value a stock option's price will diminish per day with all other factors being constant. If a stock option has a theta value of -0.012, it means that it will lose 1.2 cents a day.

The nearer the expiration date, the higher the theta and the farther away the expiration date, the lower the theta. Some

Summary

	Change in:	Due to change in:
Delta	Option price	Underlying asset value
Gamma	Delta	Underlying asset value
Vega	Option price	Volatility
Rho	Option price	Interest rate
Theta	Option price	Time to expiry

Appendix 1

Portfolio theory and the CAPM

Contents

Portfolio theory

- Risk and return in investments
- Introduction to portfolio theory
- Two-asset portfolio – Mathematics
- Possible outcomes

1 Portfolio theory

1.1 Risk and return in investments

Investors invest in shares and bonds in the expectation of making a return. The return that they want from any investment could be described as:

- a return as reward for providing funds and keeping those funds invested, plus
- a return to compensate the investor for the risk.

As a basic rule, an investor will expect a higher return when the investment risk is higher. High volatility in returns is associated with high investment risk.

For an investment, we can measure both:

- an expected or average annual return for the time period, and
- a variance or standard deviation of the returns.

The risk of variations in annual profits and dividends can be measured as either the variance or standard deviation of expected returns over a given period of time.

1.2 Introduction to portfolio theory

Portfolio theory is concerned with how investors should build a portfolio of investments that gives them a suitable balance between return and investment risk. Portfolio theory provides a theoretical basis for the capital asset pricing model, which is an important model in financial management.

Risk averse investors will accept risk provided that they are compensated for it by an adequate return. However if they could reduce their risk without a reduction in return this would be even better.

This is possible by the process of diversification.

When an investment (a) is added to an existing portfolio (b) the risk of the new portfolio formed will usually be less than a simple weighted average of the individual risks of (a) and (b) alone.

Some investments might do even more than this. Some investments can be added to an existing portfolio to give a new portfolio of lower risk than the existing portfolio. This is because of the way that the investments' returns interact with each other in different sets of economic conditions – "states of the world". Whether such investments are acceptable will depend on the effect that they have on the return of the existing portfolio.

Portfolio theory works by looking at the impact that a new investment will have on an existing portfolio. The risk/return characteristics of the existing portfolio are compared to those of the portfolio if the new investment were included.

Correlation coefficient of investment returns

The extent to which investment risk can be reduced by building a portfolio of different investments depends on the **correlation of the returns from the different investments in the portfolio**.

The correlation of the returns from different investments can be measured statistically by a **correlation coefficient**, from an analysis of historical data about returns (or from probability estimates of future returns).

A correlation coefficient can range in value from +1 (perfect positive correlation) to – 1 (perfect negative correlation).

A correlation coefficient close to zero indicates very little correlation between investment returns.

Investment risk is reduced most effectively by having investments in a portfolio whose returns are negatively correlated, or where there is not much correlation.

1.3 Two-asset portfolio – Mathematics

Consider an appraisal where A is the existing portfolio and B is a new investment under consideration.

Expected return from the two-asset portfolio

The expected return from a two-asset portfolio is the weighted average of the returns from the two investments.

$$R_P = R_A w_a + R_B w_b$$

where:

R_P is the expected return from the two-asset portfolio
R_A is the expected return from investment A
R_B is the expected return from investment B
w_a is the proportion of investment A in the portfolio (for example, 40% = 0.40)
w_b is the proportion of investment B in the portfolio

Note that $w_a + w_b = 1$ (or 100%)

Standard deviation of return for a two-asset portfolio

The overall standard deviation of the return from a two-asset portfolio can be calculated using the following formula, which is **not** given to you in the formula sheet for the examination.

$$sp = \sqrt{s_a^2 w_a^2 + s_b^2 w_b^2 + 2w_a w_b \rho_{ab} s_a s_b}$$

where:

s_a and s_b are the standard deviation of returns for investment A and investment B

ρ_{ab} is the correlation coefficient of returns for investment A and investment B

Note:

$\rho_{ab} s_a s_b$ is the covariance of returns for investment A and investment B

Example

Suppose that the portfolio of an investor consists of 70% of investment A and 30% of investment B. The expected return is 7% for investment A and 9% for investment B. The standard deviation of returns for investment A is 2.19%, and for investment B is 4.10%, and the investments are correlated with a correlation coefficient of -0.98

The expected return from the portfolio is therefore:
(7% × 70%) + (9% × 30%) = 7.6%.

The standard deviation of the returns from this portfolio would be:

$$\sqrt{(2.19)^2(0.70)^2 + (4.10)^2(0.30)^2 + 2(0.70)(0.30)(-0.98)(2.19)(4.10)} = \sqrt{0.1676} = 0.41\%$$

The portfolio therefore has an expected return of 7.6% with a standard deviation of 0.41%.

The risk in this portfolio is significantly less than the risk from the two individual investments (whose standard deviations are 2.19% and 4.10%). This is largely due to the fact that the returns from the two investments have strong negative correlation.

1.4 Possible outcomes

If the risk and return characteristics of a portfolio are compared to those of the portfolio with a new investment there are a series of possible outcomes. Not all of these would allow a decision to be made:

RETURN	RISK	CONCLUSION
Improved by new investment	Risk lowered by new investment	Accept the investment – it improves the risk/return position
Improved by new investment	Stays the same	
Stays the same	Risk lowered by new investment	
Return reduced by new investment	Risk increased by new investment	Reject the investment – it will make the risk/return position less favourable
Stays the same	Risk increased by new investment	
Return reduced by new investment	Stays the same	
↓	↓	Unable to decide. It depends on whether the fall in return is compensated by the fall in risk
↑	↑	Unable to decide. It depends on whether the increase in return is thought to be adequate compensation for the increase in risk

Example

Suppose that an investor has a choice of selecting any of the following portfolios:

Portfolio	Expected return	Risk (= σ)
	%	%
A	6.0	4.0
B	7.0	3.0
C	9.0	5.5
D	8.0	6.0

- A normal (risk-averse) investor will not select Portfolio A, because Portfolio B offers a higher return than Portfolio A for less risk
- Similarly, a risk-averse investor will not select Portfolio D, because Portfolio C offers a higher return than Portfolio D for less risk
- It is not clear whether a risk-averse investor would select Portfolio B or Portfolio C, because Portfolio C offers a higher return for greater risk, and Portfolio B offers a lower return but less risk.

Capital asset pricing model (CAPM)

- Systematic and unsystematic risk
- Measuring systematic risk
- Using the CAPM
- The beta factor of a portfolio
- Alpha factor
- Advantages and disadvantages of the CAPM
- Using the CAPM for capital investment appraisal
- International CAPM

2 Capital asset pricing model (CAPM)

The CAPM is a model that was derived mathematically from portfolio theory. You do not have to know the details of the derivation.

2.1 Systematic and unsystematic risk

Investors can reduce their investment risk by diversifying. However, not all risk can be eliminated, and there will be some risk that cannot be eliminated by diversification.

- When the economy is weak and in recession, returns from the market as whole are likely to fall. Diversification will not protect investors against falling returns from the market as a whole.
- Similarly, when the economy is strong, returns from the market as a whole are likely to rise. Investors in all or most shares in the market will benefit from the general increase in returns.

This led to the idea that there are two types of risk:

- **Unsystematic risk; and**
- **Systematic risk (market risk)**

Unsystematic risk

This is risk that is unique to individual investments or securities, that can be eliminated through diversification.

Systematic risk (market risk).

This is risk that cannot be diversified away, because it is risk that affects the market as a whole, and all investments in the market in the same way.

- A security might have a higher systematic risk than the market portfolio. This means that when the average market return rises, due perhaps to growth in the economy, the return from the security should rise by an even larger amount.

Similarly, if the average market return falls due to deterioration in business conditions, the return from the security will fall by an even larger amount.

- A security might have a lower systematic risk than the market portfolio, so that when the average market return rises, the return from the security will rise, but by a smaller amount. Similarly, when the average market return falls, the return from the security will also fall, but by a smaller amount.

This distinction together with two assumptions underpins the CAPM. The two assumptions are:

- Capital markets are perfect; and
- All investors are rational (i.e. they will try to optimise the risk/return profile of their investments by maximising return for a given risk or minimising the risk of a given return.

Based on these assumptions all investors will hold well diversified portfolios. They have perfect information and understanding so will realise that they can avoid all unsystematic risk in this way.

Implications

The only risk for which investors should want a higher return is systematic risk. This is the risk that the market as a whole will perform worse or better than expected.

All investors should appraise investments in the same way by asking *"What level of return do I want to compensate me for the systematic risk of the investment?"*

This question is answered by the CAPM equation.

$$R_S = R_f + \beta_S (R_m - R_f)$$

This is the equation of the security market line:

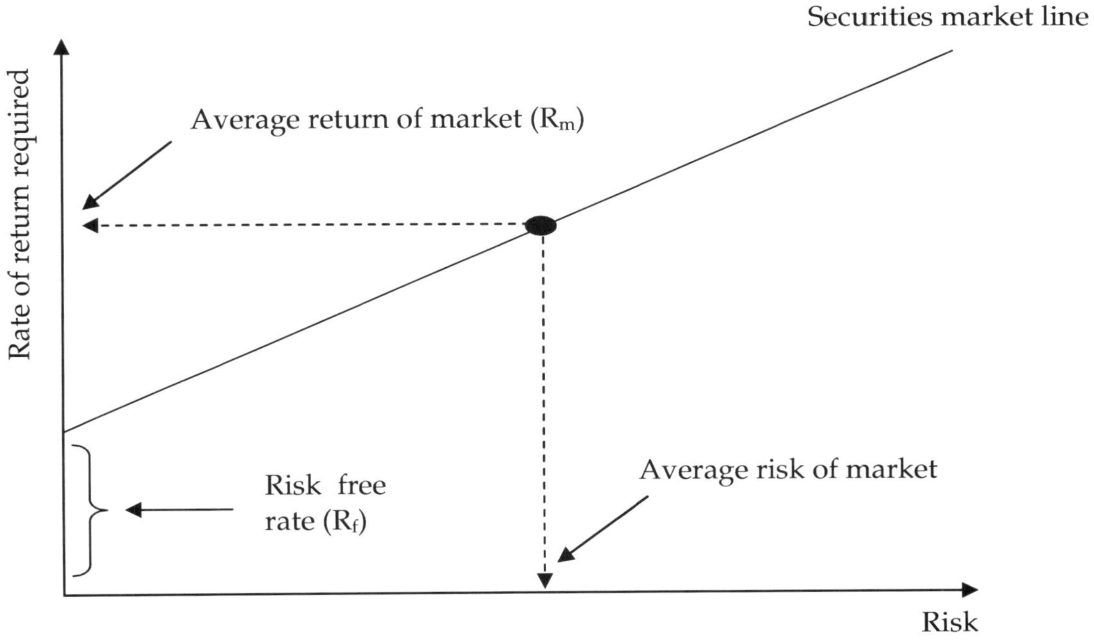

2.2 Measuring systematic risk

Systematic risk is the risk of an investment relative to that of the market. The systematic risk for an individual security is measured as a beta factor.

In practice, least squares regression analysis is used to plot a line of best fit on a plot of returns from a share vs returns from the market. This line is called the security characteristic line. β is the slope of this line

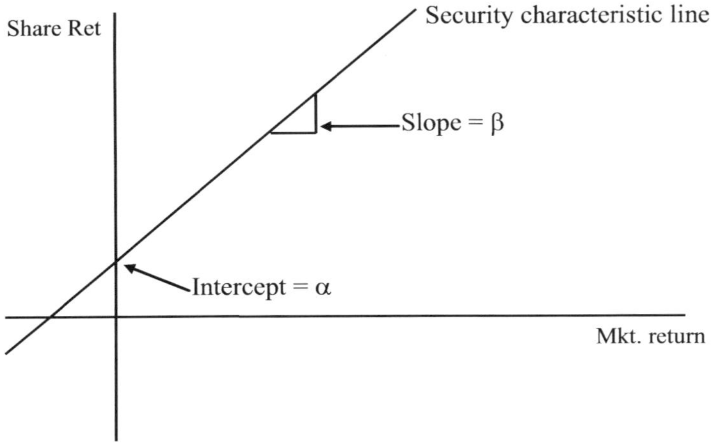

Equations

This is a measurement of the systematic risk of the security, in relation to the systematic risk of the market portfolio as a whole.

The following equations can be used to calculate a security's beta factor:

$$\beta_s = \frac{\sigma_s}{\sigma_m}$$

$$\beta_s = \frac{COV_{sm}}{\sigma_m^2}$$

$$\beta_s = \frac{\rho_{sm} \times \sigma_s}{\sigma_m}$$

where:

Cov_{sm} = the covariance of returns from Security S with the returns from the market as a whole

σ_m is the standard deviation of returns for the market portfolio

σ_s is the standard deviation of returns for Security S

ρ_{sm} is the correlation coefficient for returns from Security S with returns from the market as a whole.

Example

The annual returns on shares in Company Z have a standard deviation of 3.58% and the standard deviation of market returns is 2.72%. The correlation coefficient for returns on shares in Company Z and returns for the market as a whole is + 0.85.

The beta factor for shares in Company Z is:

$$\beta_Z = \frac{0.85 \times 3.58}{2.72} = 1.12$$

Interpreting □ values

A beta factor describes a share's degree of sensitivity to general changes in the market's returns, caused by systematic risk.

An individual security with a Beta value of 1 has the same systematic risk as the market.

When the beta factor for an individual security is greater than 1, the increase or fall in its expected return (ignoring unsystematic risk) will be greater than any given increase or decrease in the market return.

When the beta factor for a security is less than 1, the security is relatively low-risk. The expected increase or decrease in its expected return (ignoring unsystematic risk) will be less than any given increase or decrease in the market return.

The beta factor for a risk-free security = 0.

2.3 Using the CAPM

The formula for the capital asset pricing model is used to calculate the expected return from a security (ignoring unsystematic risk).

$$R_S = R_f + \beta_S (R_m - R_f)$$

where:

R_S is the expected return from a security S
R_f is the risk-free rate of return
R_m is the expected market return
β_S is the beta factor for security S.

Example

The risk-free rate of return is 4% and the return on the market portfolio is 8.5%. What is the expected return from shares in companies X and Y if:

- the beta factor for company X shares is 1.25
- the beta factor for company Y shares is 0.90?

Answer

Expected return, security X = 4% + 1.25(8.5 – 4)% = 9.625%.

Expected return, security Y = 4% + 0.90(8.5 – 4)% = 8.05%.

Example

The following information is available:

Risk-free rate of return	4.0%
Expected market return	7.5%
Standard deviation of market return	1.4%
Standard deviation of return from shares in company ABC	2.5%
Correlation coefficient for returns from shares in Company ABC and returns from the market as a whole	0.90

Required

(a) Calculate the beta factor for Company ABC shares.

(b) Estimate the returns currently expected from Company ABC shares.

Answer

(a) $\beta_{ABC} = \frac{0.90 \times 2.5}{1.4} = 1.607$

(b) Expected return, shares in Company ABC = 4% + 1.607(7.5 – 4)% = 9.6245%.

2.4 The beta factor of a portfolio

A portfolio of investments containing just a few securities will not be fully representative of the market portfolio. Its systematic risk will therefore be different from the systematic risk for the market as a whole.

The relationship between the systematic risk of a small portfolio and the systematic risk of the market as a whole can be measured as a beta factor for the portfolio.

A beta factor for a portfolio is the weighted average value of the beta factors of all the individual securities in the portfolio. The weighting allows for the relative proportions of each security in the portfolio.

Example

A portfolio contains five securities. The proportions of each security in the portfolio and the beta factor of each security are as follows:

Security	Proportion of the portfolio	Beta factor of the security
1	10%	1.20
2	25%	0.90
3	15%	0.96
4	30%	1.15
5	20%	1.06

The beta factor for the portfolio is calculated as follows:

Security	Proportion of the portfolio	Beta factor of the security	
	p	β	pβ
1	10%	1.20	0.120
2	25%	0.90	0.225
3	15%	0.96	0.144
4	30%	1.15	0.345
5	20%	1.06	0.212
Beta factor for the portfolio			1.046

2.5 Alpha factor

The CAPM assumes that capital markets are perfect. This is not the case. In practice a security might yield more or less than its expected return (based on the CAPM). The difference is an abnormal return. This abnormal return is measured as the alpha factor. The alpha factor is a measure of the model's response to capital market imperfections and is simply the balancing figure in the following formula:

$$R_S = R_f + \beta_S (R_m - R_f) + \alpha_S$$

Example

The return on shares of company A is 11%, but its normal beta factor is 1.10. The risk-free rate of return is 5% and the market rate of return is 8%.

There is an abnormal return on the shares:

$$11\% = 5\% + 1.10\ (8 - 5)\% + \alpha$$

$$\therefore\ \alpha = 2.7\%.$$

2.6 Advantages and disadvantages of the CAPM

The CAPM is based on some simplifying assumptions. For example, the CAPM assumes:

- A perfect capital market
- Uniformity of investor expectations
- All forecasts (expectations) are made in the context of just one time period.

In spite of these simplifying assumptions, the CAPM appears to be reliable in practice.

Advantages of CAPM	Weaknesses of CAPM
It provides a measurable relationship between risk and return.	It can be difficult to estimate values for the risk-free rate and market rate of return, and the beta factor for a security.
It can be used to estimate the cost of capital for securities, notably equity shares.	It focuses on systematic risk only and ignores unsystematic risk. Unsystematic risk is significant for an investor who does not have a well-diversified portfolio.
It can be adapted to establishing a required (risk-adjusted) DCF return on capital investments by a company.	It makes no distinction between the ways in which a security provides its return (for example dividends or share price increase).

2.7 Using the CAPM for capital investment appraisal

The CAPM can be used by companies for capital investment appraisal. In this situation it must be remembered that the company is spending money for the shareholders. An alternative to making the investment might be to pay a dividend instead.

The company then should look at any investment as a shareholder would. The company is acting as the shareholders' agent. The company should ask the same question each shareholder would i.e. *"What level of return would the shareholders want to compensate them for the systematic risk of the investment?"*

Some types of capital investment projects are more risky than others. For example, the systematic risk of investing in the manufacture of cars may be higher than the systematic risk of investing in a retailing business. Similarly, the risk of investing in one country may be higher than the risk of investing in another country, due to differences in the business environment or economic conditions.

If a beta factor for a particular project can be established, a risk-adjusted cost of capital can be applied to the project. This risk-adjusted cost of capital should then be used to calculate the project NPV.

For example, if a project's beta factor is 1.30, the risk-free rate of return is 4.5% and the market rate of return is 7%, the discount rate used to calculate the project NPV would be:

4.5% + 1.30 (7 – 4.50)% = 7.75%, say 8%.

Commentary

The CAPM is only valid for well diversified investors. The above approach is acceptable for companies whose shareholders are well diversified. The usual assumption is that listed companies are owned by shareholders who are well diversified. A small private company would not be. In the latter case CAPM might be an inappropriate basis to appraise capital projects.

2.8 International CAPM

The capital asset pricing model is usually applied to a single stock market, and the market portfolio represents all the securities that are traded on that market. However, the same general principles of the CAPM can be applied to international investment.

International investors build a portfolio of investments that enables them to invest world-wide. The 'world market' consists of all the main securities, such as company shares, traded in different stock markets throughout the world.
International investors may wish to monitor returns from the 'world market', and may wish to assess returns from individual securities by comparing their return with the expected return from the world market as a whole.

An international capital asset pricing model for individual securities would be:

$$R_S = R_f + \beta_S (R_{WM} - R_f)$$

where R_{WM} is the average return from the world market as a whole.

Problems with the international CAPM

There are several problems with using an international CAPM.

- A risk-free rate of return has to be selected, but which securities are risk-free? Returns on government securities vary between different countries. A risk-free security for an international CAPM might be the returns on government securities in a stable currency.
- The world market portfolio has to be identified. The world market may be based on an international (world market) stock index, but there may be different views about what should be in the portfolio.
- In practice, it is difficult for many investors to acquire a portfolio of investments that represents the world market. However, many institutional investors do attempt to do this, by:
  - investing directly in stock markets around the world
  - investing in international (global) companies, and

- possibly also investing in collective investments, such as mutual funds and open-ended investment companies (OEICs).
- whether that investment is under or overvalued.

Q&A

Practice questions

Contents

Contents

Contents

1 Corporate social responsibility

(a) What are the main issues that might be covered by a company's policy on corporate social responsibility?

(b) What types of company are most likely to face CSR risks?

(c) What is the nature of CSR risk?

2 Corporate governance

(a) What is the main purpose of statutory or voluntary codes of corporate governance?

(b) What are the main problems or issues that a code of corporate governance might be expected to cover?

3 Dividends and retentions

The directors of an all-equity company are considering the company's policy on dividends and retentions. The cost of capital is 9% and the company is able to invest in new capital projects that will earn this return. The company's shares are quoted and traded on a major stock market.

In the year just ended, the earnings per share were $2.00 per share. The company pays a dividend annually, and is about to pay a dividend for the year just ended on the basis of its selected dividend and retentions policy.

Required

Suggest what the company's share price might be if the directors select a policy of paying annual dividends that are equal to:

(a) 25% of earnings

(b) 50% of earnings

(c) 70% of earnings.

4 Financial plan

The board of directors of NNW have asked for a four-year financial plan to be prepared for Year 5 to Year 8. They have approved the following assumptions for the plan:

(1) Sales growth will be at the rate of 6% each year into the foreseeable future.

(2) Cash operating costs will be 70% of sales.

(3) Investment in new plant and equipment is expected to grow in line with the growth in sales, and the net book value of plant and equipment will grow at the same rate.

(4) Tax-allowable depreciation will grow in line with the growth in sales.

(5) Inventory, receivables, cash and trade payables will also increase at the same rate as the growth in sales.

(6) There will be no change in long-term borrowing. Interest on the bank overdraft will be payable at 7%. The interest charge for bank overdraft in the income statement each year should be calculated on the opening bank overdraft at the beginning of the year.

(7) Tax on company profits will be 30%.

(8) The company policy is to pay dividends as a constant percentage amount of earnings. This policy will not change.

(9) The cost of equity capital has been estimated as 12%.

The income statement of NNW for the year to 31st December Year 4 is as follows:

	$ million
Sales	1,800
Cash operating costs	(1,260)
EBITDA	540
Tax allowable depreciation	(160)
Earnings before interest	380
Interest	(78)
Profit before tax	302
Tax at 30%	(91)
Profit after tax	211
Dividends	(135)
Retained profit	76

The balance sheet of NNW as at the end of Year 4 is as follows:

	$ m	$ m
Plant and equipment		2,020
Current assets		
Inventory	520	
Receivables	640	
Cash	30	
		1,190
Total assets		3,210
Share capital (shares of $0.05 each)		450
Reserves		1,200
		1,650
Long term loan at 8%		800
Trade payables		450
Bank overdraft		310
		3,210

Required

(a) Prepare a financial plan for Years 5 to 8, showing the profit after tax, dividends, retained profits for each year and a summary balance sheet as at the end of each year.

(b) Calculate the expected free cash flow in each year of the financial plan.

(c) Comment briefly on the financial plan.

(d) Use the dividend growth model to estimate a market value per share as at the end of Year 8 (the end of the financial planning period). State any assumptions that you make in your estimate.

5 DCF exercises

(a) Calculate the NPV of an investment with the following estimated cash flows, assuming a cost of capital of 8%:

Years	Annual cash flow
	$
0	(3,000,000)
1 – 4	500,000
5 – 8	400,000
9 – 10	300,000
11 onwards in perpetuity (per year)	100,000

(b) The cash flows for an investment project have been estimated at current prices, as follows:

Year	Equipment	Revenue	Running costs
	$	$	$
0	(900,000)		
1		800,000	(400,000)
2		800,000	(400,000)
3		600,000	(350,000)
4	200,000	400,000	(300,000)

It is expected that the cash flows will differ because of inflation. The annual rates of inflation are expected to be:

- Equipment value: 4% per year
- Revenue: 3% per year
- Running costs: 5% per year.

The cost of capital is 12%

Required

(i) Calculate the NPV of the project ignoring inflation.

(ii) Calculate the NPV of the project allowing for inflation.

6 DCF and tax

A company is considering whether or not to invest in a four-year investment project. The project will require the purchase of equipment costing $800,000. This will have an estimated residual value of $200,000 at the end of Year 4. The equipment will be depreciated by the straight-line method.

The profits before interest and tax from the project are expected to be $250,000 each year. Tax is payable at 30% one year in arrears.

The equipment will qualify for capital allowances (tax depreciation allowances) of 25% each year, using the reducing balance method. The first claim for an allowance would be made against Year 0 profits.

The after-tax cost of capital is 15%.

Required

Calculate the NPV of the project.

7 Free cash flow

A company expects to make profits before interest and tax next year of $3 million.

Other budgeted information is as follows:

	$
Interest charges	400,000
Taxation	600,000
Dividend payments	1,200,000
Depreciation charges	550,000
Increase in working capital	150,000
Capital expenditure:	
Asset replacement expenditure	1,000,000
Discretionary expenditure	700,000

Required

Calculated the expected amount of free cash flow next year.

8 Two-asset portfolio

An investor is planning to invest in two securities, Security X and Security Y. The expected return from each security will depend on the state of the economy, as follows:

State of the economy	Probability	Return from Security X	Return from Security Y
		%	%
Strong	0.25	15	20
Fair	0.60	10	8
Weak	0.15	2	(6)

Required

(a) Calculate the mean and standard deviation of the expected return from Security X.

(b) Calculate the mean and standard deviation of the expected return from Security Y.

(c) Calculate the covariance of the returns from Security X and Security Y. The formula for a covariance is:

$$\text{Cov}_{x,y} = \Sigma r(x - \bar{x})(y - \bar{y})$$

(d) Calculate the correlation coefficient for returns from Security X and Security Y, for a portfolio consisting of 50% of the funds invested in Security X and 50% of the funds invested in Security Y. The formula for correlation coefficient is:

$$\frac{\rho_{x,y} = \text{Cov}_{x,y}}{\sigma_x \times \sigma_y}$$

where:

σ_x = the standard deviation of returns from Security X

σ_y = the standard deviation of returns from Security Y

Comment on the correlation coefficient.

(e) Calculate expected return, the variance and standard deviation of a portfolio consisting of 50% of the funds invested in Security X and 50% of the funds invested in Security Y. The formula for correlation coefficient is:

$a^2(\text{Variance X})^2 + (1 - a)^2(\text{Variance Y})^2 + 2a(1 - a)\ \text{Cov}_{x,y}$

where:

a = the proportion of the portfolio invested in Security X

(1 – a) = the proportion of the portfolio invested in Security Y

Variance X = the variance of the returns from Security X

Variance Y = the variance of the returns from Security Y

(f) Calculate expected return, the variance and standard deviation of a portfolio consisting of 80% of the funds invested in Security X and 20% of the funds invested in Security Y.

9 Risk and return

A divisional manager's attitude to investing in new projects is affected by his attitude to risk. He is prepared to invest in a project that is more risky, provided that it offers a higher expected return.

He is currently considering four mutually exclusive projects, for which the estimated returns and risk are as follows:

Project	Estimated project NPV	Risk (σ)
Project 1	80% chance of + \$4 million, 20% chance of + \$2 million	0.80
Project 2	70% chance of + \$5 million, 30% chance of + \$1.5 million	1.60
Project 3	60% chance of + \$6 million, 40% chance of + \$1 million	Not yet calculated
Project 4	50% chance of + \$8 million, 50% chance of – \$1 million	Not yet calculated

Required

(a) Calculate the risk with Project 3 and Project 4.

(b) Suggest which of the four projects the divisional manager will select.

10 Coefficient of variation

A multinational company is planning to invest in two developing countries, and it will invest equal amounts of capital in each country. It is looking at returns and risk in each of three possible countries that might be selected for investment.

The company is particularly concerned about the political risk in each country, and the threat of political risk to its expected returns. A firm of management consultants has produced the following statistical estimates of expected returns ad political risk in each of the countries.

Country	Expected investment return (%)	Political risk (%)
Country A	16	25
Country B	22	36
Country C	30	45

The expected return from investing in any of the three countries is independent of the returns that would be obtained from the other countries.

Required

(a) Calculate the risk, return and coefficient of variation of the following three investment portfolios:

(i) 50% in Country A, 50% in Country B

(ii) 50% in Country A, 50% in Country C

(iii) 50% in Country B, 50% in Country C

(b) Comment on the results.

11 Capital market line

The risk-free rate of return is 3%. The return on the market portfolio is 9%.

Suggest how an investor should create a portfolio to provide a return of 7% with minimum risk.

12 Obtaining a beta factor

A beta factor will be estimated for Security Y from the following data.

Month	Returns from the market portfolio	Returns from Security Y
	%	%
1	+ 2	+ 3
2	– 1	– 2
3	– 2	– 2
4	+ 3	+ 5
EV of monthly return	+ 0.5	+ 1.0

Required

(a) Use this data to calculate:

(i) the standard deviation of the monthly return from the market portfolio and

(ii) the standard deviation of the monthly return from Security Y.

(b) Calculate the correlation coefficient for the market returns and the returns from Security Y. This is calculated as:

$$\rho_{m,y} = \frac{Cov_{m,y}}{\sigma_m \times \sigma_y}$$

where:

σ_m = the standard deviation of returns from the market portfolio

σ_y = the standard deviation of returns from Security Y

The formula for the covariance is:

$$Cov_{x,y} = \Sigma(x - \bar{x})(y - \bar{y})$$

(c) Use this data to calculate the beta factor for Security Y. You can use either of the following formulas.

$$\beta = \frac{Cov_{m,y}}{Var_m}$$

Alternatively

$$\beta = \frac{\rho_{m,y} \times \sigma_y}{\sigma_m}$$

13 WACC

A company has just paid an annual dividend of $0.18. Investors expect the annual dividend to grow by 3% each year in perpetuity, The current share price is $1.55 and the total market value of the company's shares is $1,200,000.

The company has debt capital on which the yield is 7.8% before tax. The rate of tax is 30%. The total value of the company's debt is $350,000.

Calculate the weighted average cost of capital. Use the dividend growth model to estimate the cost of equity.

14 Optimal WACC

A company has estimated that its cost of debt capital varies according to the level of gearing, as follows:

Gearing	Cost of debt
	%
20	5.0
30	5.4
40	5.8
50	6.5
60	7.2

Gearing is measured as the market value of the company's debt as a proportion of the total market value of its equity plus debt.

The rate of tax is 30%. The ungeared equity beta factor for the company is 0.90.

The risk-free rate of return is 4% and the return on the market portfolio is 9%

Required

Identify the optimal gearing level and WACC.

15 Change in gearing

A company is all-equity financed, with 60 million shares. The current market value of the shares is $5 each. The company currently makes an annual profit before interest and tax of $40 million. There are no expectations of growth in annual profits.

The company is considering whether to raise $100 million in debt. The pre-tax interest rate would be 8% and the tax rate is 25%. The debt capital would be used to repurchase and cancel some equity shares.

Required

Use appropriate Modigliani-Miller formulas to estimate the effect the issue of debt and repurchase of shares would have on the weighted average cost of capital (WACC).

16 Geared beta

A company has $1,500,000 in equity capital and $500,000 in debt capital (at market values). The beta value of the equity is 1.126 and the beta of the debt capital is 0.

The risk-free cost of capital is 5% and the market portfolio return is 11%. The tax rate is 30%.

Required

(a) Calculate the current weighted average cost of capital (WACC).

(b) Calculate what the WACC would be if the company consisted of 60% equity and 40% debt.

17 APV method

A company in the engineering industry is considering making an investment in a telecommunications project. The investment will cost $2,000,000, and will be financed by a new issue of $1,000,000 in equity and a new issue of $1,000,000 debt capital.

The company's current gearing level is 30% debt and 70% equity.

The telecommunications industry has an average industry equity beta of 1.30625. The average gearing ratio in the industry is 20% debt and 80% equity.

The rate of taxation is 25%.

The risk-free rate of return is 4% and the average market return is 9%. The company's debt is risk-free.

The cash flows from the project before taxation are expected to be:

Year	Cash flow
	$
1	100,000
2	140,000
3	120,000

Tax is payable one year in arrears.
You should ignore tax depreciation (capital allowances) on the initial investment.
The costs of raising the equity capital will be 4% of the amount raised. The costs of raising the debt capital will be 3% of the amount raised. The debt will be in the form of a three-year loan, and the principal will be repaid in full at the end of Year 3.

Required

Calculate:

(a) the NPV of the project, using the Modigliani and Miller formulas to derive a cost of capital for the project

(b) calculate the adjusted present value (APV) of the project.

18 Adjusted Present Value

Harvey is an aluminium engineering company. It now wishes to diversify its operations into the plastics business. The proposed investment project will require the purchase of a machine costing $450,000. This will produce cash flows of $220,000 for each of the three years of its life, and it will have no residual value at the end of that time.

It is proposed to finance the purchase of the machine with a mixture of debt and equity capital. 40% of the cost will be financed by a three-year loan that will be repaid in three equal instalments. The remaining 60% of the cost will be financed by a placing of new equity.

Issue costs, which are tax-allowable, will be 5% for the equity and 2% for the debt, measured as a percentage of the net finance raised.

The plastics industry has an average equity beta of 1.356 and an average debt: equity ratio of 1:5, at market values. Harvey's current equity beta is 1.8 and 20% of its capital (at market value) consists of long-term debt which is regarded as risk-free.

The risk-free rate is 10% per annum and the expected return on an average market portfolio is 15%. Corporation tax is at 35%, payable one year in arrears. The machine will attract a 70% capital allowance in the first year, and the balance will be allowable against tax over the next three years, at an equal amount in each year.

Required

Carry out an appraisal of the investment using each of the three following methods:

(a) NPV of the project, using the company's current weighted average cost of capital (WACC)

(b) NPV of the project, using a WACC adjusted for business risk and financial risk

(c) the adjusted present value (APV) of the project.

19 More APV

Pobol Company specialises in business consultancy, but its directors are considering an investment in software development, which would represent a major diversification of the company's business activities. The following draft financial proposal has been prepared:

Year	**0**	**1**	**2**	**3**	**4**
	$000	$000	$000	$000	$000
Revenue		6,800	7,800	8,800	9,200
Cash operating costs		5,500	6,600	7,100	7,500
Allocated head office costs		100	150	150	200
Royalty payments	600	500	400	300	200
Market research costs	120	-	-	-	-
	720	6,100	7,150	7,550	7,900
Expenditure on equipment	3,000				
Working capital	400				

The following information is also available:

(1) The project will have a six-year life.

(2) All prices are calculated in money terms, allowing for inflation. After Year 4, it is expected that revenues and cash operating costs will remain unchanged in real terms, but will increase at the rate of inflation which is expected to be 3% per year. Royalty payments are expected to be $200,000 per year in Years 5 and 6.

(3) Head office cash flows will increase as a consequence of the investment by $50,000 per year in Years 1 – 3 and by $60,000 per year in Years 4 – 6.

(4) The market research costs in Year 0 have already been incurred.

(5) Highly-skilled consultancy staff will have to be switched to managing the project, resulting in lost contribution of $100,000 per year in Years 1 and 2.

(6) The working capital investment will remain unchanged. The investment in equipment and working capital will be financed by a new six-year loan at 6% interest. Issue costs for the loan will be 2% and are not tax-allowable.

(7) The cash for the royalty payments and market research in Year 0 come from internally-generated cash flows.

(8) Tax is payable at the rate of 25%, and is payable in the same year that the tax liability arises.

(9) Tax-allowable depreciation will be 20% in Year 1 and will then be a constant amount for the next five years.

(10) The average equity beta of companies in the software sector that Pobol Company is considering is 1.39. The market return is 10% and the risk-free interest rate is 6%.

(11) The average gearing of companies in the software sector that Pobol Company is considering is 80% equity and 20% debt.

Required

Calculate the adjusted present value (APV) of this project.

20 Cash flows from a foreign project

A UK company intends to invest in a foreign country, Frankland. The cost of the investment will be 45 million francs, which is £9 million in sterling at the current exchange rate. The entire cost of the investment will be paid at the beginning of the project.

A DCF analysis has been carried out on the project's expected cash flows in Frankland, and the NPV is positive.

The project is expected to generate the following dividend payments to the company in the UK:

Year	Francs
1	10 million
2	20 million
3	25 million
4	10 million

The current exchange rate is £1 = 5 francs. The expected annual rate of inflation in the UK for the next four years is 3% and in Frankland it is 5%.

Tax in the UK is 30%, and will be payable one year in arrears of dividend receipts. The company's weighted average cost of capital is 9%.

Required

Calculate the NPV of the company's expected sterling cash flows, to decide whether the project should be undertaken.

21 Foreign investment

Entity Green is a company whose domestic currency is dollars. It is considering an investment in a country, Francia, where the domestic currency is Francs (FR).

The investment will involve buying equipment in the foreign country at a cost of 1,000,000 Francs. The currency to make the purchase will be bought spot in the FX market.

The equipment and the project will have a four-year life. At the end of this time, the equipment will have no residual value. The equipment will attract an allowance for tax purposes of 25% of its cost each year. The first capital allowance will be claimed against profits in Year 1.

The cash profits from the project will be $500,000 in each of the four years. Tax is payable at 40% and is paid one year in arrears of the profits to which they relate. In addition, Entity Green will incur expenditure of $25,000 at the beginning of the project in its own currency.

There are foreign exchange restrictions in the country, and only 50% of the profits after tax each year can be paid to any shareholder in another country. The balance of the profits from the project can be paid out as a dividend to Entity Green at the end of Year 5.

Entity Green has a cost of capital of 10%, but a cost of capital of 16% is considered appropriate for evaluating the investment cash flows.

The current exchange rate is $1 = FR3.00. However, the rate of inflation is expected to be 10% in each year in the Francia and 4% each year in Entity Green's country.

Required

(a) Calculate the NPV of the project in the currency of the investment, using a discount rate appropriate to the investment.

(b) Calculate the expected annual dividend payments, in Francs.

(c) Calculate the dollar value of the expected annual dividend payments.

(d) Evaluate the NPV of the investment in dollars, using an appropriate discount rate.

22 Valuation

A company has just paid an annual dividend of 38. The board of directors has a target of increasing the share price to 800, and is considering policies for investment and growth.

Shareholders expect a return on their investment of 10% per year.

Required

Calculate the annual expected growth rate in dividends that would be required to raise the share price to 800. Use the dividend growth model to make your estimate.

23 Valuation of bonds

Assume that bond investors require a return of 9% per year on their investments.

Required

Estimate the market value of the following bonds:

(a) Irredeemable 7.5% bonds that pay interest annually.

(b) Bonds paying coupon interest of 6% per year annually, that are redeemable at par in four years' time.

(c) Bonds paying coupon interest of 10%, redeemable at par after three years, where interest is payable every six months.

Notes:

An annual cost of capital of 9% is equal to a six-monthly cost of capital of 4.4%.

DCF factor at 4.4%, periods 1 – 7 = 5.914

DCF factor at 4.4%, periods 1 – 8 = 6.623

(d) A convertible bond with a coupon of 5% and interest payable annually: these bonds are convertible after three years into equity shares at the rate of 20 shares for every $100 nominal value of bonds. The expected share price in three years' time is $7.

24 Annuities and bond prices

(a) Calculate the value of the following bonds:

(i) a zero coupon bond redeemable at par in ten years' time

(ii) a bond with an 8% coupon, with interest payable half-yearly, and redeemable at par after ten years.

Assume that the yield required by investors is 5%, and that this is 2.5% each half year for the purpose of valuing the 8% coupon bond.

(b) Calculate the value of both bonds in part (a) of the question if the yield required by investors goes up by 1%, to 6% for the zero coupon bond and 3% each half year for the 8% coupon bond.

25 EVA

A group of companies has $8,000,000 of equity capital and $4,000,000 of long-term debt capital.

Its assets include:

(a) development expenditure of $500,000

(b) goodwill $400,000, which is $1,200,000 at cost less cumulative impairment of $800,000.

During a financial year, net profit before interest and tax is $2,100,000. Interest charges are $300,000 and taxation is $450,000.

The company's weighted average cost of capital is 12%.

Required

On the basis of this data, calculate the economic value added (EVA) for the year.

26 MM, gearing and company valuation

A company has 4,000,000 equity shares in issue. The shares have a current market value of $10 each. The company is considering whether to issue $15,000,000 of debt finance and use the cash to buy back and cancel some equity shares. The tax rate is 30%.

According to Modigliani and Miller, if the company decided to issue the debt capital and repurchase shares, what would be:

(a) the total value of the geared company, and

(b) the value of equity in the company?

27 Acquisition

Big Entity is considering a takeover bid for Little Entity, another company in the same industry. Little is expected to have earnings next year of $86,000.

If Big acquires Little, the expected results from Little will be as follows:

	Year after the acquisition		
	Year 1	**Year 2**	**Year 3**
	$	$	$
Sales	200,000	280,000	320,000
Cash costs/expenses	120,000	160,000	180,000
Capital allowances	20,000	30,000	40,000
Interest charges	10,000	10,000	10,000
Cash flows to replace assets and finance growth	25,000	30,000	35,000

From Year 4 onwards, it is expected that the annual cash flows from Little will increase by 4% each year in perpetuity.

Tax is payable at the rate of 30%, and the tax is paid in the same year as the profits to which the tax relates.

If Big acquires Little, it estimates that its gearing after the acquisition will be 35% (measured as the value of its debt capital as a proportion of its total equity plus debt). Its cost of debt is 7.4% before tax. Big has an equity beta of 1.60.

The risk-free rate of return is 6% and the return on the market portfolio is 11%.

Required

(a) Suggest what the offer price for Little should be if Big chooses to value Little on a forward P/E multiple of 8.0 times.

(b) Calculate a cost of capital for Big.

(c) Suggest what the offer price for Little might be using a DCF-based valuation.

28 Takeover

Flat Company intends to make a takeover bid for Slope Company, a company in the same industry. The initial offer will be to exchange every 3 shares in Slope for 2 new shares in Flat.

The most recent annual data for the two companies is shown below.

	Flat	**Slope**
	$000	$000
Sales revenue	7,619	6,000
Operating costs	4,962	3,480
Tax allowable depreciation	830	700
Earnings before interest and taxation	1,827	1,820
Interest	410	860
Profit before tax	1,417	960
Tax at 30%	425	288
	992	673
Dividends	500	410
Retained earnings	492	263
Annual replacement capital expenditure	920	790

Other information

	Flat	**Slope**
Expected annual growth in sales, operating costs including depreciation, replacement capital expenditure and dividends for the next 4 years	5%	4%
Expected annual growth in these items from year 5 onwards	3%	2%
Gearing, measured as the ratio of debt to debt plus equity, (both debt and equity measured at market value)	25%	40%
Market price per share (cents)	320	154
Number of shares in issue (millions)	6	9
Market cost of fixed interest debt	7%	8%
Equity beta	1.20	1.35

The risk-free rate of return is 5% and the market return is 11%.

The takeover will result in some cost savings in operations so that the earnings before interest and taxation of the combined group would be $4,100,000 in Year 1 after the takeover, and growth in sales, costs, depreciation and replacement capital expenditure would by 5% per year for the following three years and then 4% per year from Year 5 onwards.

The senior financial manager of Flat Company has been assessing the value of the takeover bid for the shareholders of both companies, and has decided to use free cash flow analysis as a basis for valuing the companies before and after the takeover. He believes that the total equity value of the group after the takeover will be significantly higher than the sum of the current equity values of the two separate companies.

The weighted average cost of the combined company should be calculated as the weighted average of the current cost of capital of the individual companies, weighted by the current market value of their debt and equity.

Required

(a) Using free cash flow analysis, and making any assumptions you consider necessary, calculate a value for:

(i) the current equity in Flat Company

(ii) the current equity in Slope Company

(iii) the equity in Flat Company after the takeover.

(b) Explain the limitations of your estimates in (a).

(c) Give your views as to whether the takeover bid is likely to have the support of the shareholders in (1) Flat Company and (2) Slope Company.

29 Interest rate parity

The following are spot exchange rates:

- US$/£1 (GBP/USD): 1.8000
- €/£1 (GBP/EUR): 1.5000
- US$/ €1 (EUR/USD): 1.2000

The rates of interest for the next three years are 2.5% on the euro, 3.5% on the US dollar and 5% on sterling.

Required

If the interest rate parity theory applies, what will the spot exchange rates:

(a) after one year

(b) after three years?

30 Foreign exchange

(a) A UK company expects to pay $750,000 to a supplier in three months' time. The following exchange rates are available for the dollar against sterling (GBP/USD):

Spot	1.8570	–	1.8580
3 months forward	1.8535	–	1.8543

The company is concerned about a possible increase in the value of the dollar during the next three months, and would like to hedge its FX risk.

Required

Explain how the exposure to currency risk might be hedged, and the amount that the UK company will have to pay in sterling in three months' time to settle its liability.

(b) A German company expects to receive US$450,000 from a customer in two months' time. It is concerned about the risk of a fall in the value of the dollar in the next two months, and would like to hedge the currency risk using a forward contract.

The following rates are available for the dollar against the euro (EUR/USD):

Spot	1.3015	–	1.3025	
2 months forward	25c	–	18c	premium

Required

Calculate the company's income in euros from settlement of the forward contract in two months' time.

31 Money market hedge

A UK company expects to receive $600,000 in six months' time from a customer. It intends to convert these dollars into sterling.

The current spot rate for the dollar against sterling (GBP/USD) is 1.8800. The six-month interest rates are 5% per year for sterling and 3.5% per year for the US dollar.

Required

(a) Show how the company can create a money market hedge for its exposure to a fall in the value of the dollar.

(b) Estimate what the exchange rate should be for a six-month forward contract, GBP/USD.

32 FRA

A company will need to borrow $5 million for six months in three months' time. It can borrow at LIBOR + 0.50%. It expects interest rates to rise before it borrows the money, and so has decided to use an FRA to hedge the risk.

The following FRA rates are available:

2v5	3.82	–	3.77
3v6	3.85	–	3.80
3v9	3.97	–	3.91
6v9	3.92	–	3.87

Required

(a) How would the company use an FRA to hedge its interest rate risk, and what effective interest rate would be obtained by the hedge.

(b) What is the difference between an FRA and an interest rate coupon swap?

33 Swap

A company has a bank loan of $8,000,000 on which it pays a floating rate of US LIBOR plus 1.25%. The company believes that interest rates will soon increase and remain high for the foreseeable future, and it would therefore like to switch its debt liabilities from floating rate to fixed rate.

The loan has four years remaining to maturity. A bank has quoted the following rates for four-year interest rate swaps in dollars:

5.20% - 5.25%

Required

Show how an interest rate swap can be used to switch from floating rate to fixed rate liabilities, and calculate what the effective fixed rate would be.

34 Credit arbitrage (1)

Company X can borrow for six years at a fixed rate of 7.25% or a variable rate of LIBOR plus 1.25%. Company Y can borrow for six years at a fixed rate of 8.00% or a variable rate of LIBOR plus 1.50%.

Company X wants to borrow at a floating rate and company Y wants to borrow at a fixed rate.

The rates available on six-year swaps are 6.27 – 6.30.

Required

Show how an interest rate swap can be used by both companies to reduce their borrowing costs.

35 Credit arbitrage (2)

Entity A has an AA credit rating and Entity B has a BBB- credit rating. Both companies want to raise the same amount of long-term debt capital. Entity A wants to borrow at a floating rate of interest and Entity B wants to borrow at a fixed rate.

They are able to borrow at the following rates:

	Fixed rate	Floating rate
Entity A	6.35%	LIBOR + 0.75%
Entity B	7.25%	LIBOR + 1.25%

A bank has identified an opportunity to arrange interest rate swaps with the companies. It would expect to receive a profit margin on the arrangement of 0.10% of the notional principal amount in the swap. The remaining benefits of the credit arbitrage should be shared equally between the two entities.

Required

Explain how the interest rate swaps might be arranged, and show the effective interest rate that will be paid by each entity as a result of the swap.

36 Currency swap

Small Company, a UK company, has an opportunity to invest in Zantland for three years, by setting up and operating an operations centre on behalf of the Zantland government. The cost of establishing the centre will be 3 million zants. At the end of the three years, the Zantland government will pay 6 million zants to purchase the centre from Small Company and take over the operations. During the three years that Small Company will operate the centre, the Zantland government will pay an annual fee of 200,000 zants. The entire operation will be free from tax.
The current exchange rate is £1 = 9.00 zants spot. There is no forward market in zants. Economic conditions in Zantland are unstable, and the expected inflation rate in the country over the next three years could be anywhere between 10% and 50%. Inflation is expected to be negligible in the UK.

A bank in Zantland has identified a Zantland company that would be interested in entering a currency swap with Small Company. The swap would involve the exchange of 3 million zants at the current spot rate, at the beginning and the end of the swap. An opportunity for credit arbitrage exists, because the rates at which Small company and the Zantland swap counterparty can borrow directly for three years are as follows.

	Sterling	Zants
Small Company	6.5%	ZIBOR + 2%
Zantland counterparty	8.5%	ZIBOR + 1.5%

ZIBOR is the Zantland inter-bank offered rate, which is usually set very close to the inflation rate in Zantland.

The bank would take an annual fee of 0.5% in sterling for arranging the swap, and Small Company would receive 75% of the net arbitrage benefit from the swap.

Required

(a) Suggest how a currency swap might be arranged between the counterparties, and indicate whether Small Company would arrange the swap if it decides to invest in the project.

(b) Making whatever assumptions you consider necessary and using a discount rate of 15%, recommend whether Small Company should undertake the project.

37 Currency futures

The euro/US dollar currency future is a contract for €125,000. It is priced in US dollars, and the tick size is $0.0001.

Currency futures are not normally used by companies to hedge currency risks. However, assume that a French company intends to use currency futures to hedge the following currency exposure.

It is now February. The French company has to make a payment of US$640,000 in May to a supplier.

The price of June euro/US dollar futures is currently 1.2800.

The company is concerned that the value of the dollar will increase in the next few months, and it therefore decides to use futures to hedge the exposure to currency risk.

Required

(a) How should the company hedge its currency risk with futures?

(b) Suppose that in May when the company must make the payment in dollars, the June futures price is 1.2690 and the spot rate (US$/€1) is 1.2710.

Show what will happen when the futures position is closed, and calculate the effective exchange rate that the company has obtained for the US$640,000.

38 More currency futures

The sterling/US dollar currency future is a contract for £62,500. It is priced in US dollars, and the tick size is $0.0001.

Currency futures are not normally used by companies to hedge currency risks. However, assume that a US company intends to use currency futures to hedge the following currency exposure.

It is now October. The US company expects to receive £400,000 in January from a customer.

The price of March sterling/US dollar futures is currently 1.8600.

The company is concerned that the value of sterling will fall in the next few months, and it therefore decides to use futures to hedge the exposure to currency risk.

Required

(a) How should the company hedge its currency risk with futures?

(b) Suppose that in January when the company receives the sterling payment, the March futures price is 1.8420 and the spot rate (US$/£1) is 1.8450.

Show what will happen when the futures position is closed, and calculate the effective exchange rate that the company has obtained for the £400,000.

39 Basis

It is 1st March. The current spot exchange rate for dollars against sterling (US$/£1) is 1.8540. The exchange rate is volatile, and the June futures price for sterling/US dollar futures is 1.8760.
Assume that the settlement date for the June futures contract is 30th June.

A company has used sterling/US dollar futures to hedge two currency exposures, one relating to a cash payment on 1st May and the other relating to a cash payment in mid-June.

Required

Calculate the expected futures price for June futures:

(a) at the end of the day's trading on 30th April, if the spot sterling/dollar rate is 1.8610

(b) at the end of the day's trading on 15th June, if the spot sterling/dollar rate is 1.8690.

40 Imperfect hedge and basis

It is 20th April. A US company expects to receive £625,000 in three months' time, in July and it wants to hedge its exposure to the risk of a fall in the value of the dollar by hedging with US dollar/sterling futures.

A dollar/sterling futures contract is for £62,500 and the value of a tick is £6.25.
On 20th April, the spot exchange rate is $1.8050/£1. The company deals in the September futures contracts at a price of 1.7800. Settlement date for the September futures is in five months' time exactly.

The US company receives the £625,000 on 20th July and immediately closes its futures position. The spot rate on 20th July is 1.7700 and the futures price is 1.7600.

Required

(a) To what extent does the futures position provide a hedge for the company against currency risk, between 20th April and 20th July? To do this, compare the gain or loss on the underlying currency exposure with the gain or loss on the futures position.

(b) Explain why the hedge is imperfect.

41 Currency hedge

It is now the end of July. A UK company expects the following receipts and payments in euros at the end of the month in three months' time (at the end of October):

Receipts	€540,000
Payments	€2,650,000

The company is concerned about the exposure to a risk of a movement in the sterling/euro exchange rate, and it has decided to hedge the exposure.

It is considering three methods of hedging the exposure:

(a) with a forward exchange contract

(b) using a money market hedge

(c) using currency futures.

Relevant data is as follows:

FX rates, €/£1			
Spot	1.4537	–	1.4542
3 months forward	1.4443	–	1.4448

3-month interest rates	**Borrow**	**Invest**
Sterling (UK)	6.2%	5.6%
Euro	3.8%	3.4%

Currency futures

Currency futures for sterling/euro are each for €100,000 and are priced in sterling.

Assume that the futures contracts mature at the end of the month.

Assume for the purpose of this question that when the futures position is closed at the end of October, the basis is 0.

Futures prices as at end of July	
September futures	0.6890
December futures	0.6929

Required

Calculate the net cost in sterling of hedging the currency risk:

(a) with a forward exchange contract

(b) using a money market hedge

(c) using currency futures.

42 Hedging with STIRS

It is now December.

A UK company wants to borrow £4.5 million in two months for a period of five months. The loan period will be from a date in February to a date in July.

It wants to use short-term interest rate futures to create a hedge against a rise in short-term interest rates within the next two months.

Short sterling futures are for notional three-month deposits of £500,000.

Required

State how futures should be used as a hedge for the exposure to interest rate risk.

43 More hedging with STIRs

It is now 31st October.

A company must borrow US$12 million in three months' time, on the first day of February, for a period of four months. It can borrow at US dollar LIBOR + 1%.

The company is concerned about the risk of an increase in short-term interest rates before February, and has decided to hedge the risk with short-term interest rate futures.

Eurodollar futures are for three-month notional deposits of $1,000,000.

The current three-month LIBOR rate at the end of October is 5.5%.

The following futures prices are available at the end of October:

Futures prices as at end of July	
December futures	94.20
March futures	93.70

Assume that the settlement date for futures is the last day of the relevant month.

Required

(a) State how a hedge would be created using eurodollar futures.

(b) Suppose that at the beginning of February, three-month interest rates for the dollar (spot) have risen by 2% to 7.5%.

Allowing for basis risk, state what the effective interest rate for borrowing should be when the futures position is closed.

44 FRAs and futures

It is now 1st April. Your company will receive £8.2 million from a customer in four months' time, and it will invest this money for five months until the end of December, when it will be needed for spending on a planned capital project. The company treasurer intends to put the money on deposit for five months when it is received, and expects to be able to invest short term to earn LIBOR plus 0.40%.

The treasurer is worried about the risk of a fall in interest rates and wants to secure an effective interest rate for the investment of the £8.2 million for the five-month period.

The following information is available:

LIFFE £500,000 3 month sterling futures
Tick size (0.0001) £12.50
September: 95.35
December: 95.70

Futures contracts mature at the end of the relevant month.
The current three-month LIBOR rate is 5%.

FRA prices
4v5: 4.75 – 4.70
4v9: 4.57 – 4.52
5v9: 4.49 – 4.44

Required

(a) Explain how you would lock in an effective interest rate for the income from investing the £8.2 million, using:
    (1) FRAs
    (2) Interest rate futures

(b) Show what will happen at the end of July if the three-month LIBOR rate is 4.25% and the interest rate exposure had been hedged as indicated in part (a) of the answer, using:
    (1) FRAs
    (2) Interest rate futures

45 Traded equity options

It is mid-February. A UK investor believes that in the next few weeks, the share price of company TBA will fall by a substantial amount. The share price is currently 982.

The investor has decided to speculate on a fall in the share price using equity options, and is prepared to invest up to £12,000 in an options transaction.

On the LIFFE exchange, traded options are for 2,000 shares in a company, and the following option prices (in pence) are currently available for TBA shares:

Strike price	**March**	
pence	Calls	Puts
950	40	15
1,000	10	50

Required

(a) Explain how this investor might use options to speculate on a fall in the TBA.

(b) Show what would happen when the options expire if the TBA share price is 910.

46 Currency options

A UK company will receive US$2 million in six months' time. It is now 20th March. The company is not sure whether the US dollar will rise or fall in value against sterling over the next few months, and it has decided to hedge its exposure to currency risk using traded currency options.

On the Philadelphia Stock Exchange, traded currency options are available in a contract size of £31,250. Options are priced in cents per £1. Assume that option contracts expire on 20th of each month.

The following option prices are currently available:

Exercise price	**Calls**		**Puts**	
	June	September	June	September
1.8500	1.4	1.9	4.0	5.1

The current spot exchange rate (US$/£1) is 1.8325 – 1.8375.

Required

(a) Explain how the company's currency exposure could be hedged using traded currency options.

(b) Show what would happen if the options are still held by the company at expiry and the spot exchange rate is $1.9150 – 1.9200.

47 Interest rate hedge

A UK company will need to borrow £21 million for two months, starting in three months' time. It is now mid-March. The current LIBOR rate is 5% and the company can borrow at LIBOR + 0.75%.

The company is concerned about the possibility of an increase in short-term interest rates during the next two months, and it is looking at methods of hedging its exposure to the risk. The three methods it is considering are interest rate futures, options on interest rate futures and an FRA.

Current prices for futures, options and FRAs are as follows. (Note: Assume that all exchange-traded derivatives reach settlement on the last day of the relevant month).

Interest rate futures	
Notional three-month deposit £500,000	
Value of 1 tick = £12.50	
March	94.740
June	94.610
September	94.500

Options on interest rate futures
Premium cost expressed as an annual interest rate %

Strike price	**Calls**			**Puts**		
	March	June	September	March	June	September
94750	0.140	0.200	0.280	0.320	0.390	0.500
95000	0.124	0.080	0.120	0.470	0.560	0.850

Forward rate agreements (FRAs)	
3v5	5.38 – 5.32
3v6	5.43 – 5.46
3v8	5.52 – 5.44

Required

Show how the exposure to interest rate risk would be hedged using each of the three types of derivative.

Show what will happen in mid-June when the company borrows $21 million, assuming that the LIBOR rate has risen to 6.0%.

48 Black-Scholes

The current price of shares in FAME is 870.

Required

Use the Black-Scholes option pricing model to calculate the value of a call option maturing in six months' time and with an exercise price of 900.

The following data should be used in your calculation

(1) Risk-free interest rate = 5% per year

(2) Variance of returns on FAME shares = 9%

49 Put-call parity

The price of a call option on PWW shares, with a strike price of 600 and an expiry date in six months, is 33. The current share price is 582. The cost of capital is 4% per year.

Required

Use the put-call parity equation to calculate the price of a put option on PWW shares with a strike price of 600 and an expiry date in six months.

50 Delta hedge

(a) The delta value of shares in TER is 0.125.

Required

How might a bank use this information to construct a delta hedge for its option trading operations in TER shares?

(b) The share price of BVZ is currently 258. A bank is writing call options on BVZ shares at a strike price of 260, with an expiry date in six months' time. The risk-free rate of return is 4% per year and the variance of returns on BVZ shares is 16%.

Required

How might the bank use this information to construct a delta hedge for its option trading operations in BVZ shares?

51 Bonus scheme

The remuneration committee of Grand plc is considering a remuneration package for a new executive director. The committee want to include an attractive incentive arrangement in the remuneration package, and are considering two possible schemes.

(a) **Scheme 1**. The annual cash bonus of the executive director would be 0.5% of the economic value added (EVA®) of the company.

(b) **Scheme 2**. The executive should be given share options on 2 million of the company's shares, exercisable in one year's time. The share options would have an exercise price of the company's current market price, which is 140 cents.

The income statement of the company for the financial year just ended is as follows:

	$ million
Sales	683
Cost of sales	(421)
Depreciation	(65)
Research and development	(14)
Net interest	(35)
Profit before tax	148
Tax	(44)
Profit after tax	104

The following information is available:

(1) The capital employed of the company is reported as $525 million as at the beginning of the financial year just ended, and $570 million as at the end of the year.

(2) The research and development expenditure programme has involved spending of $14,000 for each of the past four years.

(3) Accounting depreciation and economic depreciation are about the same.

(4) The company's weighted average cost of capital is 9%.

(5) The rate of tax on profits is 30%.

(6) The risk-free rate is 5%.

(7) The members of the remuneration committee do not know the value of share options in the company, but they are aware that the current premium for an at-the-money put option on Grand plc shares, exercisable in one year, is 30 cents.

Required

Calculate the potential value of each of the incentive schemes to the executive director (and the cost to the company). State any assumptions that you make.

52 Delta neutral

Barn plc has an investment in 4 million shares of a rival UK company, Door plc. The investment has been acquired with a view to possibly making a takeover bid for Door plc, although a decision will not be taken until at least the end of November. It is now 1st July, and Door plc shares are currently trading at 635 pence

The treasurer of Barn plc is concerned about the risk of a fall in the market price of Door plc shares, and is considering the use of traded options in Door shares to hedge the risk.

Traded options: (1,000 shares)

	CALLS			PUTS		
	August	November	February	August	November	February
600	34.0	47.5	54.5	2.0	22.0	31.5
650	6.0	21.5	30.5	19.0	47.5	56.0

Required

(a) Show how Barn plc might use traded options to create a hedge against the risk of a fall in the price of Door plc shares. Assuming that at the end of November the price of Door plc shares is 580, show the outcome of your hedge.

(b) Assume that the delta of the relevant Door plc option is 0.46. Illustrate how a delta neutral hedge might be created to protect against a fall in the price of Door plc shares. Explain any practical difficulties there might be with using a delta hedge for this purpose.

Q&A

Answers to practice questions

Contents

Contents

Contents

Page

1 Corporate social responsibility

(a) (i) Ethics and behaving in an ethical manner in business (and in some cases, bribery and corruption)

(ii) Concern for employees

(iii) Concern for the community

(iv) Concern for human rights

(v) Concern for the environment: protecting the environment, creating a sustainable business.

(b) CSR issues vary between different types of company. Companies most likely to be affected include:

(i) companies that enjoy some form of monopoly, such as energy supply companies

(ii) companies that deal directly with consumers, such as banks and retail organisations

(iii) companies manufacturing food, drink and medicines

(iv) companies that extract resources from the environment: manufacturing companies whose products or manufacturing systems pollute the environment

(v) companies with a supply chain in developing countries (such as clothing manufacturers and oil exploration and extraction companies).

(c) CSR risk is the risk that a CSR issue might affect a company in any of the following ways:

(i) The company might suffer a loss of reputation (reputation risk). This could lead to a loss of customers who switch to the products of rival companies. A poor reputation could also lead to the threat of legislation.

(ii) The company might be exposed to the risk of legal action by customers and others (litigation risk). A notable example has been the litigation faced by tobacco companies, particularly in the US.

(iii) Another aspect of litigation risk is the possibility that a government will introduce legislation against a company's products (e.g. tobacco products, food products, medicines and drugs) or its production methods (e.g. anti-pollution laws).

(iv) Some investors choose to invest only in 'ethical companies'. A company with a poor CSR record might therefore attract fewer investors.

(v) Research appears to show that companies with positive CSR policies benefit financially, in terms of profits and share price.

2 Corporate governance

(a) The main aim of a code of corporate governance should be to ensure that the directors or managers of a company should run the company in the interests of its shareholders.

(b) The main issues in corporate governance, for both statutory and voluntary codes, are likely to be:

(i) the composition of the board of directors: achieving a balance of skills and experience, preventing the board from being dominated by one individual or a small group of individuals, the role of non-executive directors (and in particular independent non-executive director)

(ii) the decision-making responsibilities of the board (and how much decision-making responsibility should be delegated to management)

(iii) the process of nominating new directors for appointment to the board

(iv) the process of deciding the remuneration of directors, and trying to ensure that remuneration systems reward directors for success and do not reward them for failure

(v) the reliability of financial reporting, the independence of the external auditors, and the role of the audit committee

(vi) communications between a company and its shareholders

(vii) risk management and internal control, and the review of internal control and risk management systems

(viii) restricting the scope for insider trading or market abuse.

Corporate social responsibility and protection for whistle-blowers could also be added to this list.

3 Dividends and retentions

The dividend growth model will be used to estimate what share price might be expected.

It is assumed that the growth rate in earnings and dividends will be br, where b is the proportion of earnings that is retained and r is the return on new investment.

(a) Dividends are 25% of earnings and 75% of earnings are retained:

Growth rate = 0.75% × 0.09 = 0.0675.

$$\text{Expected share price} = \frac{0.50\ (1.0675)}{(0.09 - 0.0675)} = \$23.72$$

(b) Dividends are 50% of earnings and 50% of earnings are retained:

Growth rate = 0.50% × 0.09 = 0.045.

$$\text{Expected share price} = \frac{1.00\ (1.045)}{(0.09 - 0.045)} = \$23.22$$

(c) Dividends are 70% of earnings and 30% of earnings are retained:

Growth rate = 0.30% × 0.09 = 0.027.

$$\text{Expected share price} = \frac{1.40\ (1.027)}{(0.09 - 0.027)} = \$22.82$$

4 Financial plan

(a) **Tutorial note**. Many of the figures for the financial plan can be calculated by increasing the amount by 8% each year, in line with sales growth. The bank overdraft interest each year is calculated by taking the bank overdraft at the end of the previous year. The bank overdraft is a balancing figure in the balance sheet, that makes the equity and liabilities add up to the total assets.

Income statements		**Year 5**	**Year 6**	**Year 7**	**Year 8**
		$m	$m	$m	$m
EBITDA	(+ 8% per year)	583	630	680	735
Depreciation	(+ 8% per year)	(173)	(187)	(202)	(218)
Earnings before interest		410	443	478	517
Interest	(see workings)	(86)	(95)	(106)	(118)
Profit before tax		324	348	372	399
Tax (30%)		(97)	(104)	(112)	(120)
Profit after tax		227	244	260	279
Dividends	(64%)	(145)	(159)	(166)	(179)
Retained earnings		82	85	94	100

Balance sheets		**Year 5**	**Year 6**	**Year 7**	**Year 8**
		$m	$m	$m	$m
Plant and equipment	(+ 8% per year)	2,182	2,356	2,545	2,748
Inventory + receivables – trade payables	(+ 8% per year)	767	828	894	966
Cash	(+ 8% per year)	32	35	38	41
		2,981	3,219	3,477	3,755
Share capital		450	450	450	450
Reserves	(add retained profit)	1,283	1,368	1,462	1,562
		1,733	1,818	1,912	2,012
Long-term loan		800	800	800	800
		2,533	2,618	2,712	2,812
Bank overdraft	(balancing figure)	448	601	765	943
		2,981	3,219	3,477	3,755

Workings

(1) At the end of year 4, inventory + receivables – trade payables = 710 (in $ million). This amount will increase by 8% each year.

(2) **Interest charges**

		Year 5	Year 6	Year 7	Year 8
		$m	$m	$m	$m
Long-term loan	(8% × 800)	64	64	64	64
Bank overdraft	(7% × previous year)	22	31	42	54
		86	95	106	118

(b) There are several definitions of free cash flow. Other definitions are acceptable for your answer.

		Year 5	Year 6	Year 7	Year 8
		$m	$m	$m	$m
EBIT (1 – t)	Earnings before interest less tax at 30%	287	310	335	362
Depreciation		173	187	202	218
Increase in plant and equipment		(162)	(174)	(189)	(203)
Increase in inventory + receivables - payables		(57)	(61)	(66)	(72)
Free cash flow		241	262	282	305

(c) A feature of the financial plan that might need review is the cash position of the company. The bank overdraft is forecast to increase from $310,000 to $943,000, although the company expects to make a profit each year. The free cash flow each year, as measured, is not much more than the interest payments and dividend payments.

This suggests that the company might need to reconsider its dividend policy, and pay lower dividends. In addition, the company might possible consider alternative sources of finance, so that it does not have to rely so much on an overdraft facility. More long-term debt might be appropriate, if this can be obtained at a suitable interest rate.

(d) A possible value of the company's shares at the end of the financial planning period can be estimated using the dividend growth model, assuming that dividends will grow by about 8% per year (in line with sales growth) and the cost of equity will remain at 12%.

$$\text{Expected equity value in \$ millions} = \frac{179\ (1.08)}{(0.12 - 0.08)}$$

= $4,833 million.

There are 9,000,000 shares of $0.05 each . This gives a valuation of $537 per share.

5 DCF exercises

(a)

Annuity factor at 8%, years 1 – 8	5.747
Annuity factor at 8%, years 1 – 4	3.312
Annuity factor at 8%, years 5 – 8	2.435

Annuity factor at 8%, years 1 – 10	6.710
Annuity factor at 8%, years 1 – 8	5.747
Annuity factor at 8%, years 9 – 10	0.963

The Year 10 value of a perpetuity of $100,000 each year in perpetuity from Year 11 onwards:

= $100,000 × 1/0.08

= $1,250,000

Years	Annual cash flow	Discount factor at 8%	PV
	$		$
0	(3,000,000)	1.000	(3,000,000)
1 – 4	500,000	3.312	1,656,000
5 – 8	400,000	2.435	974,000
9 – 10	300,000	0.963	288,900
10	1,250,000	0.463	578,750
NPV			+ 497,650

(b) (i) **Ignoring inflation**

Year	Annual cash flow	Discount factor at 12%	PV
	$		$
0	(900,000)	1.000	(900,000)
1	400,000	0.893	357,200
2	400,000	0.797	318,800
3	250,000	0.636	159,000
4	300,000	0.567	170,100
			+ 105,100

(ii) **Allowing for inflation**

Year	0	1	2	3	4
	$	$	$	$	$
Equipment	(900,000)				243,101
Revenue		824,000	848,720	655,636	450,204
Running costs		(420,000)	(441,000)	(405,169)	(364,652)
Net cash flow	(900,000)	404,000	407,720	250,467	328,653
Discount factor at 12%	1.000	0.893	0.797	0.636	0.567
Present value	(900,000)	360,772	324,953	159,297	186,346

NPV = + 131,368

6 DCF and tax

Annual depreciation = $(800,000 – 200,000)/4 years = $150,000 per year.

Annual cash profits = Accounting profit + Deprecation = $250,000 + $150,000 = $400,000.

Tax depreciation allowances (capital allowances)

Year of claim		Written down value	Tax saved at 30%	Year of cash flow
		$	$	
		800,000		
0	Allowance (25%)	(200,000)	60,000	1
		600,000		
1	Allowance (25%)	(150,000)	45,000	2
		450,000		
2	Allowance (25%)	(112,500)	33,750	3
		337,500		
3	Allowance (25%)	(84,375)	25,313	4
		253,125		
4	Disposal value	(200,000)		
4	Balancing allowance	53,125	15,938	5

Year	0	1	2	3	4	5
	$	$	$	$	$	$
Equipment	(800,000)				200,000	
Capital allowance		60,000	45,000	33,750	25,313	15,938
Cash profit		400,000	400,000	400,000	400,000	
Tax on cash profit			(120,000)	(120,000)	(120,000)	(120,000)
Net cash flow	(800,000)	460,000	325,000	313,750	505,313	(104,062)
Discount factor, 15%	1.000	0.870	0.756	0.658	0.572	0.497
Present value	(800,000)	400,200	245,700	206,448	289,039	(51,719)

NPV = + $289,668

7 Free cash flow

	$ million
Profit before interest and tax	3.00
Interest	(0.40)
Taxation	(0.60)
Depreciation charges	0.55
Essential capital expenditure	(1.00)
Free cash flow	1.55

8 Two-asset portfolio

(a) **Security X**

EV of return ($\bar{x}$)

= (0.25 x 15) + (0.60 x 10) + (0.15 x 2) = 10.05.

Probability	Return	$x - \bar{x}$	$p(x - \bar{x})^2$
p	x		
0.25	15	4.95	6.1256
0.60	10	(0.05)	0.0015
0.15	2	(8.05)	9.7204
		Variance σ^2	15.8475

Standard deviation of return $\sigma_x = \sqrt{15.8475} = 3.98$.

(b) **Security Y**

EV of return ($\bar{x}$)
= (0.25 x 20) + (0.60 x 8) + (0.15 x (6)) = 8.90

Probability	Return	$y - \bar{y}$	$p(y - \bar{y})^2$
p	y		
0.25	20	11.10	30.8025
0.60	8	(0.90)	0.4860
0.15	(6)	(14.90)	33.3015
		Variance σ^2	64.5900

Standard deviation of return $\sigma_y = \sqrt{64.59} = 8.04$.

(c)

Probability	$x - \bar{x}$	$y - \bar{y}$	$p(x - \bar{x})^2$
p			
0.25	4.95	11.10	13.7363
0.60	(0.05)	(0.90)	0.0270
0.15	(8.05)	(14.90)	17.9917
		$Cov_{x,y}$	31.7550

(d) **Correlation coefficient**

$$\rho_{x,y} = \frac{31.7550}{3.98 \times 8.04}$$

= + 0.992.

This shows a high level of positive correlation between the returns from Security X and the returns from Security Y.

(e) The **EV of the return** from a portfolio consisting of 50% Security X and 50% Security Y

= (0.50 x 10.05) + (0.50 x 8.90) = 9.475%.

The **variance** of the returns from this portfolio would be:

$[(0.50)^2 \times 15.8475] + [(0.50)^2 \times 64.5900] + [2 \times 0.50 \times 0.50 \times 31.7550]$

= 3.9619 + 16.1475 + 15.8775 = 35.9869.

The **standard deviation** of the portfolio returns = $\sqrt{35.9869} = 6.0\%$.

(f) For a portfolio consisting of 80% Security X and 20% Security Y:

The **EV of the return**

= (0.80 × 10.05) + (0.20 × 8.90) = 9.82%.

The **variance** of the returns from this portfolio would be:

$[(0.80)^2 \times 15.8475] + [(0.20)^2 \times 64.5900] + [2 \times 0.80 \times 0.20 \times 31.7550]$

= 10.1424 + 2.5836 + 10.1616 = 22.8876.

The **standard deviation** of the portfolio returns = $\sqrt{22.8876}$ = 4.78%.

Note: In this example, since Security Y has a lower expected return than Security X and a higher standard deviation, expected returns will be highest and risk lowest with a 'portfolio' consisting of Security X only, and none of Security Y.

9 Risk and return

(a)

	Project 3	Project 4
Expected return	$(0.6 \times 6) + (0.4 \times 1) = +4.0$	$(0.5 \times 8) + (0.5 \times -1) = +3.5$

	Return r	Probability p	$(r-\bar{r})^2$	Return r	Probability p	$(r-\bar{r})^2$
	6.0	0.6	2.40	8.0	0.5	10.125
	1.0	0.4	3.60	– 1.0	0.5	10.125
Variance $(\sigma)^2$			6.00			20.250
σ			2.45			4.5

(b) The divisional manager will invest in projects that are more risky provided that they offer a higher return.

The manager will not invest in Project 4 because it offers a lower expected return than Project 3 but higher risk.

The expected return from Project 1 is $(0.8 \times 4) + (0.2 \times 2) = +3.6$.

The expected return from Project 2 is $(0.7 \times 5) + (0.3 \times 1.5) = +3.95$.

The highest expected return is offered by Project 3, which has a higher risk than Project 1 and Project 2. It would seem that the divisional manager will invest in Project 3 because he is prepared to take the higher risk for a higher expected return. However, Project 2 might seem more attractive: its expected return is almost as high as for Project 3 and the risk is much less.

10 Coefficient of variation

Portfolio		Expected return
50% Country A, 50% Country B	$(0.5 \times 16) + (0.5 \times 22)$	19.0
50% Country A, 50% Country C	$(0.5 \times 16) + (0.5 \times 30)$	23.0
50% Country B, 50% Country C	$(0.5 \times 22) + (0.5 \times 30)$	26.0

The standard deviation of a portfolio is:

$$\sigma p = \sqrt{\sigma_A{}^2 x^2 + \sigma_B{}^2 (1-x)^2 + 2x(1-x)\rho_{A,B}\sigma_A\sigma_B}$$

However, since the returns from each country are independent of each other, the covariance of returns ($\rho_{A,B}$) is 0; therefore the second half of the formula can be ignored because its value is zero.

Portfolio		Standard deviation of returns
50% Country A, 50% Country B	$[(22^2 \times 0.5^2) + (36^2 \times 0.5^2)]^{1/2}$	21.9
50% Country A, 50% Country C	$[(22^2 \times 0.5^2) + (45^2 \times 0.5^2)]^{1/2}$	25.7
50% Country B, 50% Country C	$[(36^2 \times 0.5^2) + (45^2 \times 0.5^2)]^{1/2}$	28.8

(Tutorial note: 'To the power of ½' is the same as 'the square root'.)

Coefficient of variation

The coefficient of variation is the ratio of the risk (standard deviation of returns) to the expected return.

Portfolio		Coefficient of variation
50% Country A, 50% Country B	21.9/19.0 =	1.15
50% Country A, 50% Country C	25.7/23.0 =	1.12
50% Country B, 50% Country C	28.8/26.0 =	1.11

The ratio of risk to expected returns is roughly the same for all three portfolios.

11 Capital market line

The investor wanting a return of 7% can invest x% of his funds in risk-free securities earning 3% and (1 – x)% in the market portfolio earning 9%.

$3x + 9(1 - x) = 7$

$6x = 2$

$x = 1/3$ or 33.33%.

The investor should invest one-third of his funds in risk-free securities and two-thirds in the market portfolio.

12 Obtaining a beta factor

(a)

Month	Market portfolio		Security Y	
	$x - \bar{x}$	$(x - \bar{x})^2$	$y - \bar{y}$	$(y - \bar{y})^2$
1	+ 1.5	2.25	+ 2	4
2	(1.5)	2.25	(3)	9
3	(2.5)	6.25	(3)	9
4	+ 2.5	6.25	+ 4	16
		17.00		38

Standard deviation of market returns = $\sqrt{17.00} = 4.123\%$.

Standard deviation of Security Y returns = $\sqrt{38} = 6.164\%$.

(b)

Month	$x - \bar{x}$	$y - \bar{y}$	$(x - \bar{x})(y - \bar{y})$
1	+ 1.5	+ 2	+ 3.0
2	(1.5)	(3)	+ 4.5
3	(2.5)	(3)	+ 7.5
4	+ 2.5	+ 4	+ 10.0
			+ 25.0

Covariance of returns = 25.0

(c) **Correlation coefficient** $\rho_{m,y}$

$$\rho_{x,y} = \frac{25.0}{4.123 \times 6.164}$$

$= + 0.984.$

(d) **Beta factor for Security Y**

$$\beta = \frac{Cov_{m,y}}{Var_m} = \frac{25}{17} = 1.47$$

Alternatively

$$\beta = \frac{\rho_{m,y} x \sigma_y}{\sigma_m} = \frac{0.984 \times 6.164}{4.123} = 1.47$$

13 WACC

$$\text{Cost of equity} = \frac{18\,(1.03)}{155} + 0.03$$

$= 0.1496$ or 14.96%.

$$\text{WACC} = \left[\frac{350}{(1{,}200 + 350)} \times 7.8(1 - 0.30)\right] + \left[\frac{1{,}200}{(1{,}200 + 350)} \times 14.96\right]$$

$= 1.23 + 11.58$

$= 12.81\%.$

14 Optimal WACC

The optimal WACC is the lowest WACC, because this will maximise the value of the company and the wealth of shareholders.

Step 1

Calculate the geared beta for equity at each level of gearing.

Gearing	Geared beta		
20%	$0.90 \times \frac{80 + 20\,(1 - 0.30)}{80}$	=	1.0575
30%	$0.90 \times \frac{70 + 30\,(1 - 0.30)}{70}$	=	1.170
40%	$0.90 \times \frac{60 + 40\,(1 - 0.30)}{60}$	=	1.320
50%	$0.90 \times \frac{50 + 50\,(1 - 0.30)}{50}$	=	1.530
60%	$0.90 \times \frac{40 + 60\,(1 - 0.30)}{40}$	=	1.845

Step 2

Use the geared beta value and the CAPM to calculate a cost of equity at each gearing level.

Gearing	Cost of equity (4% + β (9 – 4)%		
20%	4 + 1.0575 × 5	=	7.17%
30%	4 + 1.170 × 5	=	7.51%
40%	4 + 1.320 × 5	=	7.96%
50%	4 + 1.530 × 5	=	8.59%
60%	4 + 1.845 × 5	=	9.54%

Step 3

Calculate the WACC at each level of gearing, and identify the gearing level with the lowest WACC.

Gearing				WACC
20%	[20% x 5.0 (1 – 0.30)]	+	[80% × 7.17]	= 6.44%
30%	[30% x 5.4 (1 – 0.30)]	+	[70% × 7.51]	= 6.39%
40%	[40% x 5.8 (1 – 0.30)]	+	[60% × 7.96]	= 6.40%
50%	[50% x 6.5 (1 – 0.30)]	+	[50% × 8.59]	= 6.58%
60%	[60% x 7.2 (1 – 0.30)]	+	[40% × 9.54]	= 6.84%

Conclusion

The optimal gearing level is 30%, because the WACC is lowest at this gearing level. However, the WACC is almost as low at a gearing level of 40%.

15 Change in gearing

Annual earnings if the debt is issued	$ million
Profit before interest and tax	40
Interest ($100 million x 8%)	(8)
Profit before tax	32
Tax (25%)	(8)
Profit after tax = earnings	24

Value of geared company = Value of company ungeared + (Value of debt × Tax rate)

$V_g = V_u + Dt$

V_g = (60 million × $5) + ($100 million × 25%)

= $325 million

	$ million
Total value of geared company (equity + debt)	325
Value of debt	(100)
Therefore value of equity in geared company	225

Therefore cost of equity in geared company = 24/225 = 0.1067 or 10.67%.

$$WACC = \left[\frac{100}{325} \times 8.0(1-0.25)\right] + \left[\frac{225}{325} \times 10.67\right] = 9.23\%$$

(The WACC of the all-equity company is 10%. The increase in gearing reduces the WACC).

16 Geared beta

(a) The current proportion of equity in the capital structure is 1,500/(1,500 + 500) = 0.75 or 75%.

The current proportion of debt in the capital structure is 500/(1,500 + 500) = 0.25 or 25%.

Cost of equity = 5% + 1.126 (11 – 5)% = 11.756%.

Since the beta factor of debt is 0, the debt must be risk-free, with a pre-tax cost of 5%.

$$WACC = [0.25 \times 5.0(1-0.30)] + [0.75 \times 11.756] = 9.692\%, say\ 9.7\%$$

(b) **Step 1**

Convert the current geared beta into an ungeared beta:

$$B_{ungeared} = B_{geared} \times \frac{E}{E + D(1-t)}$$

$$B_{ungeared} = 1.126 \times \frac{75}{75 + 75(1-0.30)}$$

$$= 0.913$$

Step 2

Convert the ungeared beta into a geared beta for the new level of gearing

$$0.913 = B_{geared} \times \frac{60}{60 + 40(1-0.30)}$$

$$B_{geared} = \frac{0.913}{0.6818} = 1.339$$

Step 3

Use this geared beta factor to calculate the cost of equity at this gearing level.

Cost of equity = 5% + 1.339 (11 – 5)% = 13.03%.

Step 4

Calculate the WACC at this gearing level. It is assumed that the cost of debt remains risk-free.

$$WACC = [0.40 \times 5.0(1-0.30)] + [0.60 \times 13.03] = 9.218\%, say\ 9.2\%$$

17 APV method

(a) **Modigliani-Miller formula approach**

Ungeared beta for the telecommunications industry:

$$= 1.30625 \times \frac{80}{80 + 20(1 - 0.25)}$$

= 1.10

The company's gearing is 70% equity and 30% debt; therefore we need to re-gear the equity beta for the company.

$$1.10 = \text{Beta}_{\text{geared}} \times \frac{70}{70 + 30(1 - 0.25)}$$

$\text{Beta}_{\text{geared}} = 1.45$

The cost of equity for the project is therefore 4% + 1.45 (9% – 4%) = 11.25%.

WACC = (0.70 × 11.25%) + (0.3 × 4% (1 – 0.25))

= 7.875% + 0.9%

= 8.775%, say 8.8%

Year	**0**	**1**	**2**	**3**	**4**
	$	$	$	$	$
Capital expenditure	(200,000)				
Cash profits		100,000	165,000	120,000	
Tax at 25%			(25,000)	(41,250)	(30,000)
Net cash flow	(200,000)	100,000	140,000	78,750	(30,000)
DCF factor at 8.8%	1.000	1/(1.088)	$1/(1.088)^2$	$1/(1.088)^3$	$1/(1.088)^4$
Present value	(200,000)	91,912	118,269	61,145	(21,409)

NPV = $49,917

(b) **APV method**

The ungeared beta for the telecommunications industry is 1.10 (see above)

The cost of ungeared equity in the industry is 4% + 1.10 (9% - 4%) = 9.5%.

The cash flows of the project are discounted at this cost of capital, to obtain the base case NPV.

Year	0	1	2	3	4
	$	$	$	$	$
Capital expenditure	(200,000)				
Cash profits		100,000	165,000	120,000	
Tax at 25%			(25,000)	(41,250)	(30,000)
Net cash flow	(200,000)	100,000	140,000	78,750	(30,000)
DCF factor at 8.8%	1.000	1/(1.095)	$1/(1.095)^2$	$1/(1.095)^3$	$1/(1.095)^4$
Present value	(200,000)	91,324	116,762	59,980	(20,867)

Base case NPV = $47,199

PV of issue costs

Issue costs before tax:		$
Equity	$1,000,000 × 4/96	41,667
Debt	$1,000,000 × 3/97	30,928
Total issue costs		72,595

The PV of issue costs is calculated using the risk-free rate of 4% as the discount rate.

Year	Item	Cash flow	Discount factor at 4%	PV
		$		$
0	Issue costs	(72,595)	1.000	(72,595)
1	Tax saved at 25%	18,149	0.962	17,459
PV of issue costs				(55,136)

PV of tax shield

The amount borrowed will be $1,000,000 + $30,928 = $1,030,928.

The interest rate will be 4%.

The annual interest cost will be $1,030,928 × 4% = $41,237 each year, years 1 – 3.

The reduction in tax due to the interest payments = $10,309 (= 25% × $41,237) each year, years 2 – 4.

Discount factor at 4%, years 1 – 4	3.630
Discount factor at 4%, year 1	0.962
Discount factor at 4%, years 2 – 4	2.668

PV of tax shield = \$10,309 × 2.668 = \$27,504.

Adjusted present value

	\$
Base case NPV	47,199
PV of issue costs	(55,136)
PV of tax shield	27,504
APV	+ 19,567

18 Adjusted present value

Capital allowances: Workings

Year of claim		Tax saving at 35%	Year of cash flow
	\$	\$	
	450,000		
0	(315,000)	110,250	1
	135,000		
1	(45,000)	15,750	2
	90,000		
2	(45,000)	15,750	3
	45,000		
3	(45,000)	15,750	4
	0		

(a) **Current WACC**

Cost of equity = 10% + 1.8(15 – 10)% = 19%.

$$\text{WACC} = (0.80 \times 19\%) + [0.20 \times 10\%(1 - 0.65)]$$

= 16.5%

Year	0	1	2	3	4
	\$000	\$000	\$000	\$000	\$000
Machine	(450)				
Tax saved, tax allowances		110.25	15.75	15.75	15.75
Cash profits		220.00	220.00	220.00	
Tax on cash profits (35%)			(77.0)	(77.0)	(77.00)
Net cash flow	(450)	330.25	158.75	158.75	(61.25)
Discount factor at 16.5%	1.000	0.858	0.737	0.632	0.543
Present value	(450)	283.35	117.00	100.33	(33.26)

NPV = + \$17,420

(b) **WACC adjusted for business risk and financial risk**

Step 1

Calculate an ungeared beta for the plastics industry.

$$= 1.356 \times \frac{5}{5 + 1(1 - 0.35)}$$

= 1.20

The company's gearing is 60% equity and 40% debt; therefore we need to re-gear the equity beta for the company.

$$1.20 = \text{Beta}_{\text{geared}} \times \frac{60}{60 + 40(1 - 0.35)}$$

$\text{Beta}_{\text{geared}} = 1.72$

The cost of equity for the project is therefore 10% + 1.72 (15% – 10%) = 18.6%.

WACC = (0.60 × 18.6%) + (0.40 × 10% (1 – 0.35))

= 13.76%, say 14%.

Year	**0**	**1**	**2**	**3**	**4**
	\$000	\$000	\$000	\$000	\$000
Net cash flows (as in (a))	(450.00)	330.25	158.75	158.75	(61.25)
DCF factor at 14%	1.000	0.877	0.769	0.675	0.592
Present value	(450.00)	289.63	122.08	107.16	(36.26)
NPV = \$32,610					

(c) **APV method**

Step 1

The ungeared beta for the plastics industry is 1.20 (see above)

The cost of ungeared equity in the industry is 10% + 1.20 (15% – 10%) = 16%.

The cash flows of the project are discounted at this cost of capital, to obtain the base case NPV.

Year	**0**	**1**	**2**	**3**	**4**
	\$000	\$000	\$000	\$000	\$000
Net cash flow	(450.00)	330.25	158.75	158.75	(61.25)
DCF factor at 16%	1.000	0.862	0.743	0.641	0.552
Present value	(450.00)	284.68	117.95	101.76	(33.81)
Base case NPV = \$20,580					

Step 2: PV of issue costs

Issue costs before tax	Net finance obtained		Issue costs
	$		$
Debt: (40% × 450,000)	180,000	2%	3,600
Equity: (60% × 450,000)	270,000	5%	13,500
Total issue costs			17,100

The PV of issue costs is calculated using the risk-free rate of 10% as the discount rate.

Year	Item	Cash flow	Discount factor at 10%	PV
		$		$
0	Issue costs	(17,100)	1.000	(17,100)
1	Tax saved at 35%	5,985	0.909	5,440
PV of issue costs				**(11,660)**

Step 3: PV of tax shield

The amount borrowed will be $180,000 + $3,600 = $183,600.

The interest rate will be 10%.

If the loan is repaid in three equal annual instalments, the annual repayments will be:

$$\frac{\text{Loan}}{\text{PV factor, years } 1-3 \text{ at } 10\%} = \frac{\$183,600}{2,487} = \$73,824$$

Year	Balance at beginning of year	Loan payment	Interest at 10%	Loan repayment
	$	$	$	$
1	(183,600)	73,824	18,360	55,464
	(55,464)			
2	128,136	73,824	12,814	61,010
	(61,010)			
3	67,126	73,824	6,713	67,111
	(67,111)			
Balance	15	(rounding error)		

Year of interest cost	Interest	Year of tax saving	Tax saving at 35%	DCF factor at 10%	PV of tax saving
	$		$		$
1	18,360	2	6,426	0.826	5,308
2	12,814	3	4,485	0.751	3,368
3	6,713	4	2,350	0.683	1,605
PV of tax shield					10,281

Adjusted present value

	$
Base case NPV	20,580
PV of issue costs	(11,660)
PV of tax shield	10,281
APV	+ 19,201

19 More APV

It is assumed that the company's debt capital will be risk-free.

The asset beta for the industry is 1.39 × 80/[80 + 20(1 – 0.25)] = 1.17

The cost of ungeared equity in the industry is 6% + 1.17 (10 – 6)% = 10.68%. This will be rounded up to 11%.

Only relevant cash flows should be included in the DCF analysis. Non-relevant costs are the market research cost (already incurred, so a sunk cost) and head office allocated charges (a non-cash cost) – although increases in head office spending are relevant costs.

Year	**0**	**1**	**2**	**3**	**4**	**5**	**6**
	$000	$000	$000	$000	$000	$000	$000
Revenue		6,800	7,800	8,800	9,200	9,476	9,760
Operating costs		5,500	6,600	7,100	7,500	7,725	7,957
Head office		50	50	50	60	60	60
Royalty payments	600	500	400	300	200	200	200
Lost contribution		100	100				
Tax-allowable dep'n		600	480	480	480	480	480
	600	6,750	7,630	7,930	8,240	8,465	8,697
Taxable profit	(600)	50	270	870	960	1,011	1,063
Tax at 25%	150	(13)	(68)	(218)	(240)	(253)	(266)
	(450)	37	202	652	720	758	797
Add back dep'n	-	600	480	480	480	480	480
Equipment	(3,000)						
Working capital	(400)						400
Net cash flow	(3,850)	637	682	1,132	1,200	1,238	1,277
DCF factor 11%	1.000	0.901	0.812	0.731	0.659	0.593	0.535
Present value	(3,850)	574	554	827	791	734	897

The base case NPV, discounting the cash flows at the ungeared cost of equity, is (in $000) + 527.

Issue costs

Issue costs will be 2%. The net borrowing after issue costs needs to be $3,400,000; therefore the gross amount borrowed will need to be $3 million/0.98 = $3,469,400. Issue costs will be (2%) $69,000. It is assumed that this is a Year 0 cost.

There is no tax relief on issue costs

Tax shield

The annual interest cost will be $3,469,400 × 6% = $208,164.
Tax relief each year will be (25%) $52,041
Annuity factor at 6% (the risk-free cost of capital), Years 1 – 6 = 4.917.
Present value of tax shield = $255,886, say $256,000.

	$000
Base case NPV	527
PV of issue costs	(69)
PV of tax shield	256
Adjusted present value	+ 714

20 Cash flows from a foreign project

Year	Expected exchange rate		Cash flows in francs	Cash flows in £
0		5.00	(45,000,000)	(9,000,000)
1	$5.00 \times (1.05/1.03)^1$	5.10	10,000,000	1,960,784
2	$5.00 \times (1.05/1.03)^2$	5.20	20,000,000	3,846,154
3	$5.00 \times (1.05/1.03)^3$	5.30	25,000,000	4,716,981
4	$5.00 \times (1.05/1.03)^4$	5.40	10,000,000	1,851,852

Tutorial note: You may have calculated the exchange rate to three or more decimal places. Here, the exchange rate has been estimated to just two decimal places.

These cash flows in sterling should be discounted at the WACC.

Year	Cash flow	Discount factor	PV
	£	9%	£
0	(9,000,000)	1.000	(9,000,000)
1	1,960,784	0.917	1,798,039
2	3,846,154	0.842	3,238,462
3	4,716,981	0.772	3,641,509
4	1,851,852	0.708	1,311,111
NPV			+ 989,121

The NPV in sterling is positive. The project is financially viable and should be undertaken.

21 Foreign investment

(a) Calculate the NPV of the project in the currency of the investment, using a discount rate appropriate to the investment.

The annual tax allowance on the cost of the equipment is 25% of $1,000,000 = $250,000 each year for 4 years. This will result in tax savings of $100,000 (40% × $250,000) each year in years 2 – 5.

Year	**0**	**1**	**2**	**3**	**4**	**5**
	FR	FR	FR	FR	FR	FR
Equipment	(1,000,000)					
Capital allowance			100,000	100,000	100,000	100,000
Cash profit		500,000	500,000	500,000	500,000	
Tax on cash profit			(200,000)	(200,000)	(200,000)	(200,000)
Net cash flow	(1,000,000)	500,000	400,000	400,000	400,000	(100,000)
DCF factor at 16%	1.000	0.862	0.743	0.641	0.552	0.476
Present value	(1,000,000)	431,000	297,200	256,400	220,800	(47,600)

NPV = + 157,800

(b) **Dividend payments**

Year	**1**	**2**	**3**	**4**	**5**
	FR	FR	FR	FR	FR
Cash profit	500,000	500,000	500,000	500,000	
Tax on profit	(200,000)	(200,000)	(200,000)	(200,000)	
Tax saving from capital allowance	100,000	100,000	100,000	100,000	
Profit after tax	400,000	400,000	400,000	400,000	
Dividend (50%)	200,000	200,000	200,000	200,000	800,000
Retained	200,000	200,000	200,000	200,000	

(c)

Year	1	2	3	4	5
	FR	FR	FR	FR	FR
Dividend in FR	200,000	200,000	200,000	200,000	800,000
Exchange rate	3 × (1.10/1.04) = 3.1731	3 × $(1.10/1.04)^2$ = 3.3561	3 × $(1.10/1.04)^3$ = 3.5498	3 × $(1.10/1.04)^4$ = 3.7546	3 × $(1.10/1.04)^5$ = 3.9712
Dividend in $	63,030	59,593	56,341	53,268	201,450

(d) The cost of buying the equipment in Year 0 = FR1,000,000/3.00 = $333,333

Year		Cash flow	Discount factor at 10%	PV
		$		$
0	Equipment	(333,333)	1.000	(333,333)
0	Other costs	(25,000)	1.000	(25,000)
1	Dividend	63,030	0.909	57,294
2	Dividend	59,593	0.826	49,224
3	Dividend	56,341	0.751	42,312
4	Dividend	53,268	0.683	36,382
5	Dividend	201,450	0.621	125,100
NPV				**(48,021)**

The project is not worthwhile because it has a negative NPV in dollars, even though it has a positive NPV in Francs. This is because:

- the restriction on dividend payments delays returns to the parent company
- the Franc is expected to fall in value against the dollar over the next five years
- there is some additional expenditure in dollars in Year 0, that is not taken into account in the calculation of the NPV in Francs.

22 Valuation

The dividend growth model:

$$800 = \frac{38(1+g)}{(0.10-g)}$$

$800\ (0.10 - g) = 38\ (1 + g)$

$80 - 800g = 38 + 38g$

$838g = 42$

$g = 0.05$ or 5%.

An expected dividend growth rate of 5% per year is required to achieve a share price of 800.

23 Valuation of bonds

(a) (7.5/9.0) × 100 = 83.33. ($83.33 market value for each $100 nominal value of bonds.)

(b)

Year	Item	Cash flow	Discount factor at 9%	PV
1 – 3	Interest	6	2.531	15.19
4	Interest plus capital	106	0.708	75.05
				90.24

The market value of the bonds should be 90.24.

(c)

Period	Item	Cash flow	Discount factor at 4.4%	PV
1 – 7	Interest	5	5.914	29.57
8	Interest plus capital	105	$1/(1.044)^8$	74.40
				103.97

The market value of the bonds should be 103.97.

(d)

Year	Item	Cash flow	Discount factor at 9%	PV
1 – 3	Interest	5	2.531	12.66
3	Value of shares acquired	140	0.708	99.12
				111.78

The market value of the bonds should be 111.78.

24 Annuities and bond prices

Tutorial note

You might be required in the examination to remember and use the formula for the present value of an annuity. This is:

$$\text{PV of annuity} = \text{Annuity} \times \frac{1}{r}\left[1 - \frac{1}{(1+r)^n}\right]$$

(a) (i) $\text{Value of zero coupon bond} = 100 \times \frac{1}{(1.05)^{10}}$

= 100 × 0.6139

= 61.39.

(ii) PV of interest payments to maturity of the bond: interest = 4 every six months for ten years.

$$\text{PV of annuity} = 4 \times \frac{1}{0.025}\left[1 - \frac{1}{(1.025)^{20}}\right]$$

= 160 × [0.3897]

= 62.35

Period		Cash flow	Discount factor at 2.5%	PV
1 – 20	Interest	4	See above	62.35
20	Redemption	100	$1/(1.025)^{20}$	61.03
Value of bond				123.38

(b) When interest yields rise, bond prices fall.

(i) $$\text{Value of zero coupon bond} = 100 \times \frac{1}{(1.06)^{10}}$$

= 100 × 0.5584

= 55.84.

(ii) $$\text{PV of annuity} = 4 \times \frac{1}{0.03}\left[1 - \frac{1}{(1.03)^{20}}\right]$$

= 133.33 × [0.4463]

= 59.51

Period		Cash flow	Discount factor at 3%	PV
1 – 20	Interest	4	See above	59.51
20	Redemption	100	$1/(1.03)^{20}$	55.37
Value of bond				114.88

25 EVA

The adjusted capital investment is $8,000,000.

This is the equity investment. Development expenditure should be included in the total investment, and goodwill should be included at its current value (= cost less cumulative impairment). No adjustments to the amount of investment are therefore required for these items.

Net operating profit after tax = $2,100,000 – $300,000 – $450,000 = $1,350,000.

EVA = $1,350,000 – (12% × $8,000,000)

= $390,000.

26 MM, gearing and company valuation

Value of geared company = Value of company ungeared + (Value of debt × Tax rate)

$V_g = V_u + Dt$

$V_g = (4{,}000{,}000 \times \$10) + (\$15{,}000{,}000 \times 30\%)$

= $44,500,000

	$ million
Total value of geared company (equity + debt)	44.5
Value of debt	(15.0)
Therefore value of equity in geared company	29.5

The total value of the equity in the geared company is lower than when the company was geared, but there are fewer shares left in issue and the value per share will be higher.

27 Acquisition

(a) The earnings of Little next year are expected to be $86,000. A forward P/E multiple of 8.0 could be applied to this estimate, and the valuation of the equity shares in Little would be:

$86,000 × 8.0 = $688,000.

(b) The cost of equity of Big is expected to be:

6% + 1.60 (11 – 6)% = 14%.

The WACC of Big is expected to be:

[35% × 7.4 (1 – 0.30)] + (65% × 14)

= 10.913%.

(c) Since Little is in the same industry as Big, it is probably appropriate to use the WACC of Big to obtain a DCF-based valuation of Little. The WACC of 10.913% will be rounded to 11%.

The cash flows from the acquisition of Little must be calculated.

	Year 1	Year 2	Year 3
	$	$	$
Sales	200,000	280,000	320,000
Cash costs	(120,000)	(160,000)	(180,000)
	80,000	120,000	140,000
Capital allowances	(20,000)	(30,000)	(40,000)
Interest	(10,000)	(10,000)	(10,000)
Taxable profit	50,000	80,000	90,000
Tax at 30%	(15,000)	(24,000)	(27,000)
Profit after tax	35,000	56,000	63,000
Profit after tax	35,000	56,000	63,000
Add back capital allowances	20,000	30,000	40,000
	55,000	86,000	103,000
Asset replacement	(25,000)	(30,000)	(35,000)
Cash flow	30,000	56,000	68,000

Cash flows will increase by 4% each year from Year 4 onwards.

The dividend growth valuation model can be used to calculate the Year 3 value of these cash flows, using a growth rate of 4% and a cost of capital of 11%:

$$\text{Year 3 value of cash flows from Year 4} = \frac{\$68,000\,(1.04)}{(0.11 - 0.04)}$$

= $1,010,286

The expected cash flows can now be converted in to a present value:

Year	Cash flow	Discount factor at 11%	PV
	$		$
1	30,000	0.901	27,030
2	56,000	0.812	45,472
3	68,000	0.731	49,708
4 onwards	1,010,286	0.731	738,519
Total value			860,729

28 Takeover

(a) Cost of equity in Flat Company, using the CAPM = 5% + 1.20 (11 – 5)% = 12.2%

WACC in Flat Company = (12.2 × 75%) + (7 (1 – 0.30) × 25%) = 10.375%, say 10.4%

Cost of equity in Slope Company, using the CAPM = 5% + 1.35 (11 – 5)% = 13.1%

WACC in Slope Company = (13.1 × 60%) + (8 (1 – 0.30) × 40%) = 10.1%.

Free cash flow is defined here as EBIT less tax, plus tax-allowable depreciation minus replacement capital expenditure.

Free cash flows and valuation of Flat Company based on free cash flows

Year	1	2	3	4
	$000	$000	$000	$000
Earnings before interest and tax	1,918	2,014	2,115	2,221
Tax at 30%	(575)	(604)	(635)	(666)
	1,343	1,410	1,480	1,555
Add back tax-allowable depreciation	872	915	961	1,009
Less: Replacement capital spending	(966)	(1,014)	(1,065)	(1,118)
Free cash flow	1,249	1,311	1,376	1,446
Discount factor at 10.4%	0.906	0.820	0.743	0.673
Present value	1,132	1,075	1,022	973

$$\text{End-of-year 4 value of free cash flows from Year 5 onwards} = \frac{1,446\,(1.03)}{(0.104 - 0.03)}$$

= (in $000) 20,322

Present value of Year 5 onward cash flows(Year 0 value) = 20,322 × 0.673 = 13,677.

Total valuation of Flat Company equity, using the free cash flow method, is (1,132 + 1,075 + 1,022 + 973 + 13,677) = $17,879,000.

Free cash flows and valuation of Slope Company based on free cash flows

Year	**1**	**2**	**3**	**4**
	$000	$000	$000	$000
Earnings before interest and tax	1,893	1,969	2,047	2,129
Tax at 30%	(568)	(591)	(614)	(639)
	1,325	1,378	1,433	1,490
Add back tax-allowable depreciation	728	757	787	819
Less: Replacement capital spending	(822)	(854)	(889)	(924)
Free cash flow	1,231	1,281	1,331	1,385
Discount factor at 10.1%	0.908	0.825	0.749	0.681
Present value	1,118	1,057	997	943

End-of-year 4 value of free cash flows from Year 5 onwards $= \frac{1{,}385\ (1.02)}{(0.101 - 0.02)}$

= (in $000) 17,441

Present value of Year 5 onward cash flows(Year 0 value) = 17,441 × 0.681 = 11,877.

Total valuation of Slope Company equity, using the free cash flow method, is (1,118 + 1,057 + 997 + 943 + 11,877) = $15,992,000.

Combined group WACC

		Market value $m	**Cost of capital**	**MV × Cost**
Flat equity	(6m × 3.20)	19.20	0.104	1.9968
Flat debt	(19.2m/0.75) × 25%	6.40	0.049	0.3136
Slope equity	(9m × 1.54)	13.86	0.101	1.3999
Slope debt	(13.86m/0.60) × 40%	9.24	0.056	0.5174
		48.70		4.2277

WACC = 4.2277/48.70 = 0.068 or 8.68%, say 8.7%.

Free cash flows and valuation of combined company based on free cash flows

Tax-allowable depreciation in the year just ended (combined) was 1,530 and replacement capital expenditure combined was 1,710.

Year	**1**	**2**	**3**	**4**
	$000	$000	$000	$000
Earnings before interest and tax	4,100	4,305	4,520	4,746
Tax at 30%	(1,230)	(1,292)	(1,356)	(1,424)
	2,870	3,013	3,164	3,322

Year	1	2	3	4
	$000	$000	$000	$000
Add back tax-allowable depreciation	1,607	1,687	1,771	1,860
Less: Replacement capital spending	(1,860)	(1,885)	(1,980)	(2,079)
Free cash flow	2,617	2,815	2,955	3,103
Discount factor at 8.7%	0.920	0.846	0.779	0.716
Present value	2,408	2,381	2,302	2,222

End-of-year 4 value of free cash flows from Year 5 onwards $= \frac{3{,}103\ (1.04)}{(0.087 - 0.04)}$

= (in $000) 68,662

Present value of Year 5 onward cash flows(Year 0 value) = 68,662 × 0.716 = 49,162.

Total valuation of equity in the combined company, using the free cash flow method, is (2,408 + 2,381 + 2,302 + 2,222 + 49,162) = $58.475 million

Summary of free cash flow valuations	$m
Value of Flat Company equity	17.879
Value of Slope Company equity	15.992
	33.871
Value of equity in combined company	58.475
Increase in equity value	24.604

On the basis of these estimates, the value of equity (as valued on a free cash flow basis) will increase by about 72.6% as a result of the takeover.

(b) The estimates of equity value might not be reliable, for several reasons.

(1) The WACC used for the combined company, based on current market values, is lower than the WACC used for each separate company valuation. This lower WACC is questionable, and if a WACC of over 10% were used, the valuation of the company after the takeover would be much lower.

(2) The estimates for the increase in the combined Year 1 EBIT might be unrealistic, and the estimates of higher growth in sales and earnings should also be questioned.

(3) Valuations based on a dividend growth model, rather than a free cash flow model, would produce a lower valuation.

(c) Shareholders in Slope are being offered 2 shares in Flat (current value $6.40) for every three shares they hold (current value $4.62). On the basis of current market values, they are being offered a price that is 38.5% above the current share price. This is a very high premium in a takeover bid, and is likely to be very attractive to them.

For the same reason, shareholders in Flat might oppose the takeover bid, because 'value' is being given to the shareholders of Slope and a very high premium is being offered for the shares. The shareholders in Flat will only support the bid if they believe that it will 'unlock value' in the shares or result in substantial synergy gains through higher sales, cost savings or faster business growth.

29 Interest rate parity

(a) GBP/USD = 1.8000 × (1.035/1.05) = 1.7743

(Note: the interest rate is lower for the dollar than for sterling, therefore the dollar should increase in value over time against sterling.)

GBP/EUR = 1.5000 × (1.025/1.05) = 1.4643

EUR/USD = 1.2000 × (1.035/1.025) = 1.2117

(b) GBP/USD = $1.8000 \times (1.035/1.05)^3 = 1.7240$

GBP/EUR = $1.5000 \times (1.025/1.05)^3 = 1.3954$

EUR/USD = $1.2000 \times (1.035/1.025)^3 = 1.2355$

30 Foreign exchange

(a) A hedge against the risk can be obtained by entering into a forward rate agreement to buy $750,000. The forward rate is the forward rate that favours the bank. This is 1.8535 (and not 1.8543).

The cost of buying the dollars will be $750,000/1.8535 = £404,639.87.

(b) Subtract a premium, add a discount.

Spot rate	1.3025
Premium	(0.0018)
Forward rate	1.3007

The $450,000 will be sold in exchange for €345,967.56 (450,000/1.3007).

31 Money market hedge

(a) The company will receive $600,000 in six months, and will want to receive sterling and pay dollars.

It can do this with a money market hedge by borrowing US dollars now. The interest rate for six months in dollars is 3.5% × 6/12 = 1.75%. It will need to borrow now:

$600,000/1.0175 = $589,680.59.

It can immediately exchange these dollars into sterling at the spot rate of 1.8800, to obtain:

$589,680.59/1.8800 = £313,659.89.

After six months, the dollar loan will be repayable with interest. The total repayment will be $600,000, and the payment can be made from the $600,000 received from the customer.

(b) The company can do anything with the sterling it receives now from the hedging transaction. If it chose to invest the cash for six months at 5% per year (2.5% for six months), the investment of £313,659.89 would increase to:

£313,659.89 × 1.025 = £321,501.39.

To avoid opportunities for arbitrage between the money markets and the forward FX markets, the six-month forward exchange rate would therefore need to be:

$600,000/£321,501.39 = 1.8662.

32 FRA

(a) The company wants to borrow in three months' time for a period of six months; therefore to create a hedge with an FRA, it must buy a 3v9 FRA.

The interest rate for the FRA is 3.97%.

- The company will borrow in three months' time at the current LIBOR rate plus 0.50%.
- The FRA will be settled in three months' time.
  - If the six-month LIBOR rate is higher than 3.97%, the company will receive a payment from the bank to settle the FRA. The amount of this payment is the value of the difference between the FRA rate of 3.97% and the LIBOR rate.
  - If the six-month LIBOR rate is lower than 3.97%, the company will make a payment to the bank to settle the FRA, for the value of the difference between the two rates.

The effect of the FRA is therefore to 'lock in an effective interest rate of 3.97% + 0.50% = 4.47%.

(Tutorial note: For example, if the LIBOR rate in three months is 5.5%, the situation will be as follows:

	%
Company borrows at LIBOR + 0.50%	6.00
Company receives from settlement of FRA (5.50 – 3.97)	(1.53)
Effective interest cost	4.47

This is the FRA rate + 0.50%).

(b) An FRA works on the same principles as an interest rate coupon swap. The main difference is that an FRA is for one interest period only, although a company can arrange a series of FRAs. A coupon swap is longer-term, and covers several settlement dates.

33 Swap

The company should enter into a four-year interest rate coupon swap in which it receives the floating rate and pays the fixed rate (5.25%).

The effective interest rate will change from floating rate to fixed rate, as follows:

	%
Bank loan interest	(LIBOR + 1.25)
Swap	
Pay	(5.25)
Receive	LIBOR
Effective rate	(6.50)

34 Credit arbitrage (1)

	Company X		Company Y
	%		%
Borrow:		Borrow:	
Fixed rate	(7.25)	Floating rate	(LIBOR + 1.50)
Swap		Swap	
Receive fixed	6.27	Pay fixed	(6.30)
Pay floating	(LIBOR)	Receive floating	LIBOR
Net cost	(LIBOR + 0.98)	Net cost	(7.80)
Cost of variable rate borrowing	(LIBOR + 1.25)	Cost of fixed rate borrowing	(8.00)
Saving in cost	0.27	Saving in cost	0.20

35 Credit arbitrage (2)

	%
Entity A can borrow more cheaply at a fixed rate by (7.25 – 6.35)	0.90
Entity A can borrow more cheaply at a floating rate by (1.25 – 0.75)	0.50
Difference	0.40
Bank's profit	0.10
Net benefit to share between the two entities	0.30

If the entities share the benefit equally, each will be able to reduce its effective cost of borrowing by (0.30/2) 0.15%.

- Entity A wants to borrow at a floating rate. It can borrow directly at LIBOR + 0.75%. By borrowing at a fixed rate and swapping into a floating rate, its effective interest rate will be LIBOR + 0.75% – 0.15% = LIBOR + 0.60%.
- Entity B wants to borrow at a fixed rate. It can borrow directly at 7.25%. By borrowing at a floating rate and swapping into a fixed rate, its effective interest rate will be 7.25% – 0.15% = 7.10%.

For Entity A, the arrangement could be as follows:

	%
Borrow at a fixed rate	(6.35)
Swap	
Pay	(LIBOR)
Receive (balancing figure)	5.75
Effective interest cost	(LIBOR + 0.60)

For Entity A, the arrangement would be as follows:

	%
Borrow at a fixed rate	(LIBOR + 1.25)
Swap	
Pay (balancing figure)	(5.85)
Receive	LIBOR
Effective interest cost	(7.10)

The bank's profit would come from the difference between the fixed rate received from Entity B (5.85%) and the fixed rate paid to Entity A (5.75%).

This assumes that the two Entities each arrange their swap with the bank, and not directly with each other.

36 Currency swap

(a) Small company will want to borrow 3 million zants, but can borrow in sterling at a rate that is 2% lower than the rate that the Zantland counterparty can obtain. The Zantland counterparty presumably wants to borrow in sterling (the equivalent of 3 million zants), but can borrow in zants at a rate that is 0.5% lower than the rate that Small Company can obtain.

This provides an opportunity for credit arbitrage of 2% + 0.5% = 2.5%.

The bank would take 0.5% in fees, leaving 2% of net credit arbitrage for the swap counterparties to share. Small Company would have three-quarters of this amount, which is 1.5%.

The swap arrangement might therefore be as follows:

	Small Company	**Zantland counterparty**
	%	%
Borrow direct	(6.5)	(ZIBOR + 1.5)
Swap		
Pay	ZIBOR	6.5
Receive	6.0	ZIBOR
Net cost	ZIBOR + 0.5%	8.0

Small company would pay 1.5% less than by borrowing direct (at ZIBOR + 2%) and the Zantland counterparty would borrow at 0.5% less than by borrowing sterling direct at 8.5%.

(b) It is assumed that 15% is the appropriate discount rate for evaluating the project's cash flows in sterling. (A DCF rate of 15% would be very low for evaluating the cash flows in zants, considering the expected high rate of inflation in Zantland.)

It is also assumed that the swap will be undertaken, and in Year 0 Small Company will spend £333,333 (3 million zants at the spot rate of 9.00). At the end of Year 3, it is assumed that Small Company will receive the same amount (£333,333) on the termination of the currency swap, and a further 3,000,000 zants for the remainder of the sale price of the operations centre.

The project cash flows will therefore be as follows:

Year		
0	£(333,333)	
1	200,000 zants	at the end of Year 1 spot rate
2	200,000 zants	at the end of Year 2 spot rate
3	200,000 zants	at the end of Year 3 spot rate
3	3,000,000 zants	at the end of Year 3 spot rate
3	3,000,000 zants	at the swap rate of 9.00, therefore £333,333.

Year	Spot rate	
	Best case	**Worst case**
	10% inflation	50% inflation
0	9.00	9.00
1	9.90	13.50
2	10.89	20.25
3	11.98	30.38

Year	Cash flow	DCF factor at 15%	Best case		Worst case	
			Cash flow	PV	Cash flow	PV
	zants		£	£	£	£
0		1.000	(333,333)	(333,333)	(333,333)	(333,333)
1	200,000	0.870	20,202	17,576	14,815	12,889
2	200,000	0.756	18,365	13,884	9,877	7,467
3	3,200,000	0.658	267,112	175,760	105,332	69,308
3	3,000,000	0.658	333,333	219,333	333,333	219,333
NPV				+ 93,220		(24,336)

Conclusion

On the basis of the assumptions used, the project would have a positive NPV if inflation in Zantland exceeds inflation in the UK by 10% per year, but will have a negative NPV if inflation in Zantland exceeds inflation in the UK by 50% per year.

There is consequently an element of risk in the project due to uncertainty about the spot exchange rate, and this risk element should be assessed more closely before a decision is taken about the investment.

37 Currency futures

(a) The company must make a payment in US dollars in May. It must therefore buy dollars to make the payment.

Using futures, the company will therefore buy dollars and sell euros. It will therefore sell euro/US dollar futures, which are for €125,000 each.

At the futures price of 1.2800, the amount of euros to sell in exchange for $640,000 is:

$640,000/1.2800 = $500,000.

The number of contracts to sell is therefore: $500,000/$125,000 per contract = 4.0 contracts.

The company will sell 4 June contracts at 1.2800.

(b) It will close its position in May, when the futures price is 1.2690.

The value of 1 tick for this contract is 125,000 × $0.0001 = $12.50.

Original selling price	1.2800
Buying price to close the position	1.2690
Gain per contract	0.0110

Total gain on futures position = 4 contracts × 110 ticks × $12.50 = $5,500.

The French company must pay $640,000 to its supplier. It has $5,500 profit from closing the futures position. It therefore needs an additional ($640,000 – $5,500) = $634,500.

It must buy these dollars at the spot rate of 1.2710. The cost in euros will be $634,500/1.2710 = €499,213.

The effective exchange rate for the payment of $640,000 is therefore:
$640,000/€499,213 = US$1.2820/€1.

This is close to the price at which the futures were originally sold. However, the hedge is not perfect because the position was closed before the settlement date for the contract.

38 More currency futures

(a) The US company must make a payment in sterling in January. It will sell the sterling it receives in exchange for dollars.

Using futures, the company will therefore sell sterling and buy dollars. It will therefore sell sterling/US dollar futures, which are for £62,500 each.

The number of contracts to sell is therefore: £400,000/£62,500 per contract = 6.4 contracts.

The company will therefore sell either 6 or 7 March contracts at 1.8600.
In the answer in (b), it is assumed that the company will sell 6 March sterling/US dollar futures.

(b) The US company will close its position in January, when the futures price is 1.8420.

The value of 1 tick for this contract is 62,500 × $0.0001 = $6.25.

Original selling price	1.8600
Buying price to close the position	1.8420
Gain per contract	0.0180

Total gain on futures position = 6 contracts × 180 ticks × $6.25 = $6,750.

The US company will receive £400,000 which it will sell at the spot rate of 1.8450.

	$
From sale of £400,000 spot at $1.8450/£1	738,000
Profit on futures position	6,750
Total income	744,750

The effective exchange rate for the £400,000 received is therefore:

$744,750/£400,000 = US$1.8619/£1.

This is close to the price at which the futures were originally sold. However, the hedge is not perfect because the position was closed before the settlement date for the contract.

39 Basis

(a) On 1st March: Days to settlement of the June futures contracts = 31 + 30 + 31 + 60 = 122 days.

On 1 March	
Spot rate	1.8540
Futures price	1.8760
Basis	0.0220

The basis is 220 points, with the futures rate higher than the spot rate.

The basis at the end of June when the futures reach settlement will be 0.

It is assumed that basis will decrease to zero at a constant rate per day. The basis will therefore reduce by (220 points/122 days) = 1.80328 points per day.

At close of trading on 30th April, there are (31 + 30) 61 days remaining to the settlement of the June futures. The expected basis at this date is therefore:

1.80328 points per day × 61 days = 110 points.

At the end of 30th April	
Spot rate	1.8610
Expected basis	0.0110
Expected futures price (higher)	1.8720

(b) At close of trading on 15th June, there are 15 days remaining to the settlement of the June futures. The expected basis at this date is therefore:

1.80328 points per day × 15 days = 27 points.

At the end of 30th April	
Spot rate	1.8690
Expected basis	0.0027
Expected futures price (higher)	1.8717

40 Imperfect hedge and basis

(a) There is a loss on the underlying currency exposure, because sterling weakens in value between 20th April and 20th July.

	$
At 20th April: expected value of £625,000 receivable (at 1.8050)	1,128,125
At 20th July: actual value of £625,000 received (at 1.7700)	1,106,250
Loss on underlying currency exposure	21,875

The futures position is opened on 20th April by selling futures contracts (selling British pounds and buying dollars). The US company should sell 10 contracts (£625,000/£62,500 per contract). When the position is closed on 20th July, there is a gain on the position.

	$
20th April: Open position – Sell at	1.7800
20th July: Close position – Buy at	1.7600
Gain on underlying currency exposure	0.0200

Total gain (10 contracts) = 10 contracts × 200 ticks per contract × £6.25 per tick = $12,500.

The futures position has failed to provide a perfect hedge, resulting in a net 'loss' of $9,375.

Effective exchange rate	**$**
Revenue from sale of £625,000 spot on 20th July (at 1.7600)	1,100,000
Gain on futures position	12,500
Total dollar income	1,112,500

Effective exchange rate = $1,112,500/£625,000 = $1.7800.

(b) The reason why the hedge is not perfect in this case is explained by the existence of basis. When the futures position was opened, the basis was 250 points (1.8050 – 1.7800). When the position was closed, the basis was 100 points (1.7700 – 1.7600). The spot price has moved in value during the three months by more than the movement in the futures price, by 150 points. The value of this difference is $9,375 (10 contracts × 150 ticks per contract × £6.25 per tick).

41 Currency hedge

(a) **Hedging with a forward exchange contract**

Only the net exposure should be hedged. This is a net payment of €(2,650,000 – 540,000) = €2,110,000.

The entity will need to buy euros in three months' time. The three-month forward rate for the contract would be 1.4443 (the rate more favourable to the bank).

Cost in sterling = €2,110,000/1.4443 = £1,460,915.

(b) **Money market hedge**

The company must pay €2,110,000 in three months' time. To create a money market hedge, it must therefore buy euros spot and invest them for three months at 3.4% per year. The amount of euros invested, plus accumulated interest, must be worth €2,110,000 after three months.

It is assumed that the three-month investment rate for euros is 3.4% × 3/12 = 0.85%.

The amount of euros to invest now is therefore €2,110,000/1.0085 = €2,092,216.

These must be purchased spot at 1.4537, and the cost in sterling will be:

€2,092,216/1.4537 = £1,439,235.

With a forward FX contract, the payment of £1,460,915 will be made in three months' time. With a money market hedge, the payment of £1,439,235 would happen immediately. It can therefore be argued that an additional cost of a money market hedge is the loss of interest (opportunity cost) from investing £1,439,235 for three months at 5.6% per year. The lost interest would be £1,439,235 × 5.6% × 3/12 = £20,149.

The overall cost of a money market hedge would therefore be £1,439,235 + £20,149 = £1,459,384.

(c) **Currency futures hedge**

The company must pay euros. It needs to buy euros to make the payments. The futures are denominated in euros; therefore the company will buy futures.

The number of contracts required = €2,110,000/€100,000 per contract = 21.1 contracts. The company should probably buy 21 contracts.

The payments are due in October. The company should therefore buy futures with the next settlement date following. It should buy December contracts at 0.6929.

The remaining €10,000 that is not hedged by futures can be purchased forward at 1.4443, at a cost of £6,924.

If the basis is 0 when the futures position is closed in October, the effective exchange rate for the €2,100,000 will be £0.6929 = €1, or £1 = €1.4432.

The net cost in sterling will be:

	£
€2,100,000 at $1.4432/£1	1,455,100
€10,000 at €1.4443/£1	6,924
Total cost in sterling	1,462,024

The money market hedge is the cheapest method of hedging.

42 Hedging with STIRs

The company wants a hedge against the risk of higher interest rates. It should therefore sell short-term interest rate futures.

The borrowing period will begin in February; the company should therefore buy March futures, which have the next settlement date following the start of the loan period.

The planned borrowing period is 5 months, but with futures, the notional deposit period is only 3 months. To get round this difficulty, the number of futures contracts should be adjusted.

$$\text{The number of March futures to sell} = \frac{\text{£4.5 million}}{\text{£500,000}} \times \frac{\text{5 months}}{\text{3 months}}$$

= 15 contracts.

Conclusion

The company should sell 15 March short sterling futures.

43 More hedging with STIRs

(a) The company wants a hedge against the risk of higher interest rates. It should therefore sell short-term interest rate futures.

The borrowing period will begin in February; the company should therefore buy March futures, which have the next settlement date following the start of the loan period.

The planned borrowing period is 4 months, but with futures, the notional deposit period is only 3 months. To get round this difficulty, the number of futures contracts should be adjusted.

$$\text{The number of March futures to sell} = \frac{\$12\text{ million}}{\$1\text{ million}} \times \frac{\text{4 months}}{\text{3 months}}$$

= 16 contracts.

Conclusion

The company should sell 16 March eurodollar futures at 93.70.

(b) When the futures are sold, the basis is:

Spot LIBOR rate (100 – 5.5)	0.9450
Futures price	0.9370
Basis	0.0080

It is now the end of October. The March futures will reach settlement date in five months' time.

If we assume that the basis will reduce from 80 points at the end of October to 0 by the end of March at an equal amount each month, by the end of January the basis should be:

$$\frac{\text{2 months to settlement}}{\text{5 months original time to settlement}} \times 80 \text{ points} = 32 \text{ points}$$

The futures price is lower than the spot price.

At the beginning of February, if the three-month LIBOR rate is 7.5%, the futures price should be:

Spot LIBOR rate (100 – 7.5)	0.9250
Basis	0.0032
Futures price	0.9218

The futures position will be closed out, as follows:

Selling price in October	0.9370
Buying price to close	0.9218
Gain	0.0152

The gain is 152 points or 1.52%

The futures hedge is a perfect hedge, and the effective cost of borrowing can therefore be calculated as follows:

	$
Borrow $12 million at	7.50
Gain on futures position	(1.52)
Net effective borrowing cost	5.98

The net effective borrowing cost is 5.98%.

(Note: This differs from the rate in the futures contracts sold in October. In October, the interest rate in the sold futures was 6.30% (100 – 93.70). The difference is 32 points, which is the amount of the basis risk. Here, the company has benefited from the basis to obtain a lower borrowing cost).

44 FRAs and futures

(a) **FRAs**

The company can use an FRA to fix the interest rate receivable on £8.2 million. A 4v9 FRA is required, and the bank will offer a rate of 4.52%.

The company will therefore fix a rate of 4.52% for LIBOR and if it can invest at LIBOR + 0.40% this means that the effective investment rate will be 4.92%.

Futures

The company wants to fix an interest rate for income, so it should buy futures. The money for investment will be received at the end of July, so September futures should be used.

The company should buy (£8.2 million /£500,000) × (5 months/3 months) = 27.33 futures contracts, say 27 futures, and the price is 95.35.

(b) **FRAs**

At the end of July when the £8.2 million, the company will invest the money for 5 months. If it can still obtain a rate of LIBOR + 0.40%, it will invest the money at 4.65%.

The FRA contract must also be settled, as follows:

	%
Pay LIBOR	(4.25)
Receive	4.52
Profit on settlement	0.27

The company will receive a payment on settlement of the FRA equivalent to 0.27% in interest, which means that its effective interest income from investing the money for 5 months will be 4.65% + 0.27% = 4.92%.

Futures

When the futures contracts were purchased on 1st April, basis was 95.35 – 95.00 = 0.35. This is 0.05833 per month (0.35/6 months). Assuming basis changes by a constant amount each month, the expected basis at the end of July (2 months to the end of September) is 0.117.

The expected futures price at the end of July if LIBOR is 4.25% is therefore:

95.75 + 0.117 = 95.867.

The futures position will be closed as follows:

Close: sell at	95.867
Purchase price	95.350
Profit	0.517

Total profit on 27 contracts = 51.7 × £12.50 × 27 = £17,449.

The company can invest £8.2 million + £17,449 for 5 months at 4.65% (LIBOR + 0.40%) and total interest will be £159,213 (£8,217,449 × 4.65% × 5/12).

On the money received of £8.2 million, this represents an effective interest rate of (£159,213/£8.2 million) × (12/5) = 0.047 or 4.7%.

In this particular case, FRAs would be a better way of hedging the interest rate risk than futures.

45 Traded equity options

(a) The investor should buy put options on TBA shares.

Strike price	Cost per option		Number of options purchased with £12,000
		£	
950	(2,000 shares × \$0.15)	300	40
1,000	(2,000 shares × \$0.50)	1,000	12

The investor could purchase 12 put options at a strike price of 1,000 (£10) or 40 put options at a strike price of 950 (£9.50).

He is more likely to buy the out-of-the-money options at 950.

(b) If the share price is 910 at expiry and the investor still holds the options, the options will be exercised. It is assumed that he buys the options at 950.

Traded equity options are settled by physical delivery. The investor would need to buy shares at 910 and exercise the option to sell them at 950.

	£
Buy 40 × 2,000 shares at 910	728,000
Buy 40 × 2,000 shares at 950	760,000
Profit on exercise	32,000
Cost of options	12,000
Net profit on speculative investment	20,000

(**Note**: This calculation of the profit ignores the time value of money. The options are paid for when they are bought, but the profit is made only when the options are exercised).

Traded equity options can be bought and sold on the exchange, and the investor is likely to sell the put options before they expire, making a profit on the sale. As the options become increasingly in-the-money, their market value will increase.

46 Currency options

In September, the UK company will want to sell dollars and buy sterling (to convert its dollar receipts into sterling).

Since it wants to buy sterling in six months' time, it should buy call options with a September expiry.

If the strike price is $1.8500, the sterling equivalent of $2 million = £1,081,081 (2,000,000/1.85).

The contract size is £31,250; therefore for a perfect hedge, the company would want to buy 34.6 contracts (1,081,081/31,250).

Since this is not possible, it should buy either 34 or 35 contracts. In the answer that follows, it is assumed that the company will buy 35 options.

Premium cost = 35 × 31,250 × $0.019 = $20,781.25.

To pay the premium, the company would have to buy $20,781.25 spot, at a sterling cost of £11,340.38.

At the expiry date, the options are in-the-money if the spot exchange rate is 1.9200. They will therefore be exercised, at a profit of $0.07 per £1 (1.9200 – 1.8500).

Gain on exercise of 35 option contracts = 35 × 31,250 × $0.07 = $76,562.50.

The total dollar income of the company will therefore be $2,076,562.50.

This can be exchanged into sterling at the spot rate, to obtain £1,081,543 ($2,076,562.50/1.9200).

The option premium cost was £11,340, therefore ignoring the time value of money, the net revenue for the company is £1,081,543 – £11,340 = £1,070,203.

This gives an effective exchange rate for the $2 million dollar receipts of 1.8688 (2,000,000/1,070,203).

47 Interest rate hedge

(a) **Futures**

The company wants a hedge against the risk of a rise in two-month interest rates. It should therefore sell futures. Since the interest period will be 2 months and futures are for a three-month deposit, the quantity of futures sold should be:

(£21 million/£500,000) × 2/3 = 28 contracts.

The loan period will begin in mid-June; therefore sell 28 June contracts, at a price of 94.610.

Options on futures

The company will want options to sell futures; therefore it should buy put options on 28 June futures. The premium cost will depend on the strike price chosen. (Since the options are needed for two months, apply a factor of × 2/12).

Strike price		Premium
94750	(£21,000,000 × 0.500% × 2/12)	£17,500
95000	(£21,000,000 × 0.850% × 2/12)	£29,750

FRA

The company should buy a 3v5 FRA, for a notional principal amount of £21 million. The FRA rate will be 5.38%.

(Note: The FRA rate is more favourable than the futures rate of 5.39% (100 – 94.610). The company would therefore prefer to buy an FRA than sell futures. However, it might prefer to buy put options on futures rather than buy an FRA).

In mid-June, the company will borrow £21 million for two months. If the LIBOR rate is 6%, it will borrow at 6.75% (LIBOR + 0.75%) for two months.

Futures

The futures price in mid-June can be estimated as follows:

June futures price in mid-March	94.610
LIBOR rate in mid-March	95.000
Basis in mid-March	0.390

In mid-March, there were 3.5 months to settlement of the June futures. In mid-June, there are 0.5 months remaining to settlement. Basis is assumed to have reduced in size by mid-June to:

(0.5/3.5) × 39 points = 5.6 points, say 5 points.

LIBOR rate in mid-June	94.000
Basis in mid-June	00.005
Estimated futures price in mid-June	93.995

The company will close its position by buying 28 June futures at 93.995.

Original selling price	94.610
Buying price to close	93.995
Gain (ticks)	00.615

The total gain on the futures position:

= 28 contracts × 61.5 ticks per contract × £12.50 per tick

= £21,525.

(The gain on the futures position offsets the cost of the increase in the interest rate above the rate fixed by the futures contract (6% - 5.39% = 0.61%). The extra borrowing cost is £21 million × 0.61% × 2/12 = £21,350. The difference of £175 is due to the basis risk).

Options on futures

The company will exercise its options to sell futures at the strike price for the option, and will then close the futures position, giving a gain on closing the futures position.

	Strike price 94750	**Strike price 95000**
Option strike price to sell	94.750	95.000
Buying price to close	93.995	93.995
Gain (ticks)	0.755	1.005
Total gain:		
28 × 75.5 ticks × £12.50	£26,425	
28 × 100.5 ticks × £12.50		£35,175

However, after taking into account the cost of the option premiums, the net gain is reduced.

FRA

The company's FRA bank will make a payment equivalent to (6% - 5.38%) = 0.62% per year on £21 million for two months, to settle the FRA.

The gain on the FRA will offset the higher interest cost of borrowing.

48 Black-Scholes

Step 1: Calculate d_1

$$d_1 = \frac{\ln\left(\frac{870}{900}\right) + (0.05 \times 0.5)}{\sqrt{0.09} \times \sqrt{0.5}} + 0.5c\sqrt{0.09} \times \sqrt{0.5}$$

ln (870/900) = ln 0.96667. Using a calculator, the natural logarithm of 0.96667 can be obtained. This is – 0.0339.

$$d_1 = \frac{-0.0339 + 0.025}{0.30 \times 0.7071} + 0.5 \times 0.30 \times 0.7071$$

= (-0.0089/0.21213) + 0.106

=-0.042, say-0.04

Step 2: Calculate d_2

$$d_2 = d_1 - \sigma\sqrt{t} = -0.042 - \left(\sqrt{0.09} \times \sqrt{0.5}\right)$$

=-0.042-0.212

=-0.254, say –0.25

Step 3: Obtain values for $N(d_1)$ and $N(d_2)$

(a) $N(d_1)$. When $d_1 = 0.042$, the corresponding value in the normal distribution table is 0.0160. The value of d_1 is negative, so subtract from 0.50. $N(d_1) = 0.5000 - 0.0160 = 0.4840$.

(b) $N(d_2)$. When $d_2 = 0.25$, the corresponding value in the normal distribution table is 0.0987. The value of d_2 is negative, so subtract from 0.50. $N(d_2) = 0.5000 - 0.0987 = 0.4013$.

Step 4: Calculate the option price

The value of e^{-rt}

The value of rt is (0.05)(0.5) = 0.025.

The value of $e^{-0.025}$ is the same as $1/e^{0.025}$. Using a calculator, the value of $e^{0.025}$ can be obtained: this is 1.0253. Therefore $e^{-0.025} = 1/1.0253 = 0.9753$.

Option price	=	P_S N(d1)	– X e^{-rt} N(d2)
	=	870 (0.4840)	– 900 (0.9753) (0.4013)
	=	421 – 352	
	=	69	

The option price is 69.

49 Put-call parity

Value of put option + Current share price = Value of call option + PV of exercise price.

The PV of the exercise price = $600 \times 1/(1.04)^{0.5} = 600 \times 0.9806 = 588$

Value of put + 582 = 33 + 588

Value of put = 39

50 Delta hedge

(a) The bank should hold one share in TER for every 8 call options (1/0.125) that it writes.

(Alternatively, if it buys call options, it should sell one share forward for settlement on the option expiry date for every 8 options that it buys).

(b) **Calculate d_1**

$$d_1 = \frac{\ln\left(\frac{258}{260}\right) + (0.04 \times 0.5)}{\sqrt{0.16} \times \sqrt{0.5}} + 0.5 \times \sqrt{0.16} \times \sqrt{0.5}$$

ln (258/260) = ln 0.9923. Using a calculator, the natural logarithm of 0.9923 can be obtained. This is – 0.0077.

$$d_1 = \frac{-0.0077 + 0.02}{0.40 \times 0.7071} + 0.5 \times 0.40 \times 0.7071$$

=(0.0123/0.2828)+0.1414

=0.185

The bank should hold one share in BVZ for every 5.4 call options (1/0.185) that it writes.

(Alternatively, if it buys call options, it should sell one share forward for settlement on the option expiry date for every 5.4 options that it buys).

51 Bonus scheme

Bonus linked to EVA

It is assumed that research and development costs should be capitalised. The EVA in the year just ended is therefore as follows.

	$ million
Sales	683.0
Cost of sales	(421.0)
Depreciation	(65.0)
Tax: 44 + [(14 + 35) × 30%]	(58.7)
NOPAT	138.3

Interest should be calculated on the capital employed at the beginning of the year, adjusted to include the research and development costs in the previous three years that should be capitalised for the purpose of EVA calculations.

Capital employed (in $ million) = 525 + (14 × 3) = 567
Notional interest at 9% = $51.03 million, say $51.0 million.

	$ million
NOPAT	138.3
Notional interest	(51.0)
EVA	87.3

If the bonus payment is 0.5% of EVA, on the basis of the previous year's EVA the executive could expect to receive $436,500 as a cash bonus.

Share options

The share options would be call options. Their value can be estimated from the value of a similar put option, using the put-call parity theorem.

Value of put = Value of call – Current market value + Strike price × e^{-rT}.

30 = Value of call – 140 + 140 × $e^{-(0.05 \times 1)}$

30 = Value of call – 140 + (140 × 0.951229)

Value of call = 36.83cents.

The value of at-the-money call options on 2 million shares, with an exercise date in one year, is therefore about $736,600.

52 Delta neutral

(a) Barn plc could either buy put options on Door plc shares, or could write call options. With put options, the company would pay a premium to secure a worst-possible share price. With call options, the company would receive income from selling the options but would be exposed to a risk of a rise in the share price above the exercise price.

The company should choose November options, and might consider a strike price of either 600 or 650.

If Barn plc buys November put options, it will buy 4,000 contracts.

(1) If it buys put options at 600, the option premium payable will be 22.0. If the share price at the end of November is 580, the put options will be exercised for a gain of 20 (600 – 580). However, allowing for the premium, the net loss will be 2.0 pence per share or £80,000 in total compared with a strategy of not hedging the risk with options and selling the shares at the current market price of 580.

(2) If it buys put options at 650, the option premium payable will be 47.5. If the share price at the end of November is 580, the put options will be exercised for a gain of 70 (650 – 580). Allowing for the premium, the net gain will be 22.5 pence per share or £900,000 in total compared with a strategy of not hedging the risk with options and selling the shares at the current market price of 580.

(b) To establish a delta neutral position, the company should sell call options. If the share price goes up, the value of the investment in 4 million shares will rise, but this will be offset by the loss on the call options, leaving the net value of the investment unchanged. If the share price falls, the loss in the value of the shares will be offset by a gain on the options position.

The option delta for the relevant option is 0.46, which means that for every 1 share held, the company would sell 1/0.46 = 2.1739 call options on the shares, or 8,695,600 call options in total.

A problem with establishing a delta neutral hedge is that ideally at-the-money options should be sold, but these are not normally available as traded options.

Another problem is that the option delta is only applicable over a fairly narrow range of prices for a share. If the share price moves by more than a small amount, the option delta changes and options must be cancelled or written in order to re-establish a delta neutral hedge. The position therefore needs continual monitoring and adjusting if the share price is volatile.

i

Index

A

B

F

G

H

I

L

M

N

Y

Printed in Poland
by Amazon Fulfillment
Poland Sp. z o.o., Wrocław

62543864R00349